The Charmed Circle of Ideology

Anamnesis

Anamnesis means remembrance or reminiscence, the collection and re-collection of what has been lost, forgotten, or effaced. It is therefore a matter of the very old, of what has made us who we are. But *anamnesis* is also a work that transforms its subject, always producing something new. To recollect the old, to produce the new: that is the task of *Anamnesis*.

a re.press series

The Charmed Circle of Ideology:
A Critique of Laclau & Mouffe, Butler & Žižek

Geoff Boucher

re.press Melbourne 2008

re.press

PO Box 75, Seddon, 3011, Melbourne, Australia
http://www.re-press.org

© re.press 2008

British Library Cataloguing-in-Publication Data
A catalogue record for this book is available from the British Library

Library of Congress Cataloguing-in-Publication Data
A catalogue record for this book is available from the Library of Congress

National Library of Australia Cataloguing-in-Publication Data
A catalogue record for this book is available from the National Library of Australia

Author: Boucher, Geoff

Title: The Charmed Circle of Ideology :
A Critique of Laclau & Mouffe, Butler & Žižek

ISBN: 978-0-9805440-4-6

Series: Anamnesis

Designed and Typeset by *A&R*

This book is produced sustainably using plantation timber, and printed in the destination market reducing wastage and excess transport.

To Frauke and Annika

Contents

Acknowledgements

This book is the result of a doctoral dissertation and still bears some of the scars of that experience. Were I to write this from scratch today, I would probably write a different book. It remains, nonetheless, a valid immanent critique of postmarxism. I wish to acknowledge the following persons for commenting on chapter drafts: Maria Boucher, Matt Sharpe, Jeremy Moss, Justin Clemens. David Bennett read the entire thing many times and assisted greatly. Many conversations with Russell Grigg, Justin Clemens and Matt Sharpe, together with acquaintance with their work, assisted me with the development of my position on Žižek and psychoanalysis, and I wish to acknowledge their influence on my views. The remaining mistakes are those that neither reason nor friendship could part me from. Above all, I want to thank Frauke and Annika Hoffman.

Introduction

Critically Mapping the Postmarxian Field

Marxism is at the nadir of its fortunes. A new generation of militants and intellectuals is less likely to read Marx because they have resolved to struggle for a socialist revolution, than because the fashionably abstruse philosopher, Jacques Derrida, claims that "there will be ... no future without Marx" (Derrida, 1994: 13). For the last two decades—ever since the collapse of Eastern Bloc Communism—the mood of the Left has been dominated by intense rethinking and by the affects associated with the work of mourning. In the wake of 1989, the Western Left has had to contend with the ideological undertow (the impossibility and undesirability of socialism), the transformation of the major programmes for both reform and revolution (the collapse of state planning and the command economy) and the absence of progressive political alternatives (the ascendancy of neo-conservative hegemony combined with the transformation of the social democratic parties into liberal democratic formations). Sweeping inferences are drawn from the decline of the socialist tradition, on the lines of Étienne Balibar's declaration that, although "Marx will still be read in the twenty-first century, not only as a monument of the past, but as a contemporary author," nevertheless, we "have to recognise that Marxism is an improbable philosophy today" (Balibar, 1995c: 1, 118).

The procession of major theoretical figures filing past the "last instance" of the final relinquishment of Marxism is truly impressive—and depressing. The ranks of postmarxism constitute a nearly comprehensive "who's who" of the leading thinkers and activists of the 1970s New Left. Theoretical authority and conjunctural relevance appear to ballast postmarxism. Nancy Fraser, for instance, argues that "Marxism as the metanarrative or master discourse of oppositional politics in capitalist societies is finished. So too is Marxism as a totalising theory of the system dynamics, crisis tendencies, and conflict potentialities in capitalist societies" (Aronson, 1995: Fraser cited 111). The emergence of the postmarxian field from the aftermath of the avant-garde theoretical Marxism of Louis Althusser and his cothinkers seems to seal the doom of historical materialism, and to leave no alternative but to accept that the liberal-democratic "end of history" is also the finish of Marxism. Instead of the programme of democratic socialism, the Left seems to be confined to the "criticism of actually existing democracy". Renouncing the ambition to transform the world, the Left has to enter the new "postmarxian field of critical theorising": "the only possible future for Marxism is as one contributing strand among others in this new postmarxian field" (Aronson, 1995: 111).

Postmarxian Discourse Theory

Nonetheless, the new postmarxian field of discourse analysis and radical democratic politics is not, as some Marxists have claimed, just an "ex-Marxism without substance" (Geras, 1990: 127-168). In many respects, the postmarxian discourse theories of Ernesto Laclau and Chantal Mouffe, Slavoj Žižek and Judith Butler represent the most ambitious and challenging efforts to reconstruct the project of the Left. In the wake of the collapse of historical Communism and the rise of globalisation, the programme, politics and constituency of the Left is radically in question. The increasing complexity of the social field and the widespread acceptance of anti-essentialist theories in philosophy, politics, cultural studies and social theory, seem to have rendered historical materialist class-analysis untenable. Meanwhile, the emergence of new social movements around unprecedented social antagonisms mean that the political practices of the class-based Left have become marginalised, at precisely the moment when the popular base of the mainstream parties is in decline and the agenda of neo-liberalism is under questioning by radical rightwing movements. Instead of lamenting the decline of class politics and the accumulating irrelevance of the Left, Laclau and Mouffe have sought to re-articulate the conceptual framework within which radical Left politics could be imagined as a potential alternative to both social democracy and the neo-liberal conservative parties.

Elaboration of postmarxism's "radical democratic Imaginary" involved a deconstruction of Marxism, especially of the alleged tendency in Marxian theory to theorise the proletariat as the incarnation of universality. Postmarxism rejects the concept of the historical process as governed by an inexorable logic of historical necessity, culminating in rational mastery of society and the reconstruction of a transparent socialist order that would not need any political processes. Instead, Laclau and Mouffe develop an agenda that seeks to integrate socialist strategy within the social revolution inaugurated by modernity, which they claim is characterised by democratic politics and the permanence of social conflicts. Developing from their postmarxian manifesto, *Hegemony and Socialist Strategy: Towards a Radical Democratic Politics* (1985; hereafter, *HSS*) Laclau and Mouffe elaborate a new theory of discourse in support of their radical democratic programme. Butler and Žižek have made major contributions to this theory while redefining its strategic concepts. The publication of the joint work by Butler, Laclau and Žižek, *Contingency, Hegemony, Universality: Contemporary Dialogues on the Left* (2000; hereafter, *CHU*), with its declaration of a common trajectory and allegiance to the project of radical democracy, marked an important step in the consolidation of postmarxism as a distinct tendency.

This work critically maps, for the first time, the tendency of postmarxism defined by the political strategy of radical democracy, from its inception in *HSS* to its formulation as a distinct tendency in *CHU*. No previous study presents the combined work of Laclau and Mouffe, Butler and Žižek as a distinct political tendency and in the light of their total theoretical production. While valuable introductions to postmarxian discourse theory exist, these have restricted themselves to an exposition of the work of Laclau and Mouffe, with only some supplementary positions taken from Žižek (Smith, 1998; Torfing, 1999).[1] Likewise, the critical literature on Laclau and Mouffe, Butler and Žižek is limited by its restricted focus, taking these theorists serially, rather than severally, as it were. This literature is reviewed in the relevant chapters. In general, however, it is possible to say that this literature lines up "for" or "against" postmarxism (and correlatively, "against" or "for" Marxism). My investigation attempts to do something different. By

---

1. Laclau and Mouffe, Žižek and Butler are central to this project, but not alone. Their work has directly produced research in sociology, politics, economics, cultural theory and philosophy by Torben Dryberg (Dryberg, 1997), David Howarth (Howarth, 2000a), Aletta Norval (Norval, 1996), Anne-Marie Smith (Smith, 1994) and Yannis Stavrakakis (Stavrakakis, 1999). Their work has indirectly produced a growing body of research inspired by postmarxian discourse theory (Howarth, 2000b; Howarth and Norval, 1998). It has linked up with the deconstructive philosophy articulated by Simon Critchley (Critchley, 1999; Critchley, 2002) and with the feminist political philosophy of Wendy Brown (Brown, 1995; Brown, 2001). I do not analyse the entire range of the empirical studies canvassed by these authors, nor do I analyse every development in the research programme of postmarxian discourse theory. In general, I concentrate on the central statements by my primary theoreticians, drawing upon this supplementary work when necessary. Of course, Butler and Žižek are important theorists of considerable stature in their own right, with independent contributions to cultural studies and political theory. I do not engage with the important research programme in queer theory that has been strongly shaped by Butler's extraordinarily influential work, concentrating instead on her contribution to postmarxian discourse theory. Likewise, I do not investigate Žižek's contributions to film theory and psychoanalysis, although I do draw upon the productions of some of the "Ljubljana Lacanians"—Mladen Dolar (Dolar, 1993; Dolar, 1996; Dolar, 1998), Rastko Močnik (Mocnik, 1993), Renata Salecl (Salecl, 1994; Salecl, 1998; Salecl, 2000) and Alenka Zupančič (Zupančič, 2000)—where necessary to illuminate Žižek's positions. Finally, Mouffe's positions are not necessarily identical with those of Laclau, and my discussion nowhere presumes an accord that is not explicitly stated.

critically mapping the political trajectory of postmarxian discourse theory, it seeks to radicalise postmarxian discourse theories towards a postmodern Marxism. Following the US Marxist, Fredric Jameson, I contend that the postmodern is the horizon within which every radical politics develops today (Jameson, 1991: 297-418). Therefore, a contemporary socialism has to be articulated through critical engagement with postmodern politics.

Postmarxism is an effort to retrieve the legacy of Marxism for the postmodern condition. Radical democracy attempts to "describe a political project which rethinks hegemonic strategy in the new historical conditions of contemporary societies" (Laclau, 2000a: 294). The main question, therefore, is not whether postmarxism represents a fresh episode in the "treason of the intellectuals," a perfidious "retreat from class" (Wood, 1998) whose ambition is the "randomisation of history" (Wood, 1997a: 16). I accept Laclau and Mouffe's explanation that postmarxism represents a form of radical postmodern politics that seeks to recover the socialist initiative on transformed historical terrain, by articulating socialist strategy as an extension of the democratic revolution of modernity (Laclau, 1990: 97-134; Laclau and Mouffe, 1985: 149-193). In question is whether the new theories of discourse and the strategy of "radical and plural democracy" promoted by postmarxism actually *succeed* in the objective of articulating a contemporary socialist strategy. I seek therefore to intervene in the central debate on the contemporary theoretical agenda: does the advent of poststructuralism really mean the end of historical materialism? Is it the case that, as Laclau claims, postmarxism has become "an inevitable decision for anyone aiming to reformulate a political programme for the Left in [contemporary] historical circumstances" (Laclau, 1990: xii)?

To respond to this question, I critically map the tendency of radical democratic politics from a perspective informed by Structural Marxism (sometimes known as "Althusserian Marxism"), evaluating the justifications for joining the "criticism of actually existing democracy" and entering the new "postmarxian field of critical theorising". I seek to determine the "unity-in-diversity" of postmarxian discourse theory by analysing the different positions of Laclau and Mouffe, Žižek and Butler, and defining the nature of the underlying unity of radical democratic politics. According to the "joint declaration" by Butler, Laclau and Žižek, *HSS* appears as the programmatic text for the new tendency, because it "represented a turn to poststructuralist theory within Marxism" (Butler, Laclau *et al.*, 2000: 1). What are the effects of poststructuralism on Marxism and do they necessarily involve the renunciation of class analysis? What are the theoretical consequences of taking discourse as the model of social practice and what political perspectives does it open, or foreclose?

Post-Marxism and Post-Marxism

Laclau and Mouffe's characteristic claim is to retain key insights from Gramsci (hegemony) and Althusser (overdetermination) while deconstructing the history of Marxist politics and consigning the remainder "to the museum of antiquities" (Laclau, 1990: 181). The rejection of Marxist-Leninist politics, however, belies the importance of historical materialism as a social theory for the major theorists of postmarxism. Generally speaking, radical democratic postmarxism suggests not only a specifically leftwing postmodernism, but also the continued negotiation of the Marxian legacy. As Laclau explains in a conciliatory moment, postmarxism has not "rejected Marxism. Something very different has occurred. It's Marxism that has broken up and I believe that I'm holding on to its best fragments" (Laclau, 1990: 201).

Yet the very term "post-Marxism" seems to reflect a crucial ambivalence. Right from the beginning, the "post" in postmarxism was regarded as a calculated ambiguity, delineating something indeterminate, lying between temporal eclipse and intellectual supersession (Geras, 1990: 62). Stuart Sim's survey essay, "Spectres and Nostalgia: *Post*-Marxism/Post-*Marxism*" views the hyphenation as dividing the postmarxian field into two camps (Sim, 1998: 1-15). Following Sim, we can suppose that "to be *post*-Marxist is to have turned one's back on the principles of Marxism," whereas "to be post-*Marxist* is, in the style of Laclau and Mouffe, to attempt to graft recent theoretical developments ... on to Marxism, such that Marxism can be made relevant to a new cultural climate that is no longer responding to classical Marxist doctrine" (Sim, 1998: 2). Sim positions postmarxism within the political vacuum on the Left created by the collapse of historical Communism and the discrediting of classical Marxism. In this void, suggests Sim, the unity of the field of postmarxism is given by its retrospective on Marxism, whether that retrospective is positive—in which case postmarxism retains the ghost of Marx—or negative—in which case a certain nostalgia for the lost total theory can be detected. But if the nostalgic remainder active within *post*-Marxism manifests itself as a perennial aroma of lost faith and repetitions of apostasy, the spectrally Marxian dimension of post-*Marxism* seems less motivated. "One is left wondering why post-*Marxism* needs Marxism at all," Sim writes, "and what meaningful contribution it can make to a postmodern politics of the kind Laclau and Mouffe are espousing" (Sim, 1998: 2).

Contra Sim, I contend that this question can be answered precisely. Traditions are constituted through complex dialectics of betrayal and renewal, and the many strands in the Marxian tradition are no exception.[2] The lead-

---

2. For a discussion of tradition, authority and betrayal, consult Peter Osborne, *The Politics of Time* (Osborne, 1995: 127-138). Osborne's position, mediated by a reading of Walter Benjamin, implies the existence of a multiplicity of tendencies within a tradition and the political dimension of the conflict of interpretations that are adjudicated by traditionary authorities. For traditionary authority consult Hans-Georg Gadamer, *Truth and Method* (Ga-

ing example is Western Marxism, whose turn to an exploration of social subjectivity, as the antidote to classical Marxism's mechanical objectivism, constitutes the paradigm of dissidence in the Marxian tradition (Anderson, 1979). Likewise, Laclau and Mouffe's claim, to deconstructively separate the theoretical gold of radical insights from the metaphysical dross of Marxism, displays all of the contradictory elements proper to a "betrayal" of tradition that remains internal to its framework. Indeed, Laclau and Mouffe's concepts of discursive practice and hegemonic articulation are designed to operate by retaining the Marxian insight into the historicity of social relations, while avoiding the deconstructive criticism of metaphysical principles. Postmarxism's characteristic turn, from a reified totality to subjectivity as a principle of rupture, is reminiscent of Western Marxism as a whole and tends to mark postmarxism as an internal moment of the history of the Marxian tradition.

Hence the dense atmosphere of ambiguity surrounding postmarxian declarations of continued faith in, and apostasy towards, the Marxian legacy. On the one hand, postmarxism insists that it is "beyond Marxism," and therefore resolutely *post*-Marxist. It has dispensed with the centrality of the working class, the materialist postulates concerning historical existence and the importance of class relations for social structuration, and embraced postmodern ethical relativism, historicist skepticism towards foundational claims and a constructivist ontology of discourse that often borders on subjectivism. Yet, at the same time, as I show in what follows, key concrete analyses are conducted from a recognisably Marxist frame. So, on the other hand, postmarxism maintains what can only be described as a tortured loyalty to the strands of the Marxist tradition.

Laclau and Mouffe have vigorously defended themselves from accusations on the Left that they are simply ex-Marxists and have taken some pains to make their relationship to Marxism explicit. "We believe that," they argue in their reply to one such criticism:

> by clearly locating ourselves in a post-Marxist terrain, we not only help to clarify the meaning of contemporary social struggles but also to give Marxism its theoretical dignity, which can only proceed from recognition of its limitations and of its historicality. Only through such recognition will Marx's work remain present in our tradition and our political culture (Laclau and Mouffe, 1987b: 130).

Now, "our tradition and our political culture" is a notoriously vague expression. So, in response to further questioning, Laclau again returned to the theme:

---

damer, 1998: 277-285) and Paul Ricoeur, *Time and Narrative*, volume three (Ricoeur, 1988: 207-240). Laclau's grasp of the category of tradition springs primarily from Gadamer and reproduces his tendency to regard traditions as unitary, thereby depoliticising the conflict of interpretations.

as far as I am concerned, the deconstruction of Marxist tradition, not its mere abandonment, is what proves important. The loss of collective memory is not something to be overjoyed about. It is always an impoverishment and a traumatic fact. One only thinks from a tradition. Of course, the relation with tradition should not be one of submission and repetition but of transformation and critique. One must construct one's discourse as difference in relation to that tradition and this implies at the same time continuities and discontinuities (Laclau, 1990: 179).

The conclusion is as unavoidable as it is surprising: postmarxism thinks from the tradition of Marxism, in terms of a difference from and within that tradition. While postmarxism is linked to the cultural turn and postmodern politics, its radicalism springs from a continuous (deconstructive) *renegotiation* of its relation to Marxism.

Post-Althusserian Theories of Ideology

I contend that postmarxism in its emergent state remains in a relation of negative dependency upon Marxism, which it relies upon for theoretical raw material, endlessly re-traversing a deconstruction of historical material-ism so as to generate its substantive positions. This relation to Marxism can be further specified, because postmarxian discourse theory begins as a de-velopment of the post-Althusserian concept of ideology. To be exact: post-marxian theory departs from Althusser's "notes for an investigation" into "ideology and ideological state apparatuses," or the "ISAs essay" (Althusser, 1971: 127-186). This is crucial, because postmarxism prolongs and even ex-acerbates the central problem in the Althusserian theory of ideology. The problem with Althusser's essay is the incomplete synthesis between the criti-cal concept of ideology (ideology as a mystification of exploitative social re-lations) and the neutral conception of ideology (ideology as a neutral terrain on which social agents contend for hegemony) (Larrain, 1983: 88-121).

In the Althusserian problematic, the "ISAs essay" was intended to solve the difficult question of how the complex whole of the social formation, which had been described as a "structural eternity" (Althusser and Bali-bar, 1970: 107, 189), was nonetheless capable of historical transformations as a result of political interventions. Althusser's adaptation of the psychoana-lytic concept of the Imaginary[3] for the Marxist theory of ideology implied a shift beyond the supposition that ideologies are mainly conceptual systems

---

3. According to Žižek, "in the *imaginary* relation, the two poles of opposition are comple-mentary; together they build a harmonious totality; each gives the other what the other lacks … The *symbolic* relation is, on the contrary, differential: the identity of each of the moments consists in its difference to the opposite moment … it is not complementary to the other, but on the contrary, *takes the place of the lack in the other*. … Finally, the *Real* is defined as a point of the immediate coincidence of the opposite poles," that is, a traumatic impossibility, or logical inconsistency (Žižek, 1989: 171-173).

(mistaken theories of social relations), towards the hypothesis that ideologies are a modality of lived experience. According to this conception, ideology is a subject-centred body of representations that inserts individuals into social practices by aligning their social subjectivity with the requirements of their existence as mere supports of the structure. "So ideology," Althusser summarised:

> is a matter of the lived relation between men and their world. This relation, which only appears as "conscious" on condition that it is unconscious, in the same way only seems to be simple on condition that it is complex, that it is not a simple relation but a relation between relations, a second degree relation. In ideology men do indeed express, not the relationship between them and their conditions of existence, but the way they live the relation between them and their conditions of existence: this presupposes both a real relation and an "imaginary," "lived" relation (Althusser, 1969: 233).

The mystification inherent in ideology springs from its subject-centred misrecognition of decentred social structures, not from a motivated distortion of economic relations. Althusser's embrace of the neutral conception of ideology as a process of subject-formation—that is, the formation of political subjects through their interpellation, or "hailing," by the state machinery in the process of education, formal democracy, civic life and so forth—represented a breakthrough. Ideological "state" apparatuses function by "interpellating," or hailing, individuals as socialised subjects whose political subjectivity is characterised by an ineluctable misrecognition of their social existence. According to Althusser's extraordinarily influential essay, ideology consists of ritualised practices in institutional contexts and so ideology has a material existence (Althusser, 1971: 133).

In the "ISAs essay," Althusser jettisoned residual functionalist assumptions, present in *For Marx*, which made subjects into mere cultural dupes. At a stroke, Althusser's essay opened a non-reductive conception of ideology and transformed the Structural Marxist problematic, from a deterministic one dominated by structurally necessary social reproduction (Althusser and Balibar's "structural eternity"), to a probabilistic universe in which social reproduction becomes something contested by politicised social subjects. Because ideology is an ensemble of material practices producing subjects, it is impossible to reduce ideology to an epiphenomenal "false consciousness" that merely reflects the relations of production. The subject-positions produced by ideological institutions depend upon the balance of forces in the state apparatus and on the existence (or not) of counter-hegemonic ideological apparatuses—meaning that social reproduction is something contested, not something automatic. In the English-speaking world, this essay massively influenced—via the Birmingham School of sociology and film studies centred on the journal *Screen*—the programme of cultural studies, as the investigation of the cultural practices constitutive of social subjectivity.[4]

Despite its suggestive character, however, Althusser's essay did not resolve the central problem of Structural Marxism, for Althusser's position now encountered the opposite difficulty. Having dispensed with the assumption of an automatic social reproduction that might generate "structural eternities," Althusser had to explain why nonetheless, on balance, it was most probable that the social formation would continue to exist. Most likely, class relations would continue to be reproduced through the production of class-based subject-positions, unless explicitly contested (by, for instance, the French Communist Party, to which Althusser belonged). But if the state was not just an instrument in the hands of the ruling class, but instead a complex institutional structure enjoying its own relative autonomy from the relations of production, then why would the "ideological state apparatuses" produce ideologically submissive working-class subjects? What was the link between social subjectivity and the reproduction of social classes? Althusser's essay broached this question in the "Afterword" (Althusser, 1971: 183-186), but never resolved it, leading to an entire generation of post-Althusserian efforts to re-interpret this essay through the lens of neo-Marxian theory and post-structuralist philosophies.

One of the most influential efforts to solve the problem of the relation between ideological competition and class power was essayed by Laclau, who proposed to cut the Gordian Knot of the reproduction of class relations by completely separating social class and ideological subjectivity. Henceforth, Laclau declared, classes were economic and ideologies were ... well, ideological. Yet, in this operation, Laclau also severed the critical and neutral components of Althusser's theory of ideology, so as to dispense with the class element. This results in a Marxism best described as an economic reductionism of a structuralist variety (or structuralist economism), exemplified by Laclau's own *Politics and Ideology in Marxist Theory* (1977) and Mouffe's contributions to *Gramsci and Marxist Theory* (1979). This might be briefly described as the proposition that while the social relations of production and the productive forces exhaust the definition of the fundamental classes of capitalist society, classes float in a non-capitalist political and cultural environment, which they try to hegemonise as political and cultural supplements to their economic dominance. Subsequently, Laclau and Mouffe repudiated this position and turned to a deconstruction of structuralist economism in *Hegemony*.

While Laclau and Mouffe (in particular) represent structuralist economism as exhausting the totality of the Marxian legacy, this is actually not accurate. Indeed, their deconstruction of structuralist economism in *HSS* tends

---

4. The landmark text of the Birmingham school that uses Althusser's essay is Hebdige (Hebdige, 1991); for a survey of the theoretical origins of cultural studies, see Hall (Hall, 1992). For the lineage of *Screen*, consult Easthope (Easthope, 1983).

only to invert the problems of economic reductionism while dispersing the political conclusions of this form of Marxism into a politics of indeterminacy. In postmarxian theory, *Politics and Ideology in Marxist Theory* is relied upon as the definitive demonstration of the "class essentialism" and "economic reductionism" of Marxism, final evidence that historical materialism means the "disappearance of politics" into economics (Smith, 1998: 43-83; Torfing, 1999: 15-34). Indeed, Laclau has retroactively reconstructed this "Gramsci-inspired critique of Structural Marxism" as the inception of his postmarxism (Laclau, 1990: 202). *Politics and Ideology in Marxist Theory* is therefore something of an "ur-text" of postmarxian discourse theory. My contention is that this work is fundamentally flawed. Laclau arrived at a highly unstable transitional position that combines the assertion that every phenomenon is overdetermined by class with the proposition that ideology is class-neutral. Laclau's "Gramsci-inspired critique of Structural Marxism" (Torfing, 1999: 15-34) led to postmarxian historicism once the structuralist economism of this transitional phase was subjected to deconstruction in *HSS*.

Post-Althusserian theory thereby entered the charmed circle of ideology, where the ideological struggle at first displaced, and then completely subsumed, the political and economic struggles. Once the characterisation of ideology as both social foundation and societal cement is accepted, then ideological discourse becomes constitutive of both social relations and subjects' worldviews. Ideological discourse now constitutes a unity of objective institutions and discursive interpretations (Laclau and Mouffe, 1985: 107), which determines that a henceforth generalised "discourse" constructs everything (Laclau, 1990: 104), from the matter of distant stars to the terrestrial competition between ideological worldviews. I maintain that such a theory of ideological discourse creates a charmed circle, in which everything appears to be a result of political subjectivity, meaning that postmarxian discourse theory necessarily gravitates towards relativism.

The Problem of Historicism

Where Althusser claimed that the mode of production is the "absent cause" of the social formation that is "present only in its effects," post-Althusserian historicism alleges that there exists no such cause, absent or otherwise (Laclau, 1990: 59). The social field is conceptualised as a flat surface, upon which social agents inscribe different hegemonic articulations unconstrained by any hidden structural matrix (Laclau and Mouffe, 1985: 98). Lacking any reference to a determinate extra-discursive materiality, postmarxian theories of discourse necessarily include theory itself (their own included) within the charmed circle of ideology. Accordingly, for Laclau, the postmodern Left needs to "reformulate the values of the Enlightenment in the direction of a radical historicism" (Laclau, 1990: 84). By rejecting every "epistemological break" between science and ideology, postmarxism postulates that theory is merely an ideological worldview, rendered coherent by its presentation as an explicit doctrine (Laclau, 1996a: 299).

Historicism is a relativist hermeneutics, which postulates the incommensurability of historical epochs or cultural formations and therefore denies the possibility of a general history or trans-cultural universals. Best described as "a critical movement insisting on the prime importance of historical context" to the interpretation of texts, actions and institutions, historicism emerges in reaction against both philosophical rationalism and scientific theory (Hamilton, 1996: 2). According to Paul Hamilton's general introduction:

> Anti-Enlightenment historicism develops a characteristically double focus. Firstly, it is concerned to situate any statement—philosophical, historical, aesthetic, or whatever—in its historical context. Secondly, it typically doubles back on itself to explore the extent to which any historical enterprise inevitably reflects the interests and bias of the period in which it was written ... [and] it is equally suspicious of its own partisanship (Hamilton, 1996: 2).

It is sometimes supposed that a strategy of socio-historical contextualisation represents the alpha and omega of materialist analysis—e.g. Jameson's celebrated claim that "always historicise" is the imperative of historical materialism (Jameson, 1981: 11). I contend, on the contrary, that although necessary, contextualisation *alone* is radically insufficient. This strategy of historical contextualisation, as I shall demonstrate in the course of my *investigation apropos* of postmarxism, suffers from three serious defects. The historicist problematic depends upon the reduction of every phenomenal field to an immanent network of differential relations and the consequent evacuation of the category of cause from its theoretical armoury (Copjec, 1994b: 1-15). It is therefore unable to theorise the hierarchy of effective causes within an overdetermined phenomenon and must necessarily reduce to a descriptive list, progressively renouncing explanation for interpretation. Secondly, lacking a theoretical explanation of the unequal factors overdetermining a phenomenon, historicism necessarily flattens the causal network surrounding its object into a homogeneous field of co-equal components. As a consequence, historicism's description of the social structure or historical sequence gravitates in the direction of a simple totality, where everything can be directly connected to everything else. Thirdly, the self-reflexive turn to historical inscription of the researcher's position of enunciation into the contextual field results, *on these assumptions*, in a gesture of relativisation that cannot stop short of relativism. The familiar performative contradictions of relativism then ensure that historicism must support itself through an explicit or implicit appeal to a neutral metalinguistic framework, which typically takes the form of a historical master narrative or essentialist conception of the social totality. The final result of the historicist turn, therefore, is that this "materialist" analysis is in actuality a form of spiritual holism.

Historicism relies upon a variant of what Althusser called "expressive causality," which acts through "the primacy of the whole as an essence of which the parts are no more than the phenomenal expressions" (Althusser and Balibar, 1970: 187). Expressive causality postulates an essential principle whose epiphenomenal expressions are microcosms of the whole (Althusser and Balibar, 1970: 187-192). Whether this expressive totality is social or historical is a contingent question of theoretical preference. When the social field is regarded as an expressive totality, the institutional structures of a historical epoch—economy, politics, law, culture, philosophy and so on—are viewed as externalisations of an essential principle that is manifest in the apparent complexity of these phenomena. When the historical process is considered to be an expressive totality, a historical master narrative operates to guarantee that the successive historical epochs represent the unfolding of a single essential principle. Formally speaking, the problem with expressive (also known as "organic" and "spiritual") totalities is that they postulate a homology between all the phenomena of the social totality, so that the social practices characteristic of the distinct structural instances of the complex whole of the social formation are regarded as secretly "the same" (Jameson, 1981: 34-52).

In the Hegelian Marxism of Lukács, for instance, the historicist problematic begins from the *relativisation of theory*, whereby that it is claimed that historical materialism is the "perspective" and "worldview" of the revolutionary class and that, in general, theory (philosophy) is only the coherent systematisation of the ideological worldview of a social group (Lukács, 1971: 149). No distinction of kind exists between theory and ideology, opening the path for the *foundational character of ideology*, expressed through the Lukácsian claim that the ideological consciousness of a historical subject is the expression of objective relations, and that, correlatively, this historical subject (the proletariat) alienates-expresses a free society by means of a transparent grasp of social processes (Lukács, 1971: 27, 187-188). The society, as an expression of a single structure of social relations (where the commodity form and reified consciousness are theoretical equivalents) is an *expressive totality* (Lukács, 1971: 83, 85), so that politics and ideology can be directly deduced from philosophical relations. According to Lukács' directly Hegelian conception, the historical subject is the unified proletariat, which, as the "creator of the totality of [social] contents" (Lukács, 1971: 123), makes history according to its conception of the world, and thus functions as an *identical subject-object of history* (Lukács, 1971: 149). The identical subject-object and the transparency of praxis therefore form the *telos* of the historical process. Lukács reduces the multiplicity of social practices operative within the social formation to the model of an individual "making history," through the externalisation of an intellectual conception of the world. Lukács therefore arrives at the final element of the historicist problematic, namely, a theorisation of *social practice on the model of individual praxis*, presented as the historical action of a "collective individual" (Lukács, 1971: 137-140). This structure of claims is vulnerable to philosophical deconstruction (Gasché, 1985) and leads to individualist political conclusions (Althusser, 1976).

In the light of the Gramscian provenance of postmarxism, however, it is important to note that while the explicit target of Althusser's critique was the Hegelian totality, Althusser is equally critical of the aleatory posture of Gramsci's "absolute historicism," regarding it as exemplary of the impasse of radicalised historicism (Althusser and Balibar, 1970: 119-144). Althusser argues that Gramsci preserves the philosophical structure of historicism exemplified by Lukács and so the criticism of "expressive totality," or spiritual holism, also applies to Gramsci. According to Gramsci, "the philosophy of praxis is absolute 'historicism,' the absolute secularisation and earthiness of thought, an absolute humanism of history" (Gramsci, 1971: 465).[5] Gramsci's is an "absolute" historicism because it subjects the "absolute knowledge" supposed to be possible at the Hegelian "end of history" to historicisation-relativisation: instead of absolute knowledge, every truly universal worldview becomes merely the epochal totalisation of the present. Consequently, Gramsci rejects the conception that a social agent might aspire to "absolute knowledge" by adopting the "perspective of totality". If anything, this exacerbates the problems of historicism by bringing the inherent relativism of the position to the surface. Ideology, conceptualised as the worldview of a historical subject (revolutionary proletariat, hegemonic alliance), forms the foundation of the social field, because in the historicist lens a social system is cemented by the ideology of the dominant group. Philosophy (and by extension, theory) represents only the systematisation of ideology into a coherent doctrine, while politics is based on ideological manipulation as its necessary precondition. Thus, for historicism, every "theoretical" intervention is *immediately* a political act, and correlatively, theory becomes the *direct* servant of ideology.

Critically Mapping the Postmarxian Field

For Althusser, Gramsci's reconstruction of Marxism as the "philosophy of praxis" necessarily leads to historicist relativism. This is not because of some subjective defect on Gramsci's part, but because historicism is an intellec-

---

5. The best analysis of Gramsci's work remains Perry Anderson's seminal essay on the "antinomies of Gramsci" (Anderson, 1976). For an Althusserian analysis of Gramsci, see Buci-Glucksmann's (sometimes forced) extended interpretation of the *Prison Notebooks* (Buci-Glucksmann, 1980). An example of the historicist interpretation of Gramsci is provided by Boggs (Boggs, 1976).

tual structure, or "theoretical problematic". Althusser's central claim is that the theoretical problematic determines the limits of what can be articulated within a research programme. Therefore, the "project of thinking Marxism as an (absolute) historicism automatically unleashes a logically necessary chain reaction which tends to flatten out the Marxist totality into a variation of the Hegelian totality" (Althusser and Balibar, 1970: 132). Drawing upon Althusser's concept of "theoretical practice" (Althusser, 1969: 182-193), I define the postmarxian field as constituted by a process of theoretical production whose moments consist of theoretical raw materials (a specific historical and theoretical *relation to Marxism*), a theoretical problematic, or conceptual framework (postmarxian *historicism*) and a body of theoretical knowledge, or ensemble of substantive theoretical positions (the formulation of a *new theory of discourse* and the *political strategy of radical democracy*).[6] Nonetheless, despite the polemical thrust of my analysis of postmarxism, the Althusserian concept of a problematic is designed not as an excuse for denunciations, but as a research instrument. Specifically, Althusser claims to develop a structural hermeneutic capable of producing the textual unconscious of a theoretical work, locating in its ruptures and silences the existence of contradictions that are the unspoken question to which the text is a reply (Althusser and Balibar, 1970: 28). If postmarxism is an ensemble of "answers without questions," then the aim of a post-Althusserian analysis is to disclose the open question that a specific historico-theoretical moment generates. I shall

---

6. The reader may be surprised to see Althusser's old telescope being dusted off to map the theoretical debates of the twenty-first century (Thompson called it an "orrery," but it remains more than a museum-piece). While Althusser's theory of science has been immensely refined and developed in the work of Roy Bhaskar (Resch, 1992; Collier, 1994), the structure of the Althusserian concept of "problematic" remains close to Bhaskar's idea of the scientific "production of ideas from ideas" (Bhaskar, 1978; Bhaskar, 1979)—both Resch and Collier make this point (Resch, 1992; Collier, 1994). Secondly, the Althusserian distinction between the knowledge-object and the real object is similar to Bhaskar's distinction between, respectively, the transitive and the intransitive objects of science. There are two major differences between Althusser and Bhaskar. Firstly, Bhaskar maintains—and I support this conclusion— that within a realist ontology, the cycle of knowledge-generation must improve scientific knowledge of the intransitive object. This resolves the tension in the Althusserian conceptual universe between a theory of historical epistemology and Althusser's commitment to realist materialism. Secondly, Bhaskar develops a non-metaphysical materialist dialectics—Althusser is an anti-dialectician—that, while highly critical of both Hegel and Marx, represents a major contribution to historical materialism (Bhaskar, 1991: especially "Marxian Dialectic I," 344-347 and "Marxian Dialectic II," 348-353). Bhaskar's dialectics revolves upon "transformative negations," that is, determinate ontological negations, and emphasises the irreducibility of dialectical contradictions to logical contradictions (Bhaskar, 1991: 6, 56-63). Broadly speaking, Bhaskar designates processes characterised by the unity (*not* the identity) of opposite determinations, in the form of enabling constraints on action that generate "double-bind" situations, as "dialectical," and this is the sense of the word hereafter in this work (Bhaskar, 1991: 56). Dialectical theory does not support performative contradictions, which remain the "basic form of theory/practice and reflective inconsistency" (Bhaskar, 1991: 44).

show in the course of this investigation that this question revolves upon the problem of structuration, that is, the generative dialectical process whereby structures are reformed while acting as matrices of partial constraint to their own transformation, at once ground and result of transformative practices.

In other words, I intend to demonstrate that postmarxism exhibits the characteristic erasure of social complexity and reinstitution of expressive totality theorised by Althusser as the inevitable consequence of embracing the historicist problematic. I do not for a moment deny the complexity and unevenness of Laclau and Mouffe, Butler and Žižek; nor do I suppose that a theoretical problematic affects every researcher in a field identically; nor, finally, do I dispute that they are sometimes manifestly aware of the problems associated with historicism. What I claim is that the historicist problematic functions as a theoretical unconscious that prevents postmarxism from exploiting many of its own insights, and that, insofar as historicism is only criticised episodically and not structurally, it remains the centre of gravity, governing, in the final analysis, postmarxism's substantive positions. I maintain that the historicist problematic is characterised by five key positions: the relativisation of theory, the foundational character of ideology, the expressive conception of history, an identical subject-object and a theory of social practice modelled on individual praxis. These characteristics form the basis for my chapter sequence, whereby I shall demonstrate that postmarxian discourse theory is structured by the historicist problematic.

In this work, I am interested in the moment of emergence of postmarxism: broadly speaking, from *Hegemony and Socialist Strategy* (1985) through to the joint declaration of tendency in *Contingency, Hegemony, Universality* (2000). Specifically, I am interested in the way in which embrace of the historicist problematic during this formative period sets up the positions of Laclau and Mouffe, Butler and Žižek within expressive and individualist conceptions of history and praxis. In another work, I shall critique the subsequent development of these positions, starting from *Contingency, Hegemony, Universality* (2000) and tracking through to the present.

In Chapter One, I locate postmarxism in its historical context and explain how the relativisation of theory determines the postmarxian conception of the necessity for a shift "beyond Marxism". In Chapter Two, I turn to the major theoretical statements of postmarxism in the works of Laclau and Mouffe. I demonstrate that a latent expressive totality of history subtends the problematic of Laclau and Mouffe, and I show that this determines the limits to their deconstruction-inflected post-Althusserian theory of ideology. Chapter Three places Butler's Foucault-inspired post-Althusserian theory of ideology under the critical lens. I suggest that the successive waves of theorisation of Butler's influential concept of "performativity" represent so many efforts to escape from the implications of a set of assumptions regarding discourse that lead ineluctably towards a conception of social practice modeled on individual praxis. investigates the theoretical hesitations, political reversals and ethical uncertainties in Žižek's Lacanian-inspired post-Althusserian theory of ideology, to propose that Žižek's break from postmarxism towards a messianic Marxism is informed by an impossible desire to recreate the identical subject-object of history. Finally, Chapter Four investigates the theoretical hesitations, political reversals and ethical uncertainties in Žižek's Lacanian-inspired post-Althusserian theory of ideology, to propose that Žižek's break from postmarxism towards a messianic Marxism is informed by an impossible desire to recreate the identical subject-object of history.

Although the postmarxists have made some important advances in the theory of ideology, my investigation is critical of the tendency's collapse into historicism, especially its abandonment of causal historical explanation for a relativist political hermeneutics. While accepting the necessity of a Marxist engagement with poststructuralism, I contend that any post-Althusserian theory needs to fully grasp the historical and theoretical stakes involved in Structural Marxism's incomplete break from classical historical materialism. Laclau and Mouffe, Butler and Žižek radically underestimate the sophistication of Structural Marxism, which does not need to resort to a dismissal of poststructuralism in order to produce a viable contemporary class analysis. I seek to integrate many of the insights of postmarxism to outline an expanded theory of class politics that escapes the "charmed circle of ideology," that is, postmarxism's tendency to reduce politics and economics to ideological struggles.

I

"New Times": The Emergence of Postmarxism

Marx somewhere says that every incomplete revolution is followed by a crapulous depression, during which the old order regains its ascendancy by driving radical thinking into the margins of political life. When "the year of the barricades" (1968) was followed not merely by three decades of neo-liberal counter-offensive, but then by the disappointment trailing after the democratic revolutions of 1989, this crapulous depression—ably documented by Terry Eagleton (Eagleton, 1996)—turned into "desolation" and "mourning" (Aronson, 1995: 4, 9). Yet, as Freud reminds us, the transition from the desolation of melancholia to the work of mourning (and the subsequent adoption of a new ideal) is often accomplished via a moment of manic euphoria (Freud, 1984: 251-268). On the Left, this euphoria takes the form of a celebration of the supposed paradigm shift "beyond Marxism" inspired by the advent of "New Times, New Social Movements and New Democracy," of which postmarxism is supposed to be the theoretical expression.[1]

The notion that historical materialism now stands behind the "New Times," stranded by history, still speaking the discourse of a less complex society, has acquired the force of a popular prejudice. Postmarxism, aligning itself with these themes, has been celebrated as a postmodern politics in tune with the emerging realities of economic globalisation, worldwide democracy and postmodern culture (Eschle, 2001: 53-84; Nash, 2000: 1-45). This "paradigm shift" entails the transformation of social and cultural the-

---

1. The expression "new times" comes from the journal *Marxism Today*, a pioneering advocate of the thesis of the advent of a new, postmodern reality that rendered the class-struggle prognoses of the Left invalid. For a devastating critique of the politics of *Marxism Today*, consult Saville's article (Saville, 1990) and for an analysis of the "enriched Gramscianism" that forms the general context for the concept of new times propounded by *Marxism Today*, consult Harris (Harris, 1992).

ory, in line with the dominant philosophical motif (philosopheme) of radical contingency, and the abandonment of discourses of redistributive justice for the postmodern strategy of multiple struggles for cultural recognition (Fraser, 1996: 1-39). These are taken to be "self-evidently" incompatible with historical materialism. The concept of an "obviously" postmarxian social reality belongs with the idea that the collapse of "actually existing socialism" (or historical Communism) means the end of socialism as a historical movement. Together they constitute the received popular wisdom of the age.

Laclau and Mouffe accept the common sense of the epoch and systematise it philosophically. According to Laclau and Mouffe, not only has "the era of normative epistemologies come to an end," but embracing "the discourse of radical democracy [means] ... renouncing the discourse of the universal" (Laclau and Mouffe, 1985: 192). In line with postmodernism, Laclau announces that the Left needs to "reformulate the values of the Enlightenment in the direction of a radical historicism and to renounce its rationalistic epistemological and ontological foundations ... to expand the democratic potentialities of [the socialist] tradition, while abandoning totalitarian tendencies arising from its reoccupation of the ground of apocalyptic universalism" (Laclau, 1990: 84). Targeting Marxism's supposed insistence that the proletariat is the direct incarnation of political universality, Laclau announces that "the more 'universal' the idea to be embodied is, the greater the distance from the historical limitations of the social agents intended as its bearers will be, and the more likely it is that the result will be a monstrous symbiosis" (Laclau, 1990: xi). In other words, to avoid a new Stalinism, we need to embrace the relativisation of the universal that is the correlate to the postmodern "end of Enlightenment". Supposedly, the Left needs to accept the conclusions of the postmodern analysis: that there is no privileged social agent for historical change, no special structural level that holds the key to social development and no unified space of political contestation where the contradictions of the social formation condense (Laclau and Mouffe, 1985: 85). In the light of the supposed ineluctability of these historical and intellectual transformations, Laclau claims, postmarxism has become "an inevitable decision for anyone aiming to reformulate a political programme for the Left in [contemporary] historical circumstances" (Laclau, 1990: xii).

This chapter probes the justifications for a "paradigm shift" to postmarxian theory, seeking to elucidate the links between postmodern culture and radical democratic politics. Postmarxism, I maintain, relies upon a concealed historico-spiritual narrative, according to which, the new epoch of "postmodernity" is to be expressed through a shift from modern to postmodern politics and culture. This epochal "spirit of the age"—a sort of "Hegel-lite"—is represented through the concept of "New Times," which functions to frame postmarxism's empirical arguments for the redundancy of modern concepts of emancipation. Generally speaking, postmarxism's rationale for moving "beyond Marxism" is advanced by means of three major empirical claims: (1) that the main causes of social conflict in the contemporary world cannot be explained from a Marxist perspective; (2) that the agency of the new social movements renders the notion of a proletarian subject of history bankrupt; and, (3) that Marxism cannot generate a democratic programme.

Accordingly, the chapter is divided into five sections. In the first section, I examine the claims that the "New Times" represent an epochal transition beyond modernity. In the second section, I probe the related argument that the "New Times" mandate a "paradigm shift" to postmodern theory. Then, in sections three, four and five, I investigate the major social theoretical and political claims of postmarxism: the forms of social conflict in the contemporary world; the role and nature of the New Social Movements (NSM); and, the relationship between Marxism and democracy. In the relevant sections of this chapter I examine the evidence for the postmarxian claims and conclude that the postmarxian arguments exhibit some key anomalies. But I also contend the entire methodological approach of postmarxism—which I maintain is a form of cognitive and moral relativism—leads to a major conceptual problem. Postmarxism relativises theory so that theory becomes another expression of the historical process, on the same level as ideology. The erasure of the epistemological distinction between theory and ideology, especially when linked to an historico-spiritual totality, begins by supplanting explanation with description and ends by imposing structures of ideological misrecognition onto theory. I therefore not only highlight the empirical realities that constitute theoretical anomalies for the postmarxian claims, but also I seek to demonstrate that postmarxian theory regards social existence through the characteristic distortions of the ideological lens. In subsequent chapters these anomalies are explained within a theoretical framework that supplies an alternative to postmarxism.

In the first section of the chapter, I demonstrate that postmarxism relies upon an ideological conception of "postmodernity," which supports an expressive relation between history and theory. I then confront the first major postmarxian claim, that Marxism has failed to explain the crisis dynamics and the main lines of conflict in contemporary societies (Laclau and Mouffe, 1985: 149-193; Steinmetz, 1994: 176-212). In refuting this, I trace postmarxism's imposition of an imaginary unity onto diverse social phenomena, through the replacement, in successive theorisations of the contemporary conjuncture, of theoretical structures by subject-centred phenomenological descriptions. Secondly, following a widely accepted belief on the Left (Giddens, 1994a), postmarxism holds that the new social movements (hereafter, NSM)—composed of a diversity of non-class-centred social movements centred on identity politics, including urban, ecological, anti-authoritarian, feminist, anti-racist, ethnic, regional and sexual minority movements, and

so forth (Laclau and Mouffe, 1985: 159)—are the bearers of the "social revolutions of our time" (Laclau, 1985: 42). Postmarxists claim that the advent
of the NSM invalidates the Marxian conception of the historical process
and provides the definitive refutation of historical materialism (Laclau and
Mouffe, 1985: 3; Mouffe, 1988: 31; Smith, 1998: 3; Steinmetz, 1994: 177). In
the third section of the chapter, I demonstrate that, in the classical ideological style, postmarxism transforms the NSM into the specular opposite, or
inverted mirror-image, of the "traditional working class". One consequence
of this is that postmarxism is forced to advocate the untenable claim that
the NSM have nothing to do with class location. As an alternative, I propose
that the empirical evidence suggests that eliminating class from the explanation of the NSM is as futile as reducing them to class politics: the empirical evidence suggests that the NSM are the result of complex social determinations *including* class location. Finally, it is supposed that increasing social
complexity and postmodern pluralism undermine the socialist conception
of political strategy, meaning that Marxism cannot produce a democratic
political programme for contemporary society (Laclau and Mouffe, 1985:
177; Smith, 1998: 115). This is a structure of misrecognition which depends
upon a massive act of theoretical repression, namely, the elimination of postmarxism's radical dependence on the legacy of Eurocommunism. I show
that there is an actuality a long tradition of democratic theory in Marxism
and—more importantly—a number of important practical experiments in
democratic politics. I thereby demonstrate that the functional role of ideology—the concealment of contradictions—is an important aspect of the postmarxian substitution of ideological competition for theoretical debate.

THEORIES OF A NEW EPOCH OF POSTMODERN POLITICS

The Crapulous Depression of "New Times"

Postmarxian politics—the strategy of radical democracy—is generally supposed to be a postmodern politics that is the expression of a new society.
During the 1980s, Laclau and Mouffe launched the manifesto of the new
political and theoretical current of postmarxism. They proposed that the
Left stood at a turning-point between historic oblivion and a new direction,
and advocated turning towards a radical and plural democracy as a reconceptualisation of socialist strategy.

> The "evident truths" of the past—the classical forms of analysis and
> political calculation, the nature of the forces in conflict, the very meaning
> of the Left's struggles and objectives—have been seriously challenged by
> an avalanche of historical mutations which have riven the ground on
> which those truths were constituted (Laclau and Mouffe, 1985: 2).

Accordingly, the Left was faced not only with the falsification of its strategic perspectives, but also the exposure of "actually existing socialism" as a new form of domination. Nonetheless, the situation was not solely characterised in terms of the delegitimation of Marxism and the retreat of the progressive movements. To the contrary, strategically misreading the defensive conjuncture as one of advance, Laclau and Mouffe maintained that a "whole series of positive new phenomena underlie these mutations," such as the NSM and the "atypical forms of social struggle in countries on the capitalist periphery". Conjuncturally, therefore, "Western societies face a crisis of governability and a threat of dissolution at the hands of the egalitarian danger" (Laclau and Mouffe, 1985: 2). However, this conjuncture was also marked by a crisis of the classical Marxist concept of revolution, which allegedly rested upon the inaugural character of the revolutionary act, whereby the unified proletariat seizes state power and uses this as an institutional locus from which society can be rationally reconstructed (Laclau and Mouffe, 1985: 178). The Marxian schema relies upon a universal social agency (the proletariat) and a unique position from which social transformed can be effected (the state):

> What is now in crisis is a whole conception of socialism which rests upon the ontological centrality of the working class, upon the role of Revolution, with a capital "r," as the founding moment in the transition from one type of society to another, and upon the illusory prospect of a perfectly unitary and homogeneous collective will that will render pointless the moment of politics. The plural and multifarious character of contemporary social struggles has finally dissolved the last foundation for that political imaginary. Peopled with "universal" subjects and built around History in the singular, it has postulated "society" as an intelligible structure that could be intellectually mastered on the basis of certain class positions and reconstituted as a rational, transparent order, through a founding act of a political character. Today, the Left is witnessing the final act of the dissolution of that Jacobin imaginary (Laclau and Mouffe, 1985: 2).

Responding to the crisis of socialism in the broadest possible sense, then, Laclau and Mouffe proposed to jettison revolutionary insurrection, vanguard parties and the universality of the proletariat. The classical Marxist perspective is incompatible, they argued, with the increasing functional differentiation of contemporary societies, the plurality of socio-political projects brought to light by the NSM and the democratic politics of the New Left. In most respects, it seems to me that one can only agree with their broad general perspective. What is less obvious is that this critique of *classical* Marxism entails a rejection of post-classical (contemporary) forms of neo-Marxism. Equally un-argued seems to me the notion that the crisis of historical communism and classical Marxism automatically rules out any reconstruction of historical materialism and socialist strategy that might dispense with insurrectionary violence, vanguard parties and the ontological centrality of the proletariat, but retain socialist transformation, progressive organisation, universal claims and the hope of post-capitalist emancipation. But this is precisely what Laclau and Mouffe do rule out.

Curiously, despite invoking social complexity, theorists of postmarxism do not hesitate to retotalise the social field through the metaphor of "new times". Laclau and Mouffe, for instance, present an "avalanche of historical mutations" and not an explicit structural analysis, whose incompatibility with *contemporary* Marxism relies upon the massive repression of recent theoretico-political history. This invocation of a new epoch, within which Marxism could be dismissed rather than reconstructed, has an instructive precedent. Relying on metaphor to contain the dispersion of a host of perhaps unrelated developments was openly advocated in the collaboration by the former *Marxism Today* editorial collective, in their *New Times: The Changing Face of Politics in the 1990s*. According to Stuart Hall, the term "new times" was developed in the British context to embrace diverse concepts describing several structural transformations:

> If we take the "new times" idea apart, we find that it is an attempt to capture, *within the confines of a single metaphor*, a number of different facets of social change, *none of which has any necessary connection with the other*. In the current debates, a variety of different terms jostle with one another for pride of place, in the attempt to describe those different dimensions of change. They include "post-industrial," "post-Fordist," "revolution of the subject," "postmodern". None of these is wholly satisfactory. ... Each, however, signifies something important about the "new times" debate (Hall, 1989: 117 emphasis added).

In other words, the potentially divergent trajectories of these emergent developments are totalised by nothing more than the metaphor of "new times". This argument trades on the temporal dialectics of modernity—the valorisation of novelty—while introducing an epochal totalisation of history explicitly delegitimised by postmodern theory (Osborne, 1995: 1-27). Likewise, for Laclau and Mouffe the catch-all rubric of "increasing social complexity" contains phenomenal diversity in a conveniently undefined terminological unity, while at the same time masking their fundamental reliance on a vulgar Marxist methodology that reels off cultural and intellectual developments from an evolutionary logic working in the social base (Barrett, 1991: 75-76; Landry, 1991: 47). The relevant structural transformations include commodification and the introduction of scientific management of the labour process, as well as bureaucratic rationalisation and the transformation of liberal ideology (Laclau, 1990: 52-59; Laclau and Mouffe, 1985: 159-171). Astonishingly, these correspond closely to the Marxian categories of relations of production, productive forces, politics and ideology, as well as;

The decline of the classical working class in the post-industrial countries; the increasingly profound penetration of capitalist relations of production into all areas of social life, whose dislocatory effects ... have generated new forms of social protest; the emergence of mass mobilisations in Third World countries which do not follow the classical pattern of class struggle ... [and] the exposure of new forms of domination established in the name of the dictatorship of the proletariat (Laclau, 1990: 97).

These conclusions depend upon a paradoxical structure of claims whereby a fairly unreconstructed Marxism seems to be the most sensitive instrument for the diagnosis of its own irrelevance; thereafter, discursive interpretation supplants structural analysis and the enumeration and investigation of social movements and political institutions recedes to the background. Nonetheless, aggregating all of the statements in which Laclau and Mouffe make specific declarations regarding the emergence of "new times" (Laclau, 1985; Laclau, 1988: 81; Laclau, 1990: 1-4, 58-59; Laclau and Mouffe, 1985: 2, 57; Mouffe, 1988: 31; Mouffe, 1992d: 1-14; Mouffe, 1992e: 1-8), we obtain the following general structural transformations.

Philosophical. *The exhaustion of the legacy of Enlightenment metaphysics* ("essentialism") in modern philosophy and social theory brings the end of foundational universality and the advent of the postmodern shift from necessary foundations to contingent horizons (Laclau, 1988: 63-82; Mouffe, 1988: 31-46).

Social. *The increase in social complexity* consonant with "disorganised capitalism," characterised by the decline of the classical working class, leads to a condition of absolute dispersion where the structural dominance of capital accumulation dissolves (Laclau, 1990: 58-59).

Political. *The advent of the NSM* has a pluralising effect which displaces every ontologically privileged social agency (Laclau, 1985). These movements dislodge class politics, which, it turns out, "is just one species of identity politics, and one that is becoming less and less important" (Laclau, 2000a: 203).

Historical. The massive discrediting of the socialist tradition, linked to the collapse of historical Communism and decline of class politics, as a result of the exposure of "state socialism" as a new form of domination. Radical democracy, as a postmodern politics, seeks to salvage what remains viable in the Marxist tradition and to dispatch the rest "to the museum of antiquities" (Laclau, 1990: 181).

These transformations constitute the "new times," whose major theoretical expression is the "end of Enlightenment". Regardless of the increasing social complexity that these structural mutations certainly represent, postmarxism immediately reduces this to the simplicity of a shift in the "spirit of the times" by means of the historical thesis of "postmodernity," thereby linking theory and structure in an expressive relation.

Postmodern Theory and the "End of Enlightenment"

My contention is that Laclau and Mouffe remain entirely enclosed within the horizon of postmodern ideology, which postulates an epochal totality of "postmodernity". According to John Frow's exhaustive survey of the literature (Frow, 1997: 1-57), the generally accepted description of postmodern culture involves dispensing with: essentialist foundations; fixed domains of cultural values (fixed universality); the unified subject; and, history as transcendent to its textual forms. These four categories broadly correspond to Laclau and Mouffe's structural transformations.

For Frow, two significant problems attend upon most descriptions of postmodernism, namely, the tendency to deduce the content of cultural forms from the postulated existence of postmodern culture (Frow, 1997: 15)—that is, the transcendental illusion that turns a regulative hypothesis into a constitutive principle—and the construction of epochal totalities correlative to a shift in "worldview". As Frow warns:

> The problem is that of any totalising vision: ... the construction of domains of practice as massive unities ("the aesthetic") and their expressive linkage to other unified domains. Pseudo-totalities generate pseudo-histories; the epochal sense of the concept of the postmodern depends for its existence on historico-spiritual fictions (Frow, 1997: 53).

Postmodernism as an expressive concept is generally counterposed to the epochal concept of the Enlightenment. This frequently results in the sort of travesty of the history of ideas that is the hallmark of an ideological simplification. According, for instance, to the high priest of postmodern theory, Jean-François Lyotard, the postmodern "end of master narratives" means the impossibility of any totalisation of society and history, linked to the tendency of every global emancipation to turn into a new totalitarianism (Lyotard, 1997). The major themes (ideologemes) of this "end of Enlightenment" include the rejection of every foundational universality (for instance, human nature) and the supposition that society is a rational totality grounded through an essential substrate (Vattimo, 1988). Postmodern theory repudiates the concept of a unitary subject—especially any "subject of history" and all privileged social agencies—that might institute a transparent society through its control of humanity and mastery of nature (Vattimo, 1992). The utopian dream of social harmony, linked to historical teleology and the notion of a foundational act inaugurating the end of politics, is repudiated as the very root of the totalitarian temptation (Stavrakakis, 1999: 99-121).[2]

---

2. Marxist critiques of postmodernism can be divided into three categories. Criticism of postmodernism as a modality of the "lived experience" of everyday life—that is, criticism of postmodern ideology, aimed at theoretical statements as they function within a "worldview"—includes Eagleton (Eagleton, 1996), Norris (Norris, 1990; Norris, 1992, Norris, 1993) and O'Neill (O'Neill, 1995). Marxist criticism of the aesthetic productions of postmod-

Lukács, for instance, as a Hegelian Marxist, would be the very quintessence of everything that postmodernism brings into question. For Lukács, the foundational universality of the commodity form brings into existence the capitalist social totality, along with its rationally cognisable dynamics of commodity reification (Lukács, 1971: 83). This in turn brings forth the proletariat as a potential "historical subject," capable of rendering the social totality transparent through a dialectical theory grounded in social praxis, which culminates in the social revolution, considered as the founding act in the inauguration of a harmonious communist society that is beyond politics (Lukács, 1971: 149).

On the postmarxian conception, *modernity* is a historical region characterised by the incomplete emergence of the modern from the legacy of the Enlightenment. The Enlightenment, meanwhile, is considered a "re-occupation" of the modern by theology, whereas the postmodern condition becomes "modernity without illusions" (Torfing, 1999: 275). The postmarxism led by Laclau and Mouffe entirely follows this ideological conception of the relation between modernity and postmodernity. Laclau proposes the epochal thesis that the modern era is characterized by the "reoccupation" of modernity "by the medieval millennialist apocalypse" (Laclau, 1990: 74). The Hegelian-Marxist moment is dismissed along these lines, together with the Enlightenment, nineteenth-century master narratives and the totalitarianisms of the twentieth century (Laclau, 1990: 75). Where modernity— supported by Enlightenment—proposed a progressive advance in conscious mastery of the natural and social worlds, leading towards a post-political utopia, the new epoch represents "a growing awareness of limits" and the exhaustion of the discourse of the new (Laclau, 1990: 4). This enables a "radical critique of all forms of domination" and the "formulation of liberation projects hitherto restrained by the rationalist 'dictatorship' of the Enlightenment" (Laclau, 1990: 4). In the light of the abandonment of universality as a regulative ideal and the repudiation of any moment of global rupture with capitalism, postmarxism claims that the path opens to a multitude of partial solutions to particular problems—not Emancipation, but emancipations (Laclau, 1990: 215, 225; Laclau, 1995a: i-iv; Laclau, 2000c: 196). Instead of the utopian politics of global emancipation and the realization of a rational society through non-alienated subjectivity, postmodernism supposedly leads to a proliferation of localised resistances aiming to "maintain the differend" rather than to eliminate power. It promotes multiple and partial

---

ern culture include Callinicos (Callinicos, 1989), Jameson (Jameson, 1991; Jameson, 1994) and Harvey (Harvey, 1989). Finally, Marxist criticism of specifically postmodern theoretical ideologies includes Ebert on postmodern feminism (including Butler) (Ebert, 1996), Palmer on discourse theory (including Laclau and Mouffe) (Palmer, 1990), Geras (Geras, 1990) and Wood (Wood, 1998) on "postmarxism," and Wood *et. al.* on postmodern historical ideology (Wood, 1997b).

emancipation*s*, through a dispersed plurality of struggles for cultural recognition, by contesting the "microphysics of power". The totality of these theoretical shifts, linked expressively to historical transformations, is supposed to constitute a new, postmodern "paradigm".

Before investigating this new political paradigm, we need to become relatively sure that radical democracy conforms to this description of postmodernism, for Laclau and Mouffe have sometimes sought to distance postmarxism from postmodern politics. According to Laclau and Mouffe, radical democracy is politically *modern* and culturally *postmodern*. The crisis in the modern project of self-foundation (the philosophical project of modernity), far from undermining to the modern project of self-determination, actually extends it scope. At the same time, Laclau and Mouffe cautiously disengage their position from the political quietism characteristic of many postmodern theorists, such as Baudrillard (Laclau, 1990: 214).

Substantively, however, Laclau and Mouffe's postmarxism is characterised by the relativisation of the universal, while their position rejects emancipatory politics for micropolitical struggles and a plurality of relatively autonomous social antagonisms. The salient characteristic of the postmodern turn for politics is the relativisation of the universal (Feher and Heller, 1988: 12); thus, Laclau and Mouffe follow the policies of postmodernism to the letter, while denying their attachment to the programme of a postmodern politics. Steven Best and Douglas Kellner's distinction between ludic (conformist) and resistance (oppositional) postmodernism is invaluable in this context. Their encyclopedic survey characterises postmodernism as a "radicalisation of modernism" and proposes that resistance postmodernism "is a product of the new social movements" (Best, 1997: 26). Hence, Best and Kellner claim, Laclau and Mouffe's position is the leftwing of postmodern politics (Best, 1997: 271-273).

Radical Democracy as Postmodern Politics

The correctness of Best and Kellner's surmise that radical democracy is the leftwing of postmodern politics is supported by the content of Laclau and Mouffe's declarations regarding postmodernism. For Laclau, "postmodernity ... has become the new horizon of our cultural, philosophical and political experience" (Laclau, 1988: 63). Postmodernity is characterized by the weakening of foundationalism and the decline of master narratives, but does not constitute an absolute break with modernity, nor is postmodernism a complete novelty compared to modernism. Laclau claims that "postmodernity does not imply a *change* in the values of the Enlightenment modernity, but rather a particular weakening of their absolutist character" (Laclau, 1988: 67). He proposes that while the ontological status of modern categories is in question, their content is not (Laclau, 1988: 66). According to this perspective, postmodern politics retains the content of the emancipatory demands of modernity, but rejects the idea that the totality of these demands constitutes a unified whole, together with the metaphysical grounding of these in a universal and necessary foundation (Laclau, 1988: 63-82). "It is the contraposition between foundation and horizon that ... enables us to understand the change in the ontological status of emancipatory discourses," Laclau claims, where a "horizon" is a "formation without a foundation ... [that] constitutes itself as a unity only as it delimits itself from that which it negates" (Laclau, 1988: 81). Laclau rounds up the usual Enlightenment suspects—the totality of history, its rational foundation, the transparent society, global human emancipation, all based on full identities and the discourse of essences—to assert that postmodernity exposes the contents of Enlightenment to the effects of a multiplicity of contexts (Laclau, 1988: 72). With these remarks, Laclau not only locates radical democracy within the postmodern, but also explains the permanent dependence of postmodernism on the modern, which it must endlessly traverse deconstructively in order to generate any substantive positions.

We need to retain this sense of the postmodern exhaustion of novelty and its explicit yet paradoxical dependence upon the modern, as we turn to Mouffe's position. For Mouffe, "it is unlikely that Marxism will recover" from Stalinism and "the challenge to class reductionism posed by the new social movements" (Mouffe, 1988: 31). Using the distinction between self-determination (autonomy) and foundational project, it is possible to split modernity's epistemological project from its political project, because—Mouffe asserts rather than argues—there is no necessary articulation between these two aspects of modernity (Mouffe, 1988: 32). Following Claude Lefort, modernity is defined at the political level by the Democratic Revolution of Modernity (Mouffe, 1988: 33-34), which, Laclau explains elsewhere, is regarded by postmarxism as the political correlate to philosophical deconstruction (Laclau, 1990: 212-214). Indeed, according to Mouffe:

> If one sees the democratic revolution as Lefort portrays it, as the distinctive feature of modernity, it then becomes clear that what one means when one refers to postmodernity in philosophy is to recognise the impossibility of any ultimate foundation or final legitimation that is constitutive of the very advent of the democratic form of society and thus of modernity itself (Mouffe, 1988: 34).

The implication is that postmodern philosophy is the expression-recognition of an epochal totality: postmodernity as modernity at last cleansed of Enlightenment rationalism. Accordingly, contemporary political strategy "requires us to abandon the abstract universalism of the Enlightenment, the essentialist conception of the social totality and the myth of the unitary subject" (Mouffe, 1988: 44). For Mouffe, the leading effects of this deconstruction of foundations that is the correlate to the Democratic Revolution of Modernity are the dispersion of the unitary subject (Mouffe, 1988: 35) and the particularisation of the universal (Mouffe, 1988: 36).

While the particularisation of the universal raises the spectre of relativism, Mouffe replies that politics is the sphere of *doxa*, whose criterion of legitimacy and validity is not truth but persuasion (Mouffe, 1988: 37). Mouffe's reply—politics is the sphere of rhetorical persuasion and not logical truth, and therefore *always was* dominated by relativism—is exemplary of what might be called the skeptical function of postmodernism (Dews, 1987; Dews, 1995a). For it does not follow at all from the deconstruction of foundations— and therefore the contingency of the universal—that we need to renounce universality (Laclau and Mouffe, 1985: 191) as the opposite extreme from "Enlightenment fundamentalism". Universality can become a regulative ideal that is permanently subject to revision, instead of the fixed substrate of human nature. This is the argument presented by Hans Bertens,[3] who characterises postmodern politics in the following terms (Bertens, 1995: 185-208): a shift from macropolitics to micropolitics; the transition from global emancipation to local and partial emancipations; and, the gravitation from party politics to imagined communities. Although accepting that the politicisation of the social means that every social relation can potentially be contested and transformed—albeit piecemeal and nominalistically—Bertens nonetheless objects to the failure of postmodern politics to legitimate its own claims. According to Bertens, "postmodernism simultaneously undermines all traditional macropolitics, in that it rejects the metanarratives in which all macropolitics, those of the left as well as those of the right, classically ground themselves" (Bertens, 1995: 189). Nonetheless, the claim to partial emancipations requires a concept of social progress—for instance, Laclau's "construction of a more global [inclusive] social imaginary" (Laclau, 2000c: 197)—that postmarxism is no longer prepared to defend.

Despite referring to social complexity, then, postmarxism tends to reduce the complexity of contemporary social transformations to simple expressions of the "new times," thereby instigating an expressive relation between historical mutations and theoretical paradigms. This expressive conception of the history-theory relation then legitimates a new political programme— the shift from universal Emancipation to a multiplicity of partial emancipations—which is supposedly the correlate to the postmodern condition. Postmodern politics, characterised by the relativisation of political universality,

---

3. Bertens divides postmarxism into two camps: the particularisation of the universal (Best and Kellner - historicism); the universalisation of the particular (Laclau and Mouffe - particularism). While formally these possibilities represent the two anti-universal alternatives operative in postmodern politics, I am not convinced that a substantive difference exists between them. Witness, for instance, the subsequent convergence of Best and Kellner with Laclau and Mouffe (Best, 1997: 271-273).

rejects any transcendental foundation to the modern project of self-determination and exposes this project to the effects of a multiplicity of localised contexts. The result is a gravitation towards open relativism, best expressed by Mouffe's claim that politics is the domain of contingent pragmatic interventions determined by rhetoric, rather than rational interests or universal values (Mouffe, 1992e: 9-22, 135-154).

"PARADIGM SHIFT": THE PROBLEM OF COGNITIVE RELATIVISM

Theoretical Problematics versus Relativist Paradigms

Postmarxism's leap from absolutism (transcendental foundations) to relativism is unnecessary, for it neglects the possibility opened by historical epistemology, namely, a historicised conception of conceptual foundations as a replacement for transcendental philosophy. Indeed, the performative contradictions characteristic of the "postmodern paradigm" identified by Bertens (following Habermas) happen because of a conflation of the relativisation of the *contents* of universality with the abandonment of theoretical universals altogether.[4] Moreover, the relativism promoted by concepts such as Laclau's "emancipations" and Lyotard's "differend" actually depends upon the idealist conception of theoretical frameworks as systematised ideological worldviews.

I claim that by contrast with the Althusserian concept of a theoretical problematic, the relativist notion of a "postmodern paradigm," as the expression-recognition of structural transformations, imposes the structures of ideological misrecognition onto theoretical positions. According to Althusser, an "epistemological break" lies between historical science and humanist ideology, consisting in the crossing of certain thresholds of formalisation, whereby the subject-centred, practical discourse of ideology is transformed into the concept-centred, theoretical discourse of science. As I will explain in more detail in a moment, in theoretical discourse, the problems posed for formalised analysis lead to the generation of knowledge, based on the raw materials of experience (for instance, observation statements). But theoretical discourse *breaks* with the epistemological framework of its raw materials, because it refuses to accept as final data the description of phenomena observed by a subject and submits these instead to a proc-

---

4. The employment of "performative contradiction" as a criticism of postmodern theory was pioneered by Habermas (Habermas, 1987), who defines the category as follows: "a performative contradiction occurs when a constative speech act $k(p)$ rests on noncontingent presuppositions whose propositional content contradicts the asserted proposition, p" (Habermas, 1999: 80). Martin Jay glosses this less formally as "when the locutionary dimension of a speech act is in conflict with its illocutionary force," and this is the sense in which I employ the category (Jay, 1992: 29). It implies no commitment to discourse ethics. It is instead the elementary index of logical consistency.

ess of theoretical construction and then formal testing. Ideological practice, by contrast, is based on the coherence of the lived experience of a subject, and so it is necessarily subordinates theoretical re-description and hypothesis testing (when it does these at all) to the subject-centred registration of the significance of events. Where the paradigmatic expression of theoretical discourse is mathematical physics, the paradigmatic expression of ideological practice is personal narrative.

Accordingly, Althusser maintains that ideology does not pose problems but rather provide readymade solutions (to pseudo-problems), thereby reducing knowledge to a phenomenon of (mis)recognition. Drawing upon the concept of the mirror-stage from Lacanian psychoanalysis, Althusser proposes that ideological misrecognition functions exactly as the Imaginary register does in psychoanalysis. By supplying a corporeal image, unified in the mirror of language, the alienated ego functions as an instrument by which the subject intervenes in the world, at the cost of a permanent misrecognition of the decentred structures of social existence (Lacan, 1977: 1-29). Likewise, ideology is characterised by its Imaginary structures—that is, by its subject-centred construction of specular dualisms (for instance, "good" versus "evil") between imaginary unities (for instance, "postmodernity"), whose "obviousness" is the very hallmark of an ideological distortion. The standard analogy for the distinction between science and ideology is that of the Copernican Revolution, where mathematical abstraction negates the apparently blindingly obvious "fact," drawn from personal experience, that the sun rotates around the earth. Althusser conducted exactly such a revolution in Marxism with his conceptual shift from historical teleology and expressive totality, based in the unity of social praxis, to decentred social structures accessible only to formalised theoretical practice.

The equation of theory with ideology that postmarxism relies upon is made explicit in the notion of theoretical paradigms. Michèle Barrett, for instance, proposes that the relativisation of the universal—the dethroning of the working class in Marxian discourse—represents a paradigm shift and suggests that Marxists should take "a look at the world ... through the glasses of Laclau and Mouffe," instead of criticising postmarxism from the perspective of universal emancipation (Barrett, 1991: 78). To approach postmarxism with categories such as "class," "universal," "social formation," and so forth, is impossible, because a paradigm shift implies an incommensurability between theories and hence the meaninglessness of the old terms in the new discursive universe. Barrett therefore claims that to respond from the position of a global theory with an excoriation of Laclau and Mouffe as ex-Marxists is radically to fail to engage with the substance of postmarxism. This substance would appear to be a conceptual and moral relativism that is secreted by the very concept of a conceptual paradigm. How can a theoretical problematic—a research programme—form a worldview, operative in everyday life, that we might just "try out" for a few days? The idealist voluntarism of this conception of theory might alert us that we should check the label on the packet marked "paradigm" before swallowing. If conceptual "paradigms" are optative worldviews that are completely incommensurable, then what basis exists for making decisions regarding politics and theory? The danger is that this can become an ideological ruse designed to exclude debate. And does this not rely upon an expressive conception of the relation between the social complexity of everyday life and postmodern conceptual paradigms? To evade the relativist impasse implicit in this voluntarist conception of theory, we have to establish whether a rational basis for theoretical evaluations exists.

At this point I wish to introduce a distinction between relativism and relativisation. I do so because historical epistemology—rather like the postpositivist epistemology of Imré Lakatos's concept of the "methodology of scientific research programmes"—recognises that no scientific framework can claim absolute correspondence to the real. Indeed, it is a postulate of historical epistemology that the real is unknown: all science provides is more or less plausible constructions of the unknown cause of phenomenal experience. Yet these scientific frameworks are *not* conceptual paradigms, because it is possible to rationally adjudicate between them *in the historical scale*. The distinction between relativ*isation* and relativ*ism*, then, resides in whether, despite relativisation, there exist common standards of comparison or constant elements shared between theoretical frameworks. (This terminology is inspired by analogy with the Special Theory of Relativity, where despite the different results obtained in distinct frames of reference, a matrix of transformation exists that can convert the results of one frame into those of another frame, by virtue of the universal constant of the speed of light, which is the same in all frames of reference.) Likewise, the distinction between the *relativisation of theoretical problematics* and the *relativism of conceptual paradigms* rests upon the existence of a set of paradigm-neutral criteria that enables comparison between different theoretical problematics.

For proponents of postmodern relativism, conceptual paradigms are incommensurable "worldviews," and so no basis for comparison exists. But a "worldview" is exactly what a research programme is *not*—except in the idealist vulgarisations of Heideggerean and Kuhnian theories of science popular with postmodern theory. For instance, Best and Kellner, despite their perceptive remarks on Laclau and Mouffe's politics, insist that postmodern politics represents a "major paradigm shift" and so one either gets with the (new) times, or decides (equally arbitrarily) to remain stuck in the modernist paradigm. In motivating this effectively voluntarist position, Best and Kellner invoke Thomas Kuhn's *The Structure of Scientific Revolutions*, maintaining that the new paradigm is part of a postmodern epoch that includes the postmarxian politics of Laclau and Mouffe, technology, science and "emergent forms of culture and everyday life, as well as ... the advent of an expanding global economy and new social and political order" (Best, 1997: ix). According to Best and Kellner:

> Typically, one paradigm is replaced by another when a discipline reaches a crisis state that calls into question the explanatory adequacy of the existing paradigm, such that emergent problems are no longer seen only as "anomalies" and *ad hoc* solutions are no longer convincing. The shift to another paradigm is a non-cumulative, discontinuous development whereby novelty rules and tacit assumptions, theories and techniques emerge that are incommensurably different from what preceded (Best, 1997: 254).

The problem is the claim of incommensurability. If theoretical problematics in actuality obey the rules of Kuhnian conceptual paradigms—that is, the decision for a conceptual paradigm is arbitrary because the paradigm is a closed universe and no rational adjudication between paradigms is possible—then in reality, arguments about the relative merits of postmarxism are a waste of time. For it is not possible to arbitrate in this way: it is a "take it or leave it" proposition. (And this explains the frustration that many feel when confronted by the postmarxian position—it seems to be a voluntarist ultimatum based only on the suasive appeal to novelty implicit in the "New Times" rhetoric.) But the argument from Kuhnian philosophy of science in fact works against postmarxian voluntarism, for Kuhn himself quickly recognised the limitations of his position and introduced a key amendment to the theory, one that eliminated the postulate of incommensurability.

For Kuhn—accepting the legitimacy of certain subsequent modifications to the initial theory proposed in *The Structure of Scientific Revolutions* (1970)—a "paradigm" refers to the "disciplinary matrix" of a research community (Kuhn, 1970: 182-184; Kuhn, 1977: 297-299). This includes the shared symbolic generalisations unquestioningly accepted by this community (for instance, a basic accord on the historical importance of a certain theory), an agreement on heuristic models, research values (for instance, accuracy and honesty) and metaphysical assumptions—comparable to Lakatos' notion of the "hard core of metaphysical postulates" forming a scientific research programme (Lakatos, 1978). The genesis of the notion of paradigm in *The Structure of Scientific Revolutions* explains that a paradigm is centred by a practice of exemplification, which determines the core problem in the field and its best solution. The virtue of the concept of a paradigm is that it emphasises the contextual determination of theoretical propositions. The problem is that for Kuhn, scientific revolutions are akin to political revolutions in two decisive respects: they depend upon intersubjective consensus degenerating beyond a critical point (the accumulation of anomalies leading to a crisis of confidence in a paradigm); and their outcome depends *solely* upon political techniques (rhetorical persuasion) (Kuhn, 1970: 94, 102). Because paradigms are incommensurable, there exist no rational means for arbitrating which theory is *better*—leading to the proposition that even when two theories *logically* contradict each other, there are no bases for a grounded judgement that one is more justified than another (Kuhn, 1970: 198-199). In the process of withdrawing from this extreme position, Kuhn acknowledged that there exists a *singular* "shared basis for theory choice," involving accuracy, consistency, scope of application, elegance (simplicity) and productivity for new research (Kuhn, 1977: 321-322). That is, Kuhn's revised theory supplies a list of constitutive elements of a theoretical paradigm, together with a set of five paradigm-neutral criteria for judgement between paradigms. In the terms developed here, it means that the extended concept of a paradigm represents an acceptance of the relativisation of theoretical perspectives that nonetheless rejects relativism. This brings Kuhn's final theory significantly closer to the Althusserian-Bachelardian concept of a theoretical problematic (Lecourt, 1975: 1-15).

In Defense of the "Althusserian Revolution"

It follows from consideration of the possibility of comparisons between theoretical problematics that Laclau is wrong to suppose that the critique of ideology relies upon a naïve, immediate access to extra-discursive reality and that "all critique will necessarily be intra-ideological" (Laclau, 1996a: 299). Ideology critique can appeal to a rational analysis of theoretical contradictions and to the evidence that constitutes an anomaly for the theory—that is, ideology critique can proceed from internal critique to the postulation of an alternative explanatory framework. But this is a possibility that Laclau seems keen to exclude. Laclau's position states, in the clearest possible fashion, his belief that rational debate with other theoretical positions is merely a question of (ideological) assertion and counter-assertion. Indeed, the proposition that "all critique will necessarily be intra-ideological" can be decoded as follows: we only listen to the arguments of those who already share our worldview. This is not a hard-headed and practical assessment of the realities of political debate. It is a rejection of all theoretical inquiry and rational debate between research programmes and, as such, it is an open confession of dogmatism.

In elaborating his position, Laclau seeks to modify the Kuhnian position of (for instance) Barrett, Best and Kellner, adding to the incommensurability of discourses the proposition of the openness of paradigms. For Laclau, the "closure" of ideological worldviews/conceptual paradigms—their apparent existence as self-enclosed discursive universes with no outside—is the "highest form of misrecognition," for every ideological paradigm includes a hidden dialogical reference to its theoretical competitors (Laclau,

1996a: 300, 304). But this is a quite different proposition to Kuhn's opening of paradigms to rational arbitration, for Laclau is categorically not proposing that there exist paradigm-neutral standards of theoretical inquiry from which to judge competing paradigms. To the contrary: competition between paradigms is based on *ideological rivalry* and not on explanatory credibility, so that the dialogical constitution of conceptual paradigms or ideological worldviews as instrumental to the conducting social conflicts against political antagonists makes the possibility of rational debate *recede*, not advance. Instead of opening theories to rational adjudication, this reduces theoretical debate to ideological competition, supplementing the problematic notion of a conceptual paradigm with the stricture that these are dialogically constructed as ideological instruments. One only has to recall the fiasco of Lysenko's "proletarian science" in the former Soviet Union—a conceptual paradigm answering perfectly to Laclau's requirements of ideological serviceability and discursive insularity—to realise what is wrong with this description of theoretical debate.

Postmarxism's radical relativism therefore springs from the rejection of every "epistemological break" between theory and ideology. The Althusserian claim that historical materialism founds the science of history (Althusser, 1976: 151) smacks, according to postmarxism, of the "profoundly anti-democratic habits of leftwing thought," secreting "an obsolete positivism" (Laclau, 1990: 204) and a latent totalitarianism. In Leninism, this "authoritarian tendency ... can be found in its imbrication between science and politics," which "postulates a monolithic and unified understanding of the whole of the social process ... based on the ontologically privileged position of a single class—which, in turn, is transformed into the epistemologically privileged position of a single political leadership" (Laclau, 1990: 206). This accusation might characterise Lukács' position in *Lenin* (1924)—where absolute knowledge of the expressive totality, developed through the agency of the proletariat as identical subject-object of history, is deposited with its "vanguard party" (Lukács, 1970: 24-38)—but it scarcely applies to Althusser. For Althusser's anti-positivist conception of scientific (theoretical) practice was directed in opposition to the Stalinist leadership of the Communist parties and their claim to possess a final *philosophical* truth (Anderson, 1980; Elliott, 1987). Althusser's claim that Marxism is a general—not a total—history was met with accusations of apostasy, while the assertion of the relative autonomy of theoretical practice scandalised the advocates of "social praxis," that is, the "dialectical unity" of the ontological privilege of the proletariat with its special epistemological claims.

Science, unlike philosophy and religion, advances only provisional knowledge based on the best explanation and lacking the final seal of the Truth, that is, some form of Divine Guarantee of the correspondence between theoretical categories and the historical process.[5] "Every recognised science," Althusser insists, "not only has emerged from ideology but continues endlessly to do so (its prehistory remaining always contemporary, something like an alter-ego), by rejecting what it considers to be error" (Althusser, 1976: 113). For Althusser, theory constitutes "a minimum of generality necessary to be able to grasp a concrete object" (Althusser, 1976: 112) which, unlike ideology, is conducted through explicit rules and is therefore susceptible to revision (Althusser and Balibar, 1970: 59).

The specific effectivity of a science is determined by the nature of its historically produced conceptual framework, or "problematic," which constitutes the relative autonomy of a science in relation to the field of ideology from which it sprang (Althusser and Balibar, 1970: 133).

> A science can only pose problems on the terrain and within the horizon of a definite theoretical structure, its problematic, which constitutes its absolute and definite condition of possibility, and hence the absolute determination of the forms in which all problems must be posed, at any given moment in the science (Althusser and Balibar, 1970: 25).

According to Althusser, the structure of theory consists of three steps (Althusser, 1969: 182-193). In "Generalities I," always-already "worked-up," or theoretically influenced, ideological categories form the raw material for theoretical practice. In "Generalities II," these categories are subjected to a problematic, by which theoretical operations are performed on this raw material. In "Generalities III," new conceptual knowledge and substantive theoretical positions are produced.

The method developed by Althusser can be described as a "structural depth hermeneutic" (Resch, 1992: 174-178). Althusser proposes a "symptomatic" interpretation, methodologically inspired by psychoanalysis, where the text is formed through the "unconscious operation" of a problematic whose structural principles govern the relation between the latent and manifest texts of a theory. He refers to a dialectical circle of interpretation (Al-

---

5. While it is certainly correct to assert that Althusser initially lapsed into precisely this rationalist illusion—claiming that "dialectical materialism" supplied a "Theory of theoretical practice" (Althusser, 1969: 168), that is, a scientific theory of materiality that functioned as a guarantee of the truth of historical materialism—this was abandoned following Althusser's own "epistemological break" in 1967 (Althusser, 1990: 69-166). Robert Resch demonstrates that the underlying consistency of Althusser's thinking, based on the continuity of the realist and materialist concepts of theoretical practice, means that "Althusser's proposition, that science is constituted by the transformation of ideology into knowledge by means of theory, holds up even after the difference between science and ideology is reformulated in functional rather than rationalist terms" (Resch, 1992: 182). Althusser's self-criticism of "theoreticism" accepted the non-existence of every guarantee (and therefore the relativisation of knowledge), the role of philosophy as a transmission belt between theory and ideology, and that every science is constituted by breaking continuously with its (henceforth) ideological prehistory in a potentially endless series of theoretical revolutions.

thusser, 1969: 38), where progressive readings are successive approximations (Althusser and Balibar, 1970: 74). Althusser's structural hermeneutics yields a combination of textual interpretation and causal explanation, which "divulges the undivulged event in the text it reads, and in the same moment relates this to a different text, present as a necessary absence in the first" (Althusser and Balibar, 1970: 28). For instance, Marx's radical break with philosophical anthropology makes possible a "symptomatic" interpretation of political economy, whereby the lacunae of theoretical economics can be interpreted as disclosures of class interests.

So—how is debate between theoretical problematics possible? Laclau's early (Marxist) work supplies an exemplary description of this process (Laclau, 1977: 60-61). Because every theoretical problematic transcendentally constitutes the empirical object it investigates, no *direct* contrast between problematics on the basis of empirical evidence is possible. The consequence is that "a theory is only false to the extent that it is internally inconsistent, i.e., if in the process of construction of its concepts it has entered into contradiction with its postulates" (Laclau, 1977: 60). Flowing from this, Laclau concludes that "theoretical problems, to the extent that they are truly theoretical, cannot, strictly speaking, be solved: they can only be superseded" (Laclau, 1977: 60). Because the problematic determines the legitimate phenomenal field for a theory—that is, it schematises a phenomenal diversity so as to align empirical reality with theoretical categories and thereby make sensations into objects of possible experience (Jameson, 1972: 89)—"the empirical resolution of the problem consists, strictly speaking, of the negation of its existence on the theoretical plane" (Laclau, 1977: 61). Laclau suggests that empirical verification or falsification highlights the existence of anomalies (phenomena that cannot be fully grasped by the conceptual system of a theory), but that this does not inherently negate the theory. It only leads towards the alternatives of theoretical reconstruction or shift in problematic. With the emergence of a new theory, the problems generated within the horizon of the former theory are not solved, but simply superseded, that is, "dissolved as a problem with the emergence of a new theoretical system" (Laclau, 1977: 61). From this, the major logical elements in a rebuttal can be deduced: (a) the designation of empirical realities that constitute theoretical anomalies; (b) the identification of the theoretical roots of these anomalies; (c) a demonstration that these roots constitute theoretical contradictions, leading to the collapse of the conceptual system; (d) an alternative system that resolves the contradictions of the former theory (Laclau, 1977: 61-62).

The Charmed Circle of Ideology

Having established, *contra* postmarxism, that the critique of ideology is not merely intra-ideological, I want to begin to rebut postmarxism along the Althusserian Marxist lines suggested above. The remainder of this chapter therefore concentrates on the "empirical realities that constitute theoretical anomalies" for postmarxism, by examining the empirical evidence for postmarxism's major sociological and political claims. At the same time, I begin to introduce the main lines of a theoretical alternative to postmarxism, drawing upon Regulation Theory, neo-Marxist sociology and leftwing Eurocommunism.

Before doing so, however, I have to digress in order to examine a second objection to my accusation that postmarxism leads to relativism. In response to this accusation, Laclau and Mouffe reply that "'relativism' is, to a great extent, an invention of the fundamentalists" (Laclau, 1990: 104). Their reply is based on an ontology of discourse, according to which "outside of any discursive context, objects *do not have being*; they only have *existence*" (Laclau, 1990: 104). Laclau and Mouffe claim that discursive articulation is the primary ontological process in the constitution of the real, so that entities lack any determinacy unless discursively constituted as beings. "Discourse" has a general meaning and a specialised definition within their theory of hegemony. I shall discuss the specialised definition in the chapter on *HSS*; the general definition embraces both linguistic and non-linguistic elements (physical objects, human actions) (Laclau, 1990: 102), speech acts and non-discursive practices (Laclau and Mouffe, 1985: 107), considered equally as differential identities in open, relational complexes. For Laclau and Mouffe, "every identity or discursive object is constituted in the context of an action," so that, for instance, "a stone exists independently of any system of social relations, but it is ... either a projectile or an object of aesthetic contemplation only within a specific discursive configuration" (Laclau, 1990: 101-102). In other words, a thing has no natural properties aside from its social context, as the being of the object is historically transitive, while its existence is intransitive (Laclau, 1990: 103), and "natural facts are also discursive facts" (Laclau, 1990: 102). As opposed to scientific realist positions, which form the epistemological basis of the post-Althusserian forms of historical materialism I advocate in this analysis, anti-realist positions have difficulty in theoretically discriminating between science and pseudo-science, leaving them open to the charge that they conflate epistemology and politics (Chalmers, 1990).

The literature documenting scientific realism's response to social constructivism is extensive, and considerations of length prevent me from reproducing the arguments in detail. Nonetheless, the arguments proposed by advocates of scientific realism seem, in the absence of any examination of the relevant literature by Laclau and Mouffe, to be devastating. The confident assertion that it is possible to differentiate the indeterminate existence of the entity from its determinate (discursively constructed) being is the

hallmark of positivism (Newton-Smith, 1981: 19-43). From the antediluvi-
an positivism of Popper through to contemporary constructive empiricism,
the natural world is an inert posivitivity whose meaning is completely constructed through radically incommensurable theoretical paradigms (Newton-Smith, 1981: 44-101, 148-182). Philosophically, constructive empiricism
is very close to forms of neo-Kantian nominalism and forms of pragmatism
(Norris, 2001: 133-166, 167-195). Not only can the discursive claims of radical
meaning variance not be sustained, but the positivist programme (in its contemporary empiricist form) cannot manage to avoid the slide towards theoretical obscurantism and moral relativism (Norris, 1997: 6-43; Norris, 2001:
167-217; Norris, 2002: 23-57). Incapable of differentiating between pseudo-
scientific obscurantism and scientific research programmes, and unable to
explain the most striking features of the scientific enterprise (for instance,
the increasing accuracy of theories and their ability to integrate the results
of widely varying investigations), contemporary "post-positivist" anti-realism ends up converging with anti-epistemological anarchism (Feyerabend)
and political apologetics (Rorty) (Bhaskar, 1989: 146-179; Norris, 1996: 154-
179; Norris, 2001: 133-217).

Laclau and Mouffe's position appears to be a form of transcendental
argument, as they emphasise that while every phenomenon has discursive
conditions of possibility, the discursive—as horizon—has no conditions of
possibility (Laclau, 1990: 105). While Laclau is evasive when questioned (Laclau, 1990: 220), he is elsewhere happy enough to identify discourse with
the encounter of the linguistic turn and transcendental philosophy (Laclau,
1993). In keeping with neo-Kantian nominalism, then, Laclau and Mouffe
insist that discourses are only quasi-transcendental, that is, they are empirical processes that can be politically transformed, yet they transcendentally constitute the being of the object. Hence, unlike Kant, Laclau and
Mouffe suppose that the system of transcendental categories is historically
and culturally variable, effective only in localised contexts. However, their
discourse theory rests upon the epistemic fallacy, namely, "the view that
statements about being can be reduced to or analysed in terms of statements
about knowledge" (Bhaskar, 1978: 36). This fallacy is concisely reprised by
Laclau in his claim that "all truth is relative to a discursive formation" (Laclau, 1990: 196). Laclau and Mouffe avow that their position is similar to Richard Rorty's pragmatism (Laclau, 1996b: 60; Mouffe, 1996a: 1). As such,
it is vulnerable to the convincing refutation of pragmatism presented by de-
fenders of scientific realism (Bhaskar, 1989: 146-179; Norris, 2001: 133-166).

Laclau and Mouffe maintain that their position is *realist* (because objects
exist independently of thought) and *materialist* (because the being of objects,
as penetrated by historically variable and politically contested discourses, is
irreducible to conceptual relations) (Laclau and Mouffe, 1987b). These definitions of realism and materialism are unsustainable in relation to the his-

tory of philosophy and the meaning of these terms in contemporary theories of science (Geras, 1988). They are also highly problematic positions to take. By evacuating the determinacy of material objects, Laclau and Mouffe deny the possibility of any extra-discursive controls on theory and so reject the central postulate of contemporary realism, that transitive knowledge enables an exploration in depth of the intransitive object. Secondly, in insisting that the irrationality of the real is the main determinant of materialism, Laclau and Mouffe encourage conflating the irreducibility of the real to logical relations with the supposed impossibility of generating formal theoretical propositions (for instance, general natural laws of tendency, as in mathematical physics), flowing from their definition of "realism". This runs a serious risk of terminating in obscurantism.

That Laclau and Mouffe's ontology of discourse necessarily leads to relativism can be seen by considering some entities that (unlike stones) provide a test of this form of constructive empiricism: discourses and quarks. The first test, "discourses," represents a self-reflexive application of the theory to itself. This is legitimate because Laclau and Mouffe explicitly refuse any distinctions between discourse and practice, meta-theory and object language. Discourses exist, on their hypotheses, but lack any being except when specified in another (meta-)discourse. Thus, for instance, a discourse—say, *HSS*—presents a series of determinations of some theoretical objects (social agents, social relations, some historical events) while itself, as a discourse, lacking any determinacy, except when specified metadiscursively (through its insertion in a history of Marxism, or in a critical analysis). Hence, the claim that *HSS* presents an anti-essentialist discourse, while Marxism is an essentialist discourse, becomes highly problematic as a claim regarding the object, since on this ontology such claims really only disclose something about the claimant. This is an extremely improbable result, but one that follows ineluctably from their premises, for the alternative (that a discourse, taking advantage of the self-reflexive properties of language, can specify itself through nested metalinguistic statements) leads immediately to the collapse of the ontological dichotomy between indeterminate existence and determinate being. For a self-determining object is exactly what is excluded from this ontology, and Laclau and Mouffe's central postulate is that there is no difference in kind between stones and discourses, so discourses cannot be a special sort of object.

Purely theoretical entities, such as quarks in quantum physics, present Laclau and Mouffe's ontology with a special problem and expose why it is that this position secretes a form of positivism. Now it is not the being of the object, but its *existence* that is in question. This ontology should conclude that the entities do not exist, for if realism (as they construe it) reduces to the proposition that discourse can only form the being of the object, but not constitute it as an existent, then theoretical entities become only explanatory posits. In this case, the confident assertion that a clear distinction exists between the existence of objects (for instance, quarks) and their being (their properties) will gradually unravel, for the generally accepted proposition of the theory-ladenness of observations will lead to progressively calling into question the theory independence of every phenomenon. But the ontology of discourse stands or falls with the postulate that the indeterminate existence of the entity can be asserted aside from every determination of its being. Furthermore, Laclau and Mouffe have no basis for claiming any explanatory superiority for quarks over, for instance, gods. They can only claim that since, with Laclau, "all truth is relative to a discursive formation" (Laclau, 1990: 196), as a result of historical contingencies, gods simply do not belong in the discursive universe of modern science. This effectively rests the distinction between science and pseudo-science on historical facticity instead of explanatory power.

Laclau and Mouffe's position culminates in a perspectival relativism verging on sophism. They assert, as a result of their discursive ontology, that there is no rational or ethical superiority to democracy and affirm the supremacy of politics over ethics and epistemology (Mouffe, 1996a: 1, 4). Further, they affirm that the political field is characterised by groundless efforts to persuade persons (in other words, by rhetorical sallies in the spirit of sophism, perhaps modelled on contemporary media-dependent politicians, such as Tony Blair) (Mouffe, 1996a: 5). Presumably, one such purely rhetorical effort is their own claim that postmarxism promotes self-determination through acts of political identification (Laclau, 1990: 44; Laclau, 1996b: 49). At the same time, Laclau and Mouffe, as I shall demonstrate in Chapter Three, maintain an inconsistent stance in that they do not fully accept the relativism of their own position. Nonetheless, their strident insistence that theory is the direct servant of politics, and their assertion that there is no difference whatsoever between theory and ideology, is a striking instance of the historicist basis of postmarxism—and a startling demonstration of its limitations.

SOCIAL CONFLICT IN THE CONTEMPORARY WORLD

From Marxisant *Analysis to Ideological Manipulation*

The Althusserian conception that an epistemological break—consisting in the crossing of certain thresholds of formalisation—separates theoretical problematics from ideological worldviews not only explains that the problem with the postmarxian position is its subject-centred character, but also highlights the possibility (and the importance) of extra-discursive controls on theoretical debate. For many postmarxists, however, the very existence of an intransitive world is confused with "the possibility of concretely experiencing a world beyond ideology" (Porter, 2002: 43). Nothing could more graphically illustrate the subject-centred character of postmarxian phenomenology. The Althusserian idea of a distinction between science and ideology, by contrast, summarises precisely the impossibility of *experiencing* a non-ideologically constituted world, despite the structured existence of the real. Unlike the postmarxian stance, however, the Althusserian position accepts the necessity of a conflict of interpretations, but supplies methodological grounds for conducting rational debates.

A case in point is postmarxism's major social theoretical claim—that Marxism has not grasped the crisis dynamics of contemporary society. This is related to the supposition that instead of strictly capitalist social formations, "postmodernity" is characterised by dispersed "discursive formations" lacking the unity of a dominant structure (Laclau, 1990: 57-59). The problem with the postmarxian analysis is that it substitutes a political hermeneutics based in the acceptance of the postmodern ideological horizon for an explanation of the social causes underlying the relativisation of the universal. This imposes the characteristic structures of ideological misrecognition onto theoretical analysis, as postmarxism tends to conflate phenomenological description with structural analysis, and implies the legitimation of an ideologically motivated blindness. Because there is no longer a distinction between theory and ideology, a conceptual paradigm is only the coherent expression or philosophical systematisation of the ideological worldview held by a particular social agent. This leads to cognitive relativism, where the conflict between conceptual paradigms becomes the highest expression of the political competition between ideological worldviews. As a result, postmarxism resiles from historical explanations of the causes of events for interpretative "interventions" that make theory the direct servant of an ideology. The archaeology of this process can be traced in successive analyses of contemporary politics that emerged before and after the collapse of historical Communism. As ideology progressively supplanted theory, the postmarxian analysis of the political conjuncture became marked by a retreat, from a *Marxisant* analysis based in forms of post-Structural Marxism, towards a phenomenological description of the "new times" bordering on ideologically-driven celebration.

The major postmarxian claim involves rewriting theoretical history, for Laclau and Mouffe's initial assessment of the political conjuncture was based on a combination of their theory of ideological articulations with perspectives drawn from the renovation of Marxism undertaken by the post-Althusserian school of Regulation Theory (Laclau and Mouffe, 1985: 159-171). Invoking the analysis of Fordism by Michel Aglietta, the leading theoretician of the Regulation School, Laclau and Mouffe allude to the Fordist regime of accumulation as a motor for the commodification of social relations whose outcome is that "there is now practically no domain of individual or collective life which escapes capitalist relations" (Laclau and Mouffe, 1985: 161). They propose that the NSM are the result of the hegemonic postwar formation encountering structural limits to its articulation of economics, politics and ideology, combined with political resistance to the "new forms of domination" that spring from the Fordist mode of social regulation. According to *HSS*:

> One cannot understand the present expansion of the field of social conflict and the consequent emergence of new political subjects without situating both in the context of the commodification and bureaucratisation of social relations on the one hand, and the reformulation of liberal-democratic ideology—resulting from the expansion of struggles for equality—on the other (Laclau and Mouffe, 1985: 163).

According to Laclau and Mouffe's *Marxisant* analysis, then, the emergence of the NSM needs to be analysed from the "double perspective" of the transformation of social relations characteristic of the postwar hegemonic formation, and "the effects of the displacement into new areas of social life of the egalitarian imaginary constituted around liberal-democratic discourse" (Laclau and Mouffe, 1985: 165).

> The fact that these "new antagonisms" are the expression of forms of resistance to the commodification, bureaucratisation and increasing homogenisation of social life itself explains why they should frequently manifest themselves through a proliferation of particularisms, and crystallise into a demand for autonomy itself. ... Insofar as, of the two great themes of the democratic imaginary—equality and liberty—it was that of equality which was traditionally predominant, the demands for autonomy bestow an increasingly central role upon liberty (Laclau and Mouffe, 1985: 164).

The *Marxisant* element of Laclau and Mouffe's analysis is *close* to the Marxist proposition that the differential histories of the distinct social levels (economic, political, ideological) result in different effects (commodification, bureaucratisation, consumerism), that are recombined in the space of politics (hegemonic articulations). In line with their earlier revision of Structural Marxism (Laclau, 1977: 81-142; Mouffe, 1979a: 168-205), however, Laclau and Mouffe substitute ideological struggles for political conflict as the privileged terrain where social contradictions are resolved, replacing hegemonic articulations with ideological manipulation. The postmarxian element of the analysis therefore insists that the political space is governed by ideology and unified through the "permanence of the egalitarian Imaginary" in modernity (Laclau and Mouffe, 1985: 160). The emergence of the NSM is regarded in this light as "a moment of deepening of the democratic revolution" (Laclau and Mouffe, 1985: 163). The emergence of the NSM can then be regarded as a continuation of the fragmentation of the "unitary subject" of classical Marxism that highlights "the plurality of the social and the unsutured character of all political identity" (Laclau and Mouffe, 1985: 166).

Laclau and Mouffe's position is therefore *based* on Marxism, but seeks to break with the proposition that hegemonic articulations are governed by the exigencies of the accumulation of capital, and attempts to substitute ideological manipulation for the space of politics. The task of the Left is (uncontentiously) "to construct a new historic bloc in which a plurality of economic, social and cultural aspects are articulated" (Laclau and Mouffe, 1985: 170). For Laclau and Mouffe, though, the twofold character of the "democratic Imaginary" (equality and liberty) is central to this analysis, and not the constraints on hegemonic articulations imposed by the accumulation of capital, or the constitution of political space by the institution of the nation-state. Lacking an analysis of the structural constraints imposed by capitalism, their conception of the primacy of ideological struggle breaks loose from the social field and tends to suppress the relevance of economics and politics.

Laclau and Mouffe's analysis of the neo-liberal efforts to construct a new hegemonic articulation follows the same structure as their assessment of the conjuncture, especially as regards the totalising role of the ideological struggle. "It cannot be doubted," Laclau and Mouffe sum up, "that the proliferation of antagonisms and of 'new rights' is leading to a crisis of the hegemonic formation of the postwar period" (Laclau and Mouffe, 1985: 168). They indicate that, for the Left, the New Right (Thatcher, Reagan) holds the key to grasping a new political logic, because "its novelty lies in its successful articulation to neo-liberal discourse of a series of democratic resistances to the transformation of social relations" (Laclau and Mouffe, 1985: 169). Neo-liberalism is opposed to the postwar extension to the concepts of equality and liberty to include material capabilities and social rights (Laclau and Mouffe, 1985: 171). The New Right articulates liberalism to free market economics and a restricted democracy, based on the "chain of equivalences, equality = identity = totalitarianism" and the affirmation of the sequence "difference = inequality = liberty" (Laclau and Mouffe, 1985: 174). "We are thus witnessing the emergence of a new hegemonic project, that of liberal-conservative discourse, which seeks to articulate the neo-liberal defense of the free market economy with the profoundly anti-egalitarian cultural and social tradition of conservatism" (Laclau and Mouffe, 1985: 175). Drawing upon Stuart Hall's controversial analysis of Thatcher's "authoritarian populism" (Hall, 1983) and Allen Hunter's assessment of Reaganite discourse as a "specious egalitarianism" (Laclau and Mouffe, 1985: 170), Laclau and Mouffe claim that this demonstrates the "fundamental ambiguity of the social," namely, the "polysemic character of every antagonism," which exposes "the impossibility of establishing in a definitive manner the meaning of any struggle, whether considered in isolation or through its fixing in a relational system" (Laclau and Mouffe, 1985: 170). Nothing, for Laclau and Mouffe, is inher-

ently Right or Left. There are only relational social antagonisms, lacking
the strategic pole of reference that structural constraints might supply.

The Emergence of a New Mode of Social Regulation

By contrast with the postmarxian tendency to flatten social conflict onto ideological struggles alone, according to Regulation Theory—following Aglietta's pathbreaking work (Aglietta, 1979)—modes of social regulation are a
historic *bricolage* that combine a *regime of accumulation* with a diversity of *cultural institutions* and *forms of the state*, to constitute a relative unity, capable of
temporarily (in the historical scale) securing social reproduction.[6] A mode of
social regulation is defined as "the conjunction of the mechanisms working
together for social reproduction, with attention to the prevalent economic
structures and social forms" (Boyer, 1990: 20). These mechanisms can be
specified as the "general laws [of tendency]" through which "the determinant structure of a society is reproduced," by means of "the transformation
of social relations to create new forms that are both economic and non-eco-
nomic, that are organised in structures and themselves reproduce a determinant structure, the mode of production" (Aglietta, 1979: 13-16). The elements
articulated in a mode of social regulation include the regime of capital accumulation, the state form and its variations of political regime, and the hegemonic culture and dominant ideologemes.

Springing from the Structural Marxism of Althusser and cothinkers,
Regulation Theory is a "structuralist, but 'historicised' Marxism" (Boyer,
1990: 85), incorporating insights from Kalekyian (post-Keynesian) economics and the Marxist political theory of Nicos Poulantzas (Boyer, 1990: 93).
Modes of social regulation represent the post-Structural Marxist adaptation of the Gramscian concept of a "historic bloc". A historic bloc is based
on the hegemonic position of a social alliance, incorporating a mobile equilibrium of force and consent, that is, a shifting balance of forces within the
historic compromise of a determinate social settlement. Regulation Theory
begins from the Althusserian description of the social formation as a totality
of structural instances articulated on the basis of a mode of production. By

---

6. My grasp of Regulation Theory is based primarily on Michel Aglietta's exemplary *A
Theory of Capitalist Regulation* (Aglietta, 1979) and supplemented by Robert Boyer's superb
introductory work, *The Regulation School* (Boyer, 1990). Regulation Theory has been applied
to the problems of inflation and monetary theory by Alain Lipietz in *The Enchanted World*
(Lipietz, 1985) and to specific national crises of the Fordist mode of social regulation in
Boyer's *Japanese Capitalism in Crisis* (Boyer, 2000) and Bob Jessop *et. al.*, *Thatcherism* (Jessop,
Bonnett *et al.*, 1988) and *The Politics of Flexibility* (Jessop, 1991a). Alain Lipietz has explored
the major, especially monetary, dimensions of the crisis of Fordism in *Mirages and Miracles*
(Lipietz, 1987) and the main aspects of the emergent, post-Fordist mode of social regulation
in *Towards a New Economic Order* (Lipietz, 1992). A major (institutionalist) alternative theory of
the postwar boom and present crisis is provided by a persistent critic of Regulation Theory,
Robert Brenner, in "The Economics of Global Turbulence" (Brenner, 1998: 1-229).

contrast with the necessary character of social reproduction assumed by Althusser and Balibar, however, Regulation Theory regards social relations as structured by social practices that are continuously undergoing contestation and redefinition. This accords with the Marxist analysis, that the differential histories of the regional structures in the social formation are recombined on the field of "social class practices" (Poulantzas, 1973: 123-141, 275-295). Class struggles on this terrain condense at the level of the nation-state, because the political instance has the function of maintaining the unity of the social formation (and therefore acts as the nodal point where diverse social contradictions overdetermine political conflicts), which represents a "material condensation of the relation of forces" (Poulantzas, 1978: 123-153). The concept of a mode of social regulation therefore corresponds to Poulantzas' concept of the field of social practices, the diachronic complement to the synchronic structural matrix of the mode of production (Jessop, 1985: 53-148). While a mode of social regulation is a relatively unified hegemonic strategy that secures social reproduction, this constantly involves contestation of social practices and the shifting balance of the interests of the dominant and dominated within the social compromise. Therefore, it cannot be claimed that this form of Marxism overlooks the political aspect of social relations and regards politics only as a superstructural level (Laclau, 1990: 56).

The paradigmatic instance of a mode of social regulation is Fordism, which dominated the industrialised economies from the 1930s to the 1970s and is now in the process of break-up and recomposition into a new mode of social regulation. The term Fordism was coined by Gramsci in the analysis of the 1920s and refers to the structure of capitalist accumulation then becoming predominant in the United States. The Fordist mode of social regulation depended on production-line technology operated by semi-skilled process workers, combined with mass consumption, governed by means of an interventionist state based on the historic compromise of the welfare state and tripartite (state, unions, capital) bargaining institutions, and culturally conditioned by mass consumption of standardised products within nuclear family units. These relatively independent elements were selected and combined during the massive social conflicts of the 1930s and the Second World War, crystallising as a result of the emergence of a hegemonic capitalist strategy under the leadership of the internationally dominant US economy in the postwar period.

Against Laclau and Mouffe's exaggeration of the importance of ideological factors, Regulation Theory enables us to identify the social causes of postmodern politics as being anchored in the break-up of the postwar mode of social regulation. The conclusion arrived at by Regulation Theory is that capitalism in the advanced industrialised countries is in transition from the Fordist regime of accumulation, characterised by intensive accumulation and mass consumption, to a post-Fordist regime combining extensive accumulation with highly individualised (niche-marketed) mass consumption (Boyer, 1990: xv). The political conjuncture of protracted crisis and then social reconstruction that is the historical context for postmarxism springs from the unevenness of the transition from Fordism to a nascent post-Fordist mode of social regulation. Because of international and domestic rivalry between different models of post-Fordism, and the incompleteness of the transition from Fordist production to post-Fordist production in the globally hegemonic United States, post-Fordism displays greater diversity and heterogeneity than Fordism exhibited (Ruigrok, 1995). Although the United States enjoys unprecedented global dominance, there is a disparity between the military might of the world's sole superpower and its restricted economic dynamism, which has not equalled the productive gains and profitability of the postwar period.

A glance at the details of this analysis makes it possible for us to explain the phenomena described by Laclau and Mouffe as effects of the structural transformations analysed by theorists of the regulation school. Despite the lack of a unified post-Fordist hegemonic strategy, there are certain leading aspects of the rival post-Fordist paradigms that can be clearly differentiated from the Fordist social settlement (Jessop, 1991a). The competing post-Fordist modes of social regulation are characterised by extensive accumulation (flexible specialisation operated by highly skilled labour) combined with mass consumption, governed by means of a combination of the "workfare" state and the decentring of tripartite bargaining institutions, and culturally conditioned by diversified consumption of highly differentiated products within non-traditional family units. The process of transition to post-Fordist regulation involves economic globalisation, the relative decline of the nation-state and the aestheticisation of the commodity form. The relativisation of the political universal and the new importance of cultural subjectivity are both linked to the major mechanism of the break-up of Fordism, namely, the internationalisation of production. Where Fordism was a nationally centred developmental model, the post-Fordist regimes of accumulation are characterised by a new international division of labour and the globalisation of production (Dicken, 1998). This ruptures the structural integrity of national social formations by inserting them into an increasingly integrated (although highly segmented) world economy. As national economies cease to relate externally to the international division of labour and become increasingly integrated into a highly segmented world economy, the lack of structural closure of national social formations generates massive dislocations in domestic industry, social equality, mechanisms of governance and the ability of multicultural states to absorb cultural diversity. The conclusion to be drawn is that the dislocation of contemporary social formations is less a result of structural dispersion, than a consequence of a new regime of capital accumulation.

The Post-Fordist Regimes of Accumulation

The major difference between Laclau and Mouffe's initial analysis of the conjuncture and that of Regulation Theory is therefore not the concept of Fordism or the significance of the NSM, but whether the structural matrix of capitalism acts as a decisive constraint on hegemonic articulations. Laclau and Mouffe's analysis suggests that ideological manipulations are the key to a leftwing renewal and proposes that these obey a discursive logic, according to which nothing predetermines the possible articulations of a social antagonism (Laclau and Mouffe, 1985: 165). The authors, despite announcing that nothing constrains hegemonic articulations, nonetheless persist in regarding capitalist relations of production, bureaucratic authoritarianism and possessive individualism, as structural matrices whose abolition "every project for radical democracy necessarily includes" (Laclau and Mouffe, 1985: 165).[7] Laclau and Mouffe are inconsistent, then, in at once denying the existence of structural constraints and insisting that certain elements of the radical democratic programme are not negotiable. By insisting that the crisis of Fordism is the result of ethico-political struggles alone, and that the leftwing response is the extension of the democratic revolution, Laclau and Mouffe misrecognise limits of structural variation as value-decisions of the NSM. This conforms exactly to Althusser's description of ideology as a subject-centred misrecognition, in which structural roles appear as the results of autonomous decisions.

According to Laclau, the new "discursive formations" of "disorganised capitalism" are characterised by a situation whose novelty:

> lies in the fact that the nodal point around which the intelligibility of the social is articulated does not now tend to be displaced from one instance to another in society, but to dissolve.... Accordingly, articulation is constitutive of all social practice [and] ... dislocations increasingly dominate the terrain of an absent structural determination (Laclau, 1990: 59).

This absent structural determination *was* the mode of production as an "absent cause" and the "nodal point" of the social formation *used to be* the "structure in dominance". But now, in view of the fact that there is no bourgeois revolution—only "family resemblances" between democracies (Laclau, 1990: 22)—we have to conclude that there is no capitalism, only "fam-

---

7. Possessive individualism: "in all those cases where the problematic of possessive individualism is maintained as the matrix of production of the identity of the different groups, this result [specious egalitarianism] is *inevitable*" (Laclau and Mouffe, 1985: 165). Bureaucratic limitations on democracy: "it is *necessary*, therefore, to broaden the domain of the exercise of democratic rights beyond the limited traditional field of 'citizenship'" (Laclau and Mouffe, 1985: 165). Capital accumulation: "every project for radical democracy *necessarily* includes ... the socialist dimension—that is to say, the abolition of capitalist relations of production" (Laclau and Mouffe, 1985: 165). Emphasis added throughout.

ily resemblances" between economies. Indeed, Laclau stipulates expressly that this is his view. "Instead [of capitalism]," Laclau specifies:

> there are global configurations—historical blocs, in the Gramscian sense—in which the "ideological," "economic" and "political," and other elements, are inextricably fused and can only be separated for analytical purposes. There is therefore no "capitalism," but rather different forms of capitalist relations which form part of highly diverse structural complexes (Laclau, 1990: 26).

But the absence of a structural determination means the elimination of the concept of a mode of production and therefore the redundancy of the category of "capitalism," disorganised or otherwise. Hence, the occasional references to "the decline of the classical working class in the post-industrial countries" (Laclau and Mouffe, 1985: 57) in reality express what is central: the end of capitalism as the unity of a mode of exploitation and the advent of a new society, characterised by diffuse oppressions and dispersed resistances. No other sense can be made of the Panglossian claim that today, "a plurality of subjects exercise a democratic and negotiated control of the productive process on the basis of this fragmentation, thus avoiding any form of dictatorship, whether by the market, the state or direct producers" (Laclau, 1990: 83).

By contrast with the current postmarxian vision of the dispersion of the structural dominance of capital accumulation, Laclau and Mouffe's initial *Marxisant* diagnosis that "there is now practically no domain of individual or collective life which escapes capitalist relations" was correct. Regimes of accumulation can be described as the contingent articulation of a distinct labour process with certain norms of consumption, whose "combination" specifies the structural matrix for economic institutions and defines the limits of variation of class struggles for a historical period. The labour process of post-Fordism is distinct from the Fordist production line operated by semi-skilled labour. By contrast with this intensive mode of accumulation, the flexible specialisation and automated production characteristic of post-Fordism takes advantage of continuous technological innovation in information and communications equipment to accelerate the turn-over time of fixed capital (Harvey, 1989). Highly skilled operators work in production teams on the basis of constant quality improvement and multi-skilling to enable rapid re-allocation of production tasks. The mobility of capital and centrality of process innovation leads to premium on highly-skilled and "flexible" employees, with high cultural capital and the ability to learn new tasks through constant retraining. This leads to the massive restructuring of wage relations, the nation-state and everyday life generally known as "globalisation". The breakdown of the fixed mental/manual division of Fordism and the integration of worker suggestions through industrial participation has led some social democratic advocates of post-Fordism to imagine that this is a "new age of democracy" and not a new modality of exploitation (Mathews, 1988; Mathews, 1989a; Mathews, 1989b). This is belied, however, by the increasing polarisation of wealth that accompanies post-Fordist regimes of accumulation (Giddens, 1994a; Giddens, 1998; Giddens, 1999; Giddens, 2000; Giddens, 2001).

Instead of Laclau's impressionistic assertion that contemporary social formations are characterised by the dissolution of economic structures, the sociology of globalisation suggests that the world economy is gripped by intense international rivalries, which unleash significant new class struggles. Winfred Ruigrok and Rob Van Tulder conclude from their survey of international restructuring that no *uniform* "post-Fordism" can be detected in the world economy (Ruigrok, 1995: 12-35). In particular, the process of the international restructuring of capital is marked by an emerging rivalry between three powerful regional blocs, characterised by distinct variations of the post-Fordist regime of accumulation. "Toyotism" (Asia-Pacific, centred on Japan), "Macro-Fordism" (the Americas, centred on the US) and Fordism-with-"flexible-specialisation" (Europe, centred on France, Italy and Germany) are emerging as the hegemonic regimes of accumulation within the pertinent regional blocs (Ruigrok, 1995: 36-62). These can be associated with the different hegemonic strategies promoted by social forces in the relevant geographical regions, and therefore with quite different emergent articulations between cultural, political and economic social practices. This is a level of explanatory detail absent from Laclau's superficial and contradictory claim that despite the dissolution of the capitalist mode of production, "diverse" capitalist "complexes" nonetheless exist.

Secondly, and equally pointedly, class struggle is not, despite postmarxian insistence to the contrary, on the wane. Major transformations in the quality and nature of work accompany post-Fordist techniques of "flexible specialisation". Regulation Theory demonstrates by empirical methods (instead of ideological assertions) that the "renegotiation" of the relation between wage labour and capital remains the central determinant of the rate of profit, and therefore of the viability of an entire mode of social regulation (Aglietta, 1979; Bowles, Gordon *et al.*, 1983). The incorporation of the union movements into a framework of state-supervised collective bargaining might be declining, but class conflict in the industrialised democracies is not (Davis, 1999; Moody, 1988; Moody, 1997). Indeed, the Thatcherite attack on union rights has been described as the "white heat of a post-Fordist revolution" (Jessop, 1991b: 135-161). Yet, post-Fordism has both intensified class inequalities and mystified them, through social and spatial fragmentation that has undermined workers' solidarity and fragmented working-class communities (Antonio and Bonanno, 1996: 3-32). Additionally, the process of forging a new mode of social regulation is incomplete. This generates intense social conflict between the different groups included in, and those excluded from, the emerging social settlement of post-Fordism—a conflict dynamised significantly, but not exclusively, by class antagonisms.

Postmodern Politics and the Cultural Turn

The postmodern relativisation of the political universal and the postmodern fragmentation of social subjectivity therefore needs to be considered in the context of the generative social processes of the relative decline of the nation-state and the commodification of cultural practices. While the political process results in a decentring of national politics (and the rise of local antagonisms), the cultural process involves the dialectics of extreme individuation and generalised exchangeability. In line with postmodern ideology, postmarxism tends to imagine that the multiplication of the sites of social antagonism and the plurality of NSM mean the advent of an unlimited potential for democratisation (Laclau, 1985: 42; Laclau and Mouffe, 1985: 149-193). This lines postmarxism up with the mainstream ideology of a postmodern politics "beyond Left and Right" (Giddens, 1994a), which misrecognises the *decentring* of class politics for its absolute decline and predicts the relentless advance of democracy without considering the anti-democratic potentials of post-Fordism.

It is here that Laclau and Mouffe most blatantly substitute ideological misrecognition for political analysis. *HSS* proposes that in politics, "the fundamental concept is that of 'democratic struggle' and … popular struggles are merely specific conjunctures resulting from the multiplication of equivalence effects among the democratic struggles" (Laclau and Mouffe, 1985: 137). This substitutes a specifically leftwing requirement—the irreducibility of democratic struggles—for a general theory of political processes. As a description of anti-democratic populist movements and ideologies, such as fascism (Laclau, 1977: 81-142) and neo-conservatism (Hall, 1988: 19-56, 123-160), it is plainly wrong. Further, postmarxism considers that because of the "increasing complexity of the social" and the growing flexibility of subject-positions (the overdetermination of political identities), "democratic struggles tend less and less to be unified as 'popular struggles'" (Laclau and Mouffe, 1985: 133). Without the unification of democratic struggles into a popular front alliance, however, no expansive hegemony is possible. The replacement of theoretical analysis with ideological requirements results in a performative inconsistency between radical democratic theory and politics.

The task of the Left presupposes, at a minimum, an analysis of the institutional determinants of the neo-conservative embrace of "authoritarian populism" and an appreciation of the structural reforms necessary for progressive democratisation. Despite accepting that the neo-liberal effort to articulate a new hegemony involved the recuperative "divide and conquer"

strategy of sectoral concessions to social movement demands for liberty (Laclau and Mouffe, 1985: 165-166), Laclau and Mouffe restrict the Left to the
"fundamental" task of deepening and expanding "*liberal democratic ideology*"
(Laclau and Mouffe, 1985: 176). This reduction of institutional and strategic
analysis to a rapturous embrace of "liberal democratic *ideology*" evades the
difficult question of the institutional impact on representative democracy
of the emergent mode of social regulation. Laclau and Mouffe overlook the
structural constraints on liberal democracy and the increasingly authoritarian character of the post-Fordist state.

Regulation Theory, by contrast, proposes that the relative decline of
the nation-state does indeed bring about a decentring of hegemonic politics,
combined with the relativisation of the political universal (Jessop, 1990: 192-
272). Nonetheless, the new mode of social regulation imposes significant limitations on industrial democracy, the democratisation of the state and the articulation of equality with liberty (Jessop, 1991a; Jessop, Bonnett *et al.*, 1988).
Following the analysis of Poulantzas, modernity institutes politics as the field
of hegemony because capitalism excludes extra-economic coercion from the
labour process (Jessop, 1990). The nation state operates as a universalising
instance external to the economic realm and political struggle revolves upon
this "neutral arbiter," requiring the dominant class to portray its interests as
those of the nation as a whole (Poulantzas, 1973: 104-117). Popular-democratic sovereignty in the bourgeois republic nonetheless becomes explicitly politicised during the twentieth century with the advent of the interventionist
state, leading to significant concessions (social rights, formal liberties) (Poulantzas, 1973: 55-56; Poulantzas, 1975: 165-168; Poulantzas, 1978: 165-168),
combined with institutional restrictions on popular sovereignty and the retreat of democracy towards elite competition (MacPherson, 1972; MacPherson, 1977). Towards the end of the twentieth century, the growth of multinational corporations and the internationalisation of capitalism forced the
state to withdraw from economic intervention towards the management of
social crises, and mass struggles precipitated by state intervention led to the
emergence of the NSM (Poulantzas, 1978: 240-247). Poulantzas identifies
the contemporary tendency of the state form as "authoritarian statism" and
identifies its characteristics as "intensified state control over every sphere of
socio-economic life combined with a radical decline in the institutions of political democracy and with the draconian and multiform curtailment of so-
called 'formal liberties'" (Poulantzas, 1978: 203-204).

Lacking an evaluation of the trend towards plebiscitory politics orches-
trated through the mass media as something linked to corporate expansion
and the relative decline in national sovereignty (Boggs, 2000), Laclau and
Mouffe massively underestimate the significance of authoritarian populism
in the current conjuncture.[8] Indeed, Laclau and Mouffe appear to conflate

---

8. By "authoritarian populism," I mean neo-conservatism's "unceasing efforts to construct

the postmodern dispersion of the subject with the advent of a new form of subjectivity that is, effectively, a post-capitalist subjectivity beyond possessive individualism. According to Mouffe, the dispersion of the subject across a multiplicity of (potentially contradictory) subject-positions implies a post-individualist conception of democratic rights (Mouffe, 1988: 35). Amplifying these sentiments, Laclau claims that the contemporary proliferation of political identities is the condition of possibility of radical democratic politics (Laclau, 1990: 81-82). Yet, there is a link between a socially fragmented and dispersed polity and the plebiscitory legitimation of authoritarian populism, because this latter depends upon political demobilisation combined with demagogic scapegoating. Laclau and Mouffe conflate these dimensions because they do not support their analysis of the transformation of liberal ideology with an assessment of the structural transformation of parliamentary democracy.

Secondly, postmodern subjectivity needs to be related to the commodification of cultural forms. In the consumption norms of the emergent post-Fordist regimes of accumulation, a new culture plays an increasingly important role, based on the massive growth of advertising and its integration into product design (Fine and Haug, 2002; Haug, 1986). In accordance with the analysis of Fredric Jameson, we can insist that postmodernism is a new cultural dominant (hegemonic cultural style) (Jameson, 1991). Following Jameson, I contend that postmodernism is the new hegemonic culture within capitalist social formations characterised by the emergent post-Fordist modes of social regulation. This position is informed by Jameson's argument that cultural forms have to be examined from the perspective of "cultural revolution," whereby social subjects are "reprogrammed" for the lifeworld of the dominant mode of production (Jameson, 1981: 95-99); Jameson further specifies that a microcosm of this process happens during transitions between distinct stages of capitalism (Jameson, 1991: xii-xv). While the analysis presented by Regulation Theory is economically as convincing as Mandel's concept of "late capitalism" (Mandel, 1978b), relied on by Jameson, the notion of post-Fordism avoids the periodisation problems encountered in Jameson's position (Harvey, 1989: 38; Soja, 1989: 60-61).

The hegemonic cultural style of postmodernism can be characterised as a radicalisation of modernism under conditions of the commodification of

---

the movement towards a more authoritarian regime from a massive populist base," based on national-popular interpellations that are anti-democratic and anti-egalitarian (Hall, 1988: 146). Hall's basically Laclavian position on the primacy of ideology (Hall, 1988: 123-173) was subjected to devastating criticism by Jessop and cothinkers (Jessop, Bonnett et al., 1988: 57-124)—the work includes a reprint of Hall's reply to their criticisms in which he accepts their charge of a one-sided, polemical exaggeration of the importance of ideology—who did not so much object to "authoritarian populism," as to its complete independence from economics and politics (Jessop, Bonnett et al., 1988: 66-67).

the aesthetic. With the commodification of the aesthetic, the "great divide" between mass culture and high modernism is destroyed, leading to post-modern "popular" culture (Huyssen, 1986). Popular culture exists in a con-dition of "complicit critique," where the utopian potential of the modernist work is blunted by a self-reflexive knowledge of its insertion into the very sphere of commodity circulation that it criticises (Hutcheon, 1988; Hutch-eon, 1989). At the same time, grasping the aestheticisation of the commodity (and the commodification of the aesthetic) in terms of a general economy of the "commodity-body-sign," which includes the products destined for indi-vidual consumption as markers of distinction and "reified" images of mate-rial satisfaction, inserts popular culture within the total circuit of the com-modity without any nostalgia for the lost modernist utopia (Miklitsch, 1996: 5-40; Miklitsch, 1998a: 61-95). The contemporary proliferation of identities (Giddens, 1991), sometimes impressionistically described as "postmodern schizophrenia" (Jameson, 1991: xx), is therefore best regarded as an extreme individuation commensurate with the combination of extensive accumula-tion and product diversification characteristic of post-Fordism (Cross, 1993; Lee, 1993). It is in this context of the new importance of postmodern culture for social reproduction and the proliferation of commodified identities that the "rise and fall of the NSM" can be grasped as integral to the transition from Fordism to post-Fordism.

CLASS ANALYSIS AND THE NEW SOCIAL MOVEMENTS

A New Social Agency for the New Times?

In the context of the emergence of a new mode of social regulation, the cul-tural politics of the NSM cannot be considered part of a "paradigm shift" "beyond Left and Right". Instead, they appear as effects of social causes, connected to the economic structures, political dynamics and cultural di-alectics of post-Fordism. This brings us to the second major postmarxian claim, according to which the challenge posed to Marxism by the NSM is supposed to be definitive (Mouffe, 1988: 34). According to Laclau, class is completely inadequate to explain contemporary conflict. He proposes that the shift to identity politics indicates that the NSM constitute a new so-cial phenomenon which explodes the paradigm of class politics and replac-es it with identity politics (Laclau, 1985: 27-29). As supporters of the thesis that the NSM emerge from a radical structural break (Laclau, 1990: 52-55), Laclau and Mouffe hold that identity politics—driven by the "democratic Imaginary"—is the central dynamic of contemporary social conflict (La-clau and Mouffe, 1985: 149-193) and class struggle is becoming increasingly irrelevant (Laclau, 2000c: 203). Where industrial conflict emerges, this is the result of identity conflict between consumers and is not traceable to the politics of production (Laclau, 1985: 31), so identity politics is not shaped by capitalist production, but by broader cultural concerns. Capitalism does not determine the emergence of the NSM because "the capitalist system" is not a relevant theoretical determination (Laclau, 1990: 58-59), while the emergence of the NSM demonstrates the irreducibility of the social to dynamics of capital accumulation and instead, its distribution across a plurality of sites of conflict, governed by independent social logics (Laclau, 1985). Yet, as I have indicated, the combination of the globalisation of production, decline of the nation-state and increased importance of culture precipitates new forms of social conflict that have everything to do with capital accumulation and class politics.

Globally, the novelty of the NSM can be differentially determined by contrast with the "old" or traditional working-class movements. The decisive differential trait is supposed to be the new role of cultural and symbolic forms of protest, completely absent from the "old" social movements (Cohen, 1985). According to theorists of the NSM, the "traditional" social movements were centralised, hierarchical, socially homogeneous political movements, oriented to the control or transformation of the state by means of mobilisation around material needs and political demands, and lacking a focus on identity and cultural practices. By contrast, the NSM are organised in grassroots, decentred and participatory networks within civil society (Melucci, 1989) and follow the strategy of "self-limiting revolution" or localised reforms (Arato and Cohen, 1992), aiming to reduce state control rather than control the state (Touraine, 1985), by means of an orientation to the transformation of cultural signification and the constitution of new political subjectivities (Touraine, 1977). Whereas the materialist values of working-class mobilisation involve redistributive struggles in the conventional political arena, the post-materialist values of the NSM engage the quality of life and aim for the reconstruction of identity, values, lifestyles, cultural symbols and knowledge (Dalton, 1990; Giddens, 1994a; Giddens, 1998; Giddens, 2000; Inglehart, 1990a; Inglehart, 1990b; Inglehart, 1997). The NSM are focused on the new politicisation of everyday life as opposed to state politics and centred on symbolic contestation in the cultural sphere instead of power confrontation in the political domain (Melucci, 1996). According to NSM theorists, these transformations mean that the workers' movement that dominated the politics of the nineteenth- and early twentieth- centuries cannot now perform a leading role in the constitution and contestation of social structures.

Recent investigations, however, have exploded the claim of "newness" and it emerges that the category of "new" social movements cannot be empirically sustained. It overstates their novelty (Plotke, 1990; Plotke, 1995), ignores their predecessors and mistakes an early position in the cycle of protest for a new type of protest (Tarrow, 1994), neglects a long-standing historical cycle of cultural critique (Brandt, 1990), and misinterprets a generational phenomenon as a categorical shift in social action. Social movements of the traditional nineteenth-century working-class are revealed to possess all the attributes of the "new" (Calhoun, 1993; Tucker, 1991), while traditions of cultural struggles, documented in working-class historiography (Croteau, 1995; Thompson, 1963), have been deployed damagingly against the stereotyped dichotomy of "cultural" NSM and "state-centred" working-class movements. Hence, the sharp distinction between traditional working class and the NSM has not survived scrutiny.

Instead of the historical teleology of the increase of social complexity and the arrival of an expressive postmodern social totality, replete with a new social agency, reconsideration of the continuity between the "new" and traditional social movements enables us to "constitute our theoretical notion of modernity, not as a master narrative, but in a way that reflects both its heterogeneity and contestation and that takes full account of the central place of social movements within it" (Calhoun, 1993: 418). Indeed, the history of social movement struggles is coextensive with modernity and the "newness" of the social movements is partially the result of their marginalisation in the history of social theory (Wallerstein, 1990: 13). Certainly, with Laclau and Mouffe, the French Revolution catalysed the spread of mass mobilisations for liberty and equality throughout Europe and the world capitalist system, where they continue to inform contemporary social movements (Calhoun, 1993: 390-395; Wallerstein, 1990: 13-53). The historically specific rise of social movements is linked to the emergence of mass politics centred on the nation-state—like it or not, the central focus of politics in modernity—and therefore to the possibility of hegemonic strategies. Instead of a process of continuous expansion of the logic of the French Revolution, though, as Laclau and Mouffe suggest, social movement struggles have been conditioned by the structures of the world capitalist system, developing in nationalist, socialist and communist directions as a consequence of the centre-periphery division in the world economy (Shannon, 1989; Wallerstein, 1990; Wallerstein, 1991). World systems theory demonstrates the existence of six varieties of "anti-systemic movements" in response to this politico-economic distribution (Wallerstein, 1990: 13-53), while the concept of social movements as bearers of alternative modernities, including state socialism, "Islamic Jacobins" and Apartheid (Ray, 1993), adds a cultural dimension irreducible to the "expansion and deepening of liberal ideology" thesis of Laclau and Mouffe.

Beyond Left and Right?

In question, then, is not the existence and extent of "new" social movements linked to the rising importance of struggles for cultural recognition, nor the existence of non-class social antagonisms, nor yet the emergence of novel

middle-class layers. Nor can there be a dispute that the politics of many social movements are relatively autonomous from the logic of class struggles.
This means, for instance, that the fight against women's oppression cannot
be reduced to the struggle against specifically capitalist exploitation. The
Marxist claim is that the contradictions of capitalism nonetheless overdetermine the forms of women's oppression and that this non-class social antagonism exists as articulated to class structures (Barrett, 1980). Michele
Barrett's landmark *Women's Oppression Today* argued against the emergent
postmarxian position of Cutler, Hussein, Hindess and Hirst, that ideology,
politics and economics were completely independent, and that women's oppression was located in ideological relations exclusively. Barrett accepts the
non-class nature of the family as a social institution and adopts the position that women's oppression is primarily located in ideological relations of
gender construction. Drawing upon the materialist anthropology of Claude
Meillassoux and the "mixed modes of production" debate (Meillassoux,
1981; Wolpe, 1980; Kuhn and Wolpe, 1977), however, she argues that familial structures are articulated to capitalist social relations as subordinated structures, so that the wage relation and the commodity form condition
both the domestic economy and gender relations. As such, the non-class antagonism of gender relations (1) has both primary ideological and secondary
economic aspects that are conditioned by capitalism and (2) takes on a class
significance insofar as the gender division of labour in the domestic space
fundamentally conditions the segmentation of the labour market for wage
labour. However, the non-class gender opposition is an antagonistic relation
that is analytically primary in the explanation of family structures: class *conditions* gender, rather than *explains* it; gender relations have a differential history that is externally related to the histories of the economic, political and
ideological structures of capitalism; thus, the position advocated (then) by
Barrett is not a form of reductionism. In other words, non-class antagonisms
are relatively autonomous but "overdetermined" by class relations, which is
equivalent to claiming that the capitalist mode of production is a structure
in dominance.

To state all this more abstractly, then, the significant differences between contemporary Marxism and postmarxism concern the existence of
structural tendencies as determinants of social conflict and the relevance of
structural location as a conditioning factor in the adoption of subject-positions. Because postmarxism holds that identity politics arises *completely independently* of class relations, constituting an autonomous or free-floating system governed by ideology and not by material needs or state politics, Laclau
and Mouffe are forced to defend the untenable claim that capitalism is not a
relevant determinant of social conflict and to deny the pertinence of the category of structural (class) locations.

According to Laclau's major article on the NSM, "the concept of class struggle ... is totally insufficient as a way of accounting for contemporary social conflicts" (Laclau, 1985: 29). Laclau and Mouffe deny the theoretical validity of a replacement of the proletariat by the NSM within the neo-Hegelian paradigm of Gorz and Touraine, who seek a "new subject of history" and merely "invert the Marxist position" (Laclau and Mouffe, 1985: 169). Instead, the authors contend that while discourse theory reveals that workers' struggles always were a form of identity politics, nonetheless, the specificity of the politics of the NSM constitutes a democratic advance commensurate with social complexity (Laclau, 1985: 42). In support of this position, Laclau criticises classical Marxism, which determines the identity of agents in the relations of production, so that politics means the "representation of interests" (Laclau, 1985: 28). Classical Marxism designates the social agent as a pre-constituted referent of political discourse and assumes an *a priori* unity to the ensemble of subject-positions of the agent in production. The leading characteristic of the NSM is that the unity of these determinations has broken up, so that "it has become increasingly impossible to identify the group, conceived as a referent, with an orderly and coherent system of 'subject-positions'" (Laclau, 1985: 28). In other words, contemporary social clashes bring to light the multiplicity of subject-positions occupied by the agent and the conflict potential of this overdetermined ensemble.

The supposed unity of the subject in reality consists of a decentred (differential) ensemble of subject-positions (worker, Black, female, and so forth) (Laclau, 1985: 31). "It is thus impossible to speak of the social agent as if we were dealing with a unified, homogeneous entity. We have rather to approach the social agent as a plurality, dependent on the various subject-positions by which s/he is constituted within various discursive formations" (Laclau, 1985: 31-32). Because of the lack of coherence of this ensemble of subject-positions, it is impossible to regard political subjectivity as the representation of a pre-constituted interest that can be derived from the structural location of the agent. The central characteristic of the NSM is that social antagonism is determined not by the clash of interests, but by the fact that an ensemble of subject-positions has become the focal point of social conflict and political mobilisation (Laclau, 1985: 32). According to postmarxism, then, the NSM respond to the negation of identity and not to structural determinations.

In *HSS*, however, a somewhat more extended analysis is conducted in relatively evasive terms, for Laclau and Mouffe generally resort to quasi-foundational language. When explaining the causal factors operating in the emergence of the NSM, their descriptions suggest a scission between subject-positions and structural location, as in, for instance, their conjunctural analysis in terms of a "double perspective" of "the transformation of social relations" and "the effects of the displacement ... of the egalitarian Imaginary" (Laclau and Mouffe, 1985: 165). In the article on the NSM, however, Laclau is more candid. Laclau conceptualises social classes, structural levels and so forth "as complexes resulting from the *contingent* articulation of smaller entities" (Laclau, 1985: 31). The new units of analysis are "subject-positions" (Laclau, 1985: 32), that are contingently articulated together into discursive formations (social relations). This social theory can be characterised as a form of radical liberalism based on logical atomism, resulting in the complete dispersion of the social field, linked to a descriptive empiricism of the "diverse complexes" of contemporary "post-industrial" society.

The convergence of Laclau and Mouffe's position with the "beyond Left and Right" stance of the post-industrial utopians, theorists of reflexive modernity and advocates of Critical Theory should alert us to the ultimate political stakes in this debate. The "traditional" social movement of the working class has defined the agenda of the Left since the early the nineteenth-century and has meant that the Left-Right opposition tends to reflect the class division of society (Giddens, 1994a) and a principled distinction between social equality (the Left) and natural inequality (the Right) (Bobbio, 1996). Where for Giddens, for instance, the NSM appear as an adjunct to the class struggle, which remains the major dynamic of capitalism, for Laclau and Mouffe the working class is (at best) an appendage to the NSM. Once class politics becomes secondary (reflexive modernity, Critical Theory) or irrelevant (postmarxism, post-industrial theory), the Left-Right distinction ceases to be the primary political division in modern society. Laclau and Mouffe, of course, reject this entailment (Laclau and Mouffe, 2000). I endorse their refusal to abandon the Left-Right distinction, based on the sociological and philosophical reasons just considered—but it is very difficult to see how they can actually avoid it, on the basis of their position.

New Social Movements and Post-Fordism

Postmarxism's insistence on a non-class politics, combined with an exclusive concentration on ideology, functions to occlude the connection between post-Fordism and the flexible identities promoted by many of the NSM. The problem is that Laclau and Mouffe—on ideological grounds alone (Laclau, 1985: 28; Laclau and Mouffe, 1985: 150)—reject the idea that the structural tendencies of a mode of social regulation are crucial determinants of social conflict, preferring to believe that the novelty of the NSM lies in the autonomous activation of certain subject-positions as sites of contestation. It is surely significant that not only (as we have seen) do Laclau and Mouffe neglect these pronouncements when it comes to concrete analyses, but that the postmarxists who actually engage in empirical studies of the NSM also ignore them, or reverse them completely. According to a postmarxian survey conducted in the 1990s, "despite the emergence of new sites of struggle that cannot be comprehended in terms of class dynamics, capitalism remains the dominant structure of the contemporary world" (Carroll, 1994: 16-17). Indeed, many of the NSM articulate the concerns of workers left out of the Fordist social compromise and the emergent grievances of social categories of consumption (Carroll, 1994: 3-26). Another postmarxian survey of Regulation Theory and the NSM concedes that "capital accumulation remains the mainspring of advanced societies, even if the sociologically defined working class is declining in size … and … this process will continue to define the main positions in social conflict" (Steinmetz, 1994: 185). On the basis of her work on race in Britain (Smith, 1994), Smith claims to "extend" Laclau and Mouffe's position by introducing the distinction between "structural positions" and "subject-positions" (Smith, 1998: 4, 55-63)—a "supplement" that effectively repudiates the original.

Laclau and Mouffe are keen to reconceptualise workers' struggles as "always-already" identity based. They argue that workers' struggles in the nineteenth- and early twentieth- centuries were either relatively depoliticised reformist struggles in production, or radical responses "to transformations which called into question traditional forms of worker identity" (Laclau and Mouffe, 1985: 168-169). Thus the crucial determinant of the radicalisation of working-class struggles in production was political identity and not the structural determinant of capitalist exploitation. Conversely:

> Once the conception of the working class as a "universal class" is rejected, it becomes possible to recognise the plurality of the antagonisms which take place in the field of what is arbitrarily grouped under the label of "workers' struggles," and the inestimable importance of the great majority of them for the deepening of the democratic process (Laclau and Mouffe, 1985: 167).

The decisive conclusion for postmarxism is that the multiplicity of discursive contexts that informed these struggles prevent any identification of a singular and unitary working class (Laclau and Mouffe, 1985: 167). This strikes at the straw target of vulgar Marxism (for which capitalist exploitation *automatically* generates radical resistance), but is not a serious engagement with post-Althusserian Marxism at all.

The claim that workers' struggles are a form of "identity politics" is nothing new, or shocking, from an Althusserian perspective, because political subjectivity is constituted through ideological interpellations that lend the subject a social identity. It is on the basis of "lived experience" that subjects enter political conflicts, and no doubt democratic ideology is one (but not the only) determinant of the radicalisation of struggle (socialist, populist and religious radicalism, for instance, are also common). Yet, in the Althusserian perspective, the "reality shocks," engendered by the contradictions between the "Imaginary relations" constitutive of ideology and the "real conditions of existence" that ideology misrecognises, can lead to the articulation of new forms of social subjectivity that conform more closely to the structural locations occupied by a social agent (Althusser, 1990: 1-42).

Indeed, Laclau's earlier work (within the research programme of Structural Marxism) provided a superior explanation of this phenomenon, compared to the eclipse of structural factors behind ideological manipulation characteristic of the postmarxian position. From Laclau's initial position, it is clear that political crises, arising from an accumulation of structural contradictions, are experienced first and foremost as identity crises for social agents (Laclau, 1977: 103). When social agents do not belong to fundamental classes of production, the ideological crisis becomes increasingly crucial and this increases the importance of the ideological instance in the final resolution of the political crisis in the social formation as a whole (Laclau, 1977: 104). In particular, the democratic struggle represents competition for the middle classes, whose identity as "the people" is more important than their class-identity (Laclau, 1977: 114). It follows that the "struggle for the articulation of popular-democratic ideology into class ideological discourses is the basic ideological struggle in capitalist social formations" (Laclau, 1977: 114). These references to the middle classes would later be discretely erased and replaced by the entirely non-class NSM. Nonetheless, they throw significant light on the overdetermination of an ensemble of non-class subject-positions (for instance, female, Black, lesbian) by a class subject-position (for instance, working-class or middle-class), suggesting that popular-democratic identities tend to be those adopted by non-working-class subjects.

The article by Joachim Hirsch—drawing on the perspectives of Regulation Theory—supplies evidence for my analysis. Hirsch demonstrates that the NSM in Germany emerged from the crisis of Fordist social regulation and that their contradictory tendencies might be expected to lead to internal divisions if a new, post-Fordist mode of social regulation emerged as a hegemonic project. Far from dismissing the NSM, Hirsch emphasises that they "are a contradictory battle ground in the struggle for a new hegemony" and that "within these struggles, [they] play a very complex and rather contradictory part" (Hirsch, 1988: 51, 53). The NSM are both "the only real opposition" and—because of their ideological heterogeneity and dismissal of the class analyses of the "traditional Left"—potentially "the unconscious vehicles for the establishment of just this new form of capitalist exploitation and hegemony" (Hirsch, 1988: 53). In the absence of any recognition of the class dynamics and the dominance of regimes of accumulation in social life, the exclusive emphasis on the cultural politics of identity-formation (leading to new, flexible identities), linked to emergent niche-markets for products targeting specific identity choices, might easily become incorporated into post-Fordist social regulation. With particular reference to the German Greens, Hirsch warned that "the formation of a political party that relates to alternative cultures and new social movements might have the vicious effect of splitting them and domesticating them into the established forms of parliamentary politics ... the new social movements in fact might prove to be not so much radical fighters for a new and better society, but political and ideological catalysts of a really unfriendly form of capitalist post-Fordism" (Hirsch, 1988: 54). Hirsch's analysis was confirmed several years later, when the division in the Greens between "Realos" and "Fundos" became the keynote in the transformation of this "new" social movement into a political party of the old style, in government with the centre-right Social Democracy (Bramwell, 1994). What this indicates is that the connections between post-Fordism and the flexible identities promoted by the NSM generates political polarisation, which refutes Laclau's supposition that subject-positions are entirely independent of structural determinations.

The postmarxian "farewell to the working class" is only the most recent in a century of *adieus*. What has finished is not class conflict and the social agency of fundamental classes, but instead the possibility of the progressive simplification of social contradictions and the model of a homogeneous and unified proletariat in confrontation with an equally definite bourgeoisie. On this question, Laclau and Mouffe (Laclau and Mouffe, 1985: 7-46), following Althusser and Balibar (Althusser and Balibar, 1970: 183-192), are perfectly correct. Contemporary class relations are characterised by the interpenetration of multiple and conflicting determinants of structural location and the consequent heterogeneity and internal differentiation of classes, races and genders (Poulantzas, 1975; Wright, 1985). Class never appears in an unalloyed form, being instead permanently imbricated with elements from relatively independent forms of social domination (Aronowitz, 1992; Balibar and Wallerstein, 1991). The existence of structural tendencies based in the final analysis in the dynamics of the accumulation of capital means that every non-class antagonism is trapped in the "gravitational field" of class contradictions. While there is no isomorphism between structural locations and subject-positions, nonetheless the structural dynamics of late capitalism determine a polarisation within non-class and middle-class movements, leading to the emergence of tendential class-political dimensions inside the NSM. As Laclau's *Marxist* work concluded, while "not every contradiction is a class contradiction, ... every contradiction is overdetermined by the class struggle" (Laclau, 1977: 106).

The novelty of the NSM consists not in their absolute distinction from the traditional working class, but instead from a new configuration of old elements (material grievances, political demands, claims for cultural recognition), combined with historically specific activation of social layers and the emergence of new middle strata, linked to technological and economic changes. What emerges, then, is that the dynamics of social movement activism are conditioned by transformations in the structure of capitalism. Class-composition and the balance of class forces continue to overdetermine the NSM, leading to the phenomenon of the NSM articulating a politics *hegemonised* by middle-class concerns (Croteau, 1995; Eder, 1995). This is not the claim that the politics of the NSM can be *reduced* to class questions—merely that, contra postmarxism, class remains a highly relevant dimension of contemporary social conflict.

MARXISM AND DEMOCRACY

The End of the "Jacobin Imaginary"

The continued relevance of class politics and the necessity for a structural analysis of advanced capitalism expose the deficiencies in the postmarxian position, highlighting the need to reconsider the relation between Marxian theory and socialist strategy. The logic of Laclau and Mouffe's rejection of Marxism is straightforward and cumulative. Increasing complexity fragments the social field, leading to a pluralisation of social actors and political conflicts, which tends to diffuse throughout the decentred "discursive formation". Accordingly, Marxist theory supposedly cannot penetrate the non-class dynamics of contemporary social conflict; and the socialist programme, based on the ontological centrality of the proletariat, the hypothesis of increasing class polarisation and the unitary character of the political space, cannot accommodate political diversity. This leads to the necessity for a new political strategy capable of welding together sectoral demands into a relatively unified coalition. Abandoning the concepts of "privileged points of rupture and the confluence of political struggles into a unified political space" (Laclau and Mouffe, 1985: 152), radical democracy embraces the postmodern multiplicity of social antagonisms on the basis of a completely relational theory of hegemony. This chain of arguments culminates in what is, according to Laclau and Mouffe, their central thesis. They dedicate the programmatic chapter of *HSS* to the exposition of "the thesis that it is … [the] continuity between the Jacobin and the Marxist political imaginary which has to be put in question by the project for a radical democracy" (Laclau and Mouffe, 1985: 152).

Laclau and Mouffe's main contention is therefore that the Jacobin Imaginary of Marxism and the radical democratic Imaginary of postmarxism are irreconcilable opposites. Indeed, the fundamental obstacle to radical democracy turns out to be the "ultimate core" of "essentialist fixity," located "in the fundamental nodal point which has galvanised the political imagination of the Left: the classic concept of 'revolution,' cast in the Jacobin mould … [which] implied the *foundational* character of the revolutionary act, the institution of a point of concentration of power from which society could be 'rationally' reorganised" (Laclau and Mouffe, 1985: 177). Marxism, in the final analysis, cannot adapt to social complexity and democratic politics, because it is based on philosophical rationalism (Laclau and Mouffe, 1985: 3). Where classical Marxism is grounded in "*foundational* character of the revolutionary act," postmarxism defines a new, anti-essentialist social theory. This contention, and not debates around the emergence of a new mode of social regulation or the sociological novelty of the social movements, is the *ultima ratio* of the authors' position. The justification for a shift to the postmarxian field stands or falls with this claim.

There is something enigmatic about Laclau and Mouffe's presentation of this claim through a genealogy of the category of hegemony in Marxist theory (Laclau and Mouffe, 1985: 7-92). Despite claiming that the positions advanced in *HSS* could equally have been arrived at without any need for an analysis of twentieth-century Marxism (Laclau and Mouffe, 1985: 4), Laclau and Mouffe engage in endless deconstructions of Marxism (Laclau, 1995a: 84-104; Laclau, 1990: 1-85; Laclau and Mouffe, 1985: 7-92), as if exhibiting a repetition compulsion. As always, a repetition compulsion evidences the traumatic loss of an object and the desperate quest to relocate it (that is, the force of an unconscious desire).

According to Laclau and Mouffe, the concept of hegemony was introduced to supplement the economist logic of historical necessity, governing classical Marxism, with a political logic of contingency. On the basis of the "increasing complexity of the social," Marxist politics became subjected to conditions of the fragmentation of the working class, the isolation of political movements and the separation between economic and political struggles (Laclau and Mouffe, 1985: 2, 8-9). According to Laclau's subsequent summary, *HSS* demonstrates that: (1) classical Marxism rests upon the thesis of an evolutionary development leading to class polarisation and social simplification; (2) in response to a crisis of perspectives, a series of proposals for the integration of social fragmentation, through symbolic political action, emerged as means to salvage the basic theoretical schema; (3) the tactics of the united front and the socialist adoption of democratic tasks in the socialist revolution responded to increasing social complexity ("combined and uneven development"), leading to the category of hegemony; (4) "from the Leninist concept of class alliances to the Gramscian concept of 'intellectual and moral leadership,' there is an increasing extension of hegemonic tasks"; (5) this demonstrates an internal movement in Marxist theory from evolutionary essentialism towards contingent political articulations (Laclau, 1990: 120-121).

Laclau and Mouffe's analysis of this deconstructive movement follows a historical sequence and culminates with the "Gramscian watershed," which they represent as a partial break with the "essentialism" characteristic of Marxism (Laclau and Mouffe, 1985: 65-71). Their treatment of Gramsci's breakthrough is evasive, though, because this is presented as the conclusion to a historical narrative of increasing social complexity, designed to demon-

strate the replacement of class politics (and the ontological centrality of the
proletariat) by democratic politics (and the emergence of the NSM). The
discussion of twentieth-century Marxism is followed by two chapters of the-
ory-construction that begin from the anti-essentialist break of Althusserian
Marxism (Laclau and Mouffe, 1985: 95-110).

What Laclau and Mouffe have done is to invert the historico-theoretical sequence, for in the history of *effective* socialist politics, Gramsci comes
after Althusser. As Mouffe once recognised, "if the history of Marxist theory during the 1960s can be characterised by the reign of 'Althusserianism,'
then we have now, without a doubt, entered a new phase: that of 'Gram-
scism'" (Mouffe, 1979b: 1). The revival of Gramsci within the Western Left
depended upon the advent of Eurocommunism, as a political strategy, within the Western European Communist parties during the mid-1970s (Mouffe,
1979b: 1). Yet, there is only one (indirect) mention of Eurocommunism in Laclau and Mouffe's entire deconstruction of Marxist history—in a footnote
relating to Gramsci (Laclau and Mouffe, 1985: 69). Secondly, the problem
that the revival of Gramsci responds to is not *ontological* but specifically *political*: not social agency but political strategy. The central problem confronted by Eurocommunism was *not* the fragmentation of the working class, but
instead the political terrain of socialist strategy, namely, parliamentary democracy. The main debate on the Left in the 1970s concerned "whether it
was possible to reconcile the line of the hegemony of the proletariat—at the
heart of Gramsci's strategy—with the pluralist line of the [Eurocommunist]
'historic compromise'" (Mouffe, 1979b: 13). This reverses exactly the prog-
nosis of Laclau and Mouffe's central contention, namely, the continuity between Marxism and the Jacobin Imaginary, for as Mouffe says, the worry
was that the Communist Party of Italy (PCI) might have gone "too far" in
accepting democratic politics and have "abandoned" proletarian hegemony.
For Mouffe, at that time, there could be no question of presenting Marxist
hegemony in a totalitarian light, (as exclusive of pluralism), for the Gramscian conception of ideology implies hegemonic articulations between heterogeneous materials, opening the possibility for "a strategy of democratic transition to socialism: a possible Eurocommunism which avoids both
the perils of Stalinism and social democracy" (Mouffe, 1979b: 15). By a few
years later, the hopes raised by Eurocommunism had been dashed. For Laclau and Mouffe, the moment of Eurocommunism became subject to a massive theoretical repression that evacuated it completely from the landscape
of Marxist history, leaving only one, tiny, symptomatic footnote as evidence
that it had ever even existed. In the light of the previous discussion of the
continued relevance of class analysis, it is revealing that Laclau and Mouffe's
watershed document, designed to legitimate a repudiation of Marxism for
forms of postmodern politics, almost completely erases the most significant
recent development in Marxist politics—the one with the potential to refute

their insistence that Marxism is an inflexible, rationalist doctrine alien to contemporary political realities.

Eurocommunism: A Massive Gap in the Postmarxian Analysis

The "end of the Jacobin Imaginary" (that is, Leninist ideology) arrives with Eurocommunism in the 1970s (Ross, 1980: 112-134) and not with the "avalanche of historical mutations" detected a decade later by Laclau and Mouffe. Eurocommunism broke the "continuity between the Jacobin and the Marxist political Imaginary" by rejecting Leninism for democratic socialism, not by repudiating Marxism for radical democracy.[9] Of course, abandoning the Leninism in "Marxism-Leninism" is a modest historical change and not a vast metaphysical transformation that requires the theoretical vocabulary of "social Imaginaries" and "discursive formations". Nonetheless, its omission is immensely significant, for it completes the process of the imposition of structures of ideological misrecognition onto theory that characterises postmarxian historicism. The existence of Eurocommunism vitiates the specular opposition between totalitarianism and democracy that is implied by the postmarxian claim that it is impossible to separate "the Jacobin and the Marxist political Imaginary" without abandoning class politics and historical materialism. For Eurocommunism breaks with the core components of the "Jacobin Imaginary"—the singular and foundational character of the revolutionary act, the state-centred vision of social reconstruction through enlightened class dictatorship and the unification of

---

9. I am not suggesting that Eurocommunism was the first Marxist movement to embrace either parliamentary democracy or forms of participatory democracy, only that the Eurocommunist moment ruins Laclau and Mouffe's artificial teleology and indicates that mass-based democratic alternatives have existed in the Marxian tradition. Historically, the social democracy (the Second International) defended the legitimacy of parliamentary democracy, although the drift towards reformism of the social democracy makes this an ambiguous legacy. Luxemburg defended parliamentary democracy from a revolutionary perspective after the Bolshevik October, while in general the Third International under Lenin clearly advocated forms of participatory democracy. Following the Stalinisation of the Third International, Trotsky defended the necessity of revolutionary democracy in the transition to socialism; curiously, *The Revolution Betrayed* is a work not mentioned by Laclau and Mouffe (Trotsky, 1991). Nonetheless, and without any facile conflation of Lenin and Stalin, ambiguities exist in the Marxist tradition. Contemporary democratic socialists have continued to disentangle the analytical ambiguities in the Marxist tradition and extended the long work of resistance to Stalinisation by Western Marxists. Robin Blackburn's extended essay on socialism after the fall of the Berlin Wall provides a historical and political overview of the theoretical resources for contemporary democratic socialism and the major debates regarding the strands of the Marxian tradition (Blackburn, 1991). Another perspective on the possibilities for democratic socialism today is provided by Michael Harrington (Harrington, 1993). It is worth contrasting the scope and ambitiousness of these programmes with the piecemeal reforms and protest politics advocated—under the banner of socialism!—by Laclau and Mouffe.

the revolutionary subject "in the moment of proletarian chiliasm" (Laclau and Mouffe, 1985: 84)—from a Marxist perspective. This means postmarxism cannot be considered "an *inevitable* decision for anyone aiming to reformulate a political programme for the Left in contemporary historical circumstances," for instead of the specular binary of the postmarxian axiology (radical democracy or a new Stalinism), the real situation is characterised by a complex field of theoretical and political differences—including within Eurocommunism (Boggs, 1980), whose left and right wings remain invisible in *HSS*'s lonely footnote.

Indeed, despite the inflated claims to have discovered a new paradigm, postmarxism actually inherits the programme and strategy of Eurocommunism and represents a contemporary continuation of the dominant, rightward-moving tendency within the Eurocommunist "revolution in liberty". The strategy of radical democracy is substantially anticipated by the programme of "structural reforms" and "advanced democracy" advocated by the Western Communist parties in their Eurocommunist incarnation. The major difference is that postmarxian strategy substitutes the agency of the NSM for the role of the working class. Yet the postmarxian supplement—"Eurocommunism plus the new social movements"—adds nothing programmatic whatsoever to the Eurocommunist formula of the mixed economy, political democratisation and cultural hegemony, while refusing a strategic analysis of the destiny of Eurocommunism.

The major postmarxian contributions to socialist strategy are foreshadowed in the Eurocommunist-inspired rectifications to Leninist politics in the period from 1974 to 1990. Eurocommunism discarded the vanguard party, the univocal bourgeois character of the liberal democratic state and the strategic objective of the dictatorship of the proletariat. Substantively, Eurocommunism involved three major elements. (1) The *renunciation of the vanguard party* for mass formations that would participate in alliance politics with equal partners in a democratic front. (2) The *democratisation and decentralisation of the state*, through the extension of parliamentary control over the state-apparatus, linked to the *abandonment of the dictatorship of the proletariat* for *liberal socialism*. (3) Renunciation of the *command economy* for *market socialism*, involving a democratically planned mixed economy together with programmes for workers' self-management as an integral part of the extension of democracy (Boggs, 1982; Carrillo, 1978; Claudin, 1978; Marzani, 1980; McInnes, 1976). The political strategy of Eurocommunism during the 1970s embraced democratic politics and therefore went beyond the popular front led by the proletarian party. It embraced a multi-class transitional strategy including regular alternation of leaderships involved in political competition and the negotiated formulation of joint programmes representing political compromises (Napolitano, 1977). This completely discredits Laclau and Mouffe's representation of Marxist history as dominated by philosophical rationalism.

Eurocommunism abandoned the Leninist vanguard party—characterised by centralised structures and restricted debate—for a pluralist internal framework. According to Santiago Carrillo (General Secretary of the Spanish Communist Party, or PSE), political pluralism entails the renunciation by the Communist party of the claim to be the *sole* bearer of working-class interests and the acceptance of an equal partnership in an unfolding social alliance, constitutive of a "new political formation". The party seeks to remain a "leading force" that shapes state institutions and social processes without becoming identical with the state. Dictatorship is avoided by virtue of economic and political decentralisation and democratisation, combined with power sharing by alliance partners and regular elections (Carrillo, 1978: 120-137; Claudin, 1978: 166-188). Do Laclau and Mouffe (Laclau, 1990: 81-84; Laclau and Mouffe, 1985: 149-192) add anything to this?

Based on the complexity of modern society and the popular base of liberal democracy, Eurocommunist leaders theorised the liberal-democratic state as an arena of contestation, rather than as a direct instrument of political domination (Carrillo, 1978: 120-137; Claudin, 1978: 143-164; Marchais, 1977a: 182-192; Mujal-Léon, 1983: 42-87; Napolitano, 1977: 24-89). The state in advanced capitalism is traversed by class antagonisms and is the site of strategic class struggles, where diverse social forces struggle for hegemony. Therefore, the Leninist policy of frontal insurrection and the destruction of the bourgeois state was replaced by a strategy of progressive internal democratisation (Antonian, 1987: 117-135). The concept of a foundational revolutionary act was replaced by an entire historical stage of "advanced democracy," traversed by the shifting equilibrium between social forces representing a new social order (Claudin, 1978: 122-165). Taking advantage of the relative autonomy of the state, Eurocommunist strategy sought to gradually "take-over" within the apparatus, employing institutions as levers for tilting the balance of forces in the direction of the popular movement. When Laclau and Mouffe theorise that a hegemonic alliance "becomes the state" (Laclau and Mouffe, 1985: 154) through exercising discursive control of social institutions, in what does their distance from mainstream Eurocommunism consist?

Nonetheless, multiple problems persisted in Eurocommunist practice, amply supported by deficiencies in the theories outlined by the leaderships of the parties. In general, mainstream Eurocommunist doctrine was characterised by an evolutionary gradualism close to the positions of Kautsky, where parliamentary reforms would gradually broaden the basis for a national-popular alliance and narrow the support-base for pro-capitalist policies (Mandel, 1978a). In line with earlier, Stalinist doctrines of historical stages in a linear evolution, mainstream Eurocommunism supposed that socialist construction could only begin at the end of this protracted process (Mandel, 1978a). Eurocommunism's renunciation of vanguardism combined bureaucratic inertia with a democratic theory. The dominant right-wing pursued a course that subordinated mass initiatives and participation to the interests of the party apparatus, excluding militant trade-union struggle or extra-parliamentary mobilisations. In Italy, for instance, Eurocommunist electoralism degenerated into what Maria Macciocchi called a "spectacle" of ideological superficiality, involving "oratorical contests" between leaders who encouraged the passivity of their supporters (Macchiochi, 1973: 22-43). In France, the leadership sabotaged internal democratisation and thereby systematically prepared the sectarian debacle of the 1978 electoral defeat (Althusser, 1978; Antonian, 1987). Unable to internally reform and revise their strategic perspectives at the same time, the Eurocommunist movement eventually gravitated towards a form of parliamentarism.

For the leftwing of Eurocommunism, the social democracy and the Communist parties equally failed to develop a democratic political practice that might recognise the legitimacy of representative democracy while avoiding the trap of parliamentary cretinism. According to some commentators, the problem for the Left was that radicals were not able to develop forms of participatory democracy supported by a mass movement that might counter-balance the recuperative effects of participation in liberal-democratic governments (Poulantzas, 1978; Weber, 1978). Within the Eurocommunist movement, a relatively dispersed leftwing alternative existed—including theoreticians such as Althusser, Balibar, Buci-Glucksmann (Buci-Glucksmann, 1980) and Poulantzas (Poulantzas, 1978)—that promoted the strategic alternative of democratic politics combined with mass mobilisations (Antonian, 1987). While the Left Eurocommunists (Fernando Claudin, Pietro Ingrao, Lucio Magri, Rossanna Rossanda, Nicos Poulantzas) tried to form a theoretical alternative and political tendency within the developing Eurocommunist current, the Right held power in the parties (Antonian, 1987: 87-102). Instead of building on this tendency, Laclau and Mouffe shift definitively in the direction of the rightward-moving mainstream of Eurocommunism—away from socialism and towards a form of parliamentary reform politics whose explicit "aim is not to create a completely different kind of society" (Mouffe, 1990: 57).

In the absence of an institutional analysis of Communist history, Laclau and Mouffe's discursive genealogy tends to obscure the potential for bureaucratisation inherent in any protracted democratic struggle, which must necessarily happen on a parliamentary terrain profoundly shaped by the highly centralised nation-state. Lacking any analysis of the failure of Eurocommunism—beyond the ritualistic invocation of "class reductionism," which, after all, did not prevent Lenin from taking power—Laclau and Mouffe virtually condemn postmarxism to a repetition of mainstream Eurocommunism's worst defects. The Eurocommunist "Third Road" failed to materialise for *historical* and *institutional* reasons, not because of a supposed "theoretical dualism" (which played a minor role in the fiasco of Eurocommunism).[10] The concept of a historical transformation of the working-class parties engaged in parliamentary politics, as a result of the tendencies towards bureaucratisation inherent in representational forms connected to the highly centralised, modern state apparatus, supplies part of the explanation for the limitations of mainstream Eurocommunist doctrine and practice (Przeworski, 1985). The rest of the explanation is linked to the "decline of the socialist tradition" in the twentieth century, generated within the combination of theoretical restrictions springing from nineteenth-century doctrines on the state and capital, and the practical effects of Stalinist (or Maoist) Communism (Boggs, 1995b). Together, these represent a materialist alternative to Laclau and Mouffe's genealogy of a *theoretical* dualism within Marxism.

The Postmodern Strategy of Cultural Hegemony

By the mid-1980s, the Eurocommunist parties were in decline as the political conjuncture in the West shifted sharply from hegemonic crisis to a ruling-class offensive led by Thatcher and Reagan. Leftwing demoralisation was exacerbated by two overlapping factors: the theoretical "crisis of Marxism," fueled by the "New Philosophy"; and, the persistent lack of engagement of the mainstream working-class formations with the NSM. Postmarxism thus emerges at the convergence of two crises: the historico-political crisis that surrounds efforts to forge a post-Fordist hegemonic strategy, which is accompanied by the proliferation of social antagonisms in the form of the NSM; and, the theoretical crisis of historical materialism, determined by the advent of new discourses denouncing "essentialism" and advocating a postmodern epoch. These crises preserve a specificity and originality of their own and cannot be reduced to expressions of one another, for the political crisis of the Left is connected to an institutional history, while the theoretical crisis of Marxism extends beyond the mainstream parties of the working class to embrace radical theory in general.

The "rebellion of subjectivity" conducted by the "new philosophers" soon became the theoretical voice of the New Right (Benton, 1984: 173-199).[11] Its perennial themes—Marxism inevitably leads to Stalinism, "scientific politics" equals technocratic authoritarianism, Enlightenment metaphysics *is* a form of rationalist dictatorship—were soon to be found liberally distributed through postmarxian texts, following the collapse of historical

---

10. For accounts of the fate of the leading Eurocommunist parties, consult Boggs (Boggs, 1995b: 95-136) and Antonian (Antonian, 1987: 120-128). After 1990, Eurocommunism ceased to exist.

11. For critical discussions of the "New Philosophy," consult Dews (Dews, 1979; Dews, 1985), Lecourt (Lecourt, 2001). The main texts are those of Glucksmann (Glucksmann, 1980) and Lévy (Lévy, 1982).

Communism (Aronson, 1995: 51-60, 91-121; Laclau, 1990: 4, 194, 206, 225). This rightwing postmodern critique of "objectivism" purported to speak in defense of the subject—reduced in the Althusserian lens to a mere bearer of structures—but in actuality drove in the direction of epistemological relativism, typically conflating political criticism with high metaphysics in the process. The fashion for recasting socialist strategy as foremost a question of theoretical revision is exemplified by *HSS*. There was a grain of truth in all this, of course, for while economic reductionism was not the direct cause of the debacle of Eurocommunism, it was certainly a contributing factor to the disdain for the NSM displayed by the Communist and (to a lesser degree) Socialist parties (Duyvendak, 1995). Some leftists, their hopes for Eurocommunist breakthrough destroyed by the legacy of Stalinism, not only turned to the NSM as the surviving echo of the radical 1960s (Boggs, 1995a), but simultaneously turned against the theoretical materialism that—it was supposed—had framed this betrayal of revolutionary energies. "It follows," one study candidly declares, "that if a post-Marxist theory is to emerge on a foundation of new social movements, its categories will correspondingly have to be postmaterialist" (Boggs, 1986: 15).

The postmarxian tendency to relegate the NSM to the sphere of the cultural—and to equate this with the ideal—needs to be resisted. Althusser's deconstruction of the base-and-superstructure distinction involved the postulate that "ideology has a material existence" and this led to efforts to theorise, for instance, women's oppression as relatively autonomous yet articulated to the gender-biased division of labour in capitalism, and perpetuated by "ideological state apparatuses" (Barrett, 1980; Kuhn and Wolpe, 1978). The control of sexuality is therefore systematically linked to the functioning of capitalist economics. Yet, it is also relatively autonomous (which means: they are analytically separable, enjoying distinct dynamics that are contingently articulated together). It is therefore impossible to oppose cultural recognition to material oppression, as domination perpetrated through ideological practices *exists* as materialised and cannot be reduced to psychological processes. Gender is a basic structural principle of the social division of labour, because it structures a gender-segmented labour market and determines the distribution of unpaid domestic work (Fraad, Resnick *et al.*, 1994; Hartsock, 1985; Molyneux, 1979), affects the determination of the "family wage," functions as a major ideological division within the education system and familial socialisation (Foreman, 1977; Zaretsky, 1976), inflects the distinction between mental and manual labour on which the state apparatus is based (Wilson, 1977) and represents a primary distinction (masculine and feminine) between ideologically-constituted persons (Chodorow, 1978). Because the family is not a natural institution, but a social form articulated to the dominant mode of production, the sexual division of labour and the social reproduction of gendered employees cannot be divorced from an analysis of the social reproduction of capitalism. Such an analysis is in stark contrast with Laclau's assertion of the independence of subject-positions from structural determinations (Laclau, 1985).

During the 1990s, the triumphalism of the liberal-democratic "end of history" ceded to the renewal of ethnic nationalisms, religious fundamentalisms and neo-fascisms, as the conjuncture swung decisively rightwards. This is the context for the neo-conservative cultural onslaught—the "culture wars" and debates on "political correctness"—and the Left resistance in the form of multicultural "identity politics" and its theoretical arm, the politicised wing of cultural studies. [12] This resistance has been divided and ambiguous, however, and we are now in a position to suggest some reasons why. Deep divisions have opened between the "cultural Left" and the "class Left," reflecting not only the difference between NSM politics and class politics, but also the gulf between a post-Althusserian "Gramscianism" and forms of neo-classical Marxism.

For the "class Left," proponents of cultural recognition can be dismissed as merely displacing economic problems. According to the "class Left," the strategy of cultural hegemony has fragmented the Left along identitarian lines and destroyed the "common dreams" of political militants and the oppressed masses (Gitlin, 1994). This is generally linked to a wholesale rejection of poststructuralism as the antithesis of Marxism, engaged in a "descent into discourse" (Palmer, 1990) by means of the "exorbitation of language" and a "randomisation of history" (Anderson, 1984: 40, 48). For the "cultural Left," the "class leftists" are in actuality "Left Conservatives," whose cultural and intellectual agenda is often shared with neo-conservatives, and whose conception of class not only excludes real consideration of race and gender, but depends upon the regressive theoretical postulate of "secondary oppression" and "the primacy of the economic" (Butler, 1998: 47). In other words, "class leftists" are regarded as base-and-superstructure essentialists whose progressive conception of political economy is entirely vitiated by a reactionary agenda in questions "merely cultural". Meanwhile, the "cultural Left" suffers from the central problem of what might be called a psychoanalytically-inflected, post-Althusserian "neo-Gramscianism," whose theoretical sophistication is undermined by an *exclusive* concentration on ideological struggle (Harris, 1992). According to Wendy Brown (certainly not a proponent of base-and-superstructure reductionism), postmodern politics involve a "[t]heoretical retreat from the problem of domination within capitalism" (Brown, 1995: 14). We have to ask, "to what extent a critique of capitalism is foreclosed by the current configuration of oppositional politics, and not simply by the 'loss of the socialist alternative' or the ostensible 'triumph of liberalism' in the global order" (Brown, 1995: 61). She claims "class is invariably

---

12. For critical surveys of contemporary leftwing cultural politics and academic practices, see Boggs (Boggs, 1993), Harris (Harris, 1992; Harris, 1996) and Palmer (Palmer, 1990).

named but rarely theorised" in the "multiculturalist mantra" of class, race, gender and sexuality (Brown, 1995: 61). Indeed, "the political purchase of contemporary American identity politics would seem to be achieved in part *through* a certain renaturalisation of capitalism" (Brown, 1995: 60).

Where, therefore, the "class Left" *reduces* culture and ideology to political economy, by means of the base-and-superstructure metaphor, the "cultural Left," interpreting Althusser's essay on "ideological state apparatuses" through the lens of poststructuralism and after the Right-Eurocommunist "Gramsci," *reduces* Gramsci's "ethico-political hegemony" to *ideological* hegemony alone, and transforms this into a social foundation on the basis of the assumption that "everything is cultural" (Nash, 2000: 30). This represents a restrictive definition of hegemony that transforms ideology into a social foundation. It is to the roots of this position that we now have to turn.

2

Crop Circles in the Postmarxian Field: Laclau and Mouffe on Postmodern Socialist Strategy

Laclau and Mouffe's *Hegemony and Socialist Strategy* is the *History and Class Consciousness* of the postmodern.[1] In a manner highly reminiscent of Lukács, Laclau and Mouffe initiate a sophisticated synthesis of Structural Marxism and Gramscian political hermeneutics with motifs drawn from post-structuralist philosophy and contemporary theory, towards the construction of a radical postmodern social theory. It is not only that this aspires to launch a new research programme by locating the insights of Marxism within an expanded theoretical framework. It also seeks to break from the reification of mainstream Left politics and theory, especially the fragmentation of the politics of the new social movements, and the correlate essentialism of the Left's "Holy Trinity" of class, race and gender. Right from the start, the most astute commentator insisted that Laclau and Mouffe had produced a "Hegelianism with a deconstructive twist" (Dallmayr, 1989: 127). If it is so, however, it is so unconsciously. The totalising vision, characteristic of both Hegel and "the inverted Hegelianism of Marx" (Laclau, 1990: 75), of history as a "rational and intelligible structure" governed by logical or historical necessity is precisely what they aim to break from (Laclau and Mouffe, 1985: 95). Yet, despite significant steps outside of classical dialectics, this effort to move

---

1. Consult Lukács (Lukács, 1971), especially the central essay, "Reification and the Consciousness of the Proletariat" (Lukács, 1971: 83-222). My assessment of Lukács as inaugurating the paradigm of Western Marxism is based on Jay (Jay, 1984: 81-127). Additional works sympathetic to Lukács consulted for this study are Arato and Brienes (Arato and Breines, 1979) and Feenberg (Feenberg, 1981). For the Structural Marxist critique of Lukács, consult Blackburn and Stedman-Jones (Blackburn and Jones, 1972: 365-387) and the criticism advanced by Stedman-Jones (Jones, 1971).

"beyond structuralism and hermeneutics" remains unconsciously tied to a vision of history and politics of distinctly Hegelian provenance. Postmarxian historicism generates an expressive historical totality despite its insistence on the fragmentation of the postmodern social field.

When Laclau and Mouffe launched their postmarxian manifesto, they announced that they had broken with the expressive totality of Hegelian dialectics and strove to replace the vision of a necessary sequence of historical stages with a contingent series of "historical blocs," governed by the politics of hegemonic articulation. This entails the replacement of the "Jacobin Imaginary" of classical Marxism-Leninism with a political Imaginary that is "radically libertarian and infinitely more politically ambitious than the classic Left" (Laclau and Mouffe, 1985: 152). Laclau and Mouffe advocate that democratic citizenship and radical plural democracy become master signifiers in a new leftwing social Imaginary that should replace the Leninist, or "Jacobin" Imaginary. They seek to revitalise the Left project by promoting an extension of the "Democratic Revolution of Modernity" to all regions of society, while maintaining the framework of pluralism characteristic of liberal political theory. According to this conception, socialism becomes a moment in the unfolding of the Democratic Revolution, not its negation. For Laclau and Mouffe, the permanence of politics implies a post-utopian conception of historical development, as well as excluding the Hegelian expressive social totality. Yet, to the alarm of Laclau in particular, political allies Judith Butler and Slavoj Žižek have persisted in their belief that the theory of hegemony is precisely a restatement of the Hegelian notion of the "concrete universal" (Butler, 2000a: 172-175; Žižek, 2000b: 235-249).

This postmarxian return to Hegel presents an enigma. It is Kant—and anti-dialectical philosophy in general—that stands above the postmodern, precisely as a reaction against the ascendancy of the existential interpretation of Hegel in postwar France.[2] Likewise, deconstruction is not designed to "twist" Hegel in the direction of detotalisation, but to subvert dialectics completely, to effect "the destruction of the Hegelian *relève* [synthesis] *wherever it operates*" (Derrida, 1971: 40-41). Indeed, there can be no doubt that Laclau and Mouffe intend to reject both speculative dialectics and the philosophy of praxis. But their theory of discourse is incoherent and relies for its intelligibility on a latent speculative totality that is, if anything, made more explicit in subsequent rectifications of their position. The root of this speculative identity of thinking and being is Laclau and Mouffe's rejection of the distinction between discourse and practice, on the grounds that this distinction is merely a "differentiation within the social production of meaning" (Laclau and Mouffe, 1985: 107). By posing their theory of the social on the terrain of *meaning*, Laclau and Mouffe produce not a deconstructive social

2. For this interpretation of post-structuralism, consult Barnett (Barnett, 1990: 1-30), Descombes (Descombes, 1980: 1-13) and Dews (Dews, 1987: xiii-xiv).

theory, but a political hermeneutics radically at variance with key tenets of post-structuralism. The consequence is that the postmarxian field inaugurated by *HSS* is sprinkled with enigmatic "crop circles": strange patterns that seem the product of an alien intention, but are actually evidence of an elaborate theoretical "hoax," namely, the production of a "post-structuralist" social theory which makes large claims to a "materialist constructivism" while being, in reality, resolutely speculative. This chapter explores these "crop circles"—or, to adopt the Hegelian locution, "speculative germs"—so as to determine their theoretical roots. Once the core concepts of postmarxian discourse theory have been indicated—concepts of discourse, hegemony, antagonism and dislocation—the major political strategies—identity politics, radical democracy and democratic citizenship—can be evaluated. The chapter concludes by investigating recent efforts to rectify the performative contradictions in the theory of hegemony by supplementing its politics with the deconstructive ethics of Otherness.

History and Class Consciousness *in the Postmodern*

Lukács, as a Hegelian Marxist, would be the condensation of everything that is deemed politically regressive about the social theory of "the rationalist 'dictatorship' of Enlightenment" (Laclau, 1990: 4), of just about everything that the new social logic of postmodern culture brings into crisis. In this context—which is theoretically and politically hostile to the concept of totality—Laclau and Mouffe's recasting of the Gramscian concept of hegemony is designed to avoid the Lukácsian conception of society as an "expressive totality". For Lukács, a single principle is "expressed" in all social phenomena, so that every aspect of the social formation is integrated into a closed system that connects the forces and social relations of production to politics and the juridical apparatus, cultural forms and class-consciousness (Lukács, 1971: 83). By contrast, Laclau and Mouffe insist that the social field is an incomplete totality consisting of a multitude of transitory hegemonic "epicentres" and characterised by a plurality of competing discourses. The proliferation of democratic forms of struggle by the new social movements is thereby integrated into a pluralistic conception of the social field that emphasises the negativity and dispersion underlying all social identities. "Radical and plural democracy," Laclau and Mouffe contend, represents a translation of socialist strategy into the detotalising paradigm of postmodern culture.

Nonetheless, like Lukács, Laclau and Mouffe advance a new concept of social practice that aims to resolve both theoretical and practical problems thrown up by recent political setbacks. For Lukács, the objective of a new conception of praxis is to establish the dialectical unity of theory and practice, so as to demonstrate that the proletariat, as the operator of a transparent praxis, is the identical subject-object of the historical process (Lukács, 1971: 149, 206). The subject of history is therefore the creator of the contents of the social totality, and to the extent that this subject attains self-reflexivity, it is also the conscious generator of social forms (Lukács, 1971: 142 and 168). This enables Lukács to emphasise the revolutionary character of class conscious as coextensive with revolutionary action (Lukács, 1971: 46-81). Laclau and Mouffe's concept of discursive practice has the same effect—with this difference, that Laclau and Mouffe deny that discursive practices can become wholly transparent to social agents (Laclau and Mouffe, 1985: 121-122). By reinscribing the concept of praxis within a deconstruction of Marxism, Laclau and Mouffe theorise a new concept of discursive practice that "must pierce the entire material density of the multifarious institutions" upon which it operates, since it has as its objective a decisive break with the material/mental dichotomy (Laclau and Mouffe, 1985: 109). "Rejection of the thought/reality dichotomy," they propose, "must go together with a re-thinking and interpenetration of the categories which have up until now been considered exclusive of one another" (Laclau and Mouffe, 1985: 110).

Critically, this means a fusion of the hitherto distinct categories of (subjective) discourse and (objective) structure in the concept of "hegemonic articulation". This theoretical intervention is simultaneously a decisive political advance, because it now becomes clear that, for instance, "the equivalence constituted through communist enumeration [of the alliance partners within in a bid for political hegemony] is not the discursive *expression* of a real movement constituted outside of discourse; on the contrary, this enumerative discourse *is* a real force which contributes to the moulding and constitution of social relations" (Laclau and Mouffe, 1985: 110). In other words, the opposition between theory and practice, discursive practice and structural conditions, is resolved by the new theory of hegemonic articulation. The operator of these discursive practices—the new agent of social transformation—is at once the instigator of social relations and the formulator of discourses *on* the social.

The most significant difference between Lukács and Laclau and Mouffe is their respective evaluations of Hegelian dialectics. Where, for Lukács, a return to dialectical philosophy held out the prospect of a renewal of Marxian social theory, for Laclau and Mouffe it is "dialectical necessity" that constitutes the major obstacle to a radical postmodern politics. Laclau and Mouffe's fundamental objection to dialectics is to the substitution of a logically necessary sequence for the contingency of the historical process. They applaud the dialectical dissolution of fixity but deplore the supposed inversion of contingency into necessity and the imposition of a teleology of reconciliation. Hegel's work, therefore, "appears as located in a watershed between two epochs" and is evaluated as "ambiguous" rather than simply pernicious (Laclau and Mouffe, 1985: 95). On the one hand, Laclau and

Mouffe reject the Hegelian notion that "history and society ... have a rational and intelligible structure" (Laclau and Mouffe, 1985: 95). This is regarded as an Enlightenment conception fundamentally incompatible with the postmodern emphasis on contingency, finitude and historicity. On the other hand, however, "this synthesis contains all the seeds of its own dissolution, as the rationality of history can only be affirmed at the price of introducing contradiction into the field of reason" (Laclau and Mouffe, 1985: 95). Once the impossibility of including contradiction within rationality is asserted, it then becomes clear that the "logical" transitions between historical "stages" are secured contingently:

> It is precisely here that Hegel's modernity lies: for him, identity is never positive and closed in itself but is constituted as transition, relation, difference. If, however, Hegel's logical relations become contingent transitions, the connections between them cannot be fixed as moments of an underlying or sutured totality. This means that they are articulations (Laclau and Mouffe, 1985: 95).

This is not a rejection of Hegel but a re-interpretation. Interpreted in this light, Hegel's "logical" relations are the language games that frame social practices—rather than formally rational structures deducible *a priori*—and their "transitions" are only the contingent connections created by political articulations. In opposition to the logically necessary sequence of closed totalities, Laclau and Mouffe insist on a historically contingent series of open discursive formations. Resolutely contesting the category of the totality, Laclau and Mouffe declare that:

> The incomplete character of every totality leads us to abandon, as a terrain of analysis, the premise of "society" as a sutured and self-defined totality. "Society" is not a valid object of discourse (Laclau and Mouffe, 1985: 126).

So where Lukács once declared that "the category of the totality is the bearer of the principle of revolution in science" (Lukács, 1971: 15), Laclau and Mouffe now announce, by contrast, that totality is an illusion because "'society' as a unitary and intelligible object which grounds its own partial processes is an impossibility" (Laclau, 1990: 90). Where Hegel was, there deconstruction shall be—or so it would seem.

The Controversy Surrounding Hegemony and Socialist Strategy

Because the controversy surrounding *HSS* has concentrated on social fragmentation, its reliance on an expressive historical totality has tended to be overlooked. Laclau alone has managed to grasp some of the implications of his call for the Left to "reformulate the values of the Enlightenment in the direction of a radical historicism" (Laclau, 1990: 84). In a mood of belated penitence, Laclau recently explained that "if I assert radical historicism, it will require some kind of meta-discourse specifying epochal differences, which will necessarily have to be transhistorical" (Laclau, 2000a: 201). That is to say, radical historicism leads immediately to performative contradiction. But to fix a problem of this magnitude, it is not sufficient to just jump off the ground and shout "barley," for this contradiction is built into the premises of Laclau and Mouffe's entire theory. Indeed, the performative contradictions that bedevil postmarxian discourse theory are only symptoms of a deeper difficulty, located in the latent structure of the historicist problematic that subtends radical democratic politics. They are rooted in the expressive historical totality that this transhistorical meta-discourse invokes in every historicism—something that continues to elude Laclau and Mouffe. Somewhat more surprisingly, however, this has not yet come to the attention of the critics of postmarxism, whose interventions have concentrated exclusively on the postmodern social fragmentation celebrated by Laclau and Mouffe.

Of course, the break with the postulates of classical social theory, combined with the authors' declaration that "if our intellectual project in this book is *post*-Marxist, it is evidently also post-*Marxist*" (Laclau and Mouffe, 1985: 4), might have been expected to generate a furious debate.[3] *HSS* provoked a small storm of denunciations and defenses, which continues to circulate, with unabated ferocity, in the journals of the trans-Atlantic Left. From the very beginning, the conjunction of post-structuralism and Marxism implied in the designation "postmarxism" was regarded as a calculated ambiguity. Critical opinion has remained polarised into camps defined by allegiance to or rejection of postmodernism, while the Marxist part of the label has been subordinated to the question of post-structuralism. This has meant that assessment of *HSS* and its aftermath has not tended to get beyond grasping alternately at one or the other of the main valences—that is, *post*-Marxism versus post-*Marxism*—of the work.

The work was immediately scalded by Marxists as "beautifully paradigmatic" of the "retreat from class" by a disillusioned section of the Western Left (Wood, 1998: 47) and branded as "symptomatic of an intellectual malaise" and an "ex-Marxism without substance" (Geras, 1988: 42). Laclau and Mouffe were accused of a "fetishisation of dislocation" and the dispersion of subjectivity in late capitalism (Bertram, 1995: 110). This implies their theory is incapable of demonstrating the minimum basis for the

---

3. For early positive reviews of *Hegemony and Socialist Strategy*, consult Aronowitz (Aronowitz, 1988: 46-61; Aronowitz, 1992: 175-192), Ross (Ross, 1988) and Žižek (Žižek, 1990). Note that Geras' criticisms, "Post-Marxism?" (Geras, 1987) and "Ex-Marxism without Substance" (Geras, 1988), and Laclau and Mouffe's reply, "Post-Marxism without Apologies" (Laclau and Mouffe, 1987b), are reprinted in Geras (Geras, 1990: 61-126, 127-168) and Laclau (Laclau, 1990: 97-134), respectively. Laclau and Mouffe's second reply to Geras' first article, "History of Marxism" (Laclau and Mouffe, 1987a), has not been reprinted.

formation of a collective will: "the new antagonisms, as Laclau and Mouffe make clear, are best suited for the postindustrial society in which there is no opposition to a dominant system" (Bertram, 1995: 85). Indeed, denying the validity of the distinction between structural location and subject-positions, Laclau and Mouffe cannot specify why some social groups might have an interest in socialism while others (for instance, exploiters of labour-power) might not (Mouzelis, 1988: 115). Laclau and Mouffe—as is characteristic of ideology—remain silent on their own historical and institutional conditions of possibility (Callinicos, 1985). Their theory of identity as an ensemble of free-floating subject-positions "*looks* sophisticated ... but it only operates on one level" (Osborne, 1991: 219) because it cannot grasp why the ideological struggle is constituted through "the tension between the irreducible dimension of extra-discursive determinacy in the object and the plurality of its possible discursive constructions" (Osborne, 1991: 210). Indeed, the "long march from Saussure to social democracy" of postmarxism has been enabled by a discourse analysis characterised by a "fatal semiotic confusion between the *signified* and *referent*" (Eagleton, 1991: 203, 209). This could also be called a volatisation of the referent, resulting in the loss of credibility of postmarxism's claim to any normative framework from which to criticise oppression and a paradoxical "overpoliticisation" which is nothing but the mirror-reflection of vulgar Marxism's economic determinism (Eagleton, 1991: 213). This leads to a political voluntarism that spurns conjunctural analysis for ideological manipulations (Miliband, 1985; Rustin, 1988), and produces a paradoxical superabundance of political possibilities that paralyses the will (Butler, 1993b: 107).

And if that latter sounds remarkably like the negative assessment of postmodernism current in Western Marxism, then it will be unsurprising that this is also the basis for the postmodern support for Laclau and Mouffe (Ryan, 1988: 245). Indeed, *HSS* is accused from this direction of being still "too Marxist" (Barrett, 1991: 76) and, more substantially, of theoretical dualism wherein social situations are analysed from a recognisably Marxist paradigm, while theoretical questions are subjected to a post-structuralist interrogation (Landry, 1991: 41-60). A sort of postmodern *doxa* regularly claims Laclau and Mouffe for the radical wing of postmodernism on the basis of their pluralism (Nash, 2000: 1-45; Ross, 1988: vii-xxviii). Combined with the endorsement of the valorisation of the particular over the universal, this would constitute the dominant context of their reception (Zerilli, 1998). Insofar as there is criticism emanating from this direction, it is for "abstraction," a sin in the context of the nominalist celebration of the concrete (Aronowitz, 1992: 192).

Hence, the general framework of the debate has been to specify *HSS* in terms of a retreat from class or adaptation to postmodern culture. Two exceptions to this rule are Fredric Jameson's dialectical analysis of Laclau and

Mouffe as a postmodern alliance politics that can be re-inserted into a con-temporary Marxism once postmodernism is grasped as the "cultural log-ic of late capitalism" (Jameson, 1991: 297-418), and Robert Miklitsch's as-sessment of the postmarxian tendency to return to the concept of a social foundation, be that economics (Resnick and Wolff) or politics (Laclau and Mouffe) (Miklitsch, 1995: 167-196). As with Jameson's dialectical position, Miklitsch's analysis cannot be accused of hostility to postmodernism (Mik-litsch, 1998a: 57-59). This is what makes the demonstration, by both Jame-son and Miklitsch, of Laclau and Mouffe's "hyperdiscursivity" (Miklitsch), and indifference to commodification, so damaging. According to Miklitsch, postmarxism evacuates the materiality of the institutions of culture, which are the basis for any strategy of hegemony and instead focuses on a merely phenomenological "political" activism. "The irony of *HSS*," he concludes, "is that at the end, the only path left open to them is the one that they have been travelling all the time ... 'a logical pulverisation of the social, coupled with a theoretically agnostic descriptivism of the concrete situations'" (Mik-litsch, 1995: 185).

Outside of these dialectical analyses, postmodernism and the abandon-ment of class-analysis are generally taken to be synonymous, so that there is a remarkable convergence in the literature surrounding Laclau and Mouffe, differing mainly in the evaluative sign that is placed in front of the postmod-ern culture that they represent. Here, the reductionism of psychological as-cription has often met up with some of the more predictable denunciations of *HSS*. Postmarxism is politics as therapy (Cloud, 1994). It is the "opiate of the intellectuals" (McGee, 1997: 201). It is a "very substantial failure of rea-soning" and an "intellectual sickness" (Geras, 1988: 40). Why is everyone so fascinated by it then?

Surely it's clear. *HSS* acts as a screen, onto which the reader can project virtually anything they like about postmodernism and the crisis of the Western Left, because it is both politically indeterminate and theoretical-ly overdetermined. *HSS* represents a symbolic act within a conjuncture of political retreat—strategically misrecognised by Laclau and Mouffe as one of advance—and a reactivation of historical contradictions. It has to be grasped as *both* an effort to break out of the reification of Structural Marxism and as a fundamental break with historical materialism, as a theorisation of an expanded framework for Marxism and as an embrace of postmodern dispersion. I shall show that the primary symptom of this "overdetermined indeterminacy" is the oscillation of the theory of hegem-ony between two antinomic interpretations of the theory, namely, hegem-ony as a neutral frame of description of the politics of modernity and radi-cal democracy as a partisan political project (Critchley, 1999: 112; Žižek, 2000h: 173-174). Radical democracy, I contend, exists in the space of inde-terminacy created by this hesitation.

The Deconstruction of Marxism

According to Laclau and Mouffe, Marxism is an "evolutionary paradigm," centred upon the concept of "historical necessity," unfolding through the "endogenous laws" operating in the "economic base" (Laclau and Mouffe, 1985: 7-46). For Laclau and Mouffe, Kautsky constitutes the "degree zero" of Marxism, because *The Class Struggle* manages to combine class essentialism and economic reductionism into a single configuration that determines the trajectory of twentieth-century historical materialism (Laclau and Mouffe, 1985: 14-19). Economic reductionism refers to the theory of the simplification of social antagonisms leading to a final confrontation between bourgeoisie and proletariat, based on the assertion of an autonomous evolutionary dynamic operative in the economic infrastructure, which reduces politics and ideology to mere superstructural reflections of the base. For Kautsky, "the structural moments or instances of capitalist society lack any form of relative autonomy" (Laclau and Mouffe, 1985: 15). Kautsky's economic reductionism is combined with class essentialism, according to which every structural difference is fixed "through the attribution to each of a *single meaning*, understood as a precise location within a totality," yielding a singular class-belonging for every superstructural element (Laclau and Mouffe, 1985: 15).

> In the first sense, Kautsky's analysis was simply economistic and reductionist; but if this were the only problem, the corrective would merely have to introduce the "relative autonomies" of the political and the ideological, and render the analysis more complex through the multiplication of instances within a topography of the social. *Yet each one of these instances or structural moments would have an identity as fixed and singular as the instances of the Kautskian paradigm* (Laclau and Mouffe, 1985: 15).

For Kautsky, class identity is fully constituted as a unified subjectivity in the economic base so that "the working class struggles in the field of politics by virtue of an economic calculation" (Laclau and Mouffe, 1985: 15). Economic laws unfold in the base—leading to the proletarianisation of the middle classes—according to an evolutionary necessity, culminating in the moment of the terminal crisis of capitalism. The working-class party only has to take advantage of an automatic revolution. For Laclau and Mouffe, this simplistic and evolutionary schema *constitutes the paradigm for historical materialism*. According to Laclau and Mouffe:

> Faced with the rationalism of classical Marxism, which presented history and society as intelligible totalities constituted around conceptually explicable laws, the logic of hegemony presented itself from the outset as a complementary and contingent operation, required for those conjunctural imbalances within an evolutionary paradigm whose essential or "morphological" validity was not for a moment placed in question (Laclau and Mouffe, 1985: 3).

Every subsequent development in Marxism is therefore reduced by Laclau and Mouffe to an effort to complicate, extend and modify this basic
conception of society, by supplementing the logic of historical necessity with
the appendage of political contingency (Laclau and Mouffe, 1985: 47-48).
Laclau and Mouffe's major objection to Marxism, then, is that the base-and-
superstructure topography determines the supremacy of historical necessity
and the marginalisation of political contingency, leading to an evolutionary
teleology of social "stages". This implies that the base and superstructure topography is regarded as *the* Marxian contribution to social theory.

The chapters on the genealogy of the category of hegemony are easily the
most accessible and well-known parts of *HSS*. Several lucid and sympathetic
accounts have been presented (Smith, 1998: 42-83; Torfing, 1999: 35-77 and
101-119), together with some excellent critical commentaries (Geras, 1990:
61-126 and 127-168; Wood, 1998: 47-74). The critics highlight Laclau and
Mouffe's own reliance on an evolutionary logic, which inverts the Kautskian
schema (instead of progressive simplification leading to a confrontation between polar classes, we have increasing complexity leading to a proliferation
of political actors) without modifying its teleological premises (Landry, 1991:
41-60). Marxists have criticised Laclau and Mouffe's reduction of Marxism
to a single, self-enclosed strand—that of the Second International and the
Communist parties—which itself develops according to the logical restrictions of its paradigmatic opposition between historical necessity and political contingency, and is supposed to determine the limits of variation of "superstructural" mutations such as Western Marxism. Indeed, the balance of
evidence is overwhelmingly against Laclau and Mouffe's construction of the
theoretical structure of historical materialism (Geras, 1987; Miliband, 1985;
Mouzelis, 1988; Rustin, 1988). The critics also expose the dependency of Laclau and Mouffe upon a caricature of the plurality of Marx's own texts. This
rests upon Laclau's claim that historical materialism is determined by the
oscillation between historical necessity, operating through the "productive
forces" (the "1859 Preface" to *A Contribution to the Critique of Political Economy*)
and political contingency operating through the "class struggle" (*The Communist Manifesto*), which act as the fully-formed theoretical origin of Marxism
(Laclau, 1990: 6-9). Laclau and Mouffe effectively produce a deconstruction of the institutionalised mainstream of the twentieth-century Marxist
movement—the Second International and the Communist parties—but this
is not the same as a critique of historical materialism, for it tends to transpose the crisis of the parties onto the problems of the theory. It is striking to
encounter an argument that emphasises the political aspect of theory-con-
struction *for its own productions*, but refuses to accept that the ascendancy of
a travesty of Marxism during the twentieth century might have had something to do with political conditions such as the victory of Stalinism in both
the Soviet Union and the Communist parties. I regard the Marxist criticism

of the reductionism of Laclau and Mouffe's treatment of historical materialism as decisive and do not intend to traverse this territory in detail again.

I want instead to concentrate on how Laclau and Mouffe's deconstruction of Marxism goes awry because their opposition between historical totality and social fragmentation is based on the assumption that "every social configuration is *meaningful*" (Laclau, 1990: 100). Laclau and Mouffe's deconstruction of Marxism is radically incomplete and veers towards a quasi-dialectical synthesis. They do this by mediating an opposition between historical necessity and political contingency in the category of hegemony, which becomes the quasi-transcendental ground for an expanded conception of politics and history. What Laclau and Mouffe miss is the vital second move in any deconstruction, namely, the moment of "dissemination," which is "not ... polysemic dispersion," but the affirmation of "an always open ensemble of structures" that subverts every totalisation (Gasché, 1986: 237). Instead of textual dissemination, Laclau and Mouffe produce a polysemic excess, a "surplus of meaning" surrounding the social (Laclau, 1990: 90; Laclau and Mouffe, 1985: 111), that is precisely symptomatic of a speculative synthesis.

Hegemony: The Gramscian Breakthrough

These considerations become crucial once we examine Laclau and Mouffe's treatment of Structural Marxism. My contention is that in its general structure, *HSS* is exemplary for its logical clarity and strict adherence to the general form of deconstructive methodology, but that it departs from the "substance". Deconstruction consists of two, irreducibly heterogeneous movements—which I shall term "reversal" and "dissemination" —whose relation can be figured as chiasmatic crossing, or textual hybridisation (Gasché, 1986: 171-175). The opening moment of deconstruction recovers a marginalised term that supports the dominance of the central term—or transcendental signified—in a field, exposing the field as constituted through a binary opposition. Laclau and Mouffe propose that twentieth-century Marxism is dominated by the paradigmatic opposition between historical necessity (central) and political contingency (marginal) (Laclau and Mouffe, 1985: Chapter One, 7-46). Then, in conformity with the movement of deconstructive "reversal," they propose that the ascendancy of the category of hegemony in Marxist discourse evinces the subversive effects of political contingency in the field of historical necessity. Because, as they somewhat elliptically state, "this expression [hegemony] stemmed from the fracture, and withdrawal to the explanatory horizon of the social, of the category of 'historical necessity'" (Laclau and Mouffe, 1985: 7), hegemony prepares a reversal whereby a new (postmarxian) discourse becomes possible, based on the inversion of the previous hierarchy (Laclau and Mouffe, 1985: Chapter Two,

47-92). At this point the second movement in deconstruction—the phase of dissemination—begins, with the generalisation of the hitherto suppressed possibilities of the category of hegemony. Hegemony, conceptualised as condition of mutual limitation or a relation of frontiers between necessity and contingency, becomes the quasi-transcendental condition of possibility and impossibility for the dyadic relation between a field dominated by political contingency and the effect of historical necessity. The quasi-transcendental category of hegemony is linked in an infrastructural chain to several related quasi-transcendentals—social antagonism and discursive practice—in a new social theory (Laclau and Mouffe, 1985: Chapter Three, 93-148). Finally, in what should be the completion of dissemination, the subversive effects of the infrastructural chain are released within the reconstructed field of socialist strategy to work their radically democratic magic (Laclau and Mouffe, 1985: Chapter Four, 149-193). Laclau and Mouffe aim to cleave two insights—hegemony and overdetermination—from Marxism, by showing how these concepts depend upon a logic opposed to the mainstream of Marxist theory, with its supposed valorisation of historical necessity over political contingency. Laclau and Mouffe's deconstructive methodology aims to delineate a new paradigm within which the essentialism of Marxism can be consigned "to the museum of antiquities," and it does so through the proposition that the emergence of the supplement of hegemony confirms the postmodern thesis that Enlightenment essentialism is being refuted by the increasing complexity of the social (Laclau and Mouffe, 1985: 47-92).

According to Laclau and Mouffe, the concept of hegemony was introduced to supplement the economist logic of historical necessity governing classical Marxism with a political logic of contingency. The category of hegemony arose in classical Marxism in response to a crisis, where the logic of historical necessity appeared to have detoured through an "exceptional" situation, namely, the increasing fragmentation of the proletariat and the stubborn refusal of the capitalist system to terminate itself in economic catastrophe. On the basis of the "increasing complexity of the social," Marxist politics became subjected to conditions of the fragmentation of the working class, the isolation of political movements and the separation between economic and political struggles (Laclau and Mouffe, 1985: 2, 8-9). This increasing complexity determined the conditions where the supplement of political contingency acted deconstructively within the field of historical necessity. Laclau and Mouffe claim that the concept of "hegemony" in Marxism became the locus where the disruptive effects of political contingency both proliferated and remained contained within the logic of historical necessity. According to the authors, this produced four salient results: (1) the mechanism constitutive of the social agent shifts from the effect of a structural location to the result of a symbolic unification; (2) the historical necessity that assigns historical tasks to fundamental classes retreats before the contingent political articulations required by combined and uneven development; (3) the concept of class alliances is displaced by the category of hegemony; (4) the political strategy of the Communist parties moves from external combinations that "march separately" in the united front to an effort towards "moral and political leadership," where the popular front led by the proletarian party strives to accomplish national reconstruction through achieving an ideological hegemony that forges a new collective subject (Laclau, 1990: 120-121; Laclau and Mouffe, 1985: 47-92).

For Laclau and Mouffe, Gramsci's explicit theorisation of hegemony represents a watershed in the break with economic reductionism because this replaces the Kautskian notion of a progressive social polarisation, leading to the confrontation between paradigmatic classes, with the transformation of social alliances into political subjects (Laclau and Mouffe, 1985: 65-71). Gramsci suggests that a fundamental class becomes hegemonic when it articulates its sectoral interests as the general interest and begins to exert "moral and political leadership" (Gramsci, 1971: 57-58, 180-182). Gramsci refers to the articulation of a hegemonic strategy as the highest expression of political class struggle in the transition from the infrastructure to the superstructure (Gramsci, 1971: 57-58). Laclau and Mouffe's early analyses suggested that the fundamental classes struggle for hegemony principally on the ideological terrain, where new political subjects are forged. Gramsci's concept of ideology as the social cement that permeates the social formation breaks with the base-and-superstructure topology and prepares the Althusserian position that ideology is an ensemble of material practices, rather than a superstructural "false consciousness" (Laclau, 1977: 81-142; Mouffe, 1979a: 168-205). As Laclau and Mouffe conclude, "intellectual and moral leadership constitutes, according to Gramsci, a higher synthesis, a collective will, which, through ideology, becomes the organic cement unifying a historical bloc" (Laclau and Mouffe, 1985: 67). Political subjects are no longer classes but social alliances, which do not take power, but become the state by becoming hegemonic, that is, the historic bloc controls the normative and institutional framework of society by maintaining relations of consent and coercion throughout society (Laclau and Mouffe, 1985: 67). Yet, Gramsci's historical blocs can take shape only around a fundamental class, and for Laclau and Mouffe, "this is the inner essentialist core which continues to be present in Gramsci's thought, setting a limit to the deconstructive logic of hegemony" (Laclau and Mouffe, 1985: 69). Because Laclau and Mouffe hold positions of structuralist economism, they suppose that the political transformation of the fundamental class into a unifying principle within a historic bloc presupposes that fully constituted class identity is generated in the economic field. This reintroduces the dualism between the political contingencies of the hegemonic struggle, operative primarily on the ideological terrain, and the historical necessity guaranteed by the economic structure, which acts to unify the historic bloc "in the last instance".

Thus, in *HSS*, Laclau and Mouffe confront the "last redoubt of essentialism—the economy" and undertake a demonstration of the political contamination of Marxism's supposedly endogenous economic laws (Laclau and Mouffe, 1985: 75-85). "It is not the case that the field of the economy is a self-regulated space subject to endogenous laws," they conclude; "nor does there exist a constitutive principle for social agents which can be fixed in an ultimate class core; nor are class positions the necessary location of historical interests" (Laclau and Mouffe, 1985: 84-85). The consequence is that we face the dichotomy of "an absolutely united working class that will become transparent to itself at the moment of proletarian chiliasm" (Laclau and Mouffe, 1985: 84-85), or the more comforting prospect of "... the new forms of struggle in the advanced capitalist countries," that is, "precisely a context dominated by the experience of fragmentation and by the indeterminacy of the articulations between different struggles and subject positions" (Laclau and Mouffe, 1985: 13). By inverting the hierarchy between historical necessity and political contingency—by making the category of hegemony, dominated by political contingency, the centre of a new discourse and displacing the category of structure, dominated by historical necessity—Laclau and Mouffe employ a marginalised term to reverse the binary hierarchy that, they claim, constitutes the Marxist paradigm. They thereby produce a postmarxian discourse.

Laclau and Mouffe's "Speculative Germs"

The exemplary logical structure of *HSS* enables us to pinpoint exactly where Laclau and Mouffe insert their "speculative germs" into an erstwhile deconstruction of Marxism. Having asserted the subversive effects of the category of hegemony in the field of Marxist discourse, Laclau and Mouffe commence the disseminatory phase of their deconstruction by reinscribing "hegemony" into a reconfigured discursive regime, based on the supremacy of political contingency over historical necessity. Yet, instead of directly confronting this task, they "detour" (Laclau and Mouffe, 1985: 96) so as to begin to deconstruct the field of Structural Marxism, in the interests of the construction of a postmarxian identity politics (Laclau and Mouffe, 1985: 97-105). For Laclau and Mouffe, the moment of theoretical incoherence in the Structural Marxist research programme arrives with the logical contradiction between symbolic overdetermination and "economic determination in the last instance" (Laclau and Mouffe, 1985: 98). Laclau and Mouffe's recasting of overdetermination quietly deletes two crucial components of the Althusserian position: the notion that these are overdetermined *contradictions* is repudiated on the grounds of a generalised rejection of contradictions (Laclau and Mouffe, 1985: 95, 148 note 35); and, the mechanisms of ideological displacement and political condensation are shorn of any institutional determinants and assimilated to solely ideological processes. This evacuates the materialist content of Althusser's notion of overdetermined contradictions and opens the path to a speculative recapture of post-Althusserian theory.

In an assessment of the aftermath of Althusserian Marxism that implicitly critiques their own contributions to the post-Althusserian theory of ideology, Laclau and Mouffe criticise the proposition that every contradiction is overdetermined by class as "a new variant of essentialism" (Laclau and Mouffe, 1985: 98). "In the original Althusserian formulation," Laclau and Mouffe suggest, "a very different theoretical undertaking was foreshadowed," namely, "a critique of every type of fixity," by taking up symbolic overdetermination as the basis for a new concept of articulation (Laclau and Mouffe, 1985: 104). They claim that the antinomies of Althusser demonstrate the impossibility of combining ideological articulation with economic determination and propose that it follows from this that social relations have to be theorised as a "plane of signification" beyond which there exists absolutely nothing (Laclau and Mouffe, 1985: 97-105). Hence, "the symbolic—i.e., overdetermined—character of social relations implies that they lack an ultimate literality which would reduce them to necessary moments of an immanent law" (Laclau and Mouffe, 1985: 98).

As Laclau and Mouffe point out, the concept of overdetermination derives principally from psychoanalysis and in this context must not be interpreted as a mechanical multi-causal theory. Instead of the mechanical concept of a multiplicity of unequally weighted causes constituting an effect, overdetermination refers to the formation of nodal points where several chains of signification intersect in a single signifier, thereby investing this "master signifier" with the libidinal energy contained in the many discursive articulations (Laplanche, 1973: 292-293). Althusser's concept of "overdetermined contradiction" was designed to be the opposite of the Hegelian simple—or essential—contradiction, because the existence of relatively autonomous structural instances with asymmetrical effectivities led to the imprinting, in any social contradiction, of its complex conditions of existence (Althusser, 1969: 161-218). The psychoanalytic notion of a disjunction between the libidinal energy of an articulation and its conscious registration as meaning is homologous to the Marxist concept of the gap between the complex structural determinants of an effect and the subject-position(s) through which this is lived as an event by social agents. Althusser's conception of the "overdetermined contradiction" maintains, from its inception, the Marxist insistence on the ideological displacement and political condensation of economic antagonisms, and reciprocally, the ideological and political determinants of a class contradiction, so that "exceptions" to the "pure contradiction" between classes are the rule (Althusser, 1969: 87-128, especially 99-100, 104). To claim a contradiction between the essays "Contradiction and Overdetermination" and "On the Materialist Dialectic" (Laclau and Mouffe, 1985: 98) is textually insupportable—and Laclau and Mouffe do not bother to try to demonstrate this. Instead, they turn to the problems in another work altogether, Balibar's treatment of the "Basic Concepts of Historical Materialism" in *Reading Capital* (Althusser and Balibar, 1970: 199-308; Laclau and Mouffe, 1985: 99-105).

Laclau and Mouffe's Gramscian thesis that ideology is fundamental to the social formation, not only as a functional social cement, but also as the basic modality of social subjectivity that acts as a condition of possibility for politics and economics, effectively reduces politics and economics to ideology. Laclau and Mouffe insist that overdetermination:

> is a very precise type of fusion entailing a symbolic dimension and a plurality of meanings. The concept of overdetermination is constituted in the field of the symbolic, and has no meaning whatsoever outside it. Consequently, the most profound *potential* meaning of Althusser's statement that everything existing in the social is overdetermined, is the assertion that the social constitutes itself as a symbolic order (Laclau and Mouffe, 1985: 97-98).

In line with their earlier analyses of ideological articulations, Laclau and Mouffe consider that overdetermination means the formation of political subjectivity through the combination of a multiplicity of subject-positions (Laclau, 1977: 81-142; Mouffe, 1979a: 168-205). In other words, consideration of the psychoanalytic meaning of overdetermination allows Laclau and Mouffe to substitute the ideological mechanisms of subject-formation for the materialist principles of social production, as rules for the composition of the social field. Indeed, in a text published contemporaneously with *HSS*, Laclau claims that subject-positions are the social atoms from which classes, structures, nations and so forth are constructed (Laclau, 1985: 32). This claim—discreetly erased from the surface of *HSS* but distinctly present as a latent assumption—reveals the accuracy of Laclau and Mouffe's admission that their position on Structural Marxism is close to that of Hindess and Hirst (Laclau and Mouffe, 1985: 145 note 6). Indeed, it potentially understates the extent of the convergence. The authors note of Hindess and Hirst that the concept of political contingency between pre-constituted structural elements arrived at by a "rationalist deconstruction" of Structural Marxism excludes diacritical articulation (the elements remain positive social monads immune to differential relations) and therefore implies an essentialism on the lines of Leibniz (Laclau and Mouffe, 1985: 103). For Laclau and Mouffe, by contrast, the articulation of subject-positions reciprocally modifies these differential elements (on the fundamental lines of Saussurean linguistics, they are differential positions, not positive realities). In consequence, "society and social agents lack any essence, and their regularities merely consist of the relative and precarious forms of fixation which accompany the establishment of a certain order" (Laclau and Mouffe, 1985: 98). By means of such pronouncements, Laclau and Mouffe hope to evade the impasse of Hindess and Hirst, namely, "a logical pulverisation of the social, combined with a theoretically agnostic descriptivism of the 'concrete situations'" (Laclau and Mouffe, 1985: 104).

Yet, Laclau and Mouffe's invocation of psychoanalysis testifies against them, for surely the cornerstone of the Lacanian "return to Freud" is the insistence that a "sexual determination in the last instance" operates in the discursive articulation of the "formations of the unconscious," in the form of the determining role of the Real of the drive in the articulation of Symbolic desire (Fink, 1995a; Fink, 1997). The Lacanian position does not reduce overdetermination to a mechanical causality, but neither does it affirm that the discourse of the analysand is infinitely plastic. Instead, Lacan's "Gödelian structuralism" (Fink, 1995a: xiv) maps the systematic distortions of discourse onto structural diagnostic categories (psychosis, perversion, neurosis) based on distinct unconscious mechanisms (foreclosure, disavowal and repression) (Fink, 1997: 76-78). These distinct mechanisms for the production of "surplus enjoyment" (Žižek, 1989: 49-53) involve different positions of the object in discourse. By analogy with Althusser, we might say that the distinct modes of production of surplus enjoyment are manifest as the dominance of the object in a certain register of discourse. *Prima facie*, there is no theoretical inconsistency in the combination of a determination in the last instance with the overdetermined character of every differential field. By contrast, deletion of the libidinal energy contained in an overdetermined articulation means the confinement of analysis to the interpretation of meaning and implies the reduction of psychoanalysis to a hermeneutics. Laclau and Mouffe produce what is effectively a pre-Freudian position whose terminus can only be—as Ricoeur's hermeneutic "recovery" of Freud unfortunately demonstrates—the tracing back of gaps in meaning to *another*, "deeper" meaning, culminating in the speculative endeavour "to see Hegel's problematic in Freud" (Ricoeur, 1970: 468).

The "Social Production of Meaning"

The novelty of Laclau and Mouffe's politics of ideology depends upon the category of discourse, which is supposed to supersede the Marxian paradigm of labour as the model of social practice. Laclau and Mouffe's "original insight" into the consequences of the shift from structure to discourse is that discursive practice designates a new model of social acts. Broadly speaking, discursive practice refers to the selection and combination of social relations (structural elements) into articulated combinations that are deployed in space and time by social agents in the field of social practices.

By contrast with some leftwing commentators on Laclau and Mouffe's discourse theory (Callinicos, 1985; Geras, 1990; Palmer, 1990; Wood, 1997b), I do not contend that the very conception of the social field as the result of "discursive practices" is a mistake. The classical Marxian conception of labour as the paradigm of human activity (Geras, 1984; Lukács, 1978; Lukács, 1980) is not automatically superior to the postmodern concept of discourse as the model for social practice. Indeed, the postmodern model has two distinct advantages. It is impossible to arrive at the absurd position of affirming that *social* labour comes before language (Lukács, 1980: 49). Secondly, the discursive problematic includes from its inception consideration of social relations as inherently dialogical, that is, constituted in relations of dominance and subordination through dialectical processes of opposition and differentiation (Bakhtin, 1981: 259-422; Vološinov, 1973). Instead of conceiving human activity as operating directly on an inert natural "raw material," discursive practice affirms the primacy of contested social relations as the mediation between humanity and nature. Additionally, the notion of discursivity suggests human finitude, in line with Kant's conception of humanity as characterised by a merely "discursive intellect" (as opposed to an *Intellectus Archetypus*, with the god-like power to grasp intuitively the essence of things). Contrary to the ideological after-image, apparently conjured for some Marxists, of the omnipotent speaker spinning social relations at will, in a theoretical parody of magical realist literature where "anything goes," discursive practice implies a limited agent, restricted by the materiality of social relations, operating under conditions of only partial knowledge.

Nonetheless, Laclau and Mouffe's overall conceptualisation of discursive practice is seriously flawed, mainly because they simply transpose the syntax of ideological practices (the articulation of subject-positions through the action of ideological master signifiers) onto the entire field of social practices, reducing the transformation of the social formation to a question of ideological manipulation. The leading effect, therefore, of the combination of Laclau and Mouffe's selective interpretation of "overdetermination" with their Gramscian criticism of Structural Marxism, is to enable a relapse of "overdetermined contradiction" back towards the Hegelian "simple," or "essential" contradiction. The authors therefore betray their own fundamental insight.

Laclau and Mouffe's postmodern theory construction begins from the rejection of Foucault's distinction between discourse and practice on the grounds that these are merely differentiations in the "social production of meaning" (Laclau and Mouffe, 1985: 107). There are serious consequences for this position. The first is that they deny the exteriority of events to discourse, and therefore fall into the constructivist trap of being unable to specify *why* discursive regimes are historically transformed. The second is that, by insisting on textual polysemy, the centre of a hegemonic formation becomes a locus of the saturation of meaning, that is, a political symbol. We have to examine these consequences sequentially, because taken together, they constitute discourses as ideological worldviews (expressive totalities). Laclau and Mouffe's strategy is therefore to add certain provisos to the model (*relative* totality, *temporary* fixation of meaning, *incompleteness* of discourses caused by a *constitutive outside*) that are designed to prevent this relapse into expressive totality. Straightforwardly, from the perspective of Laclau and Mouffe's discourse theory, it is impossible to theorise the complexity of a social formation. Instead, as we shall see, the postmarxian version of "complexity" is a horizontal proliferation of hegemonic centres, which amounts to the multiplication of simple political antagonisms and not the complexity of an overdetermined social contradiction.

While Laclau and Mouffe affirm the existence of the external world and the materiality of discourse, they claim that the being of every object is discursively constructed (Laclau, 1990: 97-134). This blocks the path to the regional distinction between social (discursive) practices and the materiality of the object (the natural properties of objects and extra-discursive conditions of emergence of discourse). For Laclau and Mouffe, no object is given outside of a discursive condition of emergence, and so:

> if the so-called non-discursive complexes—institutions, techniques, productive organisation, and so on—are analysed, we will only find more or less complex forms of differential positions among objects, *which do not arise from a necessity external to the system structuring them* and which can only be conceived as discursive articulations (Laclau and Mouffe, 1985: 107 my emphasis).

According to Foucault's distinction between the discursive and the extra-discursive, the rules of formation of a discourse must be articulated with its extra-discursive conditions, because extra-discursive events transform the mode of existence of discourse by modifying its conditions of emergence, insertion and functioning (Foucault, 1985: 162-165; Foucault, 1991: 66-67). All that Laclau and Mouffe retain from Foucault is the concept of discursive formations as regularities in dispersion. This regularity represents an ensemble of differential positions: "This ensemble is not the expression of any underlying principle external to itself—it cannot, for instance, be apprehended either by a hermeneutic reading or structuralist combinatory—but it constitutes a configuration, which in certain contexts of exteriority can be *signified* as a totality" (Laclau and Mouffe, 1985: 106).

Laclau and Mouffe suppose that "discursive practices" involve the construction of relations of equivalence and difference whereby the identity of discursive elements is modified. They define:

> articulation [as] any practice establishing a relation among elements such that their identity is modified as a result of the articulatory practice. The

structured totality resulting from the articulatory practice, we will call discourse. The differential positions, insofar as they appear articulated within a discourse, we will call moments. By contrast, we will call element any difference that is not discursively articulated (Laclau and Mouffe, 1985: 105).

Following structural linguistics, we can say that the discursive moments have the form of a diacritical field composed of differences. Yet, the entire field of differential moments has an equivalence with respect to a master signifier that "represents" the unity of the discourse. Discourses are constituted by the tension between difference and equivalence existing within the relatively fixed discursive moments and these two logics are in a relation of mutual limitation or dynamic equilibrium. The logic of difference is the logic of social identity, whereas the logic of equivalence is the logic of frontal social antagonisms. Laclau and Mouffe align difference with the operation of metonymy, the contiguity of signifiers in the diachrony of the utterance and the psychoanalytic category of displacement. Likewise, they compress the operation of metaphor, the paradigmatic substitution of signifiers in the synchrony of the linguistic field and the psychoanalytic category of condensation. "If difference exists only in the diachronic succession of the syntagmatic pole," they claim, "equivalence exists at the paradigmatic pole" (Laclau and Mouffe, 1985: 132). In an articulated totality, the relations are necessary. This necessity derives from the regularity of structural positions rather than from an underlying intelligible principle, yet contingency and articulation are only possible because "no discursive formation is a sutured totality" (Laclau and Mouffe, 1985: 105). A discursive semi-totality has an exterior, and this "constitutive outside" functions to pierce its relational logic with contingency and renders it incomplete, ensuring that "the transition from the elements to the moments is never entirely fulfilled" (Laclau and Mouffe, 1985: 105). Indeed, Laclau and Mouffe conclude, "there is no social identity fully protected from a discursive exterior that deforms it and prevents it becoming fully sutured" (Laclau and Mouffe, 1985: 105).

The concept of discourse requires that the practice of articulation "must pierce the entire material density of the multifarious institutions" it operates on (Laclau and Mouffe, 1985: 109), so that "enumerative discourse *is* a real force which contributes to the moulding and constitution of social relations" (Laclau and Mouffe, 1985: 110). The evasions and incoherence of Laclau and Mouffe's concept of discourse—signaled here by the ambiguous words "pierce" and "contributes," when the context indicates that discourses *are* the materiality of institutions and social relations *are* discourses—have been abundantly documented (Eagleton, 1991: 210-211; Geras, 1990: 127-168). Laclau and Mouffe claim that objects exist independently of discourse, but have no extra-discursive being (so, for instance, the material properties of the object are merely discursive articulations) (Laclau, 1990: 97-134). By emptying existence of every determinacy, they arrive at a neo-Kantian idealism, because "for Laclau and Mouffe, 'objects' oscillate between determinacy and existence. What they are categorically denied is the possibility of a determinate existence" (Osborne, 1991: 209). The sophisms advanced in support of this position—"to refer ... directly to ... an extra-discursive object will always require the prior delimitation of the extra-discursive [a]nd insofar as the extra-discursive is delimited, it is formed by ... discourse" (Butler, 1993a: 11)—do not survive a moment's examination. For the delimitation of a region is not the same as its formation: this simply confuses an epistemological condition with the ontological constitution of the object.

The Concept of Discourse

The central claims of critical scientific realism—that the being of the object is *determinate* yet not in principle completely knowable and that scientific discourse, by approximating to the properties of the object, indeed refers *indirectly* to the extra-discursive—are not confronted by Laclau and Mouffe at all. They cannot therefore be said to have confronted Marxism's distinctive claim to base a politics on exactly this conception of scientific research. Laclau and Mouffe confine their reply to their critics to the accusation that Marxists make "an illegitimate detour through the referent" (Laclau and Mouffe, 1985: 118)—that is, that Marxists appeal to a pre-discursive reality as grounds for the distinction between discourse and structure. While this is true of Geras—whose appeal to a pre-discursive "human nature" as the basis for an anthropology of labour is precisely an "illegitimate detour through the referent"—it is not true of Eagleton, Jameson or Miklitsch. What Laclau and Mouffe eliminate is the possibility of a *post-discursive*, constructed referent that is not entirely covered by discourse (Eagleton, 1991: 209). Laclau and Mouffe's insistence that there is nothing outside the text involves a "tautological entrapment in the world of social construction [that] is incapable of providing an account of the cause that governs the production of social constructions of reality" (Stavrakakis, 1999: 67). Their concept of a "constitutive outside" in the form of the "field of discursivity" surrounding every discourse cannot salvage this position, because while every discursive totality has an exterior, "this exterior is constituted by other discourses" (Laclau and Mouffe, 1985: 146 note 20). Hence, for Laclau and Mouffe, there is no post-discursive referent whose properties do not endlessly dissolve once more into the labyrinth of signification. Laclau and Mouffe's conflation of ideological discourse with discursive practice means that their discourse theory is strangely indifferent to the regional syntax of social structures and unable to perform even elementary institutional analysis (Miklitsch, 1995).

Let us consider this closely for a moment. Taking a mode of social regulation as exemplary of the materialist concept of hegemonic articulation, it is possible to say that this mode, as a historic *bricolage*, results from the contingent articulation of "floating" social elements into a new configuration capable of securing social reproduction. Laclau and Mouffe's concept of discourse is therefore highly suggestive. Nonetheless, they think that relations of equivalence and difference regulate the discursive combinations of social elements, and that these "floating" elements are *subject-positions*, not structural elements. This reduces, as we have seen, the complex institutional relations that hold between, for instance, domestic units, regimes of government, norms of consumption and the regime of accumulation, to patterns of signification. Consequently, Laclau and Mouffe ignore the mobile equilibrium between institutional fixity and social dislocation within and between these structural elements—an equilibrium that depends upon financial constraints, political decisions, material limitations and ideological shifts—because their theory is only capable of thinking in terms of metaphor (equivalence) and metonymy (difference). Quite straightforwardly, this complex and shifting network of relational constraints is irreducible to merely "equivalence and difference". Laclau and Mouffe's position amounts to a "theory of discourse" indifferent to the constraints of social grammar and institutional syntax, material inequality and substantive differences, use-value and social norms, whose reduction of everything to value-like relations bears a suspicious resemblance to free-market ideologies in which every social relation is equally a commodity. Furthermore, the assertion that the "floating signifiers" articulated in discursive practices are subject-positions (Laclau, 1985), combined with the claim that discursive articulations penetrate the materiality of institutions, implies an isomorphism between subject-positions and structural elements, so that the articulation of subject-positions necessarily entails the reconfiguration of social structures. The notion that a subject-position can act as a "nodal point," or metaphor, for a complex ensemble of social practices and institutional structures implies a drastic reductionism in which this network of relations is flattened onto the regionally dominant ideogeme. Such a position gravitates towards a crass functionalism, according to which subject-positions are directly linked to social tasks, and conversely, the reconfiguration of political subjectivity itself substitutes for generalised social struggle.

It is impossible to accept that the result of discursive practice is necessarily another discourse, for this obliterates the distinction between the synchronic structure of the social formation (which is not necessarily able to be re-articulated in a conjuncture) and the diachronic horizon of action of social agents (which defines the structural elements that can be selected for discursive combinations in a political conjuncture). Nor do Laclau and Mouffe actually hold this position, for they distinguish between "sedimented" (or naturalised) structural elements and contested, discursive moments, proposing that "temporalised" discursive moments become "spatialised" into structural elements through repetition. So the structured totality resulting from a *successful* articulatory practice should in reality be called a *structure*. The advantage of this position is that it invokes a definite process of structuration—from structure to discourse to a modified structure (Giddens, 1984; Leledakis, 1995)—instead of a merely phenomenological description of the difference between structural elements and discursive moments. It also invokes the distinction between the substitution of material elements within a fixed structural configuration and the transformation of the structure through the discursive disarticulation of dominant structural matrices.

Laclau and Mouffe maintain their formal stance that discursive articulation leads only to another discourse because, despite their insistence that discourses modify material structures, they evacuate the materiality of the structural elements combined in discursive practices and treat them only as bearers of *meaning*, effectively conflating ideological discourse with discursive practices. This enables Laclau and Mouffe to deny the pertinence of the distinction between structural determinations (the totality of which cannot be articulated in a conjuncture) and subject-positions (which can be articulated) (Laclau and Mouffe, 1985: 118-120). They would object that only "floating signifiers," dislodged from a differential structure by their articulation in (socially antagonistic) relations of equivalence, can be discursively articulated in a conjuncture (Laclau, 1995a: 36-46; Laclau and Mouffe, 1985: 134-136). Laclau and Mouffe therefore relate social antagonism to the proliferation of floating signifiers (Laclau and Mouffe, 1985: 134-136) and insist that "every antagonism, left free to itself, is a floating signifier, a 'wild' antagonism which does not predetermine the form in which it can be articulated to other elements in a social formation" (Laclau and Mouffe, 1985: 171). This implies that the disarticulation of a structure results from political conflict (through ideological articulations)—meaning that, for instance, economic crisis *results from* political conflict, and correlatively, that a social crisis is always produced through the emergence of new political agents (Laclau and Mouffe, 1985: 136). Quite simply, this is nonsense (think, for instance, of the Great Depression, which in Weimar Germany *produces* a political crisis)—and Laclau and Mouffe do not believe it either, for their analysis of the NSM proposes that these emerge from the *combination* of intrinsic structural tendencies with political resistance (Laclau and Mouffe, 1985: 159-166). Yet, they cannot modify their theoretical position because accepting the existence of determinate structural locations and the materiality of structural elements conflicts with the assumption that every element is a *semanteme*, a bearer of meaning, whose articulation and disarticulation depends, not on any material properties, but on the ability of the "social text" to produce a "surplus of meaning".

The Category of Hegemony

The major problems with Laclau and Mouffe's category of hegemony flow from their idealist constructivism with its focus on textual polysemy. By inverting the master (or empty) signifier that hegemonises a discursive formation into a point of maximal saturation of meaning, Laclau and Mouffe transform hegemony into a theory of semi-expressive totality. This model is supplemented with the postmodern assertions that there exist a multiplicity of hegemonic nodes in a social formation and that consequently, no unity of rupture is possible, only a proliferation of dispersed subject-positions.

While discourses are theorised as a "regularity in dispersion," the unity of a discourse is theorised in terms of hegemony, and the formation of a discourse involves "cutting out" a partial totality from the sea of meaning, or "field of discursivity," that surrounds the social:

> The practice of articulation, therefore, consists in the construction of nodal points which partially fix meaning; and the partial character of this fixation proceeds from the ... constant overflowing of every discourse by the infinitude of the field of discursivity (Laclau and Mouffe, 1985: 113).

According to Laclau and Mouffe, the constitution of hegemony involves the construction of chains of equivalence and difference that link disparate signifying elements as moments of a relatively unified, but fundamentally incomplete, discursive totality. A dispersed ensemble of heterogeneous elements is unified by their articulation with an empty signifier, so that the identity of the elements is modified by their reciprocal interactions and thereby totalised as a differential field (a discourse). Political identities are formed within discursive totalities—historical blocs—but, flowing from the incompleteness of discourse, every political identity is inherently incomplete: the Left is decompleted by the existence of the Right, for instance.

> A social and political space relatively unified through the instituting of nodal points and the constitution of *tendentially* relational identities is what Gramsci calls a historical bloc. The type of link joining the different elements of the historical bloc—not unity in any form of historical *a priori*, but a regularity in dispersion—coincides with our concept of discursive formation. Insofar as we consider the historical bloc from the point of view of the antagonistic terrain in which it is constituted we will call it a hegemonic formation (Laclau and Mouffe, 1985: 136).

A relational field of difference and equivalence is "sutured" by the existence of master signifiers (also known as *points de capiton*, nodal points and empty signifiers). The master signifier creates and sustains identity of a certain discourse by constructing a knot of definite meanings (Žižek, 1989: 95). According to Laclau and Mouffe, the field of discursivity causes some signifiers to float as the result of the overdetermination of their meaning, until a master signifier intervenes and retroactively constitutes their identity by fixing the floating signifiers within a paradigmatic chain of equivalence.

Hegemony needs to be conceptualised, supplementing Gramsci, as both a mobile equilibrium between force and consent, and as a relation of frontiers between antagonists, where hegemonic articulations occur in a field criss-crossed with social antagonisms (i.e., negativity): "Only the presence of a vast area of floating elements and the possibility of their articulation to oppo-site camps—which implies constant redefinition of the latter—is what con-stitutes the terrain permitting us to define a practice as hegemonic" (Laclau and Mouffe, 1985: 136). Without equivalence and without relations of shifting frontiers it is impossible to consider politics as the articulation of hegemony. Laclau and Mouffe, however, reject the Gramscian assumption that a war of position happens through the division of society in two camps. Indeed, Laclau and Mouffe claim that the hegemonic form of politics only becomes dominant in modern times through a proliferation of differences and that as part of the "increasing complexity of the social," this process is primary.

> We will therefore speak of democratic struggles where these imply
> a plurality of political spaces, and of popular struggles where certain
> discourses tendentially construct the division of a single political space
> into two opposed fields. But it is clear that the fundamental concept
> is that of "democratic struggle" and that popular struggles are merely
> specific conjunctures resulting from the multiplication of equivalence
> effects among the democratic struggles (Laclau and Mouffe, 1985: 137).

Clearly, Laclau and Mouffe have abandoned the notion of fundamen-tal classes as the terrain for hegemony and the single hegemonic centre as the normal social topography. Instead, they conceptualise the social field as constrained within the poles of totality (a structure of necessary relations without antagonisms) and atomisation (a proliferation of floating signifiers through the multiplication of antagonisms). However, Laclau and Mouffe stress that "in a given social formation, there can be a variety of hegemon-ic nodal points," implying that hegemony is only ever tendential and local-ised (Laclau and Mouffe, 1985: 139). Therefore, they offer a new definition of organic crisis as a "conjuncture where there is a generalised weakening of the relational system [that] defines the identities of a given social or politi-cal space, and where, as a result, there is a proliferation of floating elements" (Laclau and Mouffe, 1985: 136). There is no single ruptural unity but rather a proliferation of antagonisms (and hence dispersion of subject-positions).

Hegemonic articulation, then, designates the practice of articulating links between discourses and modifying existing discourses, through the construction of differential and equivalential relations between existing dis-courses. Hegemonic articulation is not an aggregation of dissimilar elements into an external combination of fully constituted political constituencies, be-cause the act of hegemonic articulation entails the reciprocal modification of the identity of all of the elements involved in the articulation. The theory of hegemony therefore involves a critique of mainstream "alliance politics" and "coalition building" activities. For Laclau and Mouffe, by creating equivalences between the demands of alliance partners, and simultaneously defining the alliance in opposition to some antagonist, hegemony involves the expansion of a discourse into a horizon of social meaning. This represents a wholesale usurpation of the concept of discursive practice by the operations of ideological discourses, for what Laclau and Mouffe neglect is that the transformation of institutions and the articulation of ideological oppositions are seldom synchronised. A critical determinant of the destiny of every political strategy is its ability to maintain solidarity between alliance partners *despite* the scission between ideological discourse and institutional transformations. While the creation of equivalences between subject-positions *precedes* the reconstruction of institutions, the articulation of a new social cement, in the form of a new hegemonic ideology, *follows from* institutional reconstruction. Laclau and Mouffe's theory collapses these distinct political and ideological processes into a specious unity, generating a political voluntarism prone to mistaking ideological manipulations for institutional conquests.

Social Antagonism

For Laclau, antagonism springs from dislocation, which is the result of "the disruption of structure by forces operating outside it". Laclau and Mouffe refer to this menacing "beyond" as a "constitutive outside" and argue that every field of internal (diacritical) relations contains an implied reference to an external "social antagonism". Inspired by Staten, Laclau identifies the "constitutive outside" with both social antagonism and the conditions of existence of a discourse. According to Laclau and Mouffe, "every society constitutes its own forms of rationality and intelligibility by dividing itself; that is, by expelling outside itself any surplus of meaning subverting it" (Laclau, 1990: 51; Laclau and Mouffe, 1985: 137). Indeed, the formation of hegemony necessitates this act of exclusion, for "limits only exist insofar as a systematic ensemble of differences can be cut out as *totality* with regard to something *beyond* them, and it is only through this cutting out that the totality constitutes itself as formation" (Laclau and Mouffe, 1985: 143).

Political identities are formed within discursive totalities—hegemonic blocs—but, because the "field of discursivity" overflows every discourse, no political identity is complete: every subject-position is a floating signifier whose polysemy makes possible limitless rearticulation. Since political identities are formed through equivalential oppositions ("us" and "them"), every identity is relationally determined, or rendered incomplete, by the necessary existence of an antagonistic identity against which it is defined. Hegemonic

articulation ultimately involves the negation of identity, through the exclusion of a political opponent from the discursive universe, and this leads to
social antagonism.

The logic behind this position is straightforward. Hegemony is constructed by articulating a differential field as existing in equivalence with
respect to a master signifier. Consider a diacritical field, S, S^1, S^2, ... , S^n,
which is articulated in equivalence with a master signifier, S_1:

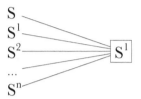

The master signifier—as a signifier—is itself binary, that is, defined
solely by its difference. Yet, this difference cannot be with respect to the field
it articulates, since the master signifier is *not* different from the field S, S^1, S^2,
... , S^n, but (*ex hypothesi*) equivalent to it. Therefore *another* signifier must exist,
"elsewhere," that diacritically defines the master signifier.

Let us call this signifier m, the excluded marginal element:

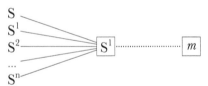

In this diagram, the dotted line S_1—m indicates that only the trace (in
the deconstructive sense) of m remains imprinted on the discursive totality
hegemonised by S_1. Yet, this trace is sufficient to deny all of the social identities articulated in the field S, S^1, S^2, ... , S^n, a complete identity. As a result,
social antagonism exists between the field hegemonised by S_1 and the excluded
margin, m. Now, presumably m is itself the master signifier of another discourse, or a floating signifier that can potentially *become* the master signifier
of another discourse.

To concretise the concept of social antagonism, consider the following
example, based on Laclau's diagram (Laclau, 2000a: 303).

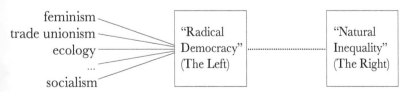

FIGURE: The social antagonism between political Left and Right, seen from the Left.

In the figure, a political alliance of the Left, hegemonised by the radical democratic Imaginary, constructs a social antagonism with the Right by excluding the signifier "Natural Inequality"—selected as *the* master signifier of the political Right following Norberto Bobbio (Bobbio, 1996: 60-81). The social identities in the alliance of the Left are decompleted by the existence of the Right, which antagonises their identity and prevents the Left alliance from becoming coextensive with the social formation.

Laclau and Mouffe claim that what distinguishes the social antagonism from both logical contradiction and real opposition is that the latter two are objective relations whereas social antagonism puts into question any objectivity. This really means that Laclau and Mouffe relapse into a perspectival relativism, whereby there is no appeal to any reality beyond one's discursive universe. Abandoning the concept of social antagonism as contradiction, they insist that the distinction between real opposition and social antagonism is that:

> Real opposition is an *objective* relation—that is determinable, definable—among things; contradiction is an equally definable relation among concepts; antagonism constitutes the limits of every objectivity, which is revealed as a partial and precarious *objectification*. ... Antagonisms are not *internal* but *external* to society; or rather, they constitute the limits of society (Laclau and Mouffe, 1985: 125).

In other words, "real opposition" implies the radically external perspective of a neutral metalanguage or "view from nowhere," whereas social antagonism is something that one is always inside. Indeed, for Laclau and Mouffe "the price of identifying 'society' with the referent would be to empty it of any rationally specifiable content" (Laclau and Mouffe, 1985: 126). If social antagonism helps to establish the boundaries of a discursive formation, it also, at the same time, prevents a discourse from constituting an objective rational and fully intelligible reality. As such, social antagonism is, at once, the condition of possibility and impossibility of society (Laclau and Mouffe, 1985: 125). Social antagonism is therefore a quasi-transcendental.

For Laclau and Mouffe, there are two main types of antagonism—popular antagonisms and democratic antagonisms. Popular antagonisms divide social space into two opposed camps, while democratic antagonisms only divide minor portions of social space (they are local or regional antagonisms). The expansion of the equivalential chain tends to polarise the social and produce a populist logic. By contrast, so-called democratic antagonisms make the world increasingly complex. The example *par excellence* is the NSM, whose democratic politics represent the wave of the future, for today, "partly because of their very success, democratic struggles tend less and less to be unified as 'popular struggles'" (Laclau and Mouffe, 1985: 133).

The intuitive plausibility of Laclau and Mouffe's phenomenology of ideology derives from the way it appeals to the experience of belonging to a political movement. Yet, *as a social theory*, this is fraught with incoherence. Laclau and Mouffe propose a fundamental symmetry between the oppressed and the oppressor, implying a perspectival relativism, according to which my judgement that the other is my oppressor is simply an expression of a relational identity (which is necessarily decompleted by the antagonist). For this reason, Laclau and Mouffe's definition of oppression involves reference to a third party, observing the conflicting parties in a social antagonism. But if discourses fix meaning, then how can there be social dialogue between discourses? How can the observer communicate their judgement to the antagonistic parties? What happens when conflicts arise between alliance partners? Secondly, if we cannot speak of social formations, but only of discursive formations, in what sense do democratic or popular antagonisms "divide social space"? What can "hegemony" (as a mobile equilibrium between force and consent, which implies dominance of a context traversed by *internal* faultlines) *mean*, when Laclau and Mouffe relegate antagonism to an *external* condition?

Political Symbolism

Laclau and Mouffe's *real* solution to the difficulty of the oscillation between an imaginary social unity and political fragmentation in the symbolic field involves reference to an expressive totality subtending every discourse. Laclau and Mouffe explain that they "have referred to 'discourse' as a system of differential entities ... such a system only exists as a partial limitation of a 'surplus of meaning' which subverts it ... [and] we will call it *the field of discursivity*" (Laclau and Mouffe, 1985: 111). The "field of discursivity" as a "surplus of meaning surrounding the social," is the totality of discourses (Smith, 1998: 85). This totality is not descriptive (an empirical register of all discourses), but transcendental (the totality constitutes every entity), for discursivity is not a collection of objects, but rather a "theoretical horizon for the constitution of the being of every object" (Laclau and Mouffe, 1987: 86). The history of philosophy supplies another name for this ultimate discursive horizon that constitutes the entirety of being: the Absolute.

For Laclau and Mouffe, instead of generating a social syntax, the "social production of meaning" culminates in a veritable "crisis of symbolic overproduction". The impossibility of a fixed centre or closed discursive totality, due to absence of a transcendental signified, results in discursivity as the "no-man's land" surrounding every discursive totality with a "surplus of meaning" (Laclau and Mouffe, 1985: 111). To define this theoretically, they rely on Derrida's influential essay, "Structure, Sign and Play in the Discourse of the Human Sciences" (Derrida, 1978: 278-293) and his demonstration that "the absence of the transcendental signified extends the domain and the play of signification indefinitely" (Laclau and Mouffe, 1985: Derrida cited 112). Following Derrida's deconstruction of the concept of structure, Laclau and Mouffe suppose that a discourse is a temporary and partial totalisation whereby the transient imposition of a structural centre creates a relative fixity in signification. Laclau and Mouffe gloss this to claim that "it is not the poverty of signifieds but, on the contrary, polysemy that disarticulates a discursive structure" (Laclau and Mouffe, 1985: 113). The "field of overdetermination," the "field of discursivity," polysemy as a "surplus of meaning" "surrounding" any discursive totality and the action of *différance* are identical in Laclau and Mouffe.

The problem is that Laclau and Mouffe interpret the "impossibility of an ultimate fixity of meaning" *not* in terms of the excess of signification over meaning, but instead in terms of an excess of meaning over signification: "it is not the poverty of signifieds but, on the contrary, polysemy that disarticulates a discursive structure" (Laclau and Mouffe, 1985: 113). While they draw upon Derrida for this position, there is no textual support in the citation offered, or in general in Derrida's work, for their interpretation. Indeed, in the article cited, Derrida explains that it is the excess of the *signifier* that replaces the transcendental signified (Derrida, 1978: 284). In the well-known *Limited Inc.*, for instance, Derrida insists that dissemination is the opposite of polysemy (Derrida, 1988: 9, 20-21). It is not the polysemic richness of the text that Derrida opens to the movement of dissemination, but rather the action of *différance* conceived as a lack, which bursts the semantic horizon with the possibility that meaning and non-meaning might be reciprocal conditions of each other's emergence. Hermeneutics, with its stress on the infinity of meaning and the endlessness of interpretation, remains, for Derrida, within the assumptions of logocentric metaphysics, since the concept of an unclosable horizon of meaning implies a determinate centre and an anticipation of coherence. Polysemy, for Derrida, can only be dispersion from some original unity. The play of dissemination consists precisely in a "disruption that bursts the semantic horizon" (Derrida, 1971: 45). Both determinate meaning and polysemic excess, for Derrida, are formed at the expense of both non-meaning and the productive play of signification that creates meanings beyond the semantic horizon of any hermeneutic procedure (Dews, 1987: 12-13; Gasché, 1986: 174, 218, 237-244). Installing a transcendental signified at the centre of a discourse is the archetypal gesture of *metaphysics*; Derrida, by contrast, enjoins us to think the concept of a decentred structure. Likewise, the Lacanian master signifier is *not* an imaginary image or transcendental signified, but a *nonsensical* placemarker for the subject's castration, or symbolic lack. The master signifier is a signifier *without signified*. It is only in the transference (in the retroactive projection by which the subject identifies with a master signifier) that this appears—in a psychoanalytic variant of ideological misrecognition—as the locus of an Imaginary Meaning.

What this means is that Laclau and Mouffe's "empty signifier" is continuously replaced in their discourse by a transcendental signified, or political symbol, that lends an imaginary unity to the discursive field. Laclau initially proposes that:

> there can be empty signifiers within the field of signification because any system of signification is structured around an empty place resulting from the impossibility of producing an object which, nonetheless, is required by the systematicity of the system (Laclau, 1995a: 43).

This is not in principle different to the Lacanian concept of the master signifier as instigating contingency, or lack. Thus far, what we have is a politicisation of Lacanian psychoanalysis and a perceptive analysis of the possible links between the Lacanian concept of the master signifier and Derrida's theory of *différance*. The difficulty in the analysis only emerges when Laclau and Mouffe attempt to square this with their concept of the field of discursivity as a surplus of meaning. For this concept of discursivity as a field of overdetermination only fits together with a logic of political symbolism.

Laclau frames the notion of an interruption in signification on the model of the sublime. The empty signifier is a result of a "blockage in the continuous expansion of the process of signification" (Laclau, 1995a: 43). This interruption is a consequence of the presence of social antagonism as the limit of any social totality. That is to say, the breakdown in signification flows from the necessity for any hegemonic identity to define itself by marginalising some term and constituting itself in opposition to this negated term. "This relation," notes Laclau, "by which a particular content becomes the signifier of the absent communitarian fullness is exactly what we call a *hegemonic relationship*" (Laclau, 1995a: 43). The role of the empty signifier, then, is discussed in terms not of its function as a placemarker for lack and a non-symbolised loss, of an inability to signify the totality, but in the capacity of representation of the utopian aspirations of a social alliance.

In every concrete example drawn up by Laclau and Mouffe, this usurpation of existential lack by political symbolism takes place. The paradigmatic case is Luxemburg, where the general strike becomes the site of the overflow of the political signifier by the ideological signified of class unity and revolutionary desire.

> [T]he mechanism of unification is clear: in a revolutionary situation, it is impossible to fix the literal sense of each isolated struggle, because each struggle overflows its own literality and comes to represent, in the consciousness of the masses, a simple moment of a more global struggle against the system. ... This is, however, nothing other than the defining characteristic of the symbol: the overflowing of the signifier by the signified. The unity of the class is therefore a symbolic unity (Laclau and Mouffe, 1985: 11).

Symbolic overdetermination becomes the concrete mechanism for the unification of the disparate subject-positions created through sectoral struggles. In the case of Perón, "Perónism ... was rather a series of symbols ... [and] the symbols of a particular group at some point assume a function of universal representation". This universal representation was that of "a pure, abstract absent fullness". "Yet the chains of equivalences constructed by the different factions of his movement had gone beyond any possibility of control" and led to the military coup as a means of retotalising the social (Laclau, 1995a: 55-56). This, again, makes the empty signifier into a political symbol that opens a crack onto the field of discursivity and permits the overflow of meaning to disrupt the social totality. Indeed, Laclau proposes that these symbols form social Imaginaries, because "once the symbol's circulation has reached a certain level of generalisation in the representation of a vast range of antagonisms, they become the necessary surface for the inscription of any new demand" (Laclau, 1990: 79).

The difference between this political symbolism, and the post-structuralism from which it is supposed to issue, could not be more stark. Following Žižek, Laclau and Mouffe's misrecognition of the master signifier (the signifier without signified) "a point of extreme saturation of meaning" is exactly an "ideological anamorphosis" (Žižek, 1989: 99). This might be passed off as a description of the political process, were it not for the combination of its reproduction in *theoretical* material and the underlying problem of the field of overdetermination as a surplus of meaning. The conclusion has to be that Laclau and Mouffe have performed an ideological inversion, amounting to the replacement of symbolic processes by an imaginary unity.

The Democratic Revolution of Modernity

For Laclau and Mouffe, the expressive historical totality that subtends every "discursive formation" is the unfolding of the Democratic Revolution of Modernity (hereafter, DRM). Following Claude Lefort, Laclau and Mouffe conceptualise modernity as inaugurated by a "democratic revolution" that invokes "the dissolution of the markers of certainty" by negating the possibility of the direct incarnation of power in the body of the Prince (Laclau and Mouffe, 1985: 152-159; Lefort, 1988: 16-18). In modernity, by contrast with the *ancien régime*, the imaginary unification of society is a function of the temporary and contingent occupation of the locus of power by some particular group and the corresponding hegemonisation of the content of the universal. According to Lefort, "this leads to the emergence of a purely social society, in which the people, the nation and the state take on the status of [ideal] universal entities" (Lefort, 1988: 18). As Žižek explains, no party can permanently embody the will of the people, so that the governing party necessarily speaks only temporarily "in the name of the people," "as a kind of surrogate, a substitute for the real-impossible sovereign" (Žižek, 1989: 147).

This means that within modernity, the locus of power is coextensive with the "Real-impossible" universality of the people, the nation and the state, that is, is rendered an empty place by the DRM. Recognition of the constitutive nature of the gap between a particular project and the impossible site of universality is the condition of possibility for democratic politics (Laclau, 1995a: 46). This power is a symbolic place that cements society by creating a myth of unification around some universal value. The empty place of power is therefore also the locus of the empty signifier. It is political symbolism—the ability to signify in the name of the absent fullness of community—that is the "empty place of power," indicating that this is a dominant ideology, or "social imaginary," and not an institutional site. Indeed, it is the "permanence of the democratic imaginary" in modernity that is the condition of possibility for the strategy of radical democracy (Laclau and Mouffe, 1985: 155).

According to Laclau and Mouffe, the "decisive mutation in the political imaginary of Western societies took place two hundred years ago and can be defined in these terms: the logic of equivalence was transformed into the fundamental instrument of the production of the social" (Laclau and Mouffe, 1985: 155). This logic of the equality of rights migrates progressively from the political to the economic, cultural and so forth, seen by Laclau and Mouffe as an extension of the "equivalential displacement peculiar to the democratic imaginary" (Laclau and Mouffe, 1985: 158). The logic of socialism, feminism and the new social movements can all be expressed as localisations of this equivalential logic. However, the DRM also entails the extension of a differential logic, the logic of liberty, in tension with the notion of equality. This logic individualises and marks the difference between moments of the social. It is the logic of autonomy, and therefore a constitutive part of the identity of the social movements that might comprise any Left project. These two logics constitute a field of tension within the social, whose poles are totalitarianism (as the end point of total equivalence) and social atomisation (as the final result of absolute difference). Radical democracy locates itself in the dynamic equilibrium that circulates between these poles, a distant echo of the French Revolution's epochal revolution in ideology—instituting a "truly new ... social imaginary" (Laclau and Mouffe, 1985: 155).

Laclau and Mouffe's theory rests upon a historical master narrative of the transition from feudalism to capitalism, according to which the shift from fixed differences and absolute equivalence, to the relation of frontiers between difference and equivalence characteristic of modernity, hinges upon the institutionalisation of the DRM (Laclau and Mouffe, 1985: 155). This master narrative of the transition from a static feudalism—where fixed differences allocate rigid social roles while millenarian equivalences generate organic totalities—to the reign of capitalist modernity—where the invisible hand of equivalence and difference allocates political power to hegemonic alliances (Laclau and Mouffe, 1985: 138), reads like a parody of vulgar Marxism transposed into the language of high metaphysics. Once the DRM creates an "empty place of power," the hegemonic form of politics predominates on the basis of constant dislocations of the structure. Nonetheless, the lost organic totality continues to haunt modernity, for the "relation by which a particular content becomes the signifier for an absent communitarian fullness is exactly what we call a *hegemonic relationship*" (Laclau, 1995a: 43). Modernity evacuates the *contents* of this totality, but not its form—that is to say, the empty signifier and the empty place of power stand in for the "communitarian fullness" which their forms continuously invoke. What replaces the substantive community of pre-modern society is, as we have seen, the "field of discursivity" as a froth of social possibilities, and "every discourse is constituted as an attempt to dominate the field of discursivity by expanding signifying chains which partially fix the meaning of [a] floating signifier" (Torfing, 1999: 98). This sea of excess signification, coextensive with the "empty place of power," is none other than the "democratic imaginary"—that is, the fundamental level of the social.

The "democratic imaginary" of the DRM forms a "discursive exterior" to *every* relation of subordination, enabling these to be transformed into relations of oppression (that is, something contested rather than merely endured) (Laclau and Mouffe, 1985: 154, 159). In a breath-taking simplification (Osborne, 1991: 210-215; Rustin, 1988: 162-173; Wood, 1998: 64-71), this thesis lets Laclau and Mouffe interpret the entire history of social struggles, from the nineteenth century onwards, as the extension and deepening of the DRM (Laclau and Mouffe, 1985: 152-159). Armed with a unitary conception of the NSM that now also subsumes "class identities," Laclau and Mouffe can propose that the task of the Left "cannot be to renounce liberal-democratic ideology, but, on the contrary, to deepen and expand it in the direction of a radical and plural democracy … [through] expanding the chain of equivalents between the different struggles against oppression" (Laclau and Mouffe, 1985: 176). In *HSS*, therefore, the new hegemonic project for the Left—the struggle for a radical and plural democracy—is conceptualised as an *expression* of the DRM.

Modernity is therefore theorised as springing from the foundational character of an inaugural political act. It is not, therefore, that Laclau and Mouffe renounce a universal revolution entirely—only that they relegate this to the historical past and erect an ethical barrier to every effort to make this happen more than once. The "dissolution of the Jacobin Imaginary," the end of the leftwing dream of an inaugural political act, announced at the beginning of *HSS*, then, is the result of Laclau and Mouffe's supposition that this act *has already happened and cannot be repeated*. The best we can do is live with the consequences, namely, engage in the critique of "actually existing democracy" and accept that "the objective of the Left should be the extension and deepening of the democratic revolution initiated two hundred years ago" (Mouffe, 1992d: 1).

The Performative Contradictions of Radical Democracy

The contradiction, between Laclau and Mouffe's claim that socialist revolution as a foundational act is the mainspring of leftwing malaise (Laclau and Mouffe, 1985: 177) and their advocacy of *another* foundational revolution as inaugurating an expressive historical totality, is only the leading edge of a series of performative contradictions. The characteristic relativist conflation of ideology (the "democratic Imaginary") and discourse theory means that performative contradiction becomes the condition of existence of postmarxism's fundamental positions. Indeed, the notion of founding a New Left politics on the basis of the generalised myth of the "radical democratic Imaginary" (Laclau, 1990: 177-196; Laclau and Mouffe, 1985: 190) should leave us feeling uneasily like we are being asked to accede to self-mystification. Postmarxism cannot justify its intervention ethically or defend its politics as something more than another particularism. It cannot substantiate its claims that the political *agon* of radical democracy is anything more than a redescription of parliamentary politics through a rose-tinted ideological lens.

The performative contradictions begin from Laclau's efforts to justify a preference for democratic politics. Modernity is not only constituted by the democratic revolution, but also by post-democratic totalitarianism. Laclau and Mouffe simultaneously claim that totalitarianism is impossible (total equivalence meaning the elimination of all differential identity) and prohibited, something that is an ethical abomination.

Postmarxism silently assumes that democracy is ethically valorized, but refuses to defend this on ethical grounds, lending Laclau's debate with English deconstructionist, Simon Critchley, its evasive quality. The substance of Critchley's argument is to ask: "if all decisions are political, in virtue of what is there a difference between democratizing and non-democratizing decisions?" (Critchley, 1999: 112; Critchley, 2002: 2). Two replies are possible: a normative response (democratic decisions are more egalitarian, pluralistic or participatory) or a factual answer (democratisation is taking place and hegemony is simply a description of this process). The normative claim is depoliticising—in Laclau's terms—because it admits a basis for political decisions outside politics. The factual account risks the collapse of the theory of hegemony into the descriptive process and the voiding of any critical claims. Thus, Critchley reads *HSS* as "Machiavellian," in the popular sense of the term: an ethically indifferent political calculus designed to secure ascendancy for any group prepared to utilise this political technology. This leaves Laclau uncomfortably close to complicity with the dislocatory logic of contemporary capitalist societies (Bertram, 1995: 82; Critchley, 2002: 2).

Laclau replies that *HSS* presents ethics and politics as a unity by virtue of a Gramscian "politicisation of ethics" (Laclau, 1995c: 93). In opposition to the ethics of infinite responsibility towards the Other promoted by Critchley's interpretation of deconstruction (Critchley, 1993), Laclau proposes that deconstruction is a decisionism (Laclau, 1995c: 94). Insofar as hegemony is the inverse of the operation of deconstruction as theorised by Laclau, this makes hegemony a theory of decision. So, for Laclau, "if deconstruction discovers the role of the decision out of the undecidability of the structure, hegemony, as a theory of the decision taken in an undecidable terrain, requires that the contingent connections existing in that terrain are fully shown by deconstruction" (Laclau, 1995a: 103). Hegemony and deconstruction are one another's inverse: hegemony goes from undecidability to the decision, while deconstruction reveals the contingent character of the original decision.

While this would seem to mean that Laclau endorses the Machiavellian interpretation of their work, their actual claim is that *HSS* is Gramscian in that it theorises hegemony as a mobile equilibrium between politics and ethics. Recently, Laclau has elaborated upon this "politicisation of ethics" (Laclau, 2000b: 79-86). Postmarxism depends upon an ethical decision to accept the transcendental status of the distinction between ethical universality and particular norms, or contextually bound maxims of conduct. The moment of ethics corresponds to the formal universality of the absent fullness of society (the impossible yet necessary dream of a harmonious, organic totality), while political contents and concrete social norms are inter-twined in particular complexes (Laclau, 2000b: 74-85). As Critchley observes, in this reintroduction of ethics into postmarxism, the distinctions ethical/normative, form/content and universal/particular line up with the distinction ontological/ontic (Critchley, 2002: 3). Not only is the alignment of ethics and ontology characteristic of Western metaphysics, but this position is incoherent—for Laclau and Mouffe, the being of every object is supposed to be discursively constructed, ruining the claim to oppose ethics to politics. Laclau denies that this system of oppositions determines his work (Laclau, 2002), but he can only do so by reiterating the claim that the ethical is linked with the empty signifier (Laclau, 2000b: 84; Laclau, 2002: 1). This means either that the ethical is linked with the *locus* of the empty signifier, the empty place of power (in which case it *is* identified with abstract universality as the locus of the ontological constitution of the social field), or that the ethical *is* the empty signifier (in which case the ethical is only a masked particular and no distinction between ethics and norms exists).

As Žižek identifies the underlying problem with Laclau's "politicisation of ethics":

> [Laclau] oscillates between proposing a neutral formal frame that

describes the working of the political field, without implying any specific *prise de parti*, and the prevalence given to a particular leftist political practice. ... Laclau's notion of hegemony describes the universal mechanism of ideological "cement" which binds any social body together, a notion that can analyse all possible socio-political orders, from fascism to liberal democracy; on the other hand, Laclau nonetheless advocates a determinate political option, "radical democracy" (Žižek, 2000h: 174).

This alternation between a formally neutral, metalinguistic claim that is belied by the partisan content of the statement is evidence of the effort to try to occupy the pure position of metalanguage at the level of the enunciation. This extends all the way through Laclau and Mouffe's position: radical democracy is a neutral theory of politics and a partisan project; democratic citizenship is the horizon of democratic politics and the aim of a new grammar of political conduct; ethics is only an effect of political decisions, but nonetheless radical democracy should be preferred as more egalitarian. For Žižek, this is the basic problem with postmodern political theory: its reluctance to adopt an openly partisan position of enunciation betrays its hysterical dependence on the demand of the Other for a legitimization of its political position. Instead of an autonomous, openly stated, partisan theory, we have the convoluted attempt to occupy the "view from nowhere" of pure metalanguage, the Imaginary position of the "impossible fullness of society".

Ethical Universality and Political Particularism

The most significant of the "crop circles" in Laclau and Mouffe's theory is that the elementary hegemonic operation (speaking in the name of the people) is theorised explicitly as a performative contradiction. For postmarxian discourse theory, "society ... is a plurality of particularistic groups and demands" (Laclau, 2000b: 55) and the universal is an empty place that it is impossible to occupy. This makes every hegemonic agent into an impostor whose "universality" is only a masked particular. According to postmarxian discourse theory, when a hegemonic agent speaks, their position of enunciation is transformed from "I speak" to "the people speaks" (Torfing, 1999: 177, 193). This implies that the position of enunciation is an abstract universal, while the content of the statement expresses a sectoral interest. But this only means that the hegemonic agent gets involved in something like the "liar's paradox," because recognition of the impossibility of universality is supposed to be constitutive of democratic politics—that is, the hegemonic agent is trapped in a performative contradiction, whereby their implied position of enunciation depends upon a universality that their statement denies. Indeed, "the assertion of universality by those who have conventionally been excluded by the term often produces a performative contradiction of a cer-

tain sort" (Butler, 2000d: 38). The hedging qualifications ("often ... of a certain sort") indicate just how uneasy the postmarxists are with this position—
yet the theoretical claim that the oppressed retain their particularity while
articulating a universal claim indicates that performative contradiction *always* happens (Butler, 2000d: 39).

The problem is that the discourse theory of Laclau and Mouffe is predicated upon the existence of an absolute gap between the abstract universal
and any concrete particular, in a reaction against the alleged teleology of the
direct incarnation of universality in the moment of "proletarian chiliasm"
(Laclau, 1995a: 22-26). While in *HSS*, Laclau and Mouffe's "renunciation of
the discourse of the universal" comes perilously close to an endorsement of
postmodern particularism (Laclau and Mouffe, 1985: 3), recently Laclau has
distanced postmarxism from strands of radical particularism in postmodern theory and multicultural politics (Laclau, 1995a: 20-35, 48-54). Laclau
brands as reactionary the identitarian "politics of authenticity" that accompanies complete rejection of the universal, because it lands the oppressed
group in the position of performatively undercutting their appeal to universal human rights and democratic entitlements (Laclau, 1995a: 48). In line
with the postmodern position on universality, however, Laclau proposes that
the definition of universality is contextually determined, and that the incommensurability of contexts ensures that there exist only local definitions
of universality (Laclau, 1995a: 34, 51-54). Nonetheless, Laclau argues that
the extreme postmodern position implies regression to a "state of nature,"
in which the competition between singularities destroys social cohesion in a
shower of antagonistic fragments (Laclau, 1995a: 33-34). Reintroduction of
social cohesion (a postmodern social contract recognising difference, for instance), while preserving the elimination universality as an explicit factor in
politics, only means its re-inscription as the ontological ground of the totality in another form (Laclau, 1995a: 58). The postmodern and multicultural
attack on universality therefore presupposes precisely what it excludes.

Yet, it is not at all clear that Laclau and Mouffe can escape the problems
of the postmodern position. Because particular identities are not fully closed,
but exist as articulated into chains of equivalence, the universal "emerges
from the particular" as an irreducible dimension of the chain of equivalence
that creates the limits of every system (Laclau, 1995a: 30-33). This serves to
partially negate particular identities by introducing "the dimension of relative universality" (Laclau, 1995a: 30-33). For Laclau, this means the dimension of universality generated by the formation of discursive equivalences is
not an *a priori* unconditional universality (Laclau, 1995a: 30-33). The relative
universality proposed by Laclau and Mouffe cannot exist before—or independently of—a chain of equivalences, formed through discursive articulations, that links particular identities (Laclau, 1995a: 30-33). In line with
Laclau and Mouffe's postmodern nominalism, this conception of universal-

ity converts every "concrete universal" into a mere generalisation lacking the key features of a transcendental (universality and necessity, constitutive capacity) (Laclau, 1995a: 30-33). The key feature of these particular social identities is that they can exist before their articulation into a chain of equivalences—and so, because this chain is contingent, they lack any *constitutive* reference to their "universal". This is why Laclau claims that "difference and particularity are the necessary starting point" for postmarxism (Laclau, 1995a: 65) and that the universal springs from the particular (Laclau, 1995a: 28). It is therefore impossible for Laclau and Mouffe to evade their own objection to postmodern theory, namely, that postmodern particularism negates the constitutive dependence of every particular upon the universal, unless the particular has reference to a *deeper* essential universal ground—in which case Laclau and Mouffe have fallen into the trap of an essentialist totality subtending the atomised field of social particulars.

Laclau and Mouffe have failed to make the elementary distinction between formal universality as a regulative ideal and the "relative universality" of the contents of the universal advanced by a determinate social alliance. In actuality, Laclau's claim that *formal* universality is not a regulative ideal is incoherent, for he immediately appends the claim that the dimension of universality is "just an empty place unifying a set of equivalential demands" (Laclau, 1995a: 30-33). This describes exactly a regulative ideal. Because the particular sectoral identity of a social agent cannot exist without its articulation to universality, as the agent becomes hegemonic by transcending corporatism, its particular identity is not just "hybridised" (as Laclau accepts, it *begins* as hybridised), but asymptotically eliminated. The example of Mary Wollstonecraft—invoked by both Laclau (Laclau, 1995a: 30-33) and Butler (Butler, 2000d: 39)—testifies against the "primacy of the particular," for this involves precisely such an articulation of an expanded content for the universal *in the name of its form*. No performative contradiction is involved in this articulation.

By contrast, the performative contradictions of postmarxism indicate the remainder of an unmediated particularism that resists universalisation, namely, the clinging of Laclau and Mouffe to the postmodern identity politics of the NSM (Osborne, 1991: 215-221). This is confirmed by Laclau's reintroduction of the problematic of representation within the theory of hegemony, which supposes the existence of a pre-discursive substance that is "represented" by a signification (Laclau, 1995a: 84-104; Laclau, 2000c: 211). Laclau claims that the hegemonic agent is "constitutively split between the concrete politics that they advocate and the ability of those politics to fill the empty place" (Laclau, 1995a: 54; Laclau, 2000b: 68). This conjures a vision of hegemonic agents "filling" the empty place, conceptualised as the insertion of a pre-constituted object into a socio-political slot. This is an incoherent position, as it supposes the existence of a split between an extra-discursive particularity that is *politically* articulated to a universal function *without fully transforming the original social particularity*. Now, according to discourse theory this split is impossible: a sectoral identity is constituted through hegemonic articulation and therefore contains internal reference to universality (Laclau, 1995a: 31). In recent interventions, Laclau has tried to salvage his position by accepting the regulative status of formal universality (Laclau, 2000c: 196), while at the same time maintaining that the universal only exists incarnated in a social particular (a sectoral identity), that universality supposes a radical exclusion, that only a social Imaginary universalises particular demands, and so the empty signifier is a representation of an impossibility (Laclau, 2000c: 207-211). This position reintroduces the absolute split between abstract, regulative universality, and the "concrete universal" of a hegemonic particular, elevated to quasi-universal status through exclusions. The basic relation between an originary particularity and an entirely unexplained regulative universality remains. Laclau claims that the postmodern relation between universal and particular is "undecidable" (Laclau, 1995a: 20-35)—because there exists a mutual conditioning of universal and particular—yet in actuality Laclau and Mouffe transform the universal into a mere generalisation subordinated to the primacy of the particular, while all the time relying upon the regulative ideal of a formal universality as "an empty place unifying a set of equivalential demands".

Democratic Citizenship and Radical Subjectivity

Where the dialectics of universal and particular explain how socially fragmented actors can form a collective will capable of instituting a new social order, the concept of democratic citizenship is intended to theorise the production of a new social cement (Mouffe, 1992e: 3-4, 60-73). The strategy of radical democracy involves the formation of a new "common-sense" through the articulation of a chain of equivalences between the struggles of the oppressed for equality and rights (Laclau and Mouffe, 1985: 182; Mouffe, 1992a: 31). This common-sense needs to be "sedimented" into a new moral and political grammar of the "way things are done" in contemporary social conflict, so that the political conquests of the Left become relatively fixed, through the generation of a new political subjectivity beyond possessive individualism. Central to this strategy is the extension of democratic rights beyond liberal practices of privatised citizenship (Laclau and Mouffe, 1985: 183-185). To theorise this strategy, Mouffe proposes a deconstructive synthesis "beyond liberalism and communitarianism" that might reconcile individual liberties with complex equality in a new form of political subjectivity.

Following Balibar's argument (Balibar, 1994c: 1-15; Mouffe, 1992a: 28-32), Mouffe accepts that democratic citizenship is *the* modern form of political subjectivity. According Balibar, the advent of a citizenship based on equal rights means that "citizenship is not one among other attributes of subjectivity; on the contrary it *is* subjectivity, *that form* of subjectivity that would no longer be identical with subjection for anyone" (Balibar, 1994c: 12). The problem for Mouffe is to integrate Kantian liberal conceptions of citizenship (based on the primacy of the individual and the neutrality of the state) with Hegelian communitarian alternatives (based on the primacy of community and the partiality of the state). Mouffe proposes that liberalism and communitarianism share a common reference to the political community of the modern nation state (Mouffe, 1992e: 23-40), that might act as the mediating ground for a progressive synthesis (Mouffe, 1992e: 41-59). She rejects both the liberal theory of the state as a neutral instrument and the communitarian postulate of the primacy of a substantive community, and wants to combine the liberal notion of democratic citizenship (political subjects as bearers of equal rights) with the communitarian concept of the partiality of the state (the "empty place of power" as hegemonised by a particular conception of the universal) (Mouffe, 1992a: 28-32). Mouffe proceeds arithmetically, claiming that Rawls cannot tolerate real political dissent (Mouffe, 1992e: 41-59) and that Walzer's complex equality implies the elimination of social antagonism (Mouffe, 1992e: 23-40). Instead of excluding political antagonisms as "irrational," radical democratic hegemony would entail the promotion of activist citizenship—a militant political subjectivity—that would support a radical democratic government through mass mobilisations within the framework of democratic contestation.

Mouffe's synthesis of liberal individualism and communitarian republicanism, however, is extremely fragile because it consists of an articulation of ideologemes lacking any institutional analysis beyond a recapitulation of the liberal conception of the political universality of the capitalist state. By introducing political conflict and social antagonism into liberalism and communitarianism, Mouffe arrives at a conception of democratic citizenship through identification with the ethico-political principles defined by a political community. For Mouffe, the political community in question is neither instrumental nor substantive, but a social Imaginary that defines a political commonwealth shaped in and through exclusionary hegemonic struggles (Mouffe, 1992a: 30; Mouffe, 1992e: 135-154).

According to Mouffe, the political community needs to be redefined in terms of "what we can call, following Wittgenstein, a 'grammar of conduct' that coincides with the allegiance to the constitutive ethico-political principles of modern democracy" (Mouffe, 1992a: 30). Reconceptualisation of the political community in terms of a grammar of conduct re-establishes the lost connection between ethics and politics (Mouffe, 1991; Mouffe, 1992b). Her deconstructive reworking of the liberal and communitarian notions of democratic citizenship suggests that she envisages democratic citizenship "as a

form of political identity that is created through identification with the political principles of modern pluralist democracy, i.e., the assertion of liberty
and equality for all" (Mouffe, 1992a: 30). That is to say, Mouffe advocates
subject-formation through identification with the DRM.

Democratic citizenship is a "common political identity of persons who
might be engaged in many different communities and who have differing
conceptions of the good, but who accept submission to certain authoritative
rules of conduct," which function as a set of procedural guarantees for democracy (Mouffe, 1992a: 31). Mouffe's position implicitly rests upon a distinction between universal form—identification with the political community as an ensemble of formal procedures for the resolution of conflicts—and
particular contents—operationalised though the notion of identification
with a specific interpretation of the democratic rules. The problem is that
democratic citizenship is at once a universal mode of subjection and a radical subjectivity corresponding to a particular politics. Hence, the contradictory imperatives to identify with *both* the universal political community
(the "empty place of power") *and* the radical principle of the DRM (Mouffe,
1992e: 71-73). This is because the concept of *radical* democratic citizenship is
supposed to supply a form of identification providing a militant political subjectivity that might form a new social cement beyond possessive individualism, by refusing the fixed boundary between private and public that in the
dominant ideology restricts the extension of the DRM (Mouffe, 1992a: 32).

It is difficult—if not impossible—to imagine how this divided identification promotes militancy beyond bourgeois civic activism or encourages
social antagonisms and political conflict. Radical democratic citizenship is
at once the particular subjectivity of the oppressed contesting domination
and the universal subjectivity of the dominant. Indeed, Mouffe's concept of
democratic citizenship as a culture of the democratic *agon* implies that politics is not about radical transformation at all, but is instead a constructive response to social frustration, a sort of steam valve. According to Mouffe, this
can be done by securing a political consensus on basic democratic values
and procedures while allowing dissent over the interpretation of the precise
meaning of these values and procedures (Mouffe, 1992e: 130-132; Mouffe,
1996b). Within such an agonistic democratic society, enemies would not
be destroyed, but turned into adversaries involved in political competition
(Mouffe, 1999: 39-55): "To envisage politics as a rational process of negotiation between individuals is to obliterate the whole dimension of power and
antagonism—what I call 'the political'—and thereby completely miss its nature" (Mouffe, 1992e: 140). At the same time, the democratic expression of
social antagonism is constrained by value consensus and a prudential morality (Mouffe, 1992e: 152), which is held to differ from liberalism in that it does
not rely upon any metaphysical foundation in a rational universality. Mouffe
opposes the equation of universality with neutrality, denying that democra-

cy requires any moral consensus grounded in universal ethics (Habermas) or political procedures grounded in a transparent rationality (Rawls). In place of these, she substitutes a prudential moral consensus and a concept of political rationality grounded in accepting equality and freedom. This seems to me identical with modern, post-metaphysical liberalism as presented by Rawls (Rawls, 1993).

Mouffe's problem once again is that the assertion that liberal citizenship is a universal form of political subjectivity performatively undercuts the "radicalism" of the postmarxian statement. This leads to an evacuation of social content, so that radical democratic citizenship becomes little more than a self-reflexive civics. The only way to escape this dilemma is to accept that the demand for a radical citizenship obeys an unconditional universal imperative—the imperative of *égaliberté*, or "equaliberty"—that transcends the contents of the universal specified by the dominant liberal ideology. Mouffe suggests this—"equality and liberty for all"—but the existence of an unconditional universal is exactly what Laclau and Mouffe deny.

Radical Democracy and Socialist Strategy

According to Mouffe, "the objective of the Left should be the extension and deepening of the democratic revolution initiated two hundred years ago" (Mouffe, 1992d: 1). Yet, the relation between the "socialist strategy" advertised by *HSS* and radical democracy has remained crucially indeterminate. The latent contradiction between the assertion that there is an anti-capitalist dynamic inherent in the extension of the democratic revolution to the state bureaucracy and the economic region of the social (Laclau and Mouffe, 1985: 178), and the simultaneous claim that within radical democracy, the elimination of constitutive antagonisms such as that between labour and capital would be a totalitarian negation of the project (Laclau and Mouffe, 1985: 186-192), suggests that this indeterminacy is the result of a structural ambivalence located in the premises of the theory. Mouffe's theory of the democratic *agon*, secured through a new form of radical subjectivity that refuses to "go all the way" to the expropriation of the means of production, indicates the kinship between radical democracy and the "self-limiting revolution" of social democratic politics. For radical democracy does not substitute for the (long vanished) "proletarian dictatorship," but for the democratic transition to socialism that Eurocommunism theorised as a stage of "advanced democracy". Postmarxism keeps the conceptual form and abandons the substantial notion of transition, replacing it with the permanent *agon* of radical democracy and democratic citizenship.

The radicalism of this democratic politics apparently springs from the "egalitarian-equivalential Imaginary" and the fundamental demand for equality. "A radical and *non-plural* democracy would be one which constituted one single space of equality on the basis of the unlimited operation of the logic of equivalence" (Laclau and Mouffe, 1985: 176). Meanwhile, a plural and *non-radical* democracy would mean the division of political space into a competing multiplicity of zones on the basis of the unlimited operation of the logic of difference. In the light of the "complexity of the social" and the "proliferation of political spaces" wrought by the new social movements, "the demand for *equality* is not sufficient, but needs to be balanced by the demand for *liberty*," which leads to respect for the separation of political spaces (Laclau and Mouffe, 1985: 176). Hence, Laclau and Mouffe conceptualise the hegemonic strategy of a New Left as "the struggle for a maximum autonomisation of spheres [of struggle] on the basis of the generalisation of the equivalential-egalitarian logic" (Laclau and Mouffe, 1985: 167).

> The logic of liberal democracy alone does not guarantee the defense of individual freedom and a respect for individual rights. It is only through its articulation with political liberalism that the logic of popular sovereignty can avoid becoming tyrannical; then one cannot speak of the people as if it was one homogeneous and unified entity with a single general will (Mouffe, 1990: 60).

It is necessary "to discard the dangerous dream of a perfect consensus, of a harmonious collective will, and to accept the permanence of conflicts and antagonisms" (Mouffe, 1990: 58). Carl Schmitt demonstrates why democracy must be plural: for Schmitt—plausibly in Mouffe's view—communism and fascism are democratic in that they homogenise the society (Mouffe, 1999: 39-52). The political implications of this concept of "democracy" are unacceptable for postmarxism. It is worth noting the category mistake—the confusion of institutionalised political processes with the ontological constitution of the social field—on which this absolutely bizarre equation of totalitarianism and democracy is based. What this reveals is a persistent slippage in postmarxian discourse, whereby the lack of attention to the distinction between politics as that dimension of social practice constitutive of social relations, and the political as an institutional terrain or structural region, leads to their conflation under the sign of the ambiguous concept of the "political institution of social relations". It also exposes the absurdities to which the abandonment of the distinction between the material aspect of social practices (the extra-discursive) and their differential aspect (the discursive) finally leads. For politics as a dimension of social existence can only ontologically homogenise the entire social field if it is granted the divine power to constitute the materiality of every object—something that Laclau and Mouffe endorse.

According to Laclau and Mouffe, "it is not in the abandonment of the democratic terrain but, on the contrary, in the extension of the field of democratic struggles to the whole of civil society and the state, that the possibility resides for a hegemonic strategy of the Left" (Laclau and Mouffe, 1985: 176). Radical plural democracy entails the pluralisation of democracy and the displacement of the DRM throughout the social. Nonetheless, despite the ambiguity of "democratic terrain," they specify that the task of the Left "cannot be to renounce liberal-democratic ideology, but on the contrary, to deepen and expand it in the direction of a radical and plural democracy" (Laclau and Mouffe, 1985: 176). Instead of defending the *institutions* of parliamentary democracy and political rights, then, we are enjoined to support the dominant ideology.

Laclau and Mouffe claim that the essential difference between liberals and postmarxists is that while liberals regard the public/private distinction as fixed, postmarxists regard it as a flexible frontier. At the same time, Mouffe's theory of the democratic *agon* makes it clear that border incursions are going to be temporary raids and not the progressive elimination of capitalism. Indeed, Laclau and Mouffe's theory of a direct conflict between the liberal principle of freedom and the democratic principle of equality implies a closed universe of inverse proportionality, where every gain in equality represents a loss of liberty, and *vice versa*. When, therefore, they claim that the struggle for a radical plural democracy seeks to displace the quest for liberty and equality to the economic sphere, we can expect that this is not going to significantly improve the prospects for socialism.

The radicalism in question here is therefore a *metaphysical* radicalism, namely, the acceptance of the groundlessness of all grounds (Laclau and Mouffe, 1985: 176) and the "indeterminate character of democracy" (Mouffe, 1996c). As Mouffe specifies, "the aim is not to create a completely different kind of society, but to use the symbolic resources of the liberal democratic tradition to struggle against relations of subordination not only in the economy, but also those linked to gender, race or sexual orientation, for example" (Mouffe, 1990: 57-58). Supposedly, the "political Imaginary" of a radical plural democracy provides the Left with a new hegemonic strategy potentially capable of engendering and unifying a broad range of progressive political struggles. However, postmarxists hastily add that this is predicated upon the unrealisability of radical plural democracy, which provides neither an actually realisable blueprint nor a utopia (Laclau and Mouffe, 1985: 190). This flows from the closed economy of equivalence (equality) and difference (liberty), so that a condition of possibility of a further democratisation of society is also its condition of impossibility. According to Mouffe, we have to conclude that radical plural democracy takes the deconstructive form of the promise of a "democracy to come," which is neither a regulative ideal, nor an indeterminate teleological judgement (Mouffe, 1996c). This messianic promise is completely empty, both socially and politically.

The Democratic Imaginary as a Social Foundation

Laclau advances the bold metaphysical claim that "every age adopts an image of itself—a certain horizon, however blurred and imprecise—which somehow unifies its whole experience" (Laclau, 1990: 3). Instead of a necessary social foundation, then, the postmodern theory of Laclau and Mouffe presents the political institution of the social field through the dominance of the "democratic Imaginary". This Imaginary, forming a "discursive exterior" to every discourse, functions as a *contingent* social foundation based not in a conception of substance (human nature, for instance), but in an institutionalised political decision. Where modernity—supported by Enlightenment—proposed a progressive advance in conscious mastery of the natural and social worlds leading towards a post-political utopia, the new epoch represents "a growing awareness of limits" and the exhaustion of the discourse of the new. This leads to a "radical critique of all forms of domination" and the "formulation of liberation projects hitherto restrained by the rationalist 'dictatorship' of the Enlightenment" (Laclau, 1990: 4). What is important about this new conjuncture, then, is the emergence of the new social movements and post-structuralist philosophy represent a *self-reflexive* break from the logic of the incarnation of universality. The critical question for Laclau, however, is recognition of the existence of the democratic Imaginary as a universal social myth:

> The imaginary is a horizon: it is not one among other objects but an absolute limit which structures the field of intelligibility and is thus the condition of possibility for the emergence of any object (Laclau, 1990: 64).

Now, this is *exactly* how we have seen the field of discursivity described. Suddenly, the reason behind the description of the field of discursivity as a surplus of meaning becomes clear: the field of discursivity is a social Imaginary that has the form of a social myth, that is, *the* meaningful space that forms the "imaginary horizon" (Laclau, 1990: 67) for a society, forming the "view from nowhere" of an atemporal principle of harmony.

To support this truly extraordinary thesis, Laclau and Mouffe theorise modernity as a historical totality, grounded in the transcendental horizon of the field of discursivity and dynamised by processes of dislocation springing from the foundational event of the Democratic Revolution. In *New Reflections*, Laclau essays a description of the contemporary social field in terms of the category of "dislocation". According to Laclau, dislocation is "the very form of" temporality, possibility and freedom (Laclau, 1990: 41, 42, 43). In an audacious metaphysical arch, Laclau connects dislocation (temporality) to myth (spatiality) to generate a new transcendental aesthetic (Laclau, 1990: 65) composed of two heterogeneous components in constant tension. Laclau envisages the social structure as proceeding through a sequence of openings (dislocatory events) and closings (hegemonic articulations) of the social field (Laclau, 1990: 41-65). This theory of localised historical "epicycles" is totalised within Laclau and Mouffe's master narrative of the "extension and deepening" of the DRM. Strictly speaking, this is impossible, for Laclau's position rules out every historical generalisation, as it adopts a postmarxian variant of the Althusserian concept of differential histories, but subtracts from this theory the unity of a structure in dominance that makes a social theory of capitalism possible. This does not detain Laclau, however, who calmly asserts the existence of "disorganised capitalism" as a new historical epoch (Laclau, 1990: 57-58). According to Laclau, the increasing complexity of the social diagnosed in *HSS* produces a multiplication of social antagonisms and a decentring of the social formation that finally culminates in postmodernity. The mode of production as an "absent cause"—together with the shifting locus of the structure in dominance—is replaced by a horizontal pluralisation of the social field.

This rapidly degenerates into a celebration of the structural dislocations caused by capitalist restructuring. In line with the political Thermidor announced by *New Reflections* (read: second thoughts) *on the Revolution*, Laclau shifts towards a politics of indeterminacy which claims that "the greater the structural indetermination, the freer the society will be" (Laclau, 1990: 44). Laclau refuses to supply a concrete political programme on the basis that "the greater the dislocation of a structure is, the more indeterminate the political construction emerging from it will be" (Laclau, 1990: 51). The paradox is that as possibilities are actualised and social agents self-determined through acts of social identification, the result is a *reduction* in liberty (Laclau, 1990: 44). Laclau proposes, then, that capitalist crisis *is* freedom, while the project of radical democracy is designed to *reduce* freedom by partially determining the social field as a discursive formation!

The postmodern condition is therefore characterised by multiple struggles for recognition, whose accomplishment constitutes so many partial and temporary emancipation*s*. After the disintegration of Emancipation, the collapse of Universality and the end of History, then, the quantum flux of micro-emancipations, contingent and particularised universalities and pocket histories ensures that this "steady state" universe is characterised by a minimum of energy fomenting in the political vacuum left by the death of master narratives. According to Laclau:

> it is not the specific demands of the emancipatory projects formulated since the Enlightenment which have gone into crisis; it is the idea that the whole of those demands constitute a unified whole and would be realized in a single foundational act by a privileged agent of historical change. ... Indeed, it is not just that emancipatory demands are diversifying and deepening in today's world, but also that the notion of their essential unification around an act of global rupture is fading (Laclau, 1990: 215).

This collapse of the "Enlightenment fundamentalism" of emancipatory demands leads to their democratisation because "the absence of a global emancipation of humanity allows the constant expansion and diversification of concrete 'emancipatory' struggles" (Laclau, 1990: 216).

> We would speak today of "emancipations" rather than "Emancipation". While the socialist project was presented as the global emancipation of humanity and the result of a single revolutionary act of institution, such a "fundamentalist" perspective has today gone into crisis (Laclau, 1990: 225).

Not surprisingly, the "end of history" looms into sight at this point in the argument, for "if the 'end of history' is understood as the end of a conceptually graspable object encompassing the whole of the real in its diachronic spatiality, we are clearly at the 'end of history'. ... In another sense, however, we can say that we are at the *beginning* of history, at the point where historicity finally achieves full recognition" (Laclau, 1990: 84). This is the familiar idealist schema whereby historical periodisation depends upon the forms of epochal self-consciousness—and, in a wonderful Hegelian inversion of Marx, the beginning of history is not the society of material abundance, but the self-reflexive grasp of the process of the spirit's self-production.

3

The Politics of Performativity:
A Critique of Judith Butler

"Performativity" has entered the lexicon in the academy as one of the most celebrated contributions to cultural theory of the last decade.[1] According to Butler, performativity combines an intentional, dramatic performance of identity (Butler, 1999a: 177), with the repetition of the institutionalised conventions of performative speech acts (Butler, 1993: 12). She draws on Foucault's insight into how power generates resistance to insist that in adopting a stance of enunciation in conformity with social norms, the subject implicitly positions themselves as rejecting the transgressive subject-positions that the dominant ideology forecloses. Accordingly, political resistance remains latent within hegemonic norms. This is supplemented by Derrida's deconstruction of speech act theory, which, Butler argues, shows how the statement, within socially accepted speech acts performed in a multiplicity of contexts, has the potential to go awry because of the differential nature of the signifier and the unlimited character of the context. It follows that performances of social identity on the borders of hegemonic norms have the subversive potential to awaken latent possibilities for political resistance. Finally, Butler brings a psychoanalytically-influenced understanding of the formation of subjectivity through power to propose that even the conformist subject, because of their never-surmounted proximity to transgression and the always-fragile character of hegemonic speech acts, remains forever a divided, "melancholy" subject, riven by the unmourned loss of foreclosed identity possibilities. Performances of identity involve, in her view, a tem-

---

1. Parts of this chapter have been published as "Judith Butler's Postmodern Existentialism: A Critique," *Philosophy Today* **48**(4) (pp. 349-363) and "The Politics of Performativity," *Parrhesia: A Journal of Critical Philosophy* (1) (pp. 112-141). For a bibliography of Butler's works to 2001, consult Eddie Yeghiayan's bibliographic website for the Wellek series of lectures given by Butler and published as *Antigone's Claim* (Butler, 2001), at http://sun3.lib.uci.edu/indiv/scctr/Wellek/butler.html (accessed on 01 May 2008).

poralised process, where the ideological rituals formative of social identities "sediment," over time, into the materiality of institutions and the surfaces of bodies (Butler, 1993: 9). The openness of the process of structuration means that subjectification is not something permanent or stable, but rather represents the precarious assertion of identity through an always-ambiguous demarcation of mainstream subjectivity from marginalised alternatives. Generally speaking, because social identities are the permanently divided result of the ritualistic repetition of conventions, the possibility for subversion of the reigning social norms remains an ineradicable potential of *all* social relations.

Butler's description of the temporalised process of structuration, which seeks to avoid recourse to political voluntarism, or the sovereign intentionality of the autonomous individual, is an important effort to rethink Laclau and Mouffe's discourse theory. Yet Judith Butler's theory of discourse is constituted by a basic tension: on the one hand, the political subversive potential of the concept of performativity requires an intentional dramatisation, where an agent selects from a repertoire of possible subject-positions; on the other hand, though, Butler insists that performativity is not reducible to a voluntarist notion of theatrical performance, but involves the insertion of subjects into discursive networks that transcend individual intentions. Butler maintains that the theory of performativity involves a "subjectless conception of agency". The problem is that Butler's subject-centred phenomenology cannot escape the historicist assumption that subjective praxis, modelled on individual identity transformations, is the principle of institutional structuration. The original formulation of the theory of performativity—in *Gender Trouble* (1999) [1990]—produced an interpretation of Foucault's discourse analytics and Derrida's deconstruction that was profoundly inflected by existential Hegelianism. Interpreting the process of subject-formation through the Hegelian lens of the "struggle for recognition," Butler proposed that social institutions are the consequence, not the cause, of social subjectivity. Consequently, the concept of agency that underlies Butler's notion of a politics of the performative remains that of abstract individualism, lacking in social specificity and continually wresting with the pseudo-problem of authorial intentionality. Thus, Butler never completely breaks from a central assumption of historicism, namely, that it is legitimate to transpose the forms of individual praxis onto social processes of institutional structuration.

Butler has made several efforts to rectify her "new existentialism" (Schrift, 1997: 153-159; Schrift, 2001: 12-23) and constrain individual praxis. Part of the problem is that Butler's point of departure remains Althusser's "ISA's Essay". Each reiteration adds new layers of post-structural theory to her interpretation of ideological interpellation (Butler, 1993a: 121-140; Butler, 1995; Butler, 1997a: 71-102; Butler, 1997b: 106-131), without confronting the major underlying conceptual issue in that essay, namely, Althusser's assignment to ideology of the responsibility for explaining major structural change. Butler compounds this by reading the "ISAs Essay" upside-down, as it were, not as an essay on how structures form subjectivity, but as the inspiration for a theory of how subjectivity shapes material institutions and corporeal realities. The notion that identity formation is the basis for institutional structuration overturns Butler's sources (Althusser and Foucault), to produce a generalised category of performativity, modelled on individual dramatic performances, whose leading characteristic is its ability to transcend its contextual determinants. In this sense, Butler can be said to have fully elaborated Laclau and Mouffe's idealist insistence on "the *material* character of every discursive structure" (Laclau and Mouffe, 1985: 95), by inverting Althusser's affirmation of the materialised existence of ideology into a theory of the ideological generation of materiality.

It is Butler's intention to develop a subjectless conception of agency. But her declarations against the sovereignty of the classical individual run in the opposite direction to the implications of her work. By confining the individual agent within discursive conventions and introducing the unconscious as a limit on conscious intentionality, Butler tried to demonstrate that "agency conditioned by ... regimes of discourse/power cannot be conflated with voluntarism or individualism, ... and in no way presupposes a choosing subject" (Butler, 1993: 15). Such strong declarations are, as I shall demonstrate in this chapter, continually undermined by the structure of theoretical claims in Butler's work. Notwithstanding the promising aspects of conceptualising discursive practices as performative speech acts, Butler's theorisation remains abstract and individualistic (McNay, 1999: 178, 189). Butler's assertion that "agency begins where sovereignty wanes" (Butler, 1997a: 16) needs to be understood, in this light, less as a claim to a post-Nietzschean, non-subjective form of agency, but as a theoretical limitation on the otherwise unconstrained power of the individual to manipulate structures. This result is diametrically opposed to the project of developing a subjectless conception of agency.

Gender Performances

Butler's theory of identity rejects the essentialist conception of gender as a substantial difference expressing an underlying natural sexual division. She conceptualises gender as constructed through social rituals supported by institutional power. In line with social constructivism, Butler proposes that gender identities are cultural performances that retroactively construct the "originary materiality" of sexuality (Butler, 1993: 10). The implication is that gender is not the expression of an "abiding substance," but a naturalised social ritual of heterosexuality (Butler, 1993: 12; Butler, 1999a: 22), and that there is a connection between the "metaphysics of substance" and the "identitarian categories of sex" (Butler, 1993: 12; Butler, 1999a: 22-25). Extending this analysis, Butler claims that the body is not a natural, material entity, but a discursively regulated, cultural construction (Butler, 1999a: 24), while gender is a performative that *produces* constative sex (Butler, 1993: 11; Butler, 1999a: 33).

Butler is resolutely hostile to the conception of an underlying substantial agent ("person") or natural entity ("body"). "[G]ender is always a doing," she asserts on the authority of Nietzsche, "though not a doing by a subject who might be said to pre-exist the deed" (Butler, 1999a: 33). According to Butler, there is no natural body before cultural inscription:

> Gender is the repeated stylisation of the body, a set of repeated acts within a highly rigid regulatory frame that congeal over time to produce the appearance of substance, of a natural sort of being. A political genealogy of gender ontologies ... will deconstruct the substantive appearance of gender into its constitutive acts and locate ... those acts within the compulsory frames set by the various forces that police the social appearance of gender (Butler, 1999a: 43-44).

Despite drawing on Freudian theory, for Butler, the psychoanalytic concept of the Law is a product of the heterosexual matrix and has to be deconstructed, to demonstrate the plurality and dispersion of social norms, and the historicity of sexual taboos. She performs a historicist reading of Lévi-Straussian anthropology and Lacanian psychoanalysis, inspired by Foucault's critique of the repressive hypothesis, to propose a conception of gender identity that is supposed to be historically specific and socially mutable (Butler, 1999a: 45-100). According to the Foucauldian critique of the repressive hypothesis:

> desire and its repression are an occasion for the consolidation of juridical structures; desire is manufactured and forbidden as a ritual symbolic gesture whereby the juridical model exercises and consolidates its own power (Butler, 1999a: 96).

The "repression of desire" actually creates a field of anticipated transgressions, because any norm is constituted through a citation of its exceptions. Rejecting psychic interiority as the correlate of the repression of desire, Butler shifts "from interiority to gender performatives," by following Foucault in the proposition that normalisation involves the body as the site of a compulsion to signify (Butler, 1999a: 171). The style of the subject is the very modality of its subjection, because this inscription of individuation, taking the form of writing on the surfaces of the body, designates the "soul" as the "prison of the body":

> The figure of the interior soul understood as "within" the body is signified through its inscription *on* the body, even though its primary mode of signification is through its very absence, its potent invisibility. ...

The soul is precisely what the body lacks; hence, the body presents itself as a signifying lack (Butler, 1999a: 172).

Butler proposes that homosexuality and bisexuality operate as the "constitutive outside" of heterosexual norms (Butler, 1999a: 98), so that "the 'unthinkable' is thus fully within culture, but fully excluded from the *dominant* culture" (Butler, 1999a: 99). Yet, the signification of heterosexual identity on the body, as a necessarily divided and recited statement of the norm and its constitutive exclusions, "effects a false stabilisation of gender" (Butler, 1999a: 172). Inspired by deconstruction, Butler claims the "citational," or repetitive and decontextualisable character of performative utterances, opens the possibility for marginal subversion of the reigning gender norms through "resignification," or the repetition of a signification in a new context. Drawing upon an analysis of drag as an instance of resignification, she concludes that "gender parody reveals that the original identity after which gender fashions itself is an imitation without origin" (Butler, 1999a: 175). The subversive repetition of gender norms in unprecedented contexts displaces and denaturalises the hegemonic universality of heterosexuality, constituting a practical deconstruction of the politics of gender normalisation. Therefore, the destabilisations effected by parodic recitation and marginal gender practices "disrupt the regulatory fiction of heterosexual coherence" (Butler, 1999a: 173). "That regulatory ideal is then exposed as a fiction," she argues, "and a norm that disguises itself as a developmental law regulating the sexual field that it purports to describe" (Butler, 1999a: 173).

The norms of heterosexuality are sustained through acts that "are *performative* in the sense that the essence or identity that they otherwise purport to express are *fabrications* manufactured and sustained through corporeal signs and other discursive means" (Butler, 1999a: 173). Drag performances reveal that genders are simulacra (copies without originals) (Butler, 1999a: 175). Gender, then, is not constative but performative, and "drag fully subverts the distinction between inner and outer psychic space and effectively mocks both the expressive model of gender and the notion of a true gender identity" (Butler, 1999a: 174). The demystification of gender identities through parodic performances leads to Butler's advocacy of a "stylistics of existence," modelled on Sartre and Foucault. In a highly revealing early formulation, Butler claimed that gender needs to be considered "as *a corporeal style*, an 'act,' as it were, which is both *intentional* and *performative*, where 'performative' suggests a *dramatic* and contingent construction of meaning" (Butler, 1999a: 177 emphasis added).

Multiple Struggles for Cultural Recognition

Before analysing the theory of gender performances in more detail, though, I want to examine its medium of propagation, because the significance and

limitations of Butler's theory can only be grasped in their politico-histori-
cal context. During the last 30 years, a shift in the political grammar of social claims has happened, from political demands for redistributive justice
to identity-based struggles for cultural recognition (Fraser, 1996: 2-3, 11-39).
According to Fraser, "the 'struggle for recognition' is fast becoming the paradigmatic form of political conflict," where "group identity supplants class
interest as the chief medium of political mobilisation" (Fraser, 1996: 11). In
this context, postmarxism, as the left wing of postmodern politics, has been
tremendously influential, with its theory that the incompleteness of identity
is the root of social antagonism.

The shift from redistributive justice to cultural recognition frames Butler's work, in particular, and conditions her ambiguous relation to identity-based struggles.[2] To anticipate somewhat, Butler's ambivalence towards
"identity politics" can be summarised by observing that while Butler formally rejects the sovereign intentionality of the autonomous individual, she
nonetheless accepts a central postulate of identity politics, that the quest for
identity is the motor force of contemporary social conflict. There is a significant difference, however, between affirming the conjunctural centrality
of struggles for cultural recognition, and making them into the generative
principle of *all* social conflict. Of course, from the perspective of psychoanalysis, the quest for self-identity underlies an individual's participation in
social movements. But that does not mean that the social movement must
be only and exclusively oriented to the affirmation of the self-identity of its
members. A trade union, for instance, might struggle for demands reflective
of the material self-interest of its members, at the same time as participation
in the union campaign bestows a social identity transcending self-interest
on campaigners. Forms of postmarxism such as Butler's, in short, conflate
recognition of the importance of cultural struggle with its supposedly exclusive generative role in social structuration, and confuse the motivations
that drive social movement participation with the aims of the social struggles themselves.

By reworking the quest for identity as a struggle for intersubjective recognition—rather than the expression of the originary freedom of the autonomous individual—Butler returns identity politics to the existential Hegelianism defended in her *Subjects of Desire* (1987). Existential Hegelianism seeks,
along lines pioneered by Alexandre Kojève, to combine the Hegelian dialectic with the individual decision on an existential project (Kojève, 1980), thus

---

2. Nancy Fraser warns that "in the United States today, the expression 'identity politics'
is increasingly used as a derogatory term for feminism, anti-racism and anti-heterosexism"
(Fraser, 1996: 17-18), and her expression, linked to Axel Honneth's pathbreaking study of the
dynamics of "cultural recognition" (Honneth, 1995), seems preferable. Nonetheless, and with
this warning in mind, the term "identity politics" *does* capture the position of one wing of this
debate, which regards individual identity as *the* mainspring of social conflict.

locating identity-formation in a matrix of cultural possibilities dominated by struggles for recognition. Butler's intervention therefore effectively decentres identity politics without producing an epistemological break.

It is Butler's preference for the Hegelian conception of the struggle for recognition as the driving force in social conflict that influences her opposition to Fraser's hypothesis of a shift from political economy to cultural struggles (Butler, 1998: 33-47). Rejecting "the neo-conservatism within the Left that seeks to discount the cultural" (Butler, 1998: 47), Butler questions whether the economic reductionism of the "class Left" seeks to violently re-impose a new orthodoxy based on vulgar materialism. She also suspects that this position secretes homophobia, because the implied equation "merely cultural equals despised sexuality" aims to "reinstitute the discredited notion of secondary oppression" (Butler, 1998: 47). But then her argument takes a surprising—and symptomatically weak—turn.

Returning to the socialist feminism of the 1970s and 1980s, Butler argues that the social regulation of sexuality, through the institution of the family and the reproduction of gendered norms in the skilling of labour power, is an essential component of the capitalist mode of production (Butler, 1998: 38-43). The political bite of this position depends upon the assertion that "homophobia [is] *central* to the functioning of political economy" (Butler, 1998: 41 emphasis added), and so the "merely cultural" turns out to be *directly* economico-political. Characteristically for forms of social interactionism (that privilege intersubjective relations above structural determinations), then, Butler's social theory relies on functionalist assumptions that are explicitly contested by the literature she cites in support of her position—for instance, Michele Barrett's *Women's Oppression Today* (Barrett, 1980: 93-96). Anti-reductionist positions based in Althusserian social theory, such as that of Barrett, opened up the possibility of sustaining the argument that cultural struggles are equally as important as economic and political ones. But the relative autonomy of cultural forms that this argument requires depends on a refusal of the economic reduction of either women's oppression or homophobic exclusion to functional components in the capitalist mode of production—precisely the move that Butler's position reverses. But if I am right that Butler's postmarxism relies on a conflation of motivation with orientation that makes the quest for self-identity through struggles for cultural recognition into the motor force of all social conflict, then this is a move that she must make.

At the same time, Butler associates "class Left" resistance to the shift from the pole of political economy to the pole of cultural recognition with the classical Marxist assumption that culture is entirely excluded from political economy. From the classical perspective, culture figures as a contingent superstructural variation, external to the operations of the mode of production. Again, the Althusserian position that originally made positions like

Butler's possible is excluded from consideration as a social theoretical alternative to the binary opposition: class Left = political economy = class Marxist economic reductionism; cultural Left = cultural recognition = post-structuralist forms of postmodern politics. And to be fair to Fraser too, Butler's criticism is a distortion of her position. Fraser's distinction between economic injustice and cultural denigration is analytic, designed to enable the construction of a system of ideal types, polarised between "exploited classes," suffering economic injustice and demanding redistributive remedies, and "despised sexualities," enduring cultural denigration and calling for symbolic recognition. Butler overlooks the analytic character of this distinction, which is based on the explicit statement that this separation is impossible in practice (Fraser, 1996: 15), and seeks to conceptualise a political shift that reflects the relative autonomy of the institutional terrains of contemporary capitalism (Fraser, 1995: 68-93). To associate Fraser—who *endorses* the struggle for cultural recognition as the demand for a new type of justice, based on the distribution of cultural goods (Fraser, 2000: 107-120)—with the denigration of cultural struggles is excessive, perhaps even egregious.

Indeed, Butler contests the division between political economy and cultural recognition by assimilating it (quite speciously in Fraser's case) to *another* opposition, between "cultural recognition and material oppression" (Butler, 1998: 41). She is then at liberty to demonstrate the cultural materialist case for the materiality of ideological apparatuses, to rehearse the argument that race and gender are modalities in which class is lived, and to assert the material aspects of the oppression of a "despised sexuality". What this demonstrates is that culture is materially linked to political economy. It does not demonstrate that they are the same, which is what Butler needs to show to defend her suggestion that an *analytic* distinction between political economy and cultural recognition is impossible (Butler, 1998: 41).

The clear entailment of Butler's claim, combined with the assumption that gender identities are *directly* functional to economic reproduction, is that the social field is a homogeneous functional whole. Such a conception, while consonant with the Hegelian notion that ethical life (the objective institutions of social life) forms an organic totality, is directly opposed to the leading contention of postmodern "identity politics," that the multiple subject-positions "adopted" by the subject are not determined by social structures (Laclau, 1985: 32; Laclau and Mouffe, 1985: 118-121). For if the adoption of a marginalised subject-position directly affects the social structure, then it follows that the relation between normal subject-positions and structural determinations is not even relatively autonomous, but actually an isomorphism. By contrast, in her work on speech act theory, Butler explicitly refuses any collapse of the regional distinction between signifier and materiality (Butler, 1993: 4-12), or between speech act and social conduct (Butler, 1997a: 72-77). Behind this inconsistent refusal of the analytic distinction between redistributive justice and cultural recognition, then, lies something else, which is prefigured in Butler's silence regarding Fraser's criticism of performativity, namely, that it theorises sexual emancipation as the liberation *from identity* (Fraser, 1998: 140-149).

While the struggles of the New Social Movements definitely combine economic, political and cultural demands, struggles for cultural recognition do not aim *directly* at political rights, universal justice, economic redistribution and so forth. By contrast with the standard political logic of modernity—the dynamic of social equality and political liberty—demands for cultural recognition rely upon claims for recognition of the worth of individual bearers of marginalised symbolic identities (Honneth, 1995). For Butler, recognition of marginalised identities cannot be solved by a redistribution of cultural goods, as a shift in the distinction enjoyed by a social identity implies the consolidation of its existence. Thus, instead of claims to redress denigration, Butler proposes the dispersion of the "identitarian" polarity of the "heterosexual matrix," which, she claims, constructs homosexual identities in the first place (Butler, 1999a: 129, 176, 185, 189). Despite the apparent radicalism of this claim, its effect, in context, is (as I shall show in this chapter) to prevent the emergence of demands for political liberation and social equality.

According to Butler, "in a sense, all my work remains within the orbit of a certain set of Hegelian questions," revolving upon desire and recognition, the subject and alterity (Butler, 1999b: xiv). For proponents of the Hegelian struggle for recognition, the realm of social signification enjoys primacy in the determination of the structures of ethical life, because the Hegelian assumption is that the development of subjectivity is the main dynamic in historical transformations. The subject can only know itself through another, but the process of recognition and constitution of self-identity impels the effort to annihilate or subordinate the other (Butler, 1987a: 37). As Butler indicates, the Hegelian shift to the cultural field generating the modern (Kantian) individual does not for a moment negate the postulate of world-constituting subjectivity. Indeed, the attributes of the "universal individual" are transposed onto social subjectivity, while a disembodied phenomenological intentionality looks on and describes the progress of consciousness. Therefore the Hegelian subject is interpreted as a "struggling individual on the brink of collective identity" (Butler, 1987a: 58), who paradoxically requires the recognition of the Other they negate. Butler's position is a postmodern variation on this line,[3] and her difference with identity politics—as

---

3. For the Hegelian exposition of mutual recognition, see Hegel (Hegel, 1952: ; Hegel, 1977). For an eloquent contemporary defense and exposition of the concept of recognition, consult Williams (Williams, 1992: ; Williams, 1997). For the Hegelian theory of history, see Hegel (Hegel, 1956). Axel Honneth's pathbreaking work on mutual recognition (Honneth, 1995) is of course the implied referent of this debate. Honneth reconstructs the Hegelian

I shall demonstrate—consists in the shift from individual to intersubjective generative mechanisms of social structures and political conflicts. While social subjectivity is the generative principle of institutional structures, individual identity is the main transformative agency. Butler's assertion of the materiality of culture, I suggest, therefore masks a fundamental defense of the primacy of individual subjectivity in the transformation of objective structures.

Beyond Identity Politics?

Butler's intervention into struggles for cultural recognition adapts an existential Hegelianism to postmodern theory, then, by recasting the master-slave dialectic as the relation between dominant identity, generated within the "heterosexual matrix," and marginalised homosexual identities. She recasts the "identitarian" categories of identity politics as relational complexes in a dialectical process and then interprets this through the lens of a Foucauldian understanding of power as multiple and productive. According to Butler, the heterosexual matrix generates a power deployed through multiple sites, and the normalisation of heterosexuality requires the prohibition and exclusion of homosexuality. Indeed, Butler proposes that all socio-political identity is dialogically structured because it includes a hidden reference to its "constitutive outside," in an abject, marginalised identity (Butler, 1993: 15-16). For instance, normative heterosexual gender identities are supported/subverted by a melancholic dis-identification with their marginalised "exterior," in homosexuality.

The concept of the quest for self-identity as the driving force in social conflict rehearses the Hegelian theory of the struggle for recognition on the terrain of so-called "postmodern identity politics". It is the primacy of subjectivity that represents the continuity between Butler's Hegelian theory and identity politics. Butler, of course, is no stranger to analysing the tenacity of a conceptual constellation—even, or perhaps especially, one consisting of a structure of misrecognition—for this was the thesis of her *investigation* on the French reception of Hegel. The "labour of the negative" of the Hegelian "subject of desire," she proposes, is preserved in negation in the successive criticisms of the teleological narrative of the *Phenomenology of Spirit* (Butler, 1987a). Butler, in *Subjects of Desire*, explains this structure of "nega-

insights in the context of post-Freudian psychoanalysis and a variant of discourse ethics, to supply a concept of the subject as produced within an intersubjective struggle for recognition whose highest form is the desire for solidarity. Where for Honneth, the struggle for recognition thereby becomes the motor force for moral progress—legitimating the notion that social conflicts represent an ethical learning experience for societies and that the progressive expansion and democratisation of ethical life springs from the resolution of these conflicts in mutual recognition—for Butler, postmodernism means the impossibility of any such unitary and linear "master narrative".

tion without transcendence," or "preservation despite negation," operative in the "general economy" of post-Hegelian theories of the subject. Despite the migration of the self-reflexive self-identity of Hegel's subject from a regulative concept (Hyppolite, Kojève) (Butler, 1987a: 63-92), to an imaginary yet necessary ideal (Sartre) (Butler, 1987a: 101-174), and its termination as a meretricious fiction to be endlessly denounced by poststructuralism (Lacan, Derrida, Foucault, Deleuze) (Butler, 1987a: 175-238), Butler contends that Hegelian self-reflexive identity nonetheless lives a return of the repressed in the poststructuralist prolongation of the subject of desire. Thus, Butler defends the relevance of the phenomenological project even while accepting the fragmentation of subjectivity and the end of the master narrative of increasing self-identity (Butler, 1987a: 230-238).

That Butler's brilliant analysis of existentialism and post-structuralism can nevertheless anticipate the trajectory of her own work, *vis-à-vis* identity politics, can be explained through her supposition that the subject of desire, as the centre of knowledge, is preserved, not exposed, by its division and decentring (Butler, 1987a: 175). What this suggests is an indifference to the distinction between subject-centred phenomenological description and the "process without a subject" of theoretical knowledge. The project of a phenomenology of subject-formation—leading to a subject-centred description of a subjectless process of agency—is inherently contradictory. In postmodern theories of the "subject-effect," the "subject" (the ego) is dispersed across a multiplicity of subject-positions and its world-constituting power is denaturalised, revealed as the product of cultural discourses. In this case, transcendental subjectivity has not been shaken, merely transferred to the field of cultural practices, which function as subject to the object of institutionalised materiality. One consequence of this strategy is that the underlying assumption of the world-constituting power of the subject—which in identity politics takes a blatantly Cartesian form—is not challenged by Butler, but merely displaced.

According to advocates of identity politics, the autonomy of subject-positions from structural determinations is the defining characteristic of the politics of the NSM (Aronowitz, 1992: 1-9; Aronowitz, 1994: 5-79; Smith, 1998: 54-86). Theories of identity-based social conflict, as we have seen in chapters One and Two, concentrate on the ability of the individual to select from a "menu" of subject-positions, asserting that the fluidity of identity is a necessary condition for democracy and that progressive multicultural politics depends upon a conceptual shift from essential identities to multiple subject-positions (Smith, 1994: ; Norval, 1996: ; Howarth, 2000). This constellation of positions defines identity politics as that particular strategy, within the broad field of cultural politics, which privileges the conscious intentionality of the autonomous individual and their ability to rationally select from a subjective menu of options. Discourses of identity therefore converge upon contemporary liberal political philosophy, which theorises procedural guarantees (the neutrality of the state and citizen rights) for individuals, whose conception of the sovereign good is held to be contextually selected from a personal hierarchy of values (Rawls, 1985: ; Rawls, 1993).

Indeed, Butler's original idea of identity as an intentional dramatic performance suggests a voluntarist conception of individual agency. When this is combined with Butler's functionalist grasp of social theory, performativity becomes reminiscent of structural-functionalism's notion of the individual's ability to obtain critical distance from their social roles. Despite Butler's subsequent disavowal of voluntarism (Butler, 1993: 15), her early work has frequently been invoked as a theoretical support for the notion that gender is a voluntary dramatic performance initiated by a conscious subject, a subject which "wears its identity as drag" (Probyn, 1995: 79) and whose intentions govern the subversive or recuperative political meanings of its acts. Many of Butler's supporters—such as, for instance, David Bell and cothinkers—apply the theory of performativity developed in *Gender Trouble* to reinstate the sovereign intentionality of the autonomous individual. Taking gay skinheads as exemplary of a "progressive identity" (Bell, Binnie *et al.*, 1994: 35), they claim that this is the result of "consciously inhabiting" an otherwise hostile cultural milieu (Bell, Binnie *et al.*, 1994: 36). This consciousness converts a subcultural uniform into subversive parody because, although the gay skinhead "passes" as straight amongst heterosexuals, their street presence surreptitiously enables "mutually constituting exchanges of glances," whereby "gay skinheads create a queer space in a heterosexual world, which is in itself empowering" (Bell, Binnie *et al.*, 1994: 37).

In an important critical analysis of identity politics, Moya Lloyd traces the reliance of Butler's supporters on authorial intention to persistent ambiguities in Butler's own position (Lloyd, 1999: 195-213). Butler at once asserts the constructed character of social identities and appears to tacitly assume that an unreconstructed strategic calculation of interests remains the basis for political interventions. In the hands of Butler's supporters, this leads to a voluntarist theory of the radical mutability of gender performances which neglects the regional distinctions between parody and politics, performance and performative, intentionality and agency (Lloyd, 1999: 199-203). In this way the sovereign intentionality of the rational agent characteristic of liberal political philosophy makes its explicit reappearance within postmarxian discourse.

Imaginary Subjects

The revealing notion of social identity as an intentional dramatic performance betrays a conviction that individual praxis is the genetic origin of social structures. In reply, Butler's supporters claim that her "Nietzschean-

Foucauldian" subjectless conception of agency is the main resource for contesting the voluntarist interpretation of performativity (Schrift, 1997: ; Mc-
Nay, 1999). According to Butler, "all signification takes place within the
orbit of a compulsion to repeat," so that the task for a subversive identity
politics "is not *whether* to repeat, but *how* to repeat and, through a radical
proliferation of gender, to displace the very norms that enable repetition itself" (Butler, 1999a: 148). The structural constraints surrounding the agent,
condemning the individual to strategies of recuperative or subversive repetition of speech acts, supposedly prevent any voluntaristic interpretation
of a subject who wilfully "decides," on a day-by-day basis, to adopt this or
that subject-position (Garber, 1996: 183-184; Salih, 2002: 43-71). Likewise, it
is claimed that the Foucauldian dimensions of Butler's theory prevent any
facile slippage from "performative speech acts" to "dramatic performances"
(Schrift, 2001: 12-23). Butler claims that the agency in question is not that
of the *subject* (as in individualist-voluntarist accounts), but of language itself,
whereby we can locate "'agency within the possibility of a variation on ...
repetition" (Butler, 1999a: 145).

Butler's supporters are insufficiently critical of her defense, however, for
what is in question is not the *omnipotence* of the subject, or their ability to determine the field of subject-positions in a postmodern form of intellectual intuition. In question is the phenomenological assumption that a free-floating
intentionality, standing aside from all processes of subjectivation, might become the launching point for the decision of "*how* to repeat". Who (or what)
decides "*how* to repeat"? On what basis is the decision to resist power made?
Assuming that it is ultimately conceded that the subject decides on the basis
of strategic calculations of material interests, or alternatively on the basis of
unconscious desires, where are these interests formed and what is the efficacy of individual resistance? Does the formation of social subjectivity actually
determine objective structures? Can it really be claimed, without lapsing into
voluntarist forms of idealism, that the adoption of identities somehow "precipitates" the materiality of institutions?

By depriving the subject of its power as genetic origin of structures and
instead analysing the process of subjectification as a variable and complex
function of power, Foucault *appears* to eliminate the autonomous individual. For Foucault, ritualised institutional practices take the form of disciplinary norms that literally conform subjects by subjecting them to regimes of
bodily signification—drills, routines, conventions—which inscribe the illusory psychic interiority of the soul on the socialised exterior of the body,
so that "the soul is the prison of the body" (Foucault, 1977: 30). Foucault's
imaginary "soul" corresponds exactly to Althusser's ideological "subject".
The resistance of the subject (now taking into account the conflation of the
psychoanalytic and political meanings) is merely a ruse of power, for power
depends upon this illusory interiority and its frustrated struggles with au-

thority for its elaboration, extension and penetration into the depth of the individual. The problem is that this results in a form of objectivist determinism that prevents the emergence of effective resistance while mechanically reducing the subject to a mere reflection of the social field (an effect of institutional socialisation, that is, a cultural dupe). Foucault's subsequent work on the "aesthetics of existence," instead of solving this problem, merely inverted it, asserting that although the subject is formed through constraints, nonetheless, the possibility remained open for "practices of liberation" of a voluntarist kind (McNay, 1994: 88-124). It might be said, then, that Foucault exposes the constitutive subject—the better to save the political individual.

Despite making some advances concerning the openness of structure as a condition for agency, Butler rehearses Foucault's trajectory in reverse, shifting from individualist voluntarism to mechanical objectivism, in part because her conception of subjectivity and objectivity remain damagingly abstract (McNay, 1999: 177-178). Drawing on the Foucault of *Discipline and Punish*, Butler claims that genealogical investigation of gender categories discloses "the political stakes in designating as an *origin* and *cause* those identity categories that are in fact the *effects* of institutions, practices, discourses, with multiple and diffused points of origin" (Butler, 1999a: viii-ix). The collocation of a (later) introduction repudiating the autonomous subject, with an (earlier) exposition of performativity in terms of an "intentional, dramatic performance" of identity, makes for interesting reading. Certainly, the sovereign subject of classical, liberal political philosophy and social theory is finished. In its place stands the post-liberal political individual, who only intervenes within an intersubjective network. Dethroned from the position of generative origin and constitutive subject, the individual in the theory of performativity nonetheless remains the primary force in the transformation of institutional materiality. In a series of displacements, Butler seeks to disperse the notion of an originary identity, which she associates with the constitutive subject. She denies the pertinence of the Cartesian pre-discursive identity of conscious intentionality and substantial entity ("I think therefore I am"), citing Nietzsche's claim that "there is no 'being' behind doing, effecting, becoming; 'the doer' is merely a fiction added to the deed—the deed is everything" (Butler, 1999a: 25). What Butler is rejecting is the notion of psychic interiority and substantive entity as constituting a pre-discursive self-identity. As she comments:

> One might be tempted to say that identity categories are insufficient because every subject-position is the site of converging relations of power that are not univocal. But such a formulation underestimates the radical challenge to the subject that such converging relations imply. For there is no self-identical subject who houses or bears these relations, no site at which these relations converge. This converging and interarticulation is

the contemporary fate of the subject. In other words, the subject as a self-identical identity is no more (Butler, 1993: 229-230).

The potential incoherence of claiming that while individuals are interpellated as subjects, there is no "site at which these relations converge," indicates the strain of simultaneously asserting the dispersion of the ego and the determination of the body by psychic structures. The problem is that in swinging from subjective voluntarism to mechanical objectivism, Butler has not, in actuality, dispensed with the assumption of a pre-discursive intentionality. She has only translated the register of its existence, from self-knowledge, to auto-affection. To see why, we need to examine the thesis that the subject is formed through Imaginary processes.

Foucault's imaginary "soul" corresponds exactly to Althusser's ideological "subject". Indeed, Althusser's reduction of the subject to exclusively Imaginary relations (that is, to the ego) prepared the multitude of post-Althusserian, postmodern conceptions, which, beginning with Foucault's work, *Discipline and Punish*, regarded the subject as reducible to a dispersed multiplicity of subject-positions. Althusser's position is revisited in Butler's important article, "Conscience Doth Make Subjects of Us All" (Butler, 1995: 6-26), where Butler expands upon the thesis that the Imaginary is solely responsible for subject-formation, by taking advantage of the paradoxes of the philosophy of reflection. Her central claim is that "for Althusser, the efficacy of ideology consists in part in the formation of *conscience*" (Butler, 1995: 13), so that "to become a 'subject' is, thus, to have been presumed guilty, then tried and declared innocent" (Butler, 1995: 16). Indeed, because this effect of "hailing" is not a singular act, but a continuous repetition of ideological interpellations, the subject-citizen is constantly demonstrating their innocence through conformist practices.

Butler grasps the anticipation of identity effected in ideological interpellation as an ambivalent relation to authority that precedes identity-formation, based on a combination of guilt and love. A passionate attachment to the image of the law that precedes subjectification is the basis for this ambivalent pre-identification, which makes it possible for subjects to recognise themselves in the call of conscience. The "subject" is "driven by a love of the law that can only be satisfied by ritual punishment" (Butler, 1995: 24). This does not solve the problem, of course, but instead merely displaces it from categories of knowledge (the problem of how I can *know* myself before the mirror image) to the register of affect (the problem of how I can *love* my existence sufficiently to want to be called into being by a guilty conscience).

Butler therefore *accepts the postulate of a pre-discursive auto-affection*, so that the subject originally desires identity. Indeed, she claims that the "I" comes "into social being … because I have a certain inevitable attachment to my existence, because a certain narcissism takes hold of any term that confers existence" (Butler, 1997b: 104). Glib references to Nietzsche notwithstanding, the postulate of a pre-discursive, narcissistic auto-affection as the mainspring of the subject originates with Fichte, who was the first to propose that the subject is initially the *deed* of self-positing (Henrich, 1982: 15-53).

Melancholy Identity: The Unhappy Consciousness

The supposition of an originary narcissism is the basis for Butler's later resurrection of psychic interiority, including a spectacular repudiation of Foucault's critique of the repressive hypothesis (Butler, 1993: 22). Butler's limited rehabilitation of psychoanalysis insists that Freud remains an indispensable resource for thinking subjection and subjectivation, because without the psyche there is no possibility of resistance. As Butler suggests, the psyche resists and exceeds the normalisation process (Butler, 1997b: 14-15):

> Does the reduction of the psychoanalytically rich notion of the psyche to that of the imprisoning soul not eliminate the possibility of resistance to normalisation and to subject formation, a resistance that emerges precisely from the incommensurability between psyche and subject? (Butler, 1997b: 87).

Butler is suggesting that something (the "psyche") exists beyond, and sometimes interrupts, the Althusserian "subject" or Foucauldian "soul". I would certainly endorse this assertion of Butler's. But what exactly is the status of Butler's psyche? Is it a restatement of the psychoanalytic concept of the unconscious? Is the philosophical notion of primordial auto-affection the same as the Freudian concept of primary narcissism, or the Lacanian mirror stage (Lacan, 1977: 1-7)? Butler's rhetoric, I suggest, resonates with psychoanalytic terminology, but without any theoretical correspondence. She constantly conflates the elementary psychoanalytic distinction between the repression of unconscious desire and the resistance conducted by the ego, generating a generalised politico-psychological "resistance". This should warn us that her relation to Freudian theory is one of syncretic appropriations through selective citation, rather than a theoretical synthesis.

Butler argues that the "sublimation" of body into soul leaves a "bodily remainder" which exceeds the processes of normalisation, and this remainder survives as a "constitutive loss" that marks the body as a signifying lack (Butler, 1997b: 92). Hence, according to Butler, "desire is *never* renounced, but becomes preserved and reasserted in the very structure of renunciation" (Butler, 1997b: 56; Butler, 1997a: 117). Her contention is that heterosexuality emerges from a simultaneous repudiation and preservation of primary homosexuality, because "renunciation requires the very homosexuality that it condemns" (Butler, 1997b: 143). Therefore, she claims, both heterosexuals and homosexuals exist in a culture of gender melancholy, unable to mourn a lost homosexual cathexis (Butler, 1997b: 139).

The central category for Butler's concept of identity is melancholia, which is distinguished psychoanalytically from mourning by the inability to acknowledge the loss of a libidinal object-cathexis (Freud, 1984: 251-268). Specifically, Butler claims that the primordial object-cathexis is homosexual, and melancholic heterosexuality is generated through the prohibition of this libidinal investment (Butler, 1999a: 63). Interpreting melancholia through the Freudian notion of the ego as a precipitate of abandoned object-cathexes (of identifications), Butler combines this with the Freudian observation that the ego is a bodily ego (Butler, 1993: 13). However, she literalises what for Freud is a body-*image* and makes the physical surface of the body coextensive with the ego (Prosser, 1998: 41). Butler also asserts—rather than demonstrates—that the taboo on incest is *preceded* by the prohibition of homosexuality (Butler, 1999a: 63). For Butler, this implies that hyperbolic gender identifications (rigid identities, or identitarianism) are instigated through the melancholic inability to mourn a lost primordial homosexuality, and so heterosexuality is characterised by the structure of self-loathing typical of melancholia.

Butler's speculations regarding the melancholic formation of subjectivity are indeed interesting. In the more rigorously theorised form of Kleinian reflections, such ideas have been productively applied within psychoanalysis to think the lost maternal object beyond the exclusive concentration on the paternal figure characteristic of some Lacanian theory (Lupton and Reinhard, 1993: 1-34). The claim, however, that before any gendering of the subject, the subject desires the parent of the same gender (for this is the structural requirement of the claim to an originary homosexuality in both masculine and feminine subjectivities) seems an impossible loop, and Butler does not try to support it with any Freudian references.

Most importantly, though, Butler's explanation of the processes of repression and identification does not sufficiently differentiate between the Freudian concept of "introjection" and the Hegelian notion of "intro-reflection". Where the Freudian process involves *metaphorisation*, the Hegelian category invokes the figure of *metonymy*. Initially, Freud supposes in "The Ego and the Id" that the mother is the object of a libidinal cathexis (Freud, 1984: 19-39). This cathexis is prohibited and the object becomes "lost" for the ego through the process of repression. In this process the image of the father as authority figure (as agent of prohibition) is taken into the unconscious substrate of the ego ("introjected"), where it is set up as an ideal identification. Thus, the Freudian process involves a substitution of an idealised figure for a libidinal object. By contrast, the Hegelian process of intro-reflection happens when the essential structure of an external process is reflected into an internal process, becoming its dynamic. The difference is immense: in Freudian identification, the psyche cannot be a microcosm of the society, whereas in Hegelian intro-reflection, this is precisely what it is.

The Hegelian "Unhappy Consciousness" is the result of the slave's internalisation of the authority of the former master, resulting in a psyche split between the universality of abstract laws and the particularity of sensuous existence (Hegel, 1977). Taking itself as an object of scorn, the Unhappy Consciousness oscillates between spiritual universality and material singularity (Butler, 1997b: 46), becoming an "incessant performer of renunciation" (Butler, 1997b: 49) and a fascinated spectator to its own abjection (Butler, 1997b: 50). Initially, as we have seen, Butler combines the Hegelian dialectics of master and slave (recast as heterosexuality and homosexuality) with the Foucauldian theory of power as multiple and productive, to theorise the conflict between the heterosexual matrix and a marginalised homosexuality. The next step is to return to *Discipline and Punish* and re-read it through the *Phenomenology of Spirit* (Butler, 1997b: 33). Just as in Hegel's *Phenomenology*, then, where the conflict between master and slave is intro-reflected in the "Unhappy Consciousness," the melancholy subjectivity diagnosed in *The Psychic Life of Power* (1997) is the intro-reflection of the struggle for identity analysed in *Gender Trouble*. The Butlerian "psychic life of power" springs from the intro-reflection of the conflict between heterosexual matrix and homosexual margin, to form a melancholic subjectivity divided between an affirmed heterosexual identity ("the subject") and a denied homosexual identity ("the psyche").

As with the Hegelian work, the main focus of Butler's reconceptualisation of the "Unhappy Consciousness" in *The Psychic Life of Power* is the emergence of intersubjective rationality (the "world of culture") from within the dialectics of self-consciousness. Butler proposes that the destructive rage of heterosexual melancholia is cultivated by the state and internalised by citizens-subjects, but that an aggressive melancholia can be productively deployed to destroy the superego agency and turn the ego's hatred outwards against the "culture of death" (Butler, 1997b: 190-191). Butler's tendency is to directly equate the positive legal framework of the society with the psychic structure of prohibitions that institutes subjectivity, reflected in the (otherwise strange) call to resist interpellation and "expose the law [of culture] as less powerful than it seems" (Butler, 1997b: 130). Thus, the "psychic life of power" turns out to be a figure for the reflection of power structures into a divided subjectivity, whereby a state-sponsored structure of marginalisation and a "culture of death" become intro-reflected into the psyche as a melancholic heterosexuality.

Furthermore, "in *Psychic* Butler seems to conflate performativity, performance and psychotherapy as she argues that what is 'acted out' in 'gender performances' is the unresolved grief of a repudiated homosexuality" (Butler, 1997b: 146; Salih, 2002: 132-133). These conflations are evidence for a systematic return to the ego-dominated politics of identity, where Butler's initial blurring of performative speech acts and intentional dramatic performances is now compounded by an identification of the resistance of the ego with political subversion. In line with this preference for the mirror relations of the Imaginary over the differential structures of the Symbolic, Butler's progressive politics display openly the dialectics of imaginary rivalry characteristic of the structure of the ego. Endorsing narcissistic rage, Butler stages a triumphant resurrection of the individual psyche while denouncing the supposed unity of the ego. She proposes that the renunciation of any claim to unitary self-identity holds open the prospect of constructive mourning instead of destructive melancholia. Recognition of melancholia involves accepting self-division and otherness, Butler claims, so that the other is installed as an identification in the ego (Butler, 1997b: 195-196). The Butlerian programme, it should be becoming clear, represents a sort of "Ego Psychology in reverse": where Ego Psychology sought to fortify the ego in the name of social adjustment (Lacan, 1988), Butler seeks to disperse the ego in the interests of permanent marginal subversion. Far from effecting a Freudian analysis of the subject, Butler's individual, driven forward by the incompleteness of an impossible desire for self-identity, rehearses the existential-Hegelian conception of the "Unhappy Consciousness," after postmodernism.

The Symbolic Law and the Phallic Signifier

Butler's critical appropriation of psychoanalysis aims to retrieve the notion of a "morphological Imaginary"—or bodily ego (Butler, 1993: 13)—from what she takes to be Lacan's "heterosexist structuralism" (Butler, 1993: 90). But, her conception of the psyche has in common with the Freudian unconscious only (as Althusser might have said) a lexicon and some theoretical opponents. It is closer to the postmodern conception of the dispersion of the formerly "unified ego": specifically, the division of the ego into multiple partitions as its specular totalisation of an ensemble of subject-positions is exposed as imaginary. Irrespective, then, of the criticisms that Butler accurately directs to Lacan (and Žižek) for their personal attitudes on particular questions (Butler, 1993a: 187-222; Butler, 2000a: 143-148), her global opposition of the imaginary morphology of the bodily ego to the unconscious instituted through a prohibition on incest effectively defends the ego from the unconscious.

It needs to be said that Butler's positioning of homosexuality as a subversive margin within a homophobic culture has a political significance as a rhetorical intervention. This rhetorical stance also explains the claim to the "subversive" potential of surrendering a coherent identity and the assertion that positioning the marginalisation of homosexuality on the same level (if not a more fundamental level) as the taboo on incest somehow opens new prospects for liberation. As with drag, homosexual desire "panics" heterosexual identity by disclosing powerful repressed desires (Butler, 1997b: 136).

Intuitively, Butler's claim that the hyperbolic identifications of "complete-ly straight" identities are symptomatic of repressed desire (Butler, 1997b: 147)—if not heterosexual melancholy—is appealing.

Nonetheless, the idea that homosexuality is "produced" to maintain heterosexuality is politically and theoretically problematic. Politically, it flirts with the reduction of queer identity to a functional role in relation to heterosexuality: "reading Butler, one occasionally gets the impression that gay desire is not complete unless it is somehow installed subversively inside heterosexuality" (Dollimore, 1996: 535). In Freudian terms, because what happens in identification is the substitution of an image of authority for a libidinal object, claiming a primary homosexuality is equivalent to the collapse of homosexual desire.

Butler's rehabilitation of psychoanalysis involves the elaboration of an "alternative imaginary to the hegemonic imaginary" (Butler, 1993: 91) centred on what she calls the "lesbian phallus". It also entails a rejection of the "sexual difference fundamentalism" that makes the phallic signifier into a phallic symbol, whose privileged referent is always the penis (Butler, 1993: 84). Butler is suspicious that a feminist rejection of the phallus (for instance, for the maternal body as privileged) reinstates the very structure of essentialism that it reacts against. Therefore, she seeks to deconstruct the phallus—and the polarity according to which men "have" the phallus while women have to "be" the phallus—by means of a relativisation and decentring of the privilege of the phallic signifier. Defending this position, Butler explains that:

> The phallus as signifier within lesbian sexuality will engage the spectre of shame and repudiation delivered by that feminist theory which would secure a feminine morphology in its radical distinctness from the masculine. ... Traversing these divisions, the lesbian phallus signifies a desire that is produced historically at the crossroads of these prohibitions, and is never fully free of the normative demands that condition its possibility and that it nevertheless seeks to subvert (Butler, 1993: 86).

In line with the general conception of performative resignification as always-already enmeshed in the heteronormative matrix it contests, Butler opts for subversion instead of separatism. As a result of her deconstructive intervention, Butler claims that "if the phallus is an imaginary effect ... then its structural place is no longer determined by the logical relation of mutual exclusion entailed by a heterosexist version of sexual difference" (Butler, 1993: 88).

To complete this retrieval of psychoanalysis, Butler confronts not only Lacan's essay on "The Signification of the Phallus" (Lacan, 1977: 281-291), but also his theory of discursive registers. Butler collapses the distinction between Imaginary and Symbolic, while rejecting the Real entirely (Butler,

1993: 78-79, 187-222). This is critical to her discursive strategy, for "Butler does not distinguish the Imaginary other from the Symbolic Other, a collapse of terminology equivalent to suggesting that there is no difference between the subject and the ego" (van Pelt, 2000: 151). Indeed, Butler's practice sometimes appears simply to be the collocation of apparently incriminating quotes, in the service of what she herself calls a "selective reading of Lacan" (Butler, 1993: 72). The effort to play off Freud against Lacan produces a theoretical syncretism that does not really come to grips with the fundamental purpose of Lacan's registers, or Freud's topography, namely, to demarcate what is strictly unconscious from that which the ego might accept.

Butler's retrieval of psychoanalysis is nonetheless strategically vital to her enterprise, because her claim to evade voluntarism rests upon the assertion that in performativity, "what is 'performed' works to conceal, if not to disavow, what remains opaque [and] unconscious," and "the opacity of the unconscious sets limits to the exteriorisation of the psyche" (Butler, 1993a: 24). Indeed, Butler probably would reject the allegation that she collapses the unconscious subject into the conscious ego, for she states that "the psyche, which includes the unconscious, is very different from the [ego]: the psyche is precisely what exceeds the imprisoning effects of the discursive demand to inhabit a coherent identity" (Butler, 1997b: 136). These formal assertions, however, are belied by the theoretical content of her efforts to theorise the unconscious, for Butler's belief in the primacy of the Imaginary—pre-eminently the register of the ego—means that she has no theoretical resources to lend substance to the claim to think a discourse beyond that of imaginary rivalries.

Indeed, while for Butler, the unity and centredness of the bodily ego exists only as sustained by the "sexually marked name" (Butler, 1993: 72), the phallic signifier performs exactly the same role in the Symbolic that the specular totality of the body plays in the Imaginary (Butler, 1993: 76, 81). When Lacan claims a disjunction between the dualisms characteristic of the Imaginary and the decentred differential order of the signifier, Butler insists that the Symbolic phallus exists by virtue of a denial of its constitution through the specular Imaginary (Butler, 1993: 79). From the *relatedness* of Imaginary and Symbolic, Butler derives, rhetorically, the textually unsupported proposition that the Imaginary is *primary* and *original*. Consistent with this position, Butler maintains that the phallic signifier is privileged because it alone has a unitary signified (Butler, 1993: 90), and that this can only be a *symbol* of the penis. The absolute determination to interpret the phallus as an Imaginary recapitulation of anatomy that is at work here is displayed when Butler cites Lacan—"*Il est encore moins l'organe, pénis ou clitoris, qu'il symbolise*" (Butler, 1993: Lacan cited 83). Instead of translating "penis *or* clitoris," Butler glosses this straightforwardly as "the phallus *symbolises* the penis" (Butler, 1993: 83).

It seems that Butler has mistakenly interpreted Lacan's position, that the phallic signifier is that which is "to designate as a whole the effect of there being a signified" (Butler, 1993: Lacan cited 82), to mean that the phallic signifier *alone has a signified*. For a symbol is nothing else except the excess of signified over signifier in an image—something which would indeed license the claim that "if the phallus is an imaginary effect, a wishful transfiguration, then it is not merely the *symbolic* status of the phallus that is called into question, but every distinction between the symbolic and the imaginary" (Butler, 1993: 79). But Lacan explains that the phallic signifier is a signifier *without signified*, a moment not of the polysemic excess of meaning, but of nonsense. Hence Lacan's progressive theoretical shift, from the "phallic signifier" to the master signifier (Fink, 1995a: 55-56). Butler claims to employ psychoanalytic categories descriptively and with no reference to clinical or empirical literature, conducting instead a "cultural engagement with psychoanalytic theory" (Butler, 1997b: 138). Let us recall *which* culture this is: that of *homo economicus*, the commodity and the ego. It should come as no surprise then, that Butler's highly imaginative and methodologically unconstrained use of psychoanalytic categories actually leads towards a denial of the specifically Freudian unconscious.

Butler's Postmodern Existentialism

Butler's denials that she has produced a new existentialism are therefore not very convincing. The affinities between performativity and existentialism are genetic, as Butler's theory of gender develops directly from existentialism (Butler, 1986: ; Heinämaa, 1997: ; Hughes and Witz, 1997), and structural, as the fundamental reliance of existential phenomenology on transcendental intentionality remains a latent assumption of Butler's work. According to her, of course, performativity is "not a return to an existential theory of the self as constituted through its acts, for the existential theory maintains a prediscursive structure for both the self and its acts" (Butler, 1999a: 181). This is a misrecognition, for there remains "a great deal of existentialist thinking still at work in Butler's philosophy," and French existentialism can be said to enjoy a "return of the repressed" in performativity (Schrift, 2001: 14-15).

The leading contention of Sartrean existentialism is that the self is constituted through its acts in a continuous movement of transcendence, so that self-identity is only an imaginary (albeit necessary) ideal, "futilely" pursued by human agents. In actuality, far from relying on a pre-discursive agent and act, Sartre defines consciousness as a "transcendental field without a subject" (Sartre, 1969: 235). Butler's criticism of the subject as a substantive agency is therefore in line with Sartre's critique of the phenomenological assumption that conscious intentionality can self-reflexively know itself as a unified ego. Sartre divides the "non-positional" transcendental intentionality of consciousness from the social identity (the ego) of the individual. As Butler herself recognises:

> Every intentional movement of consciousness towards a specific transcendental object presupposes consciousness' non-positional awareness of itself as the agent of consciousness; and yet this agency only becomes explicit through its actual deeds (Butler, 1987a: 128).

For Sartre, the retroactive construction of the subject of the action (the "me") is distinct from the agency that acts (the "I"), an opposition Sartre translates into the existential opposition between objectified identity "in-itself" and transcendental subjectivity "for-itself". Thus, Butler's claim that in existentialism the self and its acts are pre-discursive is false, as regards the social identity of the agent that is retroactively known through their actions.

Butler's target, however, is probably the Sartrean revival of the Fichtean concept of a "pre-reflexive *cogito*". According to this conception, "non-positional consciousness," as a recasting of the transcendental "unity of apperception," and the externality of the world, as the existential recasting of the transcendental "object in general," enjoy the pre-reflexive unity of the *cogito*. This *is* a pre-discursive identity, but it is quite distinct from the "self and its acts," for where the "pre-reflexive *cogito*" is transcendental, the social identity of the agent, known through its actions, is empirical.

My contention is that Butler herself, insofar as the philosophical structure of her position is basically existentialist, cannot avoid something along the lines of a non-positional consciousness, or transcendental intentionality, "behind" the multiple subject-positions adopted by the empirical agent. Indeed, as we have seen, Butler's solution to the problems of reflection is exactly the same as the neo-Fichtean and post-Sartrean position of Dieter Henrich, suggesting that she is, in reality, very far indeed from any postmodern "subjectless conception of agency". That conception is expressed through her claim that "agency conditioned by ... regimes of discourse/power cannot be conflated with voluntarism or individualism, ... and in no way presupposes a choosing subject" (Butler, 1993: 15). The idea is that the individual's intentions are constructed discursively and unconsciously constrained. But her repudiation of Foucault for psychoanalysis turned out to be a defence of the ego from the unconscious. Now I will show that Butler's discussion of the discursive construction of individual intentions makes no sense unless we suppose that a non-positional intentionality is an unstated assumption of her position.

Now, I can imagine an objection at this point, that the subject described by Butler is not only constructed in discourse through the acts it performs, but also functions only as a retroactive grammatical fiction masking a performative construct (Butler, 1999a: 25). Even when Butler claims that gender is a choice (Butler, 1987b: 128-129), this does not mean that an agent stands back from gender and voluntarily selects, for "choosing" refers to reinterpretation of gender norms (Butler, 1987b: 131). This is the basis for the distance that Butler claims to detect between performativity and existentialism. She rejects the terminology of "existential project" for "political strategy," and "linguistic expression" for "discursive performance," on the basis that the existential project, externalised in social action or linguistic expression, relies upon an underlying substantive agent (Butler, 1999a: 25).

Butler's conception of the agent is that they are always-already interpellated into a gender identity and located in an overdetermined field consisting of a multiplicity of subject-positions, confronting the problem of "*how* to repeat". Interestingly, this develops through an adaptation of the existential phenomenology of Beauvoir (Butler, 1986: ; Butler, 1987b) and Merleau-Ponty (Butler, 1989). The resources for "*how* to repeat" arrive from the polysemic excess of subject-positions in the cultural field, which acts to decomplete every identity while ensuring that the individual is always located at the intersection of multiple, overlapping discourses (Butler, 1999a: 6). Once again, though, this (high postmodern) position does not solve the problem, but merely displaces it, while at the same time raising the additional problem of moral relativism.

Once we conceptualise the agent as a field of dispersed, multiple subject-positions, then who, or what, decides which position to adopt in a context? How and why are some forms of interpretation politically progressive—a practice of liberation (Foucault)—while others are deemed to be oppressive? Butler, of course, sometimes appears to think that every form of subjection involves exclusions, which would mean that any hegemonic subjectivity is intrinsically oppressive. In this case, her position is that of the Beautiful Soul, whose permanent stance of marginal subversion is in actuality a cover for a thoroughgoing complicity (Nussbaum, 1999). However, to the extent that Butler, in recent texts, appears to revive the perspective of liberation through an increasingly inclusive universality (Butler, 2000a: ; Butler, 2000b: ; Butler, 2000c), the problem of the interests of the subject, and therefore, for Butler, of intentionality, returns.

Any *phenomenology* of the adoption, by the agent, of a multiplicity of subject-positions, must necessarily situate its description of the contents of subjective experience as a non-positional consciousness. When Butler calls for "critical desubjectivation" as an act of resistance to the law (Butler, 1997b: 130), how else are we to understand this, except than as an appeal to a disembodied intentionality somehow "behind" the dispersed multiplicity of subject-positions adopted by the individual? What else can the celebration of the dispersion, even the non-identity, of the subject entail, if we are to consider this as a *political* act (as opposed to a suicidal abdication of moral and social responsibility)? Thus, Butler seems to rehearse the existentialist conception of a permanent split between temporalised existence and spatialised essence, subjective transcendence and reified identity, in the theory of performativity. Her core proposition, that every postulation of identity is "a sign of exhaustion, as well as of the illimitable process of signification itself" (Butler, 1999a: 143), while couched in the terminology of the "linguistic turn," effectively means that the identity of the agent is continuously deposited in the wake of a movement of subjective transcendence effected by a disembodied intentionality. That "discourse" replaces the "transcendental field" does not fundamentally alter the existentialist affinities of Butler's conception of subjectivity—something celebrated by at least one of her adherents (Schrift, 1997: ; Schrift, 2001).

Speech Act Theory as a New Ontology?

The phenomenological roots of Butler's theory are clearly exhibited in the claim that performative speech acts somehow transubstantiate the referent, for this claim relies upon the assumption that transcendental subjectivity constitutes not just the epistemological forms, but also the substantial materiality of the object-world. Specifically, the theory of performativity supposes that illocutionary declaratives miraculously transform not only the social status of the speaking subject, but also the sexed materiality of the *res cogitans*. For Butler (somewhat incredibly), the performative character of social identity suggests that the ontological characteristics of the body are conferred by the discursive matrix which constitutes its gender positioning (Butler, 1999a: 136-140). Indeed, as one criticism of Butler has already noted, the deconstruction of substantialist ontology makes room for a new ontology of gender performativity (Williams and Harrison, 1998).

To grasp the limitations of Butler's theory of performativity, we need to attend closely to the technical distinctions relevant to speech act theory. The distinction between constative and performative speech acts corresponds to the difference between saying something and doing things with words. A constative utterance describes a state of affairs according to criteria of veracity (a statement of correspondence to reality that can be true or false) and so semantics is the proper domain of the constative. By contrast, a performative utterance does something (alters the status of the referent) in the enunciation. For instance, "I do" in a marriage ceremony does not report that the person is married, but instead makes (does) the bond of marriage (Austin, 1962: 13). Unlike the constative statement, the performative utterance cannot be true or false—it can only be, in Benveniste's terminology, "legitimate" or "illegitimate" (Austin uses the less politically suggestive terms "felicitous" and "infelicitous"). According to Austin's main stipulation, "there must exist an accepted conventional procedure having a certain conventional effect, that procedure to include the uttering of certain words by certain persons in certain circumstances" (Austin, 1962: 14). Searle, following Austin, refers to the institutional context within which the performance can be legitimate as the "conditions of satisfaction" of the performative aspect of the utterance (Searle, 1969).

It is well known that Austin abandoned the initial binary distinction between constative and performative for a ternary distinction between illocutionary force (performative dimension), locutionary act (constative dimension) and perlocutionary consequences (the ability of speech acts to engender consequences in partners in dialogue, for instance, persuasion) (Austin, 1962: 98-100). Austin's explicit motivation for the shift is the radical instability of the division between two distinct classes of speech acts, which necessarily yields to an analysis of the different *aspects* of every speech act. Every speech act contains both a locutionary and an illocutionary component. This effectively subverts the true/false distinction as the criterion for the validity of the locutionary act. For the veracity of a statement now depends upon the context implied by the utterance, and this context is determined by the "conditions of satisfaction" of the illocutionary act. As Austin notes, "the truth or falsity of a statement depends upon what you were performing in what circumstances" (Austin, 1962: 145). Equally, however, the duality of the speech act subverts the notion, beloved of discursive idealism, of the "magic of performatives," where the constative dimensions of speech acts can be entirely forgotten, and discourse can be held to mysteriously transmute the natural properties of the referent. For the illocutionary force of the utterance now depends upon what factually is the case in the context that supplies the "conditions of satisfaction" for the performative legitimacy of the speech act.

Indeed, the abandonment of the performative/constative distinction has important implications for the referential employment of language. The fable of the "Emperor's New Clothes" can clarify the relation between illocutionary force and locutionary accuracy. Every locutionary act ("the Emperor has new clothes on") can be trivially rephrased to make explicit the illocutionary assertion implied in the referential claim ("I believe that the Emperor has new clothes on") (Searle, 1979). The Emperor's mistake is to believe that an illocutionary assertion can completely over-rule the locutionary accuracy of the speech act, forgetting that "generally, in the performance of any illocutionary act, the speaker implies that the preparatory conditions of the act are satisfied" (Searle, 1969: 65). These preparatory conditions are institutional conventions external to the speech act (for instance, those governing rational belief-formation); making an assertion does not alter these conditions—instead, these conditions regulate the legitimacy of the illocution. Thus, Butler's assertion that "the constative claim [to describe sex] is always to some degree performative," is, strictly speaking, trivial, and does not at all demonstrate that "there is no reference to a pure body which is not at the same time a further formation of that body" (Butler, 1993: 11, 10).

Butler's reluctance to accept the full consequences of Austin's revised position is compounded by an uncritical acceptance of Derrida's deconstruction of speech act theory (Derrida, 1988). Because Butler's theory is founded on the deconstructive position, the significant limitations of Derrida's concept of "citationality" weaken the infrastructure of the theory of performativity (Butler, 1999a: 12-16). Austin makes two aspects of the illocutionary dimension of speech acts perfectly clear. Illocution depends upon convention and not intention. In the illocutionary act, "the act is constituted not by intention or by fact, but by convention" (Austin, 1962: 128). Illocutionary force depends primarily upon the conventionally sanctioned authority of the executor, and therefore upon the social and institutional context, and only secondarily upon the actual wording of the statement. Secondly, "when speech act theory contextualises utterances by directing attention to the things they do as *illocutions*, it simultaneously makes it impossible to decontextualise utterances by attending solely to what they do as *locutions*" (Petrey, 1990: 27). For instance, the appearance of the sentence, "the constitution is suspended" in a sensational pamphlet or a government decree illustrate the possibility of a single locution in entirely different illocutionary contexts (with distinct illocutionary forces). Taken together, the relative separation of illocution and locution, together with the non-decontextualisability of speech acts, means that in no sense does a word "drag its context around with it," like a snail with its shell. Thus, the context of signification, when considering the illocutionary force of the speech act, is *not* diacritically structured on the same level as the signifiers in the utterance; the signification of the utterance engages an illocutionary syntax whose reference is the analytically distinct field of the institutionally defined "conditions of satisfaction" of the illocutionary act (Searle, 1969: 54-71).

Derrida's deconstruction of Austin has rightly been described as "bizarre," for its insistence (despite the textual evidence) on the centrality of intentionality to speech act theory, and for its ambivalence regarding illocutionary force (performative success) (Dews, 1995: 54). Petrey demonstrates that Derrida's grasp of speech act theory involves the decontextualisation of the utterance and therefore a neglect of the illocutionary context of speech acts (Petrey, 1990: 131-146). Derrida attributes the force of language to its transcendence of context, with the inevitable entailment that his deconstruction of speech act theory is obliged to consider "the structure of *locution* … before any illocutionary or perlocutionary determination" (Derrida, 1988: 14). Deconstruction is, in other words, pre-Austinian, as "the abstract identity of a locutionary formulation is not pertinent to its contextual illocutionary force" (Petrey, 1990: 139). Indeed, Derrida appears sometimes to be unaware of Austin's shift from performative/ constative to illocution/ locution/ perlocution (Petrey, 1990: 148-150). Butler also ignores the implications of this shift when she continues to suggest that the performative materialises the constative. Likewise, the concept of "resignification" falls into the deconstructive trap of imagining that a decontextualised locution continues to enjoy the same category of illocutionary force (reverse interpellation as a form of declarative) regardless of institutional context.

Discursive Materialisation

In *Bodies that Matter* (1993), Butler claims to provide "a poststructuralist rewriting of discursive performativity as it operates in the materialisation of sex" (Butler, 1993: 9). For Butler, the idea of the performative expresses both the arbitrary bond between social identity and natural embodiment, and the notion that, following the Foucauldian conception of "discipline," every performance inscribes social norms upon the materiality of the body. Dramatically over-extending this conception, Butler proclaims that gender performativity materialises sex, including the anatomical reality of the natural body. Butler supports this contention with the assertion that, referring to the process of designating anatomical sex, "medical interpellation ... shifts the infant from an 'it,' to a 'she' or a 'he' [through] naming" (Butler, 1993: 7). As we have seen, this claim involves a forced interpretation of speech act theory, a misreading which mistakes a transformation in the social status of the referent for a well-nigh alchemical transmutation of its physical properties. In actuality, therefore, the work develops the phenomenology of gender performances essayed in *Gender Trouble* to its logical conclusion, in the rejection of scientific materialism for philosophical idealism.

Butler asserts that the body is "*a process of materialisation that stabilises over time to produce the effect of boundary, fixity, and surface we call matter*" (Butler, 1993: 9). Imperceptibly, Butler's rhetorical shifts shade "the effect of boundary" into the quite different claim that discourse enters the depths of matter and invests the organs with a function. In particular, Butler seems to be saying that through the "interpellation" of sex at birth, the infant is discursively "assigned" a biological sexuality (Butler, 1993: 7-8). To the extent that she indeed *does* flirt with just such a claim, we have to agree that "[t]he assertion that sexual difference is discursively constructed strains belief" (Epstein, 1995: 101). Butler's discussion of genetics in *Gender Trouble*, for instance, risks obscurantism. Characteristically arguing through rhetorical questions, rather than explicit declaratives, she asks: "is it not a purely cultural convention ... that an anatomically ambiguous XX individual is male, a convention that takes genitalia to be the definitive 'sign' of sex?" (Butler, 1999a: 140).

Despite having identified elements of ideology in the genetic inquiry she analyses, Butler's contention that the genitalia (and therefore, biological reproductive functions) have nothing to do with sex is indeed strange. It is the rhetorical slippage from "small testes which totally lacked germ cells, i.e., precursor cells for sperm" (Butler, 1999a: medical report cited 137), to "anatomically ambiguous," that enables this fragile construction. The individuals in question are anatomically definite although underdeveloped and sterile. Gender relates to a cultural subject-position that includes sexual pleasure, while sex designates the organic functions that enable the biological reproduction of the species. The "sex organs" designate my sex, whether I am naturally sterile or medically sterilised, or not. This is not to deny the existence of an anatomical continuum, or of statistically rare cases of dual, ambiguous or transient genitalia. But sex refers to the statistically overwhelming poles constituting this continuum. Why is it politically progressive to deny the results of scientific inquiry? It seems to me more like a politically regressive anti-scientific prejudice that denies the possibility for any epistemologically robust empirical realism. Butler's (accurate) point is that the existence of a polarised continuum of anatomical structure cannot directly determine the variegated and historically variable spectrum of gendered subject-positions. It is also indicated, by the research that she canvasses, that chromosomal variation may have an only refracted impact on anatomical forms and functions. The relation between DNA sequences and physical morphology may well obey a complex relation, rather than a linear determination. How this dematerialises the anatomical bearers of organic functions into gendered subject-positions is left hanging, unanswered, in her characteristic rhetorical question.

Butler seems incapable of making the elementary distinction between medical intervention into natural processes and the transcendental constitution of their cultural significance. This would be a step backwards compared to, for instance, Kant, whose transcendental idealism does not preclude the results of science because material reality is only constituted by the categories of the understanding, rather than entirely formed by discourse. Indeed, the title of her book positively trades on the semantic ambivalence of "matter" (materiality/significance), apparently deliberately conflating the two. In *Gender Trouble*, for instance, she claims that the "external genitalia" are "essential to the *symbolisation* of reproductive sexuality" (Butler, 1999a: 140 emphasis added). Strange to relate, the genitalia also have a functional relation to reproductive sexuality; they are not reducible to cultural symbols. *Bodies that Matter*, instead of retracting this claim, extends it, by enhancing the ability of "performativity" to go beyond merely conforming surfaces, to invest matter in depth (Ebert, 1996: 113-149).

Butler preserves a margin of ambiguity in her theorisation, insisting that "the point has never been that 'everything is discursively constructed'" (Butler, 1993: 6). She rejects the "divine performative" that exhaustively forms a pliant materiality, insisting that a remainder of materiality escapes construction (Butler, 1993: 6). In *Bodies that Matter*, Butler proposes the substitution of the model of the "constitutive outside" to discourse (Butler, 1993:

8) for the "cultural construction of everything". This deploys Laclau and Mouffe's terminology within a radically different ontology, since for Laclau and Mouffe the "constitutive outside" is another discourse, not the extra-discursive referent. Nor is it entirely clear where this revision leaves Butler, for this constitutive outside is nothing else than the construction of identities through exclusionary means, whereby "a set of foreclosures" is "refused the possibility of cultural articulation" (Butler, 1993: 8). Butler's new position tends to undermine the Foucauldian account of performativity, for the political potentials of the former theory depended upon the radical *inclusion* in the cultural field of the excluded transgressions constitutive of the norm. Indeed, the claim that power necessarily cited its transgressions formed the basis for subversive resignification within the cultural field and the consequent displacement and proliferation of norms. At other times, the indeterminacy of Butlerian "matter" seems to indicate that this position is only the standard positivist opposition between an inert materiality and the transcendental constitution of its significance (Butler, 1996: 108-125). It is easy to see why. Once the excluded, abjected sexualities, as a "constitutive outside," are regarded as something on the order of matter itself—a matter that resists articulation—it is difficult to see how a subversive politics can develop at all.

The Politics of Performativity

Excitable Speech (1997) tries to redress the lack of historico-political specificity in Butler's theory by outlining a politics of the performative. Butler examines several categories of illocutionary act—including "hate speech" and gay declaratives in the military—to redeem the claim that effective performances of alternative identities defy calculation and the assertion that these acts transform institutional structures (Butler, 1993: 8). The centrepiece for this demonstration is her theorisation of resignification through the category of the perlocutionary consequences of speech acts. Where the illocutionary force of a speech act is conventional, the perlocutionary consequences are unconventional, depending on the mobilisation of affect in dialogue partners (as in the distinction between warning someone and generating the side-effect of alarming them). For Butler, the basic idea is that the subject is generated through interpellation-subjection, in a process whereby individuals are assigned "injurious names" (for instance, "queer"), but that by taking up these names as affirmations a "reverse interpellation" can be effected, generating militant subjectivities instead of conformist subjects. This is the meaning of Butler's condensed claim that "insurrectionary speech becomes the necessary response to an injurious language" (Butler, 1997a: 163). What in one context is injurious speech ("queer") becomes, in another context, the hearer of insurrectionary language, not, it is implied, directly through its illocutionary force, but rather through the unpredictable consequences of us-

ing it *as if it were* a different illocution. Butler's claim, therefore, treats illocution as if it was locution, and neglects the all-important institutional context
of the speech act. Indeed, the collapse of the illocution/locution distinction
is directly stated in Butler's assertion that "the critical and legal discourse
on hate speech is itself a restaging of the performance of hate speech" (Butler, 1997a: 163). Unfortunately, the entailment is that her "reverse interpellation," or "resignification," is a locutionary pseudo-declarative, lacking the
required illocutionary force, and so the promised politics of performativity
do not actually materialise.

Butler's major thesis is that speech is constitutively "out of control," because its effects exceed the "sovereign" intentionality of the conscious agent
(Butler, 1997a: 15). As Butler states, "agency begins where sovereignty wanes.
The one who acts ... acts precisely to the extent that he or she is constituted
as an actor and, hence, operating within a linguistic field of enabling constraints from the outset" (Butler, 1997a: 16). While such claims are enthusiastically received by Butler's supporters as evidence of her subjectless conception of agency (McNay, 1999: 178-181; Salih, 2002: 100), her position actually
does nothing more than restate the fundamental contention of speech act
theory, that the illocutionary force of the utterance depends on social context and not individual intention. Recognition of the importance of social
context might be expected to generate a "politics of performativity" oriented
to a radical reconstruction of institutions. The twist is, however, that Butler's conception of the politics of speech acts depends on the radically untenable claim that social context is *irrelevant* to the political implications of
the utterance. As we shall see, far from developing a subjectless conception
of agency, this enables Butler to return to her perennial theme of the individual resisting their subjection through oppositional cultural practices; like
Foucault, Butler dethrones the omnipotent subject so as to save the political
individual.

Butler rejects both the ability of sovereign intentionality to govern
speech, and the simultaneity of utterance and injury supposedly required
by the construction of hate speech as illocutionary acts (Butler, 1997a: 16).
She opposes the theory of the performative employed by legal theoreticians
such as Catherine McKinnon, for whom, Butler claims, the performative
is an immediately efficacious expression of the sovereign intentionality of
the individual agent, and equivalent to a physical action (Butler, 1997a: 15).
We have already seen that any interpretation of speech act theory such as
McKinnon's must be specious. Instead of directly contesting the legal reading of speech act theory, however, Butler reasserts her deconstructive criticism of Austin, to imply that performatives are generally inefficacious and
temporally delayed, beyond the conscious control of the speaker and distinct
from physical acts. The rationale for this position is to create a gap between
the existence of hegemonic norms and their employment by social agents in

speech acts, preventing any monolithic conception of the social field. Its effect, however, is that Butler uses the speech act/social conduct distinction to
drive a wedge between hate speech and acts of violence.

Butler cites legal theory to the effect that what is really at stake in hate
speech is an illocutionary force, operative in certain contexts, directed at
negating the social identity of the victim (Butler, 1997a: 16), which suggests
that the question of sovereign intentionality is a pseudo-problem. Instead of
directly intervening into the debate on how speech act theory supports legal judgements, however, she maintains that the power of words to wound
resides in unanticipated effects generated through a *loss* of context and *opposes* every effort to link illocutionary force to institutional conditions (Butler,
1997a: 16). She proposes the adoption of a perlocutionary model, according
to which the injury done to the victim of hate speech results unpredictably
and in a delayed way (Butler, 1997a: 16). Because her deconstructive interpretation of speech act theory neglects any taxonomy of illocutionary acts,
Butler is in no position to contest the conservative assertion that these acts
have the force attributed to them by the Right. Indeed, the consequence of
her stance is that she attacks as "conservative" Bourdieu's effort to connect
speech to institutions so as to raise the question of social equality (Butler,
1997a: 16), and rejects his "amplification of the social dimension of the performative" (Butler, 1997a: 16). By contrast, Butler insists on the break with
context supposedly performed by "insurrectionary" resignification, thanks
to its ability to act in unconventional ways (Butler, 1997a: 16). In other words,
Butler restricts speech act theory to decontextualised locutions and unconventional perlocutions, discarding illocution entirely as "conservative" and
insufficiently "insurrectionary". As usual, however, when ultra-revolution-
ary rhetoric becomes a means whereby social questions are rejected for an
"autonomous" dimension of language (Butler, 1997a: 16), Butler's position
masks a thorough-going political individualism.

By insisting on the distinction between speech and conduct (Butler,
1997a: 15), Butler retreats from the central claim of discursive materialisation, that no clear boundary between speech acts and material reality exists. Indeed, the assertion that the speech act does not, after all, "constitute
the referent to which it refers" (Butler, 1997a: 16), effectively admits that
the effort to elaborate a politics of performativity entails the collapse of the
metaphysics articulated in *Bodies that Matter.* Now Butler, in her anxiety to
deny the effects of social context on illocutionary force, moves in the opposite direction. In the instance of "coming out" in the military, where the authorities decreed that to say "I'm gay" is equivalent to a sexual act, Butler,
instead of contesting this ludicrous interpretation of expressive illocutions,
maintains a rigid split between speech and conduct (Butler, 1997a: 112). Unfortunately, therefore, Butler does not even mention that an assertive declaration ("I'm gay") attaches a declarative illocution to a state of affairs by,

in this instance, attributing a property to the speaker (Searle, 1979: 18-20). Such a declaration cannot, under any circumstances, be considered to be "homosexual conduct" equivalent to sexual intercourse, since this latter presupposes two persons—intercourse is not something that I have with myself. She makes some excellent points regarding homosociality in the military and the repression of homosexual desire in hyperbolic masculinity (Butler, 1997a: 121), but entirely fails to contest the abuse of speech act theory relied upon by the military authorities.

Butler is resolutely opposed to most (but not all, as we shall see) forms of legal redress and official censorship, on the grounds that state intervention may strengthen those institutions while being deployed against the victims of hate speech. In opposition to racial vilification, Butler proposes not state intervention (legislation), but radical mobilisation and practices of resignification. Her concern is that speech act legislation functions as state censorship and becomes the precedent for banning homosexuality in the military and censoring pornography. In line with the deconstructive indifference to the locution/illocution distinction, she claims that the state, by reiterating hate speech acts, repeats discursive violence and prosecutes the victim, finally protecting hate speech as "free speech" (Butler, 1997a: 121). Her insensitivity to the possibility that a single locution can have different illocutionary force in distinct contexts encourages Butler to directly equate legal discourse and hate speech, leading to an apparently ultra-left dismissal of all legal redress and state protection as counter-productive. At the same time, Butler claims that she "is not opposed to any and all regulations," such as, for instance, "hate speech regulations that are not state-centred, such as those that have restricted jurisdiction within a university" (Butler, 1997a: 102, 101). This is an interesting position to take, considering that (1) she works in one, and (2) according to the Althusserian model of ideological interpellation, the education system is *the* modern ideological *state* apparatus.

The ethico-political consequences of Butler's stance are disturbing. Butler proposes that the model of the sole originator of speech is a consequence of the juridical model, which needs to fabricate an author so as to find them guilty (Butler, 1997a: 50). Hence, the law produces hate speech so as to legislate censorship and fabricates a culpable subject so as to prosecute them. Subjects, Butler claims, are not uniquely accountable for their speech because the subject is a "belated metalepsis," or subject effect (Butler, 1997a: 50), a retroactively installed substitution of a "guilty party" after the citation of a speech act. The immediate implication of taking this seriously in a legal context would be that it is possible for every speaker to plead diminished responsibility. Butler claims that the citationality of speech amplifies ethical responsibility for hate speech, however, by making individuals accountable for "the *manner* in which such speech is repeated" (Butler, 1997a: 50 my italics). This returns us once again to the loop of "*how to repeat*," and the pseudo-problem of the "remaking of language *ex nihilo*" (Butler, 1997a: 50); my earlier comments regarding the distinction between the omnipotence of the subject and a non-positional intentionality apply once again, with full force. In *Excitable Speech* Butler claims that the question of responsibility is "afflict-ed with impurity from the start" and "intimates an ethical dilemma brew-ing at the inception of speech" (Butler, 1997a: 28). It is more likely, however, that the ethical dilemma springs from Butler's posing of the question.

An immediate index of this is the logical contradiction involved in the concept of resignification. As an alternative to police protection and legal redress, Butler suggests that victims of hate speech exploit the open tem-porality of the sign (Butler, 1997a: 121). Speech acts do not take place in the punctual instant of the utterance, but represent a "condensation" of the his-toricity of a social ritual and a semantic history, and so an utterance may be "excessive to the moment it occasions" (Butler, 1997a: 14), raising the possibility of resignification as a political alternative. Resignification, she suggests, "depletes" the term of derogatory history and converts it into an affirmation (for instance, queer, black, woman) (Butler, 1997a: 158). This possibility springs from the hypothesis of the contextual determination of the value of the sign. Nonetheless, despite these theoretical ruminations, Butler in actuality rehearses the leftwing commonsense, that resignifying "queer" is something different to deploying "nigger," and that citing a por-nographic image is different to burning a cross. She claims this is because of the significance of the historicity of the sign (Butler, 1997a: 57). The two claims (the contextually determined value of the sign, and the historicity of the sign) are in logical contradiction. Likewise, Butler asserts that when the oppressed lay claim to their universal human and political rights, from which they have hitherto been excluded, they produce a performative con-tradiction (Butler, 2000d: 38). Even for supporters, "*Excitable Speech* does not provide a clear idea of how interpellatives may be replayed or their mean-ings altered" (Salih, 2002: 115).

"On the whole," Lois McNay concludes, "there is a tendency in Butler's work to confine discussion of the politics of the performative to a series of dualisms ... which are far from adequate to capturing the complex dynam-ics of social change" (McNay, 1999: 178). We might add that the abstract and formal theory of agency provided by performativity restricts gender politics to the question of symbolic identity (Fraser, 1995), to the exclusion of considerations of material equality and social practices (Hull, 1997). But-ler's efforts to concretise agency and salvage performativity tend to con-solidate these problems rather than rectify them. The consequence is that "the primacy that Butler's model accords to the process of symbolic identi-fication results ... in a disregard of the specificity of socio-political power" (McNay, 1999: 181).

The problems in Butler's theory spring from the combination of the historicist assumption that individual praxis can be transposed onto social structuration, and the existential-Hegelian roots of her phenomenology of subjectivation. For Butler, the incompleteness of identity is the result of the dialectics of the self and other in the social field, so that—in classic Fichtean-Sartrean style—the shock of the encounter with the other sets permanent limits to my self-identity. Butler claims that:

> The "incompleteness" of each and every identity is a direct result of its differential emergence: no particular identity can emerge without presuming and enacting the exclusion of others, and this constitutive exclusion or antagonism is the shared and equal condition of all identity-constitution (Butler, 2000c: 31).

The permanent stance of marginal subversion follows from this conception of the *necessity* for the self to exclude the other, so that while Butler formally advocates the development of an inclusive universality, no new social order can be imagined that would not, in fact, be based upon domination. Sartre's impasse—that ethics is both necessary and impossible—is here repeated on the terrain of discourse theory, so that the social norms that make sociality possible can only be conceptualised as a constraint upon the spontaneity of the self. The problem with this theory is that it reduces the social field to the sum of dyadic interpersonal collisions, flattening the complexity of social formation and institutional contexts onto a pseudo-dialectic of narcissistic identification and sibling rivalry. No wonder, then, that the "collective dimension is missing from Butler's account of performative resignification, whose underpinnings in a theory of psychic dislocation confine its explanatory force to the private realm of individual action" (McNay, 1999: 189).

As a consequence, Butler's theory oscillates between voluntarism and determinism, swinging between strategic calculations based in transparent intentionality and the assertion that effective performances defy calculation entirely. This does not lead to an effective politics. Instead, it can only repeat the impasse of Foucault's "aesthetics of existence," condemned to a series of performative contradictions that culminate in explicitly supporting liberal anti-censorship struggles against any effort to raise the question of substantive equality. As her supporters concede, Butler's "position ... primarily addresses politics at the level of the individual agent enacting their gender while subjected to various cultural constraints" (Schrift, 1997: 157). Instead of lending substance to Laclau and Mouffe's excessively formal theory of discourse, performativity evacuates the social content of different practices, with a consequent inability to specify their institutional context. Indeed, in this sense, performativity is to be strictly opposed to performative speech acts, for the latter only operate in a social context, whereas performativity enjoys the veritably miraculous power to generate performative effects irrespective of conventions. The repercussion is that rather than clarifying the relation between discursive practice and institutional structures, performativity tends to disperse all structural constraints. The global result of these difficulties is that the trajectory of Butler's theory describes a series of unsuccessful efforts to evade the deadlock of what can only be called a postmodern existentialism, while the politics of performativity remain within the envelope of radicalised liberalism.

4

Radical Negativity: Žižek's Lacanian Dialectics

In *The Sublime Object of Ideology* (1989) and subsequent books, Žižek complete-ly rewrites Laclau and Mouffe's deconstructive theory of discourse in terms of Lacanian psychoanalysis.[1] Žižek's intervention proposes that the uncon-scious subject is the unruly by-product of ideological interpellation. He com-bines this reconstructed theory of ideology with Hegelian philosophy, to cre-ate a remarkable new social theory based in "Lacanian dialectics" (Dews, 1995). At the same time, he makes strenuous efforts to escape the metaphysi-cal implications of the historicist problematic. By developing a structural concept of the autonomous subject, Žižek not only supplies a sophisticat-ed extension of the theory of ideological interpellation, but also furnishes an ethical basis for democratic socialism. Žižek's intervention identifies the missing link in post-Althusserian theories of ideology—the unconscious sub-ject as the unruly by-product of ideological interpellation—while making strenuous efforts to escape the gravitational field of the historicist problem-atic of postmarxian discourse analysis.

Nonetheless, the conclusions towards which Žižek is driven, apparent-ly on the basis of Lacanian psychoanalysis, are nothing less than extraor-

---

1. Parts of this chapter have been published in "The Antinomies of Slavoj Zizek," *Telos: A Quarterly Journal of Critical Thought (129)* (2004), pp151-172, and "The Law as a Thing: Zizek and the Graph of Desire," in Geoff Boucher, Jason Glynos and Matt Sharpe (Ed.'s), *Travers-ing the Fantasy: Critical Essays on Slavoj Žižek, with a Reply* (London: Ashgate, 2005), pp. 25-46. Žižek's reply is "Ethical Socialism? No, Thanks! Reply to Boucher," *Telos: A Quarterly Journal of Critical Thought (129)* (2004), pp173-189. I have not altered my position because—as the reader may judge for themselves—Žižek does not appear to me to have a reply. To say, as he does, that this expresses a political difference is not to defend *his* side of that difference—only to state the obvious. As for the expressly Kantian character of my position, as opposed to Žižek's Hegelianism, I continue to hold to this and would add that it was Žižek who claimed that Hegel is the most consequent of Kantians.

dinary, and tend to undermine any confidence we might have in the theoretical machinery that permits such deductions. In Žižek's "philosophical manifesto of Cartesian subjectivity," *The Ticklish Subject* (2000), we are cheerfully informed by the author that embracing this reinvigorated Cartesianism necessarily leads to ethical decisionism and political voluntarism (Žižek, 2000h: 114-115). These are condensed, for Žižek, into the figure of a "voluntarist decisionism," which is to be combined with "Cartesian mechanism" to produce, in what must rate as an alchemical triumph, a "materialist theory of Grace" (Žižek, 2000h: 116-119). Indeed, Žižek's recent espousal of a "politics of Truth," that would subvert contemporary capitalism, just as Christianity undermined the Roman Empire (Žižek, 2001d: 4-5), is part of a package deal. This comes complete with a defence of the excesses of Leninism (Žižek, 2001e), a theory of the proletariat as the "singular universal" of capitalist society that is reminiscent of Georg Lukács' notion of the proletariat as the identical subject-object of history (Žižek, 2000h), an intellectual return to the speculative heights of Schelling's Romantic philosophy (Žižek, 1996), and a metaphysically well-endowed revival of Pauline theology (Žižek, 2000e; Žižek, 2001d).

I am not convinced that this quasi-religious politics of redemption is the only (or the best) conclusion that can be drawn from Žižek's work. My question: will the real Žižek please step forward? My strategy: to play Žižek off against Žižek, so as to recover a non-Cartesian Žižek. To do this, I interrogate Žižek's interpretation of Lacanian psychoanalysis. The basic thrust of my argument is that—*contra* the neo-Cartesian Žižek—the Lacanian "divided," or unconscious, "subject before subjectivation" is not a mirror-image, in the unconscious, of the ego. The unconscious subject does not possess the properties of transparent self-reflexivity, punctual unity and world constituting agency supposedly possessed by the Cartesian ego. Lacanian psychoanalysis does not—as its critics suppose (Lacoue-Labarthe, 1992)—reinstate the philosophy of consciousness by transposing the unitary subject into the unconscious. But this, as I shall demonstrate, is exactly what Žižek has recently begun to claim. My analysis retraces what might be described as a "cascade of errors" in Žižek's work. From the very beginning, a series of tiny mistakes and minor omissions have begun to accumulate. They all point in a single direction: dispersion of the ego, unity of the unconscious. Uncorrected, they have acquired a momentum of their own and begun to colonise Žižek's theoretical apparatus. To trace the evolution of this problem, I begin from an analysis of Žižek's interpretation of Althusser via the "Graph of Desire," showing how his treatment of the subject results in an antinomic conception of the relation between Symbolic and Real. This condemns Žižek to lurch between these antinomic poles, hesitating between the alternatives of total complicity with "obscene enjoyment" or a catastrophic rupture with existing symbolic structures. Then I investigate the theoretical consequences of this conception and examine the political and ethical dilemmas that result. Finally, I trace these problems to Žižek's recent, neo-Cartesian embrace of the unified unconscious and show how this impedes the search for a political strategy in today's conditions.

I.

Drawing on the Lacanian theory of the subject, Žižek explains the mechanism of ideological interpellation with reference to Lacan's "Graph of Desire" (Žižek, 1989: 87-129; Lacan, 1977: 292-325). Designed to replace the Freudian topography of the ego, superego and id,[2] Lacan's topology of the "subject of the signifier" formalises the fundamental operations of social discourse. It theorises the Imaginary and Symbolic identifications of the subject, as well as the "subversion of the subject" through the logic of unconscious desire driven by the Real of libidinal investments, or "enjoyment".[3]

---

2. Richard Boothby's *Death and Desire* (1991) provides a useful first approximation to the relation between the Freudian subject and the Lacanian subject, one that allows us to provisionally map Lacan's often arcane topological "registers" (the Imaginary, the Symbolic and the Real) onto the more familiar psychic agencies of the Freudian topography of the psyche. The Freudian agencies of the ego, the (social) superego and the id map onto the Lacanian registers of the Imaginary, Symbolic and Real (Boothby, 1991: 106, 172-174). "From a Lacanian point of view, the source of what Freud called a 'death drive' is to be located in the tension between the real and the imaginary, between the 'real of the body and the imaginary of its mental schema' (Lacan). The pressing toward expression of somatic energies alienated by imaginary identification constitutes a force of death insofar as it threatens the integrity of that identity" (Boothby, 1991: 67). Indeed, "the death drive may be said to involve the emergence of the real in the disintegration of the imaginary—a disintegration that is effected by the agency of the symbolic" (Boothby, 1991: 136). The symbolic actualises the unbinding of energies bound in the alienated structure of the ego: therefore, Lacan claims that "the signifier ... materialises the agency of death" (Lacan, 1972: 52). From a Lacanian perspective, the concept of the death drive, as a drive towards difference beyond identity, fragmentation over wholeness, heterogeneity as subversive of homogeneity, "is identifiable with the drive to signification" (Boothby, 1991: 136). The opposition between Symbolic signification and the non-symbolised Real coincides with the distinction between desire and drive. The Real is both the fullness of enjoyment that can be postulated as existing before the advent of the Symbolic and the remainder that persists after symbolisation, evident in the persistence of impossibilities within the symbolic (Fink, 1995a: 26-29). Yet, there exists a major difference between the Lacanian subject and the Freudian subject. For Lacan, the psyche is not composed of an ensemble of agencies: indeed, the agency of the subject of modernity tends to exist only momentarily, as a "surging forth" of something unexpected within the articulation of a discourse. If there is any agency, it is the agency of the letter, of the signifier.

3. I have consulted Bruce Fink's lucid exposition of Lacanian psychoanalysis extensively in the preparation of this dissertation (Fink, 1995a; Fink, 1995b; Fink, 1995c; Fink, 1995d; Fink, 1996a; Fink, 1996b; Fink, 1997). Also useful was Joël Dor's introduction to Lacan (Dor, 1997). Both official English translations of Lacan's seminars and papers (Lacan, 1974; Lacan, 1977; Lacan, 1986; Lacan, 1987; Lacan, 1988a; Lacan, 1988b; Lacan, 1993; Lacan, 1996) and some unofficial translations of material not available in English (Lacan, 1989a; Lacan, 1989b) were consulted for this dissertation. Jacques-Alain Miller's articles on the master sig-

The "Graph of Desire" can be regarded as consisting of two analytically dis-

nifier and "extimacy" (Miller, 1978; Miller, 1994) represent authoritative commentaries on key Lacanian concepts. Needless to say, Žižek's popular introductions form the best possible entry point into Lacanian theory (Žižek, 1991b; Žižek, 1992b; Žižek, 2001c). The wonderful, discursive introductions to desire, sexuation and the object (*a*) by Darian Leader are unsurpassed for their accessibility, conceptual accuracy and sheer wit (Leader, 1996; Leader, 1998; Leader, 2001). Other material on Lacanian psychoanalysis consulted included the following. Joan Copjec's presentation of the opposition between Lacanian theory and postmodern historicism was decisive in the formation of my main contention regarding postmarxian theory, although she deals with the impact of Foucault on film theory and not with postmarxian social theory (Copjec, 1994b). See also her introduction to *Supposing the Subject* (Copjec, 1994a). Mark Bracher's accessible exposition of Lacanian discourse theory presents the "four discourses" and major Lacanian concepts (divided subject, object (*a*), master signifier, knowledge) was invaluable (Bracher, 1994), as was Russell Grigg's entry on discourse in *A Compendium of Lacanian Terms* (Glowinski, Marks *et al.*, 2001: 61-70). Yannis Stavrakakis' essay on Lacanian politics is valuable, although it subjects Lacan to the problematic of Laclau and Mouffe without recognising that Lacan cannot be aligned with historicism (Stavrakakis, 1999). I confess to a strong affinity for Richard Boothby's unorthodox interpretation of Lacan through the lens of Freudian libido theory (Boothby, 1991), not least because it supplies a working model through which one can *derive* and *confirm* Lacanian propositions (as opposed to merely accepting the word of the master). Tamise van Pelt's introduction to Lacan's three registers is insightful, although she tends to conceptualise the relations between Imaginary, Symbolic and Real as a musical score (as different "instruments" or "melodies" inhabiting a homogeneous space) and not as a formal topology (as a system of formal relations between heterogeneous operations inhabiting disjoint spaces) (van Pelt, 2000). On Lacanian concepts, I have relied especially on Eric Laurent for the distinction between alienation and separation (Laurent, 1995) and Maire Jaanus for the drives (Jaanus, 1995). These concepts are further explicated by the excellent contributions to the collection entitled *Reading Seminar XI* (Feldstein, Fink *et al.*, 1995). Lacan's seminars on desire (Lacan, 1989a; Lacan, 1989b) are available as unofficial translations by Dr. Cormac Gallagher; Žižek and Dor on the "graph of desire" (Dor, 1997: 195-245; Žižek, 1989: 87-129) are extremely useful introductions. The relation of desire between subject and object is raised especially in the contributions to the collection entitled *Reading Seminars I and II* (Feldstein, Fink *et al.*, 1996). Two of Fink's students, Julia Lupton and Kenneth Reinhard, develop a Lacanian interpretation of tragedy that concretises key Lacanian concepts, especially the "graph of desire" (Lupton and Reinhard, 1993). The essays presented in the *Sic* series (from Verso) are highly useful introductions to the subject (Žižek, 1998b), the object (*a*) (Žižek and Salecl, 1996) and the "formulae of sexuation" (Salecl, 2000). Several collections of Lacanian essays can be found (Apollon and Feldstein, 1995; Malone and Friedlander, 1988; Pettigrew and Raffoul, 1996), containing contributions of varying quality. Shoshana Felman's work on Lacan and speech act theory is now a classic (Felman, 1983), and John Forrester's work on Lacan and Derrida, while not really Lacanian, develops an insightful commentary on the psychoanalytic concepts of the temporality of speech (Forrester, 1990). Jonathan Lear produces an existential Lacan in support of a relatively depoliticised psychoanalytic ethics (Lear, 2000). A related shift happens in Stuart Schneiderman's homage to Lacan as a philosopher of "being towards death," which minimises the problem of *sexuality* as the final determinant in the psychoanalytic field (Schneiderman, 1983). These compare unfavourably with Alenka Zupančič's brilliant reconstruction of Lacanian ethics from a Kantian perspective informed by Žižek's work (Zupančič, 2000). A feminist introduction to Lacanian theory is presented by Elizabeth Grosz (Grosz, 1990) and Patricia Elliot writes a critical introduction to the often highly unorthodox appropriations of Lacan in psychoanalytic feminism (Elliot, 1991). Finally, somewhat dated introductions that

tinct, but actually connected levels, which broadly correspond to the distinction between conscious and unconscious: "the level of [discursive] meaning and the level of [libidinal] enjoyment" (Žižek, 1989: 121). As Žižek explains, the major advance in his work identifies that:

> The crucial weakness of hitherto "(post-)structuralist" essays in the theory of ideology descending from the Althusserian theory of interpellation was to limit themselves to the lower level, to the lowest square of Lacan's graph of desire—to aim at grasping the efficiency of an ideology exclusively through the mechanisms of Imaginary and Symbolic identification. The dimension "beyond interpellation" which was thus left out has nothing to do with some kind of irreducible dispersion and plurality of the signifying process—with the fact that the metonymic sliding always subverts every fixation of meaning, every "quilting" of the floating signifiers (as it would appear in a "poststructuralist" perspective). "Beyond interpellation" is the square of desire, fantasy, lack in the Other and drive pulsating around some unbearable surplus-enjoyment (Žižek, 1989: 124).

Žižek opposes the postmodern reduction of the subject to a dispersed multiplicity of subject-positions, lent a merely imaginary unity by a political symbol. The concept of dispersed, multiple subject-positions promulgated by Laclau and Mouffe concentrates on ideological misrecognition of decentred discourses, theorising the formation of the subject in terms of a "subject-effect" of the multiplicity of discursive practices constitutive of the interpellated individual. By contrast with postmarxian theory, Žižek maintains that the Lacanian (divided) subject is the quasi-transcendental condition of possibility and impossibility for the relative unity of an ensemble of subject-

---

tend to present Lacan as a structuralist, but that still make a valuable contribution to the literature on Lacan, come from Anthony Wilden (Wilden, 1968), Ellie Sullivan (Ragland-Sullivan, 1986) and Annika Lemaire (Lemaire, 1977). Early efforts to come to grips with Lacan whose importance today is strictly limited include Jane Gallop's largely mystified commentary on *Écrits* (Gallop, 1985) and the somewhat more solid work by John Muller and William Richardson (Muller and Richardson, 1982). For the historical context for the development of Lacanian theory consult Catherine Clement's critical history (Clement, 1983). The best of the critical material on Lacan is without doubt the deconstructive essay, *The Title of the Letter* (Lacoue-Labarthe, 1992), which develops Derrida's comments in *The Post Card* (Derrida, 1987: 411-496). The limitation of Lacoue-Labarthe and Nancy's treatment is that they allege, on the basis of a single seminar in Lacan's *Écrits*, that the unconscious subject is a centred subject (that is, that Lacan transposes the classical subject to the domain of the unconscious). This ignores the significance of the object (*a*) and the concept of "extimacy," which precisely *decentre* the unconscious subject. The opposite criticism is produced by Manfred Frank (Frank, 1989), who claims that the decentring of the unconscious subject prevents the development of a subjective identity and effectively disperses the subject into the text of its utterances. For a reply to this position, see Peter Dews (Dews, 1987). For hostile criticisms of Lacan's work, consult Marcelle Marini (Marini, 1992), Mikkel Borch-Jacobsen (Borch-Jacobsen, 1991) and François Roustang (Roustang, 1990). This is not, of course, a comprehensive bibliography of works on Lacan; for a more complete bibliography, consult Marini (Marini, 1992).

positions. Instead of focusing on the relation between Imaginary mirror-im-
ages and Symbolic differences, he concentrates on the dimension "beyond
interpellation" that forms in the intersection of the symbolic field with the
"Real of enjoyment".

Lacan provocatively interpreted the Cartesian *cogito* as a disjunctive syl-
logism ("I think where I am not, and I am where I do not think") to emphasise the distinction between the "substanceless subjectivity" of the subject
of the enunciation, and the embodied existence of the human individual (Dolar, 1998: 11-40; Lacan, 1998: 13). Following Lacan's interpretation,
Žižek supposes that there exists a permanent discord, or irreducible alienation, between social subjectivity and material existence. In other words, the
dimension "beyond interpellation" that subverts every ideological form of
social subjectivity arises not from textual dissemination, but from the un-
bridgeable gulf between subjection to the signifier and the materiality of the
body. For Žižek, therefore, post-Althusserian theories of subjectivation flowing from Derrida and Foucault miss both the "I think" and the "I am". They
thereby degenerate into a discursive idealism that concentrates on the effects
of textual polysemy on a dispersed ensemble of subject-positions, to the exclusion of both transcendental subjectivity and embodied existence.

Žižek's work is undoubtedly a breakthrough. Following Mark Bracher,
we can anticipate that "Lacan's formulation of … a circular causality between the Symbolic and the Real makes it possible to account for the fact
that individual subjects are produced by discourse and yet manage to retain some capacity for resistance" (Bracher, Alcorn *et al.*, 1994: 1). Contrary
to postmarxian discourse analysis, political resistance arises from the subject, not from the "undecidability" of the text. Yet, like all breakthroughs,
Žižek's Lacanian dialectic is unevenly developed, stamped with its origins
in the historicist-relativist problematic of Laclau and Mouffe. In the end, despite abandoning postmarxism for Marxism, Žižek does not manage to go
beyond historicism.

This chapter performs a symptomatic analysis of a series of political
reversals, ethical hesitations and theoretical uncertainties that betray the
existence, in Žižek's work, the reinstatement of the identical subject-object
of history. Žižek's politicisation of Lacanian psychoanalysis relies upon a
slight, yet significant, vacillation in the relation between the Lacanian subject and its object. The strategy of this chapter is to demonstrate that Žižek's
work can be divided into two periods: the postmarxian period of "radical
democracy" and the Marxist period of "Pauline Materialism". The period of "radical democracy" runs from *The Sublime Object of Ideology* (1989) to
The Metastases of Enjoyment (1994), while the period of "Pauline Materialism"
spans *The Indivisible Remainder* (1996) to *The Ticklish Subject* (2000), as well as
more recent, minor works. Contra Žižek, the two periods are not absolutely
distinct, but instead express different articulations between the divided sub-

ject to the "eternally lost," "sublime object," the Lacanian object (*a*). The articulation between Žižek's construction of Lacanian psychoanalysis and his political ideology is crucial. Because an effective critical "division of la-bour" operates between Lacanian psychoanalysis and theories of ideology, critical reception of his work has grasped alternatively at its politics, or its Lacanian theory, without fully connecting the two.[4] In the postmarxian pe-

---

4. My position develops the insights of Sharpe into the antinomies that plague Žižek's position (Sharpe, 2001a; Sharpe, 2001b). By demonstrating that the poles of the "antinomies of Slavoj Žižek" correspond to two distinct periods, I resolve Žižek's apparent self-contradic-tions into *technical* (as opposed to descriptive) antinomies, that is, opposite conclusions from identical premises. I then demonstrate that the latent philosophical assumption upon which this antinomic structure rests is that of "intellectual intuition". That is, I show how a critical solution to the antinomy is possible. Postmarxian critics of Žižek include Laclau's exasper-ated claim that Žižek regresses to a Lukácsian Marxism devoid of concrete programmatic suggestions (Laclau, 2000b: 195-206), combined with the allegation that Žižek's Lacanian dialectics effect a reduction of the social field to an allegory of the psyche (Laclau, 2000a: 288-296). For Daly, a reconciliation between deconstructive pan-textualism and the psycho-analytic category of enjoyment is possible once the Real is recast as the fantasy accompani-ment of textual formations (Daly, 1999: 87) (which is psychoanalytic terms means, once the Real is domesticated for deconstructive consumption by being reduced to the Imaginary). Thus Žižek is to be criticised for not noticing that (with Laclau and Mouffe) the universal grows from the particular, enabling a democratic "extension" of nationalism (Daly, 1999: 89). (Žižek's actual position is that the particular *subverts/supports* the universal, sufficiently indicating the limits of Daly's "radicalism".) Glynos endorses some of the most problematic aspects of "Žižek's anti-capitalism" on the basis of an uncritical acceptance of the thesis of a "deep structural homology" between capitalism and hysteria (Glynos, 2001: 78). Late capitalism is therefore (by inference) the descent into perversion, leading to an effort to cast Žižek's proposal for a social "cure" as an ethical opposition to capitalism. Glynos explains that "if the dynamic logic of capitalism serves as one of Žižek's central targets, it is because it relies upon a certain sort of subjectivity"—literally so, for in this perspective, desire is the motor of capitalism (Glynos, 2001: 86-88). Glynos is not alone: Soto-Crespi claims to detect (following Žižek) a homology not only between surplus value and "surplus enjoyment," but also between the psychic operations of alienation (lack) and separation (loss), and the eco-nomic functions of commodification and exploitation (Soto-Crespo, 2000). Donahue, like-wise endorses Žižek's "late Marxism" as a critical expression of the postmodern condition (Donahue, 2001). Thus, for supporters and critics of Žižekian postmarxism alike, "the Real" designates the homology between social subjectivity and political economy, something to be deplored or explored, according to theoretico-political preference. Butler's postmarxian-feminist critique of Žižek is a major statement of feminist suspicion towards the category of the Real and its link to the "phallic" signifier (Butler, 1993: 196-211, 216-220; Butler, 2000: 140-151). While I am critical of Butler's position on psychoanalysis, as canvassed in detail in Chapter Three above, her position on Žižek exposes the *political* (as opposed to theor-etical, which I believe she misrecognises) stakes in the "Real of sexual difference". In briefest compass, Lacan's "formulae of sexuation" appear to be symbolisations of the two possible logical stances towards totality: inconsistency and completeness ("masculine"); consistency and incompleteness ("feminine"). There is absolutely no justification for assigning sexes to these logical operations—a position which, as Butler proposes, necessarily encourages the notion that natural biological differences in reproductive organs form the zero-degree of human difference. That this is not exactly what Lacan states (Copjec, 1994b: 201-236), has not prevented the conservative wing of Lacanian theory from developing what can only be

riod of radical democracy, following Lacan, this relation is a disjunction. In the period of "Pauline Materialism," this becomes an identity of subject and object. The hinge between the two periods—the moment of the break—is the encounter with the metaphysics of the philosopher of German Romanticism, F. W. Schelling, in Žižek's *The Indivisible Remainder* (1996) and *The Abyss of Freedom* (1997).

In the Lacanian terms developed by Žižek, an identical subject-object appears as an identity of the "subject before subjectivation" and the "sublime object of ideology" in the moment of the political decision. This effectively makes the subject the "creator of the totality of contents" (Lukács) of the entire social field—an idealist position that involves an explicit rehabilitation of the discredited doctrine of "intellectual intuition" pioneered by Schelling. I contend that it is this impossible desire that keeps Žižek within the "event horizon" of the historicist problematic despite his recent rejection of postmarxism, trapped in the paradoxical position of denouncing postmodern politics whilst launching joint declarations of tendency with Laclau and Butler.

---

called a "sexual difference fundamentalism". Note that my brief is against the "Real of sexual difference," not the category of the Real, whereas Butler conflates the two without realising that it is only the later Lacan who makes sexual difference into the stake of the Real. Note also that the assumption that Žižek somehow "represents" the masculine position and Butler the feminine is inaccurate: Clemens demonstrates that, in Lacanian terms, the opposite is true (Clemens, 2003: 113-132). Žižek's reliance on the politically-suspect positions of Laschian social psychology (the dethroning of paternal authority in the decline of the nuclear patriarchal family leads to the rise of the incomparably more ferocious "maternal superego" and the "pathological narcissist" of late capitalism), combined with dismissals of the NSM as mere cultural displacements of class antagonisms, support the suggestion that a reactionary cultural agenda is latent in the Žižekian Real. For Porter, the notion of a non-ideological reality is a contradiction in terms, and so Žižek's Real can only mean a "non-place" (a utopia of disalienation, maintained as the necessary-impossible ethical standard that generates the imperative to engage in ideology-criticism) (Porter, 2002). Herbold combines Butler's arguments with a variant of this "there's no such thing as a non-ideological reality" argument to propose that Žižek's reliance on patriarchal theories vitiates his ideology-critique by gendering the non-position "outside ideology" (Herbold, 1995: 112). Thus, for Žižek's feminist and postmodernist critics, the Real is some-thing, although disagreement exists as to whether this is ultimately nature or utopia.

For the Lacanian critics—for whom the Real is a *relation* irreducible to a worldly referent, whether a natural object or a social space—Žižek's politics are irrelevant or "inconsistent" with psychoanalytic neutrality. From this perspective it is questioned whether psychoanalysis can make a meaningful contribution to social theory (Bellamy, 1993) and whether psychoanalytic categories have any really extra-clinical referents (Nicol, 2001). While many psychoanalytic thinkers salute Žižek's popularisation of Lacanian psychoanalysis (Reinhard, 2001), deplore its criticism of the postmodern dispersion of the subject (Flieger, 2001), express their fascination with its religious overtones (Moriarty, 2001; Wright, 2001), or try to align Žižek with the themes of *Lacan et la Philosophie* (is it philosophy? Anti-philosophy? Continental philosophy? Or perhaps—incredibly—Anglo-American philosophy?), the common denominator is a withdrawal from analysis of Žižek's politics. Thus the Lacanians invert the most frequent criticism of Žižek—that his cultural and political investigations are only illustrations for psychoanalytic propositions—into an implied or explicit endorsement of this practice.

Three Centres of Gravity ... and Death

The problems with Žižek's ethico-political stance are rooted in a philosophical anthropology of the death drive as the "real kernel" of human existence. This anthropology secretes the metaphysics of "intellectual intuition," or the notion of an identical subject-object of history, as its "philosophical unconscious". In philosophical terms, the notion of an identical subject-object belongs to the problem of "intellectual intuition," a possibility, according to Kant, excluded for humanity's merely "discursive intellect" (Žižek, 1993: 18-19, 38-39; Kant, 1993: 61-68 (B59-B72), 106 (B44), 228-30 (A83/B339-A287/B343)). In intellectual intuition, instead of regulative fictions, the Ideas of reason become principles directly constitutive of phenomena, and correlatively, the subject capable of "intellectual intuition" can directly intuit the noumenal aspect of the object. For an intellect capable of "intellectual intuition," then, the Ideas of reason would immediately be objects of possible experience, forming a sensible nature, and so such an architect of the universe would effectively generate the forms of the world from its intentional positing of objectivity. In other words, such a subject "expressively" generates the social totality from the contents of its intentions. This idea, revived by Fichte in the form of the "identical subject-object," transforms the finite human into a demi-god able to mould sensible nature into a moral world order, in conformity with the Ideas of the subject. What German philosopher Dieter Henrich calls "Fichte's original insight" into the supposed possiblity of intellectual intuition (Henrich, 1982), formed, according to some interpretations, the basis for Schelling's philosophy. Intellectual intuition was rehearsed in the twentieth century in the form of Lukács' Hegelian Marxism, which found in the proletariat an "identical subject-object of history" (Lukács, 1971: 149).

For Žižek, the Lacanian "Real of enjoyment", explains the openness of the historical process and replaces Laclau and Mouffe's category of the "field of discursivity" as the explanation of why discursive totalities cannot become "structural eternities". The subversion of symbolic structures by the force of desire (dynamised in the final analysis by the death drive) explains the "restlessness" of the subject within *every* discursive structure. Instead of the "end of history" characteristic of, for instance, Alexandre Kojève's interpretation of Hegel (Kojève, 1980), in Žižek's Lacanian dialectics the agonic process of social struggle is endless.

To anticipate somewhat, the basic Lacanian idea of the death drive can be summarised under the Freudian heading of the "absence of an ideational representation of the drives". Because a direct representation is missing, contingent empirical objects are "elevated to the dignity of the Thing," functioning, through sublimation, as substitute-representations constitutive of the libidinal goals of the subject (Lacan, 1986).[5] In Žižek's social theory, these material objects are ideological rituals (connected to master signifiers), by which individuals are interpellated as subjects.

Žižek theorises the logical zero-degree of human subjectivity, the moment between two master signifiers, as the zone "between the two deaths" (between symbolic death, where the absence of any master signifier equals the non-existence of social identity, and real, natural death). This is graphically captured in the "sublime" image of Eastern European rebels in 1990 "waving the national flag with the red star, the Communist symbol, cut out, so that instead of the symbol standing for the organising principle of the national life, there was nothing but a hole in its centre" (Žižek, 1993: 1). "It is difficult to imagine," Žižek adds, supporting the claim that the death drive replaces Laclau and Mouffe's field of discursivity, "a more salient index of the 'open' character of a historical situation 'in its becoming'" (Žižek, 1993: 1). At the risk of labouring the point, the hole in the flag figures the absence of the ideational representative of the drives, the "void" of the "Thing" (the id, or drives), contingently filled by various master signifiers (red stars, radical democracy, The American Way of Life…).

Despite the exasperation Žižek seems to generate in his critics, the relation between the "hole" of the death drive and the "political symbol" of the master signifier maintains the unity of his theory, preventing his complex synthesis from collapsing into a competing multitude of inconsistent positions. According to Žižek, his work contains:

> three centres of gravity: Hegelian dialectics, Lacanian psychoanalytic theory, and contemporary criticism of ideology. … The three theoretical circles are not, however, of the same weight: it is their middle term, the theory of Jacques Lacan, which is—as Marx would say—"the general illumination which bathes all the other colours and modifies their particularity" (Žižek, 1991a: 3).

I conjecture that there is a functional distribution of theoretical roles amongst these "three centres of gravity," into, respectively, historical dialectics, the unconscious subject and postmarxian politics. This distribution can be related to the Lacanian theory of the three registers: the Symbolic order of the signifier (Hegelian dialectics); the Real of enjoyment structured by fantasy (Lacanian psychoanalysis); and, the Imaginary order of ideological misrecognition (postmarxian theory). Why, then, does the middle term define the "specific gravity" of the rest of Žižek's theoretical ensemble? My claim is that the death drive forms a supplementary fourth centre of gravity, which ballasts the Žižekian problematic, forms the very "substance" of Žižek's work, links Žižek's "three centres of gravity" into a theoretical configuration and centres his research on the problem of the subject-object relation. Inso-

---

5. See (Žižek, 1994c: 87-112) for Žižek's commentary.

far as the death drive is coextensive with the Real of enjoyment (Žižek, 1989:
132), and this is located in the slot marked "Lacan," Žižek can legitimately
claim that his work consists of three components, but that one part determines the specific gravity of the other parts. The category of the Real overdetermines Žižek's entire theoretical ensemble, leading Žižek to successively
(and dangerously) identify the Real with the dialectical concept of the historical violence that founds a social totality, the psychoanalytic hypothesis of the
death drive as a disruptive "third domain" between nature and culture, and
the postmarxian hypothesis of ineradicable social antagonism.

According to Žižek, psychoanalysis explains how the multiplicity of social antagonisms generating postmodern struggles for cultural recognition
are actually "a multitude of responses to the same impossible-real kernel"
(Žižek, 1989: 4). He enlarges on this proposition:

> The subject is constituted through his own division, splitting, as to the
> object in him; this object, this traumatic kernel, is the dimension that we
> have already named as that of "death drive," of a traumatic imbalance,
> a rooting out. Man as such is "nature sick unto death," derailed, run off
> the rails through fascination with a lethal Thing (Žižek, 1989: 181).

The "lethal Thing," Žižek's "kernel of the Real," stimulates/cataly-
ses constant, but incomplete, efforts to symbolise the unnatural nature at
the centre of human existence. According to him, this core is "radically
non-historical: history itself is nothing but a succession of failed attempts to
grasp, conceive, specify this strange kernel" (Žižek, 1989: 5). In keeping with
all philosophical anthropologies, therefore, Žižek postulates an ahistorical
foundation for the unity of the concept of Man:

> In this perspective, the "death drive," the dimension of radical negativity,
> cannot be reduced to an expression of alienated social conditions, it
> defines *la condition humaine* as such: there is no solution, no escape from it;
> the thing is not to "overcome," to "abolish" it, but to learn to recognise
> it in its terrifying dimension and then, on the basis of this fundamental
> recognition, to try to articulate a *modus vivendi* with it (Žižek, 1989: 5).

The death drive, in other words, is the anthropological basis for the (negative) unity of the "human condition". Interpreting the "discontents of civi-
lisation" as a "hole" in every symbolic order, Žižek makes the death drive
into the basis of everything from political revolutions to cultural styles. The
"kernel of the real" is therefore also the theoretical kernel of Žižek's work—
it is not a speculative annex, but its fundamental basis—as demonstrated by
the overdetermination, by the Real, of Žižek's "three centres of gravity".

That the category of the Real overdetermines Žižek's interpretation of
Lacan is clear: his Lacan is the "third period" Lacan of the Real as a hole
in the Symbolic field—the Lacan of the logic of fantasy, identification with
the *sinthome*, the incompleteness of the Other and the mysteries of the Bor-

romean knot (Žižek, 1989: 131-136). It is also the Lacan of an increasingly strident insistence on the "Real of sexual difference" as the deadlock structuring every symbolisation. For Žižek, the concept of the Real is also crucial to preventing his Lacanian dialectic from relapsing into the speculative metaphysics of intellectual intuition.

The problem is, however, that the conceptual architecture of Žižek's synthesis secretes a philosophical unconscious that relies upon "intellectual intuition" as its fundamental structure. The moment we have made the "Real kernel" of human nature into the root of both social antagonism and the historical process we risk a philosophical anthropology where the Hegelian thesis of the "substance as subject" designates a "vanishing," "repressed" moment of identity between the subject and object. Žižek's social theory and cultural anthropology is therefore constantly menaced by a relapse into the supposition of an identical subject-object of history.

Lacan: The Real of Enjoyment

Žižek's fundamental strategy for evading an identical subject-object of history is to insist on the permanent alienation of subject from object. According to him, the gap between Symbolic and Real, historical social formations and human nature never closes, and so no society is ever the direct expression of the "subject of history," just as there is no form of social antagonism that directly manifests the "kernel of the Real" in social relations. Indeed, Žižek's Lacanian dialectic seems to reject any philosophical anthropology of an "identical subject-object of history," where the Hegelian dictum of the "substance as subject" entails the alienation-expression, by the "subject of history," of the social totality.

Žižek's energetic denials of speculative metaphysics are apparently sustained by the Lacanian inverse proportionality between subject and object, because the mutual exclusion (and paradoxical imbrication) of symbolic desire and the "Real of the drives" generates a permanent unruliness in the subject, effectively preventing any final reconciliation of subject and object. I am convinced that, despite Žižek's "non-metaphysical" orientation to dialectical theory, it is fundamentally the Lacanian relation between the "divided subject" and its "eternally lost object" that maintains the separation of subject and object, and prevents the emergence of an "identical subject-object". The subject of desire is alienated from the structure and separated from an eternally "lost" object, condemned to a futile quest for completeness. The self-identity of the Lacanian subject is as impossible, from this perspective, as the identity of subject and object. So long as Žižek sticks to the Lacanian subject, he avoids metaphysical relapse.

To grasp how the relation between Symbolic and Real works in Žižek's dialectics, then, we need to attend to some theoretical propositions of Lacanian psychoanalysis, for my contention will be that, at a certain point, Žižek's position involves a significant revision of basic principles. Freud arrived at the concept of the death drive as a regulative hypothesis designed to account for the phenomena that could only be explained by the categories of repetition compulsion and traumatic re-enactment (Freud, 1984: 269-340 especially 295). Yet, in the characteristic slippage from regulative hypothesis to constitutive principle that vitiates many of Freud's anthropological insights, "Beyond the Pleasure Principle" moves inexorably towards the "death instinct" and a speculative discussion of the government of necessity within the "living substance" (Freud, 1984: 316-317). Before long, we are on the terrain of the speculative opposition between construction and destruction (life and death), proper to Schopenhauerian philosophy (Freud, 1984: 322). The "elemental" struggle between speculative principles as directly constitutive of the subject's acts is precisely what a regulative hypothesis does not license, as this cannot constitute empirical reality, but only provide an ideal focus for the convergence of theoretical categories.

Now, as is well known, the hypothesis of the death drive is a central component of Lacan's return to Freud. Lacan's revision of the concept of the death drive transforms Freud's biological instinct into a denatured drive and thereby restores its status as a regulative hypothesis. The Lacanian subject is not only divided in the Symbolic through "lack" (alienation)—the "lack" of a proper signifier—but also decentred in the Real through "loss" (separation)—the "loss" of an ideational representative of the drives.[6] The category of "lack" (alienation) is based on Lacan's identification of the distinction between the "subject of the statement" and the "subject of the enunciation". The Lacanian subject—radically distinct from the conscious ego, or "subject of the statement"—is identified with the "subject of the enunciation" as a "fading" in discourse that results from the permanent split between the irreducible temporality of the enunciation and the synchronic network of propositions into which the statement is inserted (Fink, 1995a: 36-41; Žižek, 1991a: 155; Lacan, 1998: 26). The effect of the insertion of the human individual into language is not only the generation of an unconscious subject, however, but also the evacuation of libidinal satisfaction from the body, leaving only rem(a)inders in the form of the erogenous zones.[7] Phenomeno-

---

6. The Lacanian subject maintains a tenuous link with the material existence of the human subject as a natural being, but refuses any direct access to natural need and biological instinct as a delusive immediacy. The human being's entry into language involves not only the division of the subject into consciousness and the unconscious, but also the bending of the instincts into the repetitive motion of the drives. This aligns the satisfaction of the drives with the concept of a "primal scene" or traumatic encounter with a master signifier and suggests that the drives are "warped" into their circular path by the action of this signifier. Lacan's revision of the concept of the death drive transforms Freud's biological instinct into a denatured drive and thereby restores its status as a regulative hypothesis.

7. Symbolically-constructed desire aims for this "real object" as that which lies "beyond"

logically, the unconscious "subject of desire" is alienated into language and forced to seek, through a series of substitute-objects, for an eternally lost "object". This (logically) second operation of "loss" (separation) invokes the figure of the "death drive," for despite the "montage" of a multiplicity of drives (oral, anal, scopic, invocatory), these can be regulatively totalised through their identification in the last instance with the generative cycle of sex and death. The libidinal satisfaction of the drives is conceptualised by Lacan as "enjoyment"—the "only substance known to psychoanalysis" (Lacan)—and theorised as *structurally* distinct from "substanceless subjectivity"—hence Lacan's recasting of the *cogito* as *disjunctive*. Jacques-Alain Miller figures this paradoxical relation of "internal exclusion," between divided subject and object (*a*), as "extimacy," designating the impossibility of an irruption into the Symbolic Order of the "Real of enjoyment," or libidinal object of the drives, in any form other than hallucination (Miller, 1994).[8]

The Lacanian conception of the death drive, as the absent cause of the compulsion to repeat, is a regulative fiction and not a substantive entity (i.e., a biological instinct) (Fink, 1995c: 232-239). A repetition compulsion implies a "fault" in the differential process of signification—something that "resists symbolisation" and "returns to the same position"—and licenses Lacan's topological interpretation of the death drive as "Real" (Žižek, 1989: 132). The Real of enjoyment therefore designates a remainder, a surplus enjoyment that escapes the network of the signifier and fastens to a signifying formation, rendering it porous. As Žižek explains:

> The Real is therefore simultaneously both the hard, impenetrable kernel resisting symbolisation *and* a pure chimerical entity which has in itself no ontological consistency. ... This is precisely what defines the notion of

the metonymic object of desire. The drive, by contrast, accomplishes its goal—the achievement of satisfaction through repetition—in the structurally missed encounter with this "real object" (Lacan, 1998: 177-181). Drive and desire, therefore, work at cross-purposes, and it follows (somewhat paradoxically) from the endless rotary motion of the drive that the drive *is* this "object," that is, in the final analysis, the libido as object-cause of desire, the object (*a*) (Lacan, 1998: 197-199). Consequently drive, identified by Lacan with sexuality and death (Lacan, 1998: 199), thrives on the paradoxical satisfaction of the missed encounter, while desire only exists when it can pursue the metonymic object of desire that is effectively a screen concealing the object of the drives. The collapse of this linguistically mediated screen threatens the annihilation of desire, registered by Lacan as the "aphanisis," or eclipse, of the divided subject before the approach of the object (*a*) (Lacan, 1998: 207-208, 216-219). Colloquially, for psychoanalysis, we might say that "getting what we *really* want" would represent a catastrophe, namely, the extinction of desire, the inability to "want anything anymore". The Lacanian divided subject is therefore elementally social: were the subject whole, undivided, able to "get off" on itself—equivalent to the coincidence of the divided subject with the object of the drives—this would represent the implosion of the subject's relation to language, equivalent to a psychotic break.

8. Lacan explains this conception of psychosis as a linguistic disorder, caused by the invasion by the Real into an imperfectly formed Symbolic Order, in Seminar III (Lacan, 1993).

traumatic event: a point of failure of symbolisation, but at the same time never given in its positivity—it can only be constructed backwards, from its structural effects (Žižek, 1989: 169).

In Žižek's postmarxian period, the Real receives a materialist definition, because it is identified with the traumatic event of a missed encounter and with political contingency (which Žižek figures as a "surplus"), and with "Real-impossible" structural contradictions in the social formation (which Žižek describes as a "substance"). As Žižek explains, "the Real is an 'entity' which must be constructed afterwards so that we can account for the distortions of the symbolic structure" (Žižek, 1989: 162), something that does not exist, but nonetheless exercises a structural causality (Žižek, 1989: 163). The Real is simultaneously posed and presupposed by the Symbolic as its "absent cause": the Real possesses both "corporeal contingency" as the substance of (pre-symbolic) enjoyment *and* "logical [in]consistency," as a series of disruptive effects in the symbolic texture (Žižek, 1989: 171).

While Žižek sustains the relation of mutual exclusion between Lacanian subject and object, the Real, as an absent cause, remains an "empty grave," a structural impossibility. More recently, however (and perhaps with some warrant from the later Lacan), the death drive is transformed from a *hypothesis* unifying certain analytic *categories*, to a distinct *domain* animating the living substance, that is, the *place* (and not the logical zero-degree) "between the two deaths". This necessarily involves the transformation of the Real from a regulative hypothesis into something directly constitutive of phenomenal reality—that is, into a speculative principle. "The place 'between the two deaths'," Žižek affirms, is "a place of sublime beauty as well as terrifying monsters, is the site of *das Ding*, of the real-traumatic kernel in the midst of the symbolic order" (Žižek, 1989: 135). It must not be thought that this domain is the empty space beyond the Limit, the depopulated space of a purely theoretical unity (regulative ideas as "concepts without objects"). Instead, for Žižek, Lacan's later work licenses a systematic exploration of the Beyond and its intensive population with uncanny monsters and sublime heroes. The chief exhibit in this bestiary is the "excremental" figure of the Žižekian "saint," whose most important attribute is that he or she is a subject who has become an object—that is, an undivided subject who is simultaneously an object in the Real (Žižek, 1997a: 79; Žižek, 2000e: 374-375). The suspicion that this odd character is nothing less than a postmodern (i.e., abject) version of the identical subject-object will be confirmed in the course of this chapter. No wonder, then, that Žižek claims that in Lacan's (read, Žižek's) final work, the Real approaches what formerly was the *Imaginary* (Žižek, 1989: 162). It does so, I suggest, because the emergence of fantastic entities is precisely the index of the step from the legitimate employment of reason into transcendental illusion.[9]

---

9. Žižek defends Hegel from the Kantian accusation that dialectics is a protracted relapse

The Hegelian Performative

Nonetheless, Žižek categorically denies that the Hegelian "speculative iden-tity" of the "substance as subject" entails regression to the pre-modern meta-physics of expressive totality posited by an identical subject-object, or "cos-mic spirit," along the lines of Charles Taylor's influential reading of Hegel (Žižek, 1993: 29-33, 125-161; Žižek, 2000h: 70-124; Taylor, 1975). On lines consistent with contemporary "non-metaphysical" dialectics, Žižek produc-es a non-teleological interpretation of the "negation of negation" as ground-ing every identity in its quasi-transcendental conditions of possibility and impossibility (Žižek, 1989: 176-177; Žižek, 1991a: 30; Žižek, 1993: 120-124; Žižek, 1994c: 190).[10] Seeking to defend Hegel from the allegation that dia-

into pre-Critical metaphysics on the grounds that Hegel is actually a more consequent Kant-ian than Kant, for instead of plunging into speculations regarding the noumenal beyond, what Hegel does is to disperse the supposition of an inaccessible absolute truth. (Hegel dis-perses the *inaccessibility* of absolute truth, not the illusion of a final Truth—hence the claim of the *Logic* to conceptualise the very Being of God *qua* Logos.) This is the significance of Žižek's repetition of the Hegelian proposition that "the supersensible is appearance *qua* appearance" (Žižek, 1989: 193-199). The notion that truth forms a standard of knowledge beyond the phe-nomenal field is a *postulate*, revealing that this impossible standard is an *effect* of the decision to limit knowledge, and so with this recognition "Truth is already here" (Žižek, 1989: 191). Žižek can therefore bring together Hegelian dialectics and the Lacanian registers to suggest that this impossibility, paradoxically located *within* the symbolic field, but only cognisable by means of a self-reflexive "shift of perspective," is what Lacan means by the Real. The Real—especially the object (*a*)—is a "mere semblance" that adds nothing to the phenom-enon, consisting of a non-existent anamorphic object "that can be perceived only by a gaze 'distorted' by desire" (Žižek, 1991b: 12). It is worth noting that Žižek's Hegelian solution to the division between noumenon and phenomenon, Truth and knowledge (absolute Truth, as opposed to relative truths), is the opposite of contemporary scientific conceptions of dialect-ical processes. Where Žižek tries to save Truth by sacrificing knowledge—by discovering an object that does not exist for an objective gaze (Žižek, 1991b: 12)—materialist dialectics saves knowledge by sacrificing Truth (Bhaskar, 1991: 15). In question is not Žižek's description of the subjective logic of the object (*a*), but its linkage with Hegelian metaphysics in the service of a social theory and political strategy.

    10. The non-metaphysical dialectics developed by Klaus Hartmann and followers re-sponds to the metaphysics of "cosmic spirit" with two critical moves: the elimination of meta-physical explanations and the introduction of contingency into the structure of the dialectic, considered as a category theory. Hartmann's works in translation are relatively limited (Hart-mann, 1966; Hartmann, 1972; Hartmann, 1988). The English-speaking non-metaphysical school includes—directly—Terry Pinkard's reconstruction of the *Phenomenology* (Pinkard, 1994) and the *Logic* (Pinkard, 1989), Richard Winfield's investigation of the *Philosophy of Right* (Winfield, 1988), Alan White's analysis of the post-Hegelian (Schellingian) criticism of Hegel's ontology (White, 1983)—and indirectly—Robert Pippin's reconstruction of Hegelian social philosophy (Pippin, 1989; Pippin, 1999) and Robert Williams' studies on the theory of recog-nition (Williams, 1992; Williams, 1997). Tony Smith has applied non-metaphysical dialectics to a reconstruction of the logic of *Capital* (Smith, 1989). Žižek is explicitly influenced by Pip-pin (Žižek, 1993: 265 note 10), but his theory of ethical life is very close to Williams' contention that mutual recognition involves the dynamism of the identity and difference of the Other, that is, the Other is recognised, but not known, or known, but not recognised, instigating the

lectics produces an expressive totality driven by the historical teleology of

dialectics of the struggle for recognition as a permanent feature of ethical life (Williams, 1997). According to the non-metaphysical school, a metaphysical explanation involves proposing a suprasensible entity as the explanatory ground for a phenomenon: the phenomenon "x" is only possible if "Φ" exists. By contrast, a category theory reconstructs the intelligibility of a domain of social practice (including natural science) by producing a systematic arrangement of interlocking categories as the explanatory conditions of possibility for the intelligibility of the phenomenon: the phenomenon "x" is only intelligible if the category "Φ" is employed (Pinkard, 1989: 15). That is, Hartmann interprets Hegel as a "transcendental ontology" paradoxically "devoid of existence claims" (Hartmann, 1988: 274). In the light of this research, it emerges that Taylor's is the "Fichtean" interpretation of Hegel initially promoted by Hegel's rival, the theological philosopher Schelling (Pinkard, 1989; White, 1983). This is a somewhat forced reading of Hegel. As Hartmann recognises, the "non-metaphysical" interpretation of Hegel is forced to discard the philosophies of nature and history as "speculative" in the bad, Kantian sense. Further, for Kant, post-critical metaphysics divides into two camps: theology (or special metaphysics) concerns metaphysical entities as explanatory grounds; ontology (or general metaphysics) concerns existence claims for being as the ground of phenomena. Kant, for instance, claims in the metaphysical exposition of the transcendental categories of space and time to have deduced the *existence* of space and time as aspects of being. This is a metaphysical ontology on Kant's terms. The difference between pre- and post-critical metaphysics is that for Kant, a metaphysical ontology can only be inferred from the transcendental examination of human rationality—not deduced from the divine rationality or the structure of nature independently of human knowledge. After Kant, metaphysical ontology remains, but only as a *postulate* of reason and not as a foundational claim. White concedes that Hegel retains a general metaphysics or metaphysical ontology, but defends the proposition that this is an inference from the immanent examination of rationality—that is, a post-critical ontology (White, 1983: 15). Pinkard demonstrates that, from a consistent non-metaphysical perspective, this is unnecessarily defensive (Pinkard, 1989; Pinkard, 1994). Nonetheless, both are compelled to accept that Hegel *does* sometimes lapse into expressive conceptions of totality and teleological constructions of the dialectic. The idea of dialectical rationality as a "transcendental ontology" is useful, however, because it focuses attention on the infamous "logical hierarchy" in Hegel in a way that explains the dialectical sequence of categories without reference to an externally imposed teleology. The interpretations offered by both Pippin and Pinkard sharply differentiate between a transcendental and speculative argument. While the transcendental argument can supply the necessary and universal conditions of possibility, a speculative argument supplies a *better* explanation, but not the only *possible* explanation. Dialectical theories are therefore retrospectively justified in precisely the same way that scientific theories are. Once Hegel is grasped as a post-critical "completion" of the Kantian programme of demonstrating the universal and necessary conditions of possibility for experience, it becomes clear that "Hegelian dialectic is no mysterious form of logic that transcends or is an alternative to ordinary logic. It is a strategy of explanation for a philosophical program that attempts to reconcile most of the major dualisms in the history of philosophy. ... [B]ecause Hegel took himself to be engaged in something like the Kantian "science of reason," he was mistakenly led to see his dialectic as providing not only explanations of the *possibility* of categories but also derivations of the *necessity* of that set of categories" (Pinkard, 1989: 6). Pinkard's non-metaphysical reconstruction of dialectical category theory as an "explanation of possibility" has significant implications for the conception of the "negation of the negation". In this context, then, "contradiction" and "negation" are discursive operators for ordering categories systematically, as opposed to logical operators for making formal inferences. Dialectical contradiction, in the context of constructing a systematic theory of categories implies that a category, considered as a general principle that unifies a the divers-

social reconciliation, Žižek performs a "Hegelian critique of Marx" (Žižek, 1993: 26). He affirms that:

> "Substance as subject" ultimately means that a kind of ontological "crack" forever denounces as a semblance every "worldview," every notion of the universe *qua* totality of the "great chain of being". ... In short, "Hegel as absolute idealist" is a displacement of Marx's own disavowed ontology (Žižek, 1993: 26).

The "lack" in the structure—the inconsistency of every totality, the existence of social antagonism—prevents any automatic social reproduction that might exclude the dimension of political subjectivity. On Lacanian lines, Žižek proposes that what Marx lacks (and Hegel supplies) is a concept of the hysterical subject as correlative to the inconsistency of the social structure. Provocatively proposing that Hegel is the original postmarxist (Žižek, 1989: 5-6), Žižek reads "substance as subject" as a Hegelian anticipation of Althusser (Žižek, 1993: 139-140), whom Žižek interprets as a partial rectification of the *Marxian* ontology of social reconciliation. "Substance as subject," therefore really means the permanence of alienation, interpreted after Lacan as *castration*. As a result, Žižek regards the dialectical process as governed by contingency and driven by the "Real kernel" of the death drive:

> The absolute negativity which "sets in motion" dialectical movement is nothing but the intervention of the "death drive" as radically non-historical, as the "zero-degree" of history—historical movement includes in its very heart the non-historical dimension of "absolute negativity" (Žižek, 1989: 144).

Žižek insists that every dialectical totalisation brings a rem(a)inder that renders the totality incomplete. This is the Lacanian equivalent of Derrida's celebrated shift from the "restricted economy" of classical dialectics to the "general economy" of the signifier. Hence, the inclusion of the death drive within the process of dialectical negation implies a breach in the "restricted economy" of the dialectic, breaking with historical teleology and expres-

---

ity of a manifold, contains a "contradiction" between what it inherently is *qua* category (a unifier of a manifold) and what it is explicitly (the moment of unity alone). By unfolding the moments of unity, difference and unity-in-difference, a series of interconnected categories can be developed that represent "determinations" (specifications) of some category, whereby the category is expanded from an abstract simplicity to a concrete complexity. Because, for Hegel, determination is negation, the three moments of categorical reconstruction (abstract unity, abstract difference, concrete unity-in-difference) develop the "negation of the negation". Yet, in the non-metaphysical perspective, this is not a unique and necessary rational exfoliation of being from thought, but instead a contingent (hypothetical) reconstruction of a field of knowledge that "explains possibility" through this sequence of quasi-transcendental categories. The "negation of the negation" is *not* teleological in non-metaphysical dialectics. This does not negate the force of Althusser's criticism of "expressive totality" as a condemnation of vulgar Hegelian metaphysics, whose real object, however, may very well have been Stalinism (Jameson, 1981: 34-39).

sive totality. Therefore, Žižek claims, dialecticians need to learn to "count to four," by locating the dialectical triad (thesis, antithesis, synthesis) in the fourfold matrix that includes "the non-dialecticisable excess, the place of death ... supposedly eluding the dialectical grasp" (Žižek, 1991a: 179). The means for this transformation is the death drive, which restructures the dialectical triad from "thesis, anti-thesis, synthesis" to "Imaginary, Real, Symbolic" (Žižek, 1993: 120-124); following cothinker Mladen Dolar, "the imaginary balance changes into a symbolically structured network through a shock of the Real" (Žižek, 1989: 183). The inclusion of the "supplementary fourth" element of the death drive into the dialectical triad so transforms Hegel that Žižek's Lacanian dialectics becomes, for several commentators, completely unrecognisable (Dews, 1995: 236-257; Gasché, 1994: 213, 278-279 note 214). This is not a problem for Žižek, however, who avers that "the only way to 'save' Hegel is through Lacan" (Žižek, 1989: 7).

The effect on dialectics is startling: dialectics becomes a "squared totalisation," a meta-narrative of a historical sequence of failed integrations, enabling Žižek "to discern the strange 'logic' that regulates the process by means of which the breakdown of a totalisation itself begets another totalisation" (Žižek, 1991a: 99). In other words, dialectics becomes the philosophy of an impossible existential quest for a complete identity, instead of the historical master narrative of the ascent to absolute knowledge (Žižek, 1991a: 61-68; Žižek, 1993: 171). Instead of a linear evolution, history is cyclically structured by an endless series of incomplete political revolutions.

Žižek's paradigmatic critical intellectual is Hegel, whose *Phenomenology of Spirit* is interpreted as "an 'existential dramatisation' of a theoretical position whereby a certain *surplus* is produced: the 'dramatisation' gives the lie to the theoretical position by bringing out its implicit presuppositions" (Žižek, 1991a: 142). Indeed, Žižek praises Hegel as "the most sublime of hysterics," because Hegel managed to articulate the dialectical logic governing the permanent disjunction between enunciation and statement (Žižek, 1989: 191). In hysteria, an impeded traumatic kernel is converted into a somatic symptom:

> [And] a homologous conversion is what defines the "figures of consciousness" in Hegel's *Phenomenology of Spirit* ... In "dramatising" his position, the subject renders manifest what remains unspoken in it, what *must* remain unspoken for this position to maintain its consistency. Therefore every "figure of consciousness" implies a kind of hysterical theatre (Žižek, 1991a: 142).

The "elementary matrix" of Žižek's ideology-criticism is exactly this process of dramatising theoretical "figures of consciousness"—*a problem disappears when we take into account* (when we 'stage') *its context of enunciation*" (Žižek, 1991a: 145)—as indicating a subjective position of enunciation in relation to a "form of life". The hysteric (the critical intellectual) exposes the castration of the master by disclosing that the truth of subjects' adherence to the master signifier is not grounded upon its ultimate rationality, but instead on the secret yield of libidinal satisfaction ("enjoyment") that sustains their allegiance. Žižek's Lacanian dialectics is designed to expose the contingency of every master signifier and its dependence upon the libidinal investments of the subject (Žižek, 1993: 2).

Instead of teleological metaphysics, then, Žižek interprets Hegel as supplying a "logic of the signifier" (Žižek, 1991a: 74-100; Žižek, 1994c: 47-50) that coincides with the concept of a "Hegelian performative". Dialectics, Žižek insists, reveals the radical contingency of every performative inauguration of a new social order. The "Hegelian performative" designates the moment in which the subject, whose hegemonic articulation succeeds in founding a new social order, acts as a "vanishing mediator" in the historical process (Žižek, 1991a: 195-215). Dialectics therefore disperses the mirage of historical teleology by revealing the repressed historical violence that founds every social totality. In the aftermath of the traumatic event of inauguration, the historical violence of social institution is "gentrified," transformed from the radical negativity of social antagonism into the political positivity of a differential structure (Žižek, 1991a: 195-215). The means for this is the ideological fantasy of a harmonious society, or "social fantasy," which "closes the gap" between the chain of signification and the master signifier. But what exactly *is* this "repressed violence," and in what way is this cyclical theory of history supposed to be *dialectical*?

As Žižek explains, it is generally supposed that Hegel converts Fichte's speculative equation, "I = I" into something like "the absolute subject = the expressive totality of society and history". Not so, Žižek claims: "Hegel converts the Fichtean I = I into the absolute contradiction Spirit = Bone ... the subject is posited as correlative to an object which precisely cannot be considered as the subject's objectivisation" (Žižek, 2001c: 88). But what exactly *is* this foreign body that prevents the emergence of an expressive totality?

Everything hinges, according to Žižek, on the dialectical circle of "presupposing the positing" and "positing the presuppositions". Every performative speech act requires the existence of an institutional or conventional background, with the implication that an inaugural declaration (for instance, the Declaration of the Rights of Man) must necessarily misfire. The paradox is that an institutional background is a presupposition of a declarative speech act, yet in order to inaugurate a new social order, this background must be posited by the declaration itself. For Žižek, this implies the existence of "impossible" performatives—pure inaugural declarations—that coincide with the creation of new social orders and new master signifiers. The corollary is that the performative status of the declaration is "originally repressed," appearing as a constative (Žižek, 2001c: 96-99). In other words, the "stain on the mirror" correlative to the subject, the foreign body that resists incorporation in an expressive totality, is nothing other than the *act* of positing an expressive totality! This act, the act of a subject capable of generating forms of objectivity from "the absolute self-transparency of a pure performative," is what is "originally repressed" as a traumatic deed of self-positing (Žižek, 2001c: 88). Thus, the identical subject-object is the "originally repressed" ground of the division between subject and object, enunciation and statement, which necessarily appear phenomenally as opposites. Is it necessary to add that this "solution" to the problems of the philosophy of reflection is "Fichte's original insight," served up by Žižek as Lacanian dialectics?

Postmarxism: Hegemonic Dialectics and Political Subjectivity

We have seen that Žižek relies upon the Lacanian relation of inverse proportionality between subject and object for his claim that "saving" Hegel through Lacan prevents a return to metaphysical dialectics. Yet Žižek also affirms that in the Act of social inauguration, subject and object coincide in the figure of a "headless subject," a "saint" possessed by the death drive. This completely cancels any inverse proportionality between subject and object, invoking instead the Romantic demigod capable of an act of "intellectual intuition". Likewise, we have seen that Žižek conceptualises the historical process as an endless dialectical sequence, in which the subject appears as phenomenally estranged from the structural "substance". Every dialectical totalisation results in a non-dialectical remainder, he claims, thus squaring the circle of a Lacanian dialectics. But this non-dialectical remainder turns out to be nothing other than the originally repressed act of an identical subject-object.

We therefore have to ask whether an endless dialectical progression, based on a quest for self-identity that departs from an original fusion and returns to an impossible unity, is not, after all, a repetition of the Hegelian "struggle to the death for pure prestige," recast in the language of psychoanalysis.[11] In Žižek's opening intervention into the postmarxian field (Žižek, 1990: 249-260) he proposes, in a variation on the "substance as subject" motif, to read postmarxism not only as political competition, but also as social division. Žižek distinguishes the social reality of the antagonistic fight—a political competition between apparently symmetrical opponents—from the Real of social antagonism—where the radically asymmetrical antago-

---

11. For Alexandre Kojève, for instance, the lesson of the existential reading of Hegelianism was the interpretation of the "end of history" not as a determinate historical terminus, but as the abandonment of the search for a divine guarantee for human rationality (Kojève, 1980). The Kojèvian "sage" combines existential resoluteness in the teeth of the "mineness" of death with the dialectical recognition that the quest for identity culminates in the spiritual substance of universal ethical life, thus celebrating the lack of metaphysical supports for social institutions as a personal conquest with general implications.

nists, master and slave, engage in a fight to the death for social recognition (Žižek, 1990: 253). He aligns this opposition with the distinction between conscious subject-positions (the social reality of the antagonistic fight as political competition) and the unconscious subject (hegemonic dialectics as the Real of social antagonism). Žižek can then propose that the division in the subject leads to an unconscious drive to annihilate the other, who appears before the subject as an object blocking self-identity. As Žižek subsequently explains, the divided subject encounters the other as embodying their lost "sublime" object, with the consequence that the subject is driven by the phantasmatic desire for wholeness to destroy the corporeal body of the other, so as to recapture the subject's "lost" object (Žižek, 1993: 68-69).

Žižek's interpretation of hegemonic politics through the master-slave dialectic, as something like the "elementary matrix of intersubjectivity," generates significant problems, compounding his uncritical acceptance of the transposition of concepts drawn from the psychology of individuals onto the field of political agency. Strictly speaking, the master-slave dialectic is not a form of intersubjectivity at all, because instead of having reference to a shared universality, the master *is* the universal, while the slave is "nothing," a singularity. In Hegel's discussion, therefore, the master-slave dialectic is the transcendental genesis of the field of intersubjectivity, not its paradigmatic form (Hegel, 1977: 111-119; Hyppolite, 1974: 168-177; Pinkard, 1994: 55-62). Worse still, Žižek lacks the dialectics of servile labour that enables Hegel to make the transition from the master-slave dialectic to the opening form of intersubjectivity, the "unhappy consciousness" (Hegel, 1977: 119-138; Hyppolite, 1974: 190; Lukács, 1975: 480-481, 537-567). Not only does this mean that for Žižek, the social formation is regarded as entirely constituted by the master's universal—literally, the "master's signifier"—and hence, the social formation is an expressive totality, but there is no way to get from the "dialectics" of universal and singular to hegemonic politics. Instead, Žižek's social theory can only generate the perspectives of total revolt or servile complicity: this is a "dialectics" incapable of elaborating increasingly complex forms of ethical life. In this optic, history appears as an endless cycle of overthrows, generating no progress, which can be modelled on the Lacanian "formulae of sexuation"—the "Real of sexual difference" between masculine and feminine (Žižek, 1993: 45-80)—that is, an eternal opposition between fixed principles, "master-masculine" and "slave-feminine".

Perhaps these considerations explain Žižek's extraordinary indifference to the critical Hegelian distinction between the "absolute negativity" of "the natural negation of consciousness ... which remains without the required significance of recognition" (Hegel, 1977: 114) and the "radical negativity" of self-consciousness, which generates a continuous movement of transcendence in quest of self-reflexivity through mutual recognition. Žižek employs "absolute negativity," or "abstract" negation, as if it were equivalent to "radical negativity," or "determinate" negation, because, for him, the "absolute negativity" of the death drive dynamises the historical process, by energising the "radical negativity" of the "substanceless subjectivity" of the unconscious subject. It is not the desire for recognition, but the drive to annihilate the other, that supplies the fundamental dynamism, if not of progress, at least of "the eternal return of the same," namely, the endless cycle of political revolutions. Yet, if desire is the desire of the Other, while drive is a pure desire, desire of desire itself, then *on this dialectical schema*, drive will be the return of desire into itself—conditional upon the recognition of the "non-existence," that is, the contingency, the inconsistency, of the Other. But this is precisely the schema whereby Reason, taking itself as an object, finally returns from the long exile of the Spirit into Hegel's "end of history," once it realises that rationality is not resident in God or Nature, but is the product of intersubjective consensus.

Žižek's reliance on the Hegelian dialectic to develop a social theory, then, implies that the struggle for recognition (the master-slave dialectic) is finally a desire for self-identity, that is, for the coincidence of subject and object. According to Hegel, "the object of Desire is ... the universal indestructible substance ... the Notion of *Spirit*" (Hegel, 1977: 110)—that is, the universal medium of intersubjective community, in which "I" is "we" and conversely (Hegel, 1977: 110). And as we shall discover, the "universal Truth" that Žižek will deliver himself of consists exactly in the revelation that the highest deed of self-reflexive subjectivity is the production of a new master signifier, whereby the subject who refuses to give way on their desire indeed arrives at the "spirit of community". There is surely no warrant for this in Lacan. What is lost in Žižek's translation of psychoanalysis into spiritual dialectics is the relation of mutual interference between desire and drive, and therefore the counter-finality dominating the Lacanian conception of the "dialectic of desire". For Lacan, the self-reflexive culmination of the dialectic in an identical subject-object is structurally impossible as a *social* act. For Žižek, by contrast, the articulation of an "impossible," performative contradiction turns out to disclose the Absolute itself, in a "vanishing" moment of social inauguration.

Radical Negativity: The Philosophical Anthropology of the Death Drive

Despite Žižek's denials, then, the major elements of the metaphysical interpretation remain in position: an expressive relation between theoretical ideologies and cultural formations, combined with the agency of the subject, as "vanishing mediator" in the generation of discursive totalities, implies a theory where the social totality is the alienation-expression of a "subject of history". Again, Žižek's explicit anthropology appears to refuse this conclusion, while in actuality relying on the structure of "intellectual intuition" for its truth-claims.

Žižek employs the concept of the Real of enjoyment as a hole in the Symbolic field to present a post-structural anthropology that departs from Lévi-Strauss.[12] Instead of the Symbolic field delineated by structural anthropology, which exhibits the closure characteristic of a centred structure, he conceptualises the socio-symbolic field as decentred, perforated by a hole at its centre. This hole is the Real of social antagonism, and at the centre of the structure we find not an ahistorical governing principle, but instead an empty signifier, a zero-symbol that is the site for political contestation and contingent articulations. Although Lévi-Strauss' two tribal moieties seem to inhabit different discursive universes, "the very splitting into the two 'relative' perceptions implies a hidden reference to a constant"—not, Žižek anxiously assures us, "to the objective, 'actual' disposition of buildings, but to a traumatic kernel, a fundamental antagonism"—which happens to be ideology as the social "zero-institution" (Žižek, 2001c: 221). The modern political Left and Right, Žižek adds helpfully, behave as do these two moieties. The struggle for hegemony, then, "is … precisely the struggle for how this zero-institution will be overdetermined, coloured by some particular signification" (Žižek, 2001c: 222).

At the same time, this is a *post*-structural anthropology, in that the root of social divisions is not some positively existing characteristic of human nature, but instead the "negative essence" of the signifier. Social antagonism is an expression of the Real of social difference (whose root, Žižek proposes, is sexual difference), which can ultimately be explained through the very existence of difference *per se*, as a difference that retroactively appears to pre-exist every differential signification (Žižek, 2001c: 223). This difference "in-itself"

12. (Žižek, 2000c: 112-113; Žižek, 2001c: 221-222). According to Žižek, "a tribe is divided into two subgroups, "those who are from above" and "those who are from below"; when we ask an individual to draw … the plan of his village (the spatial disposition of cottages), we obtain two quite different answers, depending on his belonging to one or the other subgroup. Both perceive the village as a circle, but for one subgroup, there is, within this circle, another circle of central houses, so that we have two concentric circles, while for the other subgroup, the circle is split in two by a clear dividing line. In other words, a member of the first group (let us call it "conservative corporatist") perceives the plan of the village as a ring of houses more or less symmetrically disposed around the central temple, whereas a member of the second ("revolutionary antagonistic") subgroup perceives the village as two distinct heaps of houses separated by an invisible frontier. The central point of Levi-Strauss is that this example should in no way entice us into cultural relativism, according to which the perception of social space depends on the observer's group membership: the very splitting into the two "relative" perceptions implies a hidden reference to a constant—not to the objective, "actual" disposition of buildings, but to a traumatic kernel, a fundamental antagonism that inhabitants of the village were unable to symbolize, to account for, to "internalize" and come to terms with; an imbalance in social relations that prevented the community from stabilizing itself into a harmonious whole. The two perceptions of the village's plan are simply two mutually exclusive attempts to cope with this traumatic antagonism, to heal its wound via the imposition of a balanced symbolic structure" (Žižek, 2001c: 221-222).

forms the core of Žižek's anthropology. As we have seen from Žižek's (post-) structural anthropology, the only certainty is that social division exists. But once social division (pure difference) is grasped as certain knowledge, we have arrived at the (absolute) Truth. Indeed, it is by means of the basic matrix of self-reflexive inversion that Žižek can denounce the effort to occupy a neutral metalinguistic position of enunciation while at the same time producing a theory of the Truth of ideology. Žižek correlates the shift from the desire for a neutral-universal stance to recognition of its impossibility with the move from desire to drive, Symbolic to Real (Žižek, 1994d). This suggests a phenomenology of ideology, whereby the subject strives towards the limits of subjectivity, without for a moment abandoning the valorisation of subject-centred descriptions of experience characteristic of Žižek's rejection of science for philosophy (Resch, 2001). Such a position is grounded in idealist assumptions regarding the primacy of thinking over materiality, so that "logical inconsistency" gradually, but inevitably, supplants "corporeal contingency" as the basic definition of the Real (Resch, 1999).

Žižek accepts the postmodern criticism that ideology-critique implies a privileged position of enunciation from which the agent can denounce ideological mystification, but proposes that nonetheless we must not renounce the concept of an extra-ideological reality (Žižek, 1994d: 17). According to Žižek:

> "I am a replicant" is the statement of the subject at its purest—the same as in Althusser's theory of ideology, where the statement "I am in ideology" is the only way for me to truly avoid the vicious circle of ideology (Žižek, 1993: 41).

Robert Pfaller shows how Žižek equates an ambivalent self-reflexivity with non-ideological truth, implying that the subject, by manifesting their grasp of the impossibility of non-ideological subjectivity, nonetheless manages to "vanishingly" enunciate a non-ideological proposition (Pfaller, 1998: 225-246). This "vanishing" form of (non-)subjectivity is theorised by Žižek as "subjective destitution," the "place between the two deaths" occupied by those sublime heroes (who are equally abject monsters) reduced to automata of the death drive. According to Žižek, then, the performative contradiction inherent in the self-reflexive claim to a "universal ideology" is less an index of delusion than a testimony to truth—as Pfaller shows, Žižek relies upon the claim that the "liar's paradox," *qua* impossible statement, is self-reflexively inverted into the enunciation of an impossibility (Pfaller, 1998: 233-234). Thus, just as "the supersensible is appearance *qua* appearance," the non-ideological is ideology *as* ideology. That is, the moment a universal stance is conceptualised as merely relative, only the result of subjective positioning "in ideology," we have already grasped the truth of ideology by self-reflexively enunciating a performative contradiction. Žižek can therefore maintain that "stepping out of … ideology is the very form of our enslavement to it" (Žižek, 1994d: 6), while conducting the criticism of ideology: non-ideological objectivity is a limit condition *of subjectivity* ("subjective destitution"), whose existence can be self-reflexively inferred from within ideology.

The circular character of Žižek's position generates a link between the "leap of faith" and "absolute knowledge," reminiscent of Lukács' "wager on communism" before writing *History and Class Consciousness*. It is therefore not surprising that Žižek's constant polemical denunciations of "historicism," for its lack of recognition of the "non-historical kernel of human existence," are laced with bold claims to have adopted a "dogmatic" stance, so that, for instance, we are informed that "Marxism and psychoanalysis are 'infallible' at the level of their enunciated content" (Žižek, 1994c: 183). To claim that Žižek remains within the gravitational field of historicism will perhaps generate consternation, for the dominant tendency in criticisms of Žižek is to take a position for or against his supposed *anti*-historicism. Crusader for Cartesian certainty, defender of the *cogito* and supporter of the Truth-Event of militant materialism (the October Revolution), Žižek has produced numerous critiques of "postmarxian historicism" and "postmodern sophism" (Žižek, 1993: 1-5; Žižek, 1996b: 214-218; Žižek, 2000c: 112-114; Žižek, 2001c: 80-81). In opposition to the historicist tendency of radical democratic postmarxism, Žižek has from the beginning proposed that "over-rapid historicisation makes us blind to the real kernel that returns as the same through diverse … symbolisations" (Žižek, 1989: 50). His position is that it is impossible to entirely contextualise a phenomenon: the dissolution of every event into its socio-historical context implies the positioning of the analyst in the "view from nowhere," the god's-eye position of pure, neutral metalanguage situated "above" the historical texture. The apparently modest perspectival relativism of the historicist therefore masks an extraordinarily immodest claim to perfect neutrality, to possess the "master's gaze, which viewing history from a safe metalanguage distance, constructs the linear narrative of 'historical evolution'" (Žižek, 2001c: 80). Žižek connects the metanarrative of legitimation that supports historicism with the fundamental operation of ideology (Žižek, 1991a: 130) and regards deconstruction as the "highest expression" of contemporary historicism, because its endless recontextualisations engage precisely such a metalinguistic claim (Žižek, 1989: 153-155; Žižek, 1991a: 87-90). What historicism overlooks is the eternal return of the same of *difference itself* in every historico-symbolic text, conceptualised psychoanalytically as "lack" (the absence of a presence) (Žižek, 2000c: 114; Žižek, 2001c: 223).

The problem is that this definition of the Symbolic as based in a pure, non-conceptual difference, besides having surprisingly Deleuzian overtones (Deleuze, 1994), coincides with Žižek's definition of the Real, collapsing "lack" into "loss," Symbolic into Real—and subject into object.

II.

Against the conceptual background of Žižek's Hegelian tendency to close the gap between subject and object, it should not be surprising that despite the brilliance of his Lacanian interpretation of ideological interpellation, several small, but significant, revisions lead to a reversal of the Lacanian "agency of the letter" into a Hegelian "agency of the subject". Žižek's extension of the Althusserian concept of ideological interpellation is a powerful Lacanian reformulation of the process of subject formation. By introducing an unconscious dimension to the Althusserian subject, Žižek can explain the hidden dependence of the subject on libidinal investments that are denied in conscious discourse. My contention is, however, that Žižek's exposition of the Lacanian graph of desire as an extension of the theory of interpellation drifts subtly from Althusser and Lacan towards Hegel and Schelling. We therefore have to examine this discursive inversion—which determines Žižek's theoretico-political impasse—very closely in the next sections. I investigate the accuracy of Žižek's interpretation of the Lacanian "Graph of Desire," in the light of the influence of the historicist problematic of Laclau and Mouffe on his work. Then, I propose to clarify the opposition between the Althusserian-Lacanian "agency of the letter" and the Hegelian "agency of the subject" by means of Lacan's matrix of the four discourses (Bracher, 1994: 107-128; Žižek, 1998c: 74-113). I claim that Žižek's reformulation replaces the Lacanian discourse of the master with a hysterical discourse on interpellation.

Beyond Interpellation: The Lacanian Interpretation of Althusser

The Lacanian interpretation of Althusser involves two significant rectifications to the concept of ideological interpellation. (1) Althusser's imaginary relation to the real conditions of existence becomes less important, in interpellating the subject, than the role of an ideological "master signifier" (for instance, "God," or "Communism"), which is held to form the horizon of expectations for the subject by totalising every chain of signification. (2) The material rituals of ideological practice are considered to be effects of an unconscious repetition-compulsion, generated by the trauma of interpellation, so that the unconscious dimension in ideology is rooted less in its subject-centred character, than in the existence of psychic division and intrapychic conflict.

The Althusserian vignette of "hailing," however, involves the paradox that individuals *recognise themselves* as the object of an interpellation *before* they have acquired the minimal self-identity constitutive of subjectivity. The Lacanian interpretation of Althusser accepts the force of this paradox, namely, that the subject's entry into language happens by means of the intervention of an initially *meaningless* command. This interpellation primordially wounds the subject, permanently dividing the subject between an ineffable singular existence and an anticipatory social identity that is structurally incomplete. The nature of this wound is the absence of the "ideational representative of the drives": the drives cannot be directly represented in the psyche, only appearing through delegates, suggesting to Lacan the model of a "hole" that is contingently filled by substitute objects.

Adapting Lacan's notion to the theory of ideology, Mladen Dolar suggests that the interpellation of subjects proceeds by means of the introjection of the ideological command as an uncomprehended alien *object*—a meaningless material *voice*, a blind authoritarian *gaze* (Žižek, 1996a)—that is only *retroactively* accepted as the locus of Meaning (Dolar, 1993: 75-96). Žižek proposes that "belief is an affair of obedience to the dead, uncomprehended letter," and expands upon this *apropos* of "Kafka as critic of Althusser":

> Of course, in his theory of Ideological State Apparatuses, Althusser gave an elaborated, contemporary version of this Pascalian "machine"; but the weak point of his theory is that he or his school never succeeded in thinking out the link between the Ideological State Apparatuses and ideological interpellation ... The answer to this is, as we have seen, that this external "machine" of State Apparatuses exercises its force only in so far as it is experienced, in the unconscious economy of the subject, as a senseless, traumatic injunction. ... *That leftover, far from hindering the full submission of the subject to the ideological command, is the very condition of it* (Žižek, 1989: 43).

The persistence of an enigmatic ideological interpellation in the unconscious tends to hystericise the subject, thus instigating an existential questioning with the potential to undermine the ideological interpellation itself. The after-effects of this traumatic process of division between the signifier and enjoyment continue to resonate in the unconscious, which is "structured like a language," composed of introjected representations, leading to a variety of "formations of the unconscious," ranging from everyday parapraxes to hysterical symptoms. Lacan's conception that "the unconscious is structured like a language" depends upon the distinction between the signifier (the Symbolic Order that consists of differences without positive terms) and the letter (the material support of signification that is inherently meaningless). For Lacan, the unconscious is composed of *letters* which function as objects in the drives (Fink, 1995c: 223-229; Žižek, 1994c: 173). These letters are the depository of the subject's unconscious identifications to a sequence of introjected master signifiers, considered not as elements of the chain of signification, but as *objects* lodged in the unconscious (Fink, 1995a). Paradigmatically, these letters are objects (*a*) (Lacan, 1974: 83-100). According to Lacan, the object (*a*) is both the object *in* desire—the phantasmatic substance of the desired object, which is always the desire of the Other, that is, the desire to be desired by the Other—and the cause *of* desire—a void in the subject that converts the linearity of instincts into the circularity of drive. The unconscious therefore consists of a chain of master signifiers that simultaneously function as objects (*a*), material letters in the combinatory of the unconscious. Hence, the Lacanian subject is both *divided* between the master signifier (meaning) and the object (*a*) (being) (Žižek, 1996b: 79), and *decentred*, because of the non-coincidence of the metaphorical master signifier with the object (*a*) as metonymy of an impossible desire. If the master signifier is the "metaphor of the subject," substituting in discourse for the material existence of the subject, and this master signifier is also the metonymy of the desire of the subject, then whenever the subject designates an object of desire in a chain of signification governed by this master signifier, they constitutively absent themselves from this discourse even as they indicate that their "real" object lies perpetually beyond the horizon of what they are speaking about.

Following Dolar, the object (*a*), or "sublime object of ideology," is the objectival aspect of the master signifier—its material existence as a letter—and it functions as the "rigid designator" within, or "objective correlative" to, the signification governed by the master signifier (Žižek, 1989: 95-100). Approximately, the sublime object—the Lacanian object (*a*)—is the phantasmatic "referent" of the master signifier, the impossible desire that the master signifier "fixes" into position as a sublime "beyond" to the ideological field, while the "subject before subjectivation" is the vanishing "final signified" of the master signifier (Žižek, 1991a: 27). An ideological interpellation, introjected into the psyche of the subject as a meaningless command, instigates a compulsion to repeat the senseless material rituals of ideology. The force of ideological interpellation depends effectively on the lodgement of a fragment of the state machine within the subject, in the form of a senseless, traumatic stain, a dead letter, an unintelligible command to obey.

By means of this conceptual apparatus, Žižek claims to theorise "enjoyment as a political factor," that is, the material rituals of ideological practices as effects of a repetition-compulsion. Because the master signifier is an object for the drives, there is a libidinal satisfaction in the repetition of the rituals associated with ideological practices: the acting out of the material aspect of the symbolic ideological ritual gratifies the libidinal investments of the subject. For Žižek, the paradigmatic instance of this libidinal investment is the Fisher King from the Grail legend, whose performative incompetence exposes a *senseless* repetition-compulsion, that is, an enactment of an ideological ritual lacking the master signifier. This "enjoyment," the libidinal investment in the material ritual, shorn of the formal screen of performative signification, is externalised as the suppurating wound in the Fisher King's thigh (Žižek, 1989: 76-84; Žižek, 1993: 145-199). The basic idea is that we are held to the ideological mystification not *just* because it "explains" the "real conditions of existence" from a subject-centred perspective, nor even because the ideological master signifier totalises the discursive field and enables meaning to emerge, but because we "get off" on, obtain libidinal satisfaction from, the stupid material ritual. The Althusserian thesis that ideology consists precisely of such institutional rituals and material practices ("kneel down and you shall believe") exposed, for instance, the mode of operation of the Stalinist regimes, as well as the most effective path towards generalised resistance (Žižek, 1993: 229; Žižek, 1994c: 59-65), and can be applied to commodity fetishism, where we persist in mystified practices *despite* formal knowledge of the mechanisms of exploitation (Žižek, 1989: 11-53).

The Lacanian "Graph of Desire"

In Chapter Three of *The Sublime Object of Ideology*, Žižek provides a virtuoso exposition of the "Graph of Desire" as a Lacanian extension to the Althusserian theory of ideological interpellation (Žižek, 1989: 87-129). Despite my fundamental agreement with Žižek's intentions, I want to draw attention to two aspects of Žižek's demonstration that introduce a shift towards an identical subject-object. The first is Žižek's understatement of the unconscious Symbolic Law, which leads him to treat the unconscious as consisting exclusively of libidinal enjoyment, neglecting to stress the fundamental generative role of the prohibition of incest. The second is Žižek's substitution of the agency of the subject—who is supposed to "anticipate" their interpellation in an act of decision—for the Lacanian agency of the letter—where the subject has their name effectively imposed on them as an alien destiny. The main stake in Žižek's discussion is his demonstration that "beyond" the dispersed, multiple subject-positions occupied by the agent, there lies not only the logical quasi-transcendental of the empty ("barred," or unconscious) "subject before subjectivation," but also the materiality of the object of the drives and the unconscious libidinal investments of the subject. In general, in the post-marxian field, Žižek's concepts of the "subject before subjectivation" and the "sublime object of ideology" depend upon the category of the Real of enjoyment as the hidden support for, and subversion of, the Symbolic field. On this basis, Žižek aims to theorise "enjoyment as a political factor," that is, the hidden dependence of the reigning master signifier upon a now "vanished" intervention of the "subject before subjectivation," whose current hysterical posture is sustained by a secret yield of enjoyment gained from their subjection. The aim of this analysis will be to liberate the subject from the illusion of the existence of a "sublime object of ideology" and to force recognition of the world-constituting power of the subject *qua* vanishing mediator in the historical process. By employing the Lacanian "Graph of Desire," Žižek therefore aims to demonstrate why enjoyment is the truth of ideology and to explain how it is possible for the critical intellectual, on the basis of this revelation, to preserve critical distance from the master signifier.

Completed Graph

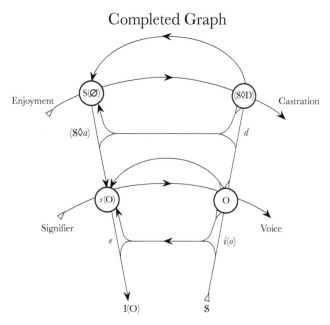

FIGURE: The completed form of the Graph of Desire (Žižek, 1989: 121; Lacan, 1977: 313).

In the lower "level" of the Graph of Desire, the vector running from the "Signifier" to the "Voice" represents the diachronic dimension—or syntagmatic axis of selection—of a differential chain of signification. The synchronic dimension of the process of anchoring—or paradigmatic axis of combination—is represented as an equivalential chain running from the divided subject, S, to the Ego-Ideal, I(O). (This vector travels through the strictly unconscious upper "level" of the Graph of Desire, discussed below.) What Lacan designates as the "effect of retroversion" indicates that the intervention of a master signifier fixes the meaning of the chain of signification: "the *point de capiton* represents, holds the place of, the big Other, the synchronous code, in the diachronous signifier's chain" (Žižek, 1989: 103). The retroactive result of the intervention of the master signifier is symbolic identification, I(O), which stands both for an Imaginary Other and for the Ego-Ideal that is the locus of the symbolic identification of the subject. The intersections of the diachronic chain and synchronic field—where S_2 is replaced by s(O), the meaning of the locution, and S_1 by O, the Other, that is, locus of the code, or "treasury of the signifier"—define at once the minimal differential articulation, S_2—S_1, and the equivalential relation created between these terms by the operation of the master signifier. The point $i(o)$—or ideal ego—is the locus of the metonymic object—the object that metonymically designates the object of desire. The point e—or ego—denotes the "me" of intersubjective discourse. The ego is constituted through the imaginary misrecognition of a differential (decentred) subject-position as a centred identity. Lacan refers to the loop travelling through the points $, *e*, O, s(O), *i(o)*, and I(O), as the "chatterbox," because this represents an ego-dominated discourse wherein the subject, trying to express themselves, primarily makes an effort to realise an ideal that is supported by an imaginary self-conception (Lacan, 1989a: Seminar of 6 November 1957). Less prejudicially, it is the circuit of rational discourse, for "apart from being the circuit of the transmission of information … it is the locus of the concrete discourse of the 'speakingbeing' trying to make themselves understood" (Dor, 1997: 200).

It cannot be over-emphasised that for post-Althusserian theories of ideology, *the circuit of rational discourse is all there is*. For postmodernism, the chain of signification is a chain of "floating" subject-positions, articulated within the horizon of action of a political conjuncture, totalised by means of a political symbol. According to Ernesto Laclau, for instance, a dispersed ensemble of subject-positions (gay, black, worker, etc.) attains its relative unity through the exceptional position of one of the subject-positions (for instance, radical democrat), which acts as a universal equivalent and thereby homogenises the otherwise heterogeneous sheaf of identities. Žižek opposes the postmodern reduction of the subject to a dispersed multiplicity of subject-positions, lent a merely imaginary unity by a political symbol. The thrust of Žižek's argument is, however, that the "subject before subjectivation" and the "sublime object of ideology" *cannot* be reduced to a question of the identity of the agent. In the Lacanian terms developed by Žižek, this debate can be explored by means of the following question: given that the Lacanian "Graph of Desire" consists of two analytically distinct "cells," or levels, *why is there a second level, "beyond" the interplay of Imaginary identity and Symbolic identification?*

The opposition between the signifier and the letter—and the persistence of the letter in the unconscious—provides the basis for the Lacanian explanation of why there is something more than the "circuit of rational discourse". The lack of a final signifier in the process of interpellation implies the incompleteness of identity—leading to quest for a guarantee in the Real for the singular existence of the subject. The subject experiences their lack of a final signifier as the loss of an object, paradigmatically, the loss of fusional unity with the mother correlative to their entry into language. Bruce Fink refers to this eternally lost object—the object (*a*)—as a rem(*a*)inder from the entry into language, and it can be described (approximately) as the unconditional demand for an impossible fullness (Fink, 1995a: 60-61). The existence of a phantasmatic, or "sublime" referent of the master signifier explains "why Lacan developed his graph of desire *apropos* of … a drama of *failed interpellation*" (Žižek, 1989: 120): in "alienation," the subject loses its fusional unity with the mother and enters language under the sign of an incomprehensible master signifier; in "separation," the master signifier is experienced as a contingent placeholder for a lost plenitude that the subject desperately seeks.

The subject of desire is the void of an empty placemarker in discourse—
the logical space occupied by successive (incomplete) identities. At the same
time, these identities, successively adopted by the subject, are bound into a
relative unity by the characteristic stance that the subject takes up towards
these identities—in short, by the way that the subject "gets off" on various
subject-positions, by the characteristic libidinal investment that the subject
makes in an identity. Hence, every interpellation-subjectivation is haunted
by the possibility for the emergence of a hysterical question, addressed to the
master signifier: "is that *it?*" As Žižek explains:

> the only problem is that this "square of the circle" of interpellation, this
> circular movement between symbolic and imaginary identification,
> never comes out without a certain leftover. After every quilting of the
> signifier's chain, which retroactively fixes its meaning, there always
> remains a certain gap, an opening which is rendered in the third form of
> the graph by the famous *Che Vuoi?*—"You're telling me that, but what do
> you want with it, what are you aiming at?" (Žižek, 1989: 111).

The (hystericising) question—"*Che Vuoi?*" "What do you want?"—is experienced by the subject as an unbearable anxiety. Anxiety—the only emo-
tion that never lies (Lacan)—bears witness to the dimension of the death
drive, the dimension of the Real of enjoyment. It is critical to stress that the
anxiety generated by the enigmatic (non-)reply of the Other points beyond
identity: the hysterical question is not "what am I," but "what do I want,"
not just a question of the incompleteness of identity, but primarily of the
libidinal investments that subvert every identity. "The hysterical question
opens the gap of what is 'in the subject more than the subject' of the *object in
subject* which resists interpellation-subordination of the subject, its inclusion
in the symbolic network" (Žižek, 1989: 113). Hence, the hysterical question,
by highlighting the contingency of the master signifier, refers to the failure
of interpellation, to the inability of the subject to fully assume their symbolic
mandate. According to Žižek:

> This is the dimension overlooked in the Althusserian account of
> interpellation: before being caught in the identification, in the symbolic
> recognition and misrecognition, the subject ($) is trapped by the Other
> through a paradoxical object-cause of desire in the midst of it, through
> this secret supposed to be hidden in the Other: ($ ◊ *a*)—the Lacanian
> formula of fantasy (Žižek, 1989: 44).

For Žižek, this "what does the Other want from me?" indicates the Symbolic dimension of desire, as opposed to Imaginary demand (Žižek, 1989:
112). Desire, defined by Lacan as what in demand is irreducible to need, is
borne by the signifier and takes the form of an enigma, for it is ultimately
the desire of the Other.

The subject is always fastened, pinned, to a signifier which represents him for the other, and through this pinning he is loaded with a symbolic mandate, he is given a place in the intersubjective network of symbolic relations. The point is that this mandate is ultimately always arbitrary: since its nature is performative, it cannot be accounted for by reference to the "real" properties and capacities of the subject. So, loaded with this mandate, the subject is automatically confronted with a certain *Che Vuoi?*, with a question of the Other (Žižek, 1989: 113).

Žižek's explanation is consistent with Lacan's explication of the Graph of Desire *apropos* of Shakespeare's *Hamlet* (Lacan, 1989b), which Lacan interprets as the drama of the reluctant adoption, by the subject, of an arbitrarily imposed symbolic mandate. The subject can only enter the Symbolic (the social field) by means of a *retroactive* identification that results in an *anticipatory* (Imaginary) self-identity—an anticipation that can only be ratified in the "future anterior" as what the subject discovers itself as "having meant". The fractured dialectic of alienation into an anticipatory, imaginary identity and retroactive, symbolic identification with an enigmatic signifier, determines the perpetual undercurrent of anxiety that pertains to the existence of the subject. The subject enters the social field, then, by assuming a symbolic mandate, and, since the reply of the Other is necessarily enigmatic, what the subject finds upon thus entering the Symbolic Order is automatically the disjunction between their anticipatory identification and the enigmatic (non) confirmation in the reply of the Other. This disjunction marks out the space of the question mark, *Che Vuoi?*

($ ◊ a): "Divided Subject Desperately Seeks Lost Object …"

The completed form of the "Graph of Desire" illustrates the final form of the libidinal economy of the Lacanian subject. Paradigmatically, the two levels of Lacan's graph represent the permanent gap between the enunciation and the statement (Lacan, 1998: 138-139), recast by Žižek in terms of the illocutionary force (the performative dimension) and the locutionary content (the constative dimension) of that speech act by which a person assumes a social mandate (Žižek, 1989: 113; Žižek, 2001c: 69-110). The two resulting levels of the graph (meaning and enjoyment) articulate the different aspects of the perforation of the Symbolic Order by "a pre-symbolic (real) stream of enjoyment—what happens when the pre-symbolic 'substance,' the body as materialised, incarnated enjoyment, becomes enmeshed in the signifier's network" (Žižek, 1989: 122). As Žižek summarises, the general result of the insertion of the human body into the realm of the signifier is that:

> by being filtered through the sieve of the signifier, the body is submitted to *castration*, enjoyment is evacuated from it, the body survives as dismembered, mortified. In other words, the order of the signifier (the big Other) and that of enjoyment (the Thing as it embodiment) are

radically heterogeneous, inconsistent; any accordance between them is structurally impossible (Žižek, 1989: 122).

The second stage of the Graph is unconscious and the line passing from "Enjoyment" to "Castration" represents an unconscious chain of signification that persists beneath the conscious articulations of the subject. This suggests the existence of an unconscious positioning of the subject, at the level of the enunciation, with respect to the field of the Other and the objects of unconscious desire. To grasp what Lacan means by the *discontinuous* line of unconscious signification, it is worth noting that he considers paradigmatic a dream of Anna Freud, aged two years old (recounted by Freud), which connects the subject to a string of objects denied her during the day. Without hesitation, Lacan locates the surname at the symbol S(Ø) and the forbidden objects at ($ ◊ D), the symbol for the drives (Lacan, 1989b: Seminar of 3 December 1958). The signifier of the incompleteness of, or lack in, the Other, appears at the intersection of enjoyment and the signifier:

> as soon as the signifier is penetrated by enjoyment, it becomes inconsistent, porous, perforated—the enjoyment is what cannot be symbolised, its presence in the field of the signifier can be detected only through the holes and inconsistencies of this field, so the only possible signifier of enjoyment is the signifier of the lack in the Other, the signifier of its inconsistency (Žižek, 1989: 122).

Correlative to this inconsistency of the signifier stands the inconsistency of the social—the unconscious recognition that the symbolic social structure is "crossed-out by a fundamental impossibility, structured around an impossible/traumatic kernel, around a central lack" (Žižek, 1989: 122). This inconsistency in the field of the social prevents any closure and implies that the subject is *not* radically alienated in the structure as a mere bearer of structures. On the right hand side of the intersection of enjoyment and the signifier stands the formula of the drive, ($ ◊ D), indicating the incompleteness of the evacuation of enjoyment from the body. The drive and its satisfactions— obtained in the endless circuit around the object (*a*)—are inscribed on the body as the erogenous zones and designated by D, symbolic demand (as opposed to natural need). Žižek interprets ($ ◊ D) as the formula of *sinthome*: "a particular signifying formation which is immediately permeated with enjoyment—that is, the impossible conjunction of enjoyment and the signifier" (Žižek, 1989: 123).

Žižek's proposition is that fantasy is the means by which the gap between the upper and the lower levels of the "Graph of Desire" is closed. As Žižek explains, "fantasy … is a construction enabling us to seek maternal substitutes, but at the same time a screen shielding us from getting too close to the maternal Thing" (Žižek, 1989: 119-120). For Žižek, this supplies "the key" to the loop of enjoyment, the unconscious circuit of the second stage of the graph:

instead of imaginary identification (the relation between imaginary ego and its constitutive image, its Ego-Ideal) we have here desire (*d*) supported by fantasy; the function of fantasy is to fill the opening in the Other, to conceal its inconsistency. Fantasy conceals the fact that the Other, the symbolic order, is structured around some traumatic impossibility, around something which cannot be symbolised—i.e., the real of *jouissance*: through fantasy, *jouissance* is domesticated, "gentrified" (Žižek, 1989: 123).

Fantasy appears as the response to the dreadful enigma of the desire (or lack) in the Other and, at the same time, fantasy constructs the frame within which it is possible to desire. As the subject's response to the intolerable anxiety provoked by the incompleteness of the Other:

fantasy functions as a construction, as an imaginary scenario filling out the void, the opening of the *desire of the Other*: by giving a definite answer to the question "What does the Other want?" it enable us to evade the unbearable deadlock in which the Other wants something from us, but we are at the same time incapable of translating this desire of the Other into a positive interpellation, into a mandate with which to identify (Žižek, 1989: 115).

In other words, we reconcile ourselves to our social position by means of a fantasy of participation in a meaningful whole: indeed, "society as a Corporate Body is the fundamental ideological fantasy" (Žižek, 1989: 126). By virtue of the role of fantasy in linking the empty enunciation of the Law to its concrete statement in a particular master signifier, in the final loop of the synchronic arc, the divided subject rejoins the Ego-Ideal through the detour of the unconscious structure:

First we have S(Ø): the mark of the lack of the Other, of the inconsistency of the symbolic order when it is penetrated by enjoyment: then ($ ◊ a), the formula for fantasy; the function of fantasy is to serve as a screen concealing this inconsistency: finally, *s*(O), the effect of the signification as dominated by fantasy; fantasy functions as "absolute signification" (Lacan); it constitutes the frame through which we experience the world as consistent and meaningful (Žižek, 1989: 123).

Fantasy defends the subject from the pure desire characteristic of the death drive, by constructing the frame for reality, within which symbolically mediated desire becomes possible. Fantasy is the key to the conversion of a contingent, retroactive identification into an apparently necessary, anticipatory identity—but it must not be forgotten that fantasy is in the last instance an illusion, masking the radically disjunctive character of the dialectics of symbolic identification and imaginary identity. To reduce the unconscious to fantasy *alone* represents a grave error, for it obscures the fundamental conflict—between a Law of prohibition and the objects of the drives—active in the unconscious psychic economy. Such a reduction would effectively make the unconscious into a unity, transposing the self-identity of the classical subject into the register of the unconscious.

Political Strategy and Social Identification

Žižek's motivations for introducing the "agency of the subject" into his Lacanian dialectics are clear: the ambition of ideology criticism is to replace conformity to the existing structures with identification with the new social order. If ideological interpellation represents an *imposition*, governed by the dialectics of retroactive identification, then how is the subject supposed to swap acceptance of existing domination for a proleptic identification with liberation? The Althusserian conception of a political struggle between and within the ideological state apparatuses might have supplied the key to this question. Žižek, however, having conceptualised the unconscious as rotating solely around the ideological *sinthome*, cemented by (the old) social fantasy, is in a position where his answer to this question has to involve supplying the subject with an entirely new unconscious.

Žižek suggests that fantasy, as "a screen masking a void," is fundamentally meaningless and therefore cannot be demystified through the standard leftwing procedures of ideological criticism (historical contextualisation and institutional analysis of "who benefits"). The social fantasy cannot be reduced to a differential chain of signification structured by "nodal points," or master signifiers, because these are supported, in the final analysis, by "the non-sensical, pre-ideological kernel of enjoyment" (Žižek, 1989: 124). For Žižek, nationalism occupies the place of the unconscious Thing that supplies the centre of gravity and hidden support for democracy (Žižek, 1993: 222). Nationalist enjoyment, Žižek claims, is the inherent opposite of the neutral-universal liberal democratic framework, "in the sense that the very project of formal democracy opens the space for fundamentalism" (Žižek, 1993: 221). Once again, we see Žižek's tendency to align formal universality with the (pre-)conscious discursive field and to make this dependent upon a non-universalisable singularity in the Real. Indeed, in the paradigmatic instances of neo-Nazi racism and ethnic nationalism, Žižek criticises leftwing "discursive idealism" for actually reinforcing these identifications (Žižek, 1993: 202-208). By discursively identifying the inconsistency behind ideology, the Left effectively highlighted the yield of stupid enjoyment gained through material rituals, and in the absence of institutional reconstruction, this acted to *promote* these ideologies (Žižek, 1993: 209-211).

Because every discursive field is ultimately sutured by a real kernel of enjoyment—because every ideological meaning is supported by an institutional ritual—Žižek develops what might be called, slightly ironically, the "two tactics of postmarxian radicalism in the democratic revolution". These tactics are to "search and destroy," or, as Žižek explains, the interpretation of symptoms and the traversal of the fantasy:

> One is discursive, the "symptomal reading" of the ideological text, bringing about the "deconstruction" of the spontaneous experience of its meaning—that is, demonstrating how a given ideological field is a result of a montage of heterogeneous "floating signifiers," of their totalisation through the intervention of certain "nodal points"; the other aims at extracting the kernel of enjoyment, at articulating the way in which—beyond the field of meaning but at the same time internal to it—an ideology implies, manipulates, produces a pre-ideological enjoyment structured in fantasy (Žižek, 1989: 125).

Assuming that politics provides an extra-clinical instantiation of these procedures—an assumption that rests upon the dubious analogy between party and analyst, and depends on a highly tendentious interpretation of the "difference" between Lenin and Kautsky on class consciousness (Žižek, 2001d)—what happens then? The leftwing political problematic involves not only forging new symbolic identifications, but also a reconfiguration of the subject's basic relation to ideological fantasies in general, without which ideological struggle degenerates into mere manipulation. Take for instance the Marxian "fundamental fantasy," expressed in Marx's *Economic and Philosophical Manuscripts of 1844*, of communism as disalienation in a harmonious society. By contrast with the postmarxian demand to completely abandon all utopias (Stavrakakis, 1999: 99-121),[13] psychoanalytically-informed leftist commentators have suggested that "traversal of the fantasy" means recasting utopia as an indeterminate teleological judgement, that is to say, its retreat from foundation to a horizon (Copjec, 1996: xxv-xxvi; Homer, 1998). Socialist politics retains the vision of communism as a regulative goal and not a social blueprint.

Žižek's answer to this problem is "subjective destitution". For Žižek, the reduction of the subject to an "excremental remainder" reveals the elementary matrix of subjectivity: "if the Cartesian subject is to emerge at the level of the enunciation, he must be reduced to the 'almost nothing' of disposable excrement at the level of the enunciated content" (Žižek, 2000h: 157). This

---

13. The postmarxian position is that the subject has to accede to their castration, to the human condition of lack. Translated into contemporary theory, this means recognition that the empty place of power cannot be permanently occupied by a social force claiming to incarnate universality, that is, acceptance that parliamentary elections are the final horizon of radical politics (Stavrakakis, 1999: 134-136). For Stavrakakis, developing these sentiments to their final conclusion, the problem is utopia: traversal of the fantasy means rejection of every utopia, especially communism (Stavrakakis, 1999: 99-121). Lumping together the dreams of fascist conquerors with the hopes of the oppressed in "one reactionary mass," Stavrakakis advocates a post-utopian politics that (surprise!) bears a suspicious resemblance to liberal democratic parliamentarism. This implies a post-ideological condition that is not post-political—surely a contradiction in terms, redolent of the liberal multiculturalist desire to reduce political conflict to the management of neutralised differences.

picturesque description supports two distinct strands of argument in Žižek's work. "Subjective destitution," as the desolation of narcissism and the disclosure of the contingency of identifications, means the revelation, to the subject, that every ideology is to some extent arbitrary, and the corresponding recognition that the sublime beyond, menaced by the social antagonist, never existed. This is equivalent to the Lacanian ethical stance of "not giving way on one's desire," as a persistence in the struggle for the Cause, despite a radical renunciation of the richness of wish-fulfillment dreams of plenitude (Žižek, 1989: 120). On these lines, Žižek says that traversal of the fantasy means the "loss of loss," the recognition that the object (a) is an object that exists only in fantasy and that the Other is also lacking (a final answer) (Žižek, 1989: 122).

Žižek, however, in line with the broadly Lukácsian variant of "anti-historicism" he espouses, *also* wants an anti-scientific and post-ideological subjectivity, "beyond fantasy," but not necessarily beyond utopianism. Therefore, he introduces a *third* stage, which is effectively the double negation of the starting point in symptomatic analysis:

> First, we had to get rid of the symptoms as compromise formations, then, we had to "traverse" the fantasy as the frame determining the coordinates of our enjoyment: ... i.e., our access to "pure" desire is always paid for by the loss of enjoyment. In the last stage, however, the entire perspective is reversed: we have to identify precisely with the particular form of our enjoyment (Žižek, 1991a: 138).

For Žižek, the traversal of the fantasy brings the subject to the pulsion of the death drive around the ideological *sinthome*. "Going through the fantasy" is, for Žižek, therefore strictly correlative to identification with a *sinthome* (Žižek, 1989: 124), as "the truth about ourselves" (Žižek, 1989: 128). Identification with the *sinthome* means identification with the singular marginalised element that sustains the dominant ideology—for instance, identification with the persecuted Jew or immigrant worker—and its elevation to a new universal. This relatively innocuous looking New Left politics of sympathetic identification makes a class politics impossible (as the most oppressed are not necessarily in the best position to change the system) and implies a decision grounded in *Truth*, correlative to an act in the Real. Indeed, it follows ineluctably from Žižek's postulates that traversal of the fantasy involves a step beyond sociality. The consequence is not subjective realignment, but the step into psychosis. This is such a significant step that Žižek hesitates on the lip of this conclusion from some time.

III.

Now that we have an accurate understanding of the meanings of the symbols in the second stage of the Graph of Desire, we are in a position to grasp the significance of a slight, but crucial, omission in Žižek's exposition. In brief, while many Lacanians identify the symbol S(Ø) with the Symbolic Law (as an empty enunciation, a non-fungible "No!") (Fink, 1995a: 57-58; Zupančič, 2000: 140-169), Žižek associates it only with the dimension of the incompleteness of the symbolic order. What Žižek has done is to make the "loop of enjoyment," the second stage of the Graph of Desire, rotate solely around the ideological *sinthome* (for instance, the racist enjoyment of ethnic ultra-nationalism), supported by the ideological fantasy, which as an unconscious sequence of material letters is immune to every interpretive demystification. The consequences are serious, because this makes the Žižekian unconscious the exclusive domain of a non-universalisable, singular enjoyment, which is supported by unconscious fantasy. The Žižekian subject is therefore a "Dr. Jekyl and Mr. Hyde" monster: on the surface, a defender of rational universality, but beneath this veneer, a secret devotee of obscene nationalism, vicious anti-semitism and/or patriarchal sexism. Because of the way Žižek has structured this subject, there is no way to get beyond the oscillation between democratic politics and obscene enjoyment, except by dispensing completely with the unconscious. The entailment of Žižek's position is therefore that challenging the reigning "social fantasy" means a movement beyond the Symbolic Law. Not surprisingly, his position is plagued by a series of antinomies—political reversals, ethical hesitations and theoretical uncertainties—that betray the existence of an identical subject-object, located in the upper level of the Graph of Desire.

Symbolic Law versus Superego Enjoyment

Žižek's exposition of the "graph of desire" substantiates his claim that beyond identification-interpellation lie both the unconscious "subject beyond subjectivation" and the materiality of the drives. Hence the significance of Žižek's contentions that "the last support of the ideological effect ... is the non-sensical, pre-ideological kernel of enjoyment" and that "an ideology implies, manipulates ... a pre-ideological enjoyment structured in fantasy" (Žižek, 1989: 124-125). This pre-ideological enjoyment, aligned by Žižek with the enjoyment of the mother (that is, with incestuous enjoyment, or fusional unity with the mother), is connected in his work with the Lacanian concept of the Thing, that is, the id and the drives. As Lacanians have commented, this puts the "id" back in "ideology," with a vengeance (Lupton and Reinhard, 1993). By linking ideological subjectivity to the existence of extra-ideological enjoyment, structured by unconscious fantasy, Žižek hopes to explain the longevity of political systems that seem to lack popular legitimacy, and to develop a political strategy capable of confronting the astonishing resilience of pro-capitalist ideologies. He also proposes to demarcate the space of effective anti-capitalist resistance from the "inherent transgressions," the pseudo-radical diversions (for instance, racism), built-in to the structure of contemporary multinational capitalism. The problem is that Žižek's interpretation of the unconscious subject in terms of a "pre-ideological enjoyment" tends to neglect the strictly Freudian aspect of the unconscious, namely, the *prohibition* of incest (as opposed to incestuous enjoyment), recast by Lacan as the "Symbolic Law". The result of Žižek's treatment is that the unconscious reduces to a singular (that is, non-universalisable, non-dialecticisable) enjoyment, one that is impervious to discursive intervention because it is located before, or beyond, culture—surely a strange position to take for someone influenced by Freud's "talking cure".

Under the influence of the historicist problematic of Laclau and Mouffe, Žižek proposes to theorise the "dependence of Law on the process of enunciation, or ... its radically contingent character" (Žižek, 1989: 37). While not formally incorrect, the conclusions Žižek develops from this interpretation conflate the *necessity* of the enunciation of the Symbolic Law (for every non-psychotic) with the *contingency* of the statement which is its vehicle. Lacan's "*Nom du Père*," by contrast, with its deliberate homophonic play on the relation between the paternal "no!" (to incest) and the paternal name, highlights this analytic separation between the (necessary and universal) enunciation of a prohibition and the (contingent and particular) baptismal statement. Indeed, according to Bruce Fink, Lacan not only analytically separates these two aspects into alienation and separation, but also aligns the dialectics of primary and secondary repression with these two logical moments. In alienation, a non-displaceable "No!" (the incest prohibition), as an empty enunciation without a statement whose matheme is $S(\emptyset)$, is substituted for enjoyment of the (m)Other, whereas in separation, the paternal signifier, whose matheme is S_1, substitutes for the desire of the (m)Other. The mathemes of the Lacanian "graph of desire" can therefore be assigned a Freudian interpretation, where $S(\emptyset)$ stands for primary repression, in the advent of the incest prohibition and the formation of the unconscious, while O, the Other, is the locus in which the Oedipal conflict is resolved by means of the paternal name, S_1, in the process of secondary repression and identification with the paternal image, or Ego Ideal. It follows that the opposition between the Symbolic Law and the Real of enjoyment is a division (a decentring) *within* the upper, strictly unconscious, "cell" of the "graph of desire" and not an opposition between the upper and lower levels.

By contrast, Žižek tends to present the distinction between Symbolic Law and the Real of enjoyment as coextensive with the opposition between ideological meaning (lower level of the graph) and superego enjoyment (upper level of the graph). Žižek systematically maps this distinction onto several case studies, meaning that the division between symbolic field and real enjoyment has many incarnations. These include: "enlightened cynicism" (Symbolic) and "ideological enjoyment" (Real) (Žižek, 1989: 28-33); "cynical distance" (Symbolic) and "ethnic nationalism" (Real) (Žižek, 1993: 200-216); "democratic politics" (Symbolic) and "bureaucratic enjoyment" (Real) (Žižek, 1991a: 231-252), and; the "official public law" (Symbolic) and its "supplementary framework of illegal transgressions" (Real) (Žižek, 1994c: 54-85). Since the opposition between ideological meaning and superego enjoyment is aligned with the distinction between consciousness and the unconscious, his move has very serious implications. Indeed, a series of equivalences is created, which reproduces precisely the split between ideological meaning and unconscious enjoyment, Symbolic and Real, lower level and upper level of the Graph of Desire, at work in Žižek's conception of the divided subject. At the highest theoretical level, however, this distinction takes the form of the opposition between "symbolic public Law" (Symbolic) and the "superego transgressions" (Real) that support the Law (Žižek, 1994c: 54).

> In so far as superego designates the intrusion of enjoyment into the field of ideology, we can also say that *the opposition of symbolic Law and superego points towards the tension between ideological meaning and enjoyment*: symbolic Law guarantees meaning, whereas superego provides enjoyment which serves as the unacknowledged support of meaning (Žižek, 1994c: 56).

Implied in Žižek's conception of the relation between superego enjoyment (the enunciation) and ideological meaning (the statement) is the phenomenalisation of the unconscious Symbolic Law (its replacement with the master signifier), and the conflation of primary and secondary identifications. Indeed, Žižek explicitly aligns the lower level of the graph ("the level of ideological meaning") with the symbolic Law and on this basis claims to theorise the "predominance of the superego over the law" (Žižek, 1991a: 241). The basis for this claim is the proposition that:

> superego emerges where the Law—the public Law, the Law articulated in the public discourse—fails; at this point of failure, the public Law is compelled to search for support in an *illegal* enjoyment. Superego is the obscene "nightly" law that necessarily redoubles and accompanies, as its shadow, the "public" Law (Žižek, 1994c: 54).

Žižek's condensation—"public Law," as a collapse of Symbolic Law into public legality—indicates exactly the conflation at work in his fundamental insight. According to Žižek, in filling out the contents of the universal, the master signifier necessarily stages a sequence of exclusions, which, instead of undermining the reigning ideology and/or legal framework, actually support it and legitimate forms of extra-legal coercion (Žižek, 1993: 46-47). He claims that this obscene superego supplement "represents the spirit of community," compelling the individual's identification with group identity, despite (or because of) its violation of the explicit rules of community life (Žižek, 1994c: 54). Žižek risks a second revision:

> What holds together a particular community most deeply is not so much

identification with the Law that regulates the community's "normal" everyday circuit, *but rather identification with a specific form of transgression of the Law, of the Law's suspension* (in psychoanalytic terms, with a specific form of enjoyment) (Žižek, 1994c: 55).

Inverting the entire discussion of the role of the master signifier in the process of interpellation, Žižek now claims that identification happens not to the master signifier, but with its exclusions, or inherent transgressions. Claims to oppose "postmodern anti-Enlightenment *ressentiment*" and its celebration of particularism notwithstanding, Žižek makes the "loop of enjoyment" supreme with respect to the Symbolic Law, so that the only effective resistance to power is a complete exit from the field of universality.

For Žižek, the splitting of the Law into "Symbolic Public Law" and an obscene superego supplement is a consequence of modernity, for the advent of a neutral-universal law implies the repression of the "authoritarian-patriarchal logic that continues to determine our attitudes" (Žižek, 1994c: 56). According to this account, Kant is the decisive marker of the modern splitting of the political field into a formal, empty universality (democracy, autonomy) and the prohibited Thing that supplies its unacknowledged support (the national Thing, the supreme good), because formal democracy and Kantian autonomy are both constituted by the evacuation of the locus of the supreme value (of the empty place of power, of the supreme good) (Žižek, 1993: 220-222). Kant both designates the space of the National Thing (the ideological supreme Good) and prohibits the crucial step into nationalism. Indeed, "filling out the empty place of the Thing by the Nation is perhaps the paradigmatic case of the inversion which defines radical Evil" (Žižek, 1993: 222). Žižek's claim is that nationalism occupies the place of the unconscious Thing that supplies the centre of gravity and hidden support for democracy. Nationalist enjoyment, Žižek claims, is the inherent opposite of the neutral-universal liberal democratic framework, "in the sense that the very project of formal democracy opens the space for fundamentalism" (Žižek, 1993: 221). Once again, we see Žižek's tendency to align formal universality with the discursive field and to make this dependent upon a non-universalisable singularity in the Real. This connects with the claim that:

> It is a commonplace of Lacanian theory to emphasise how this Kantian moral imperative conceals an obscene superego injunction; "Enjoy!"— the voice of the Other impelling us to follow our duty for the sake of duty is a traumatic irruption of an appeal to an impossible *jouissance* ... The moral Law is obscene insofar as it is its form itself which functions as a motivating force driving us to obey its command—that is, insofar as we obey moral Law because it is law and not because of any positive reasons: the obscenity of moral Law is the obverse of its formal character (Žižek, 1989: 81).

Despite explicitly acknowledging the inadequacy of every representation of the Law, Žižek cannot resist the temptation to draw conclusions from
the representation (S_1) regarding the relation represented (the moral law,
equals the Symbolic Law). From Žižek, then, we learn that the *moral law* is
supported by meaningless, obscene enjoyment (Žižek, 1989: 80-81) and that
the obscene, perverse dimension of Kantian moral formalism finally appears in fascism (Žižek, 1989: 82).

By contrast, Žižek's cothinker Alenka Zupančič, demonstrates that the
Kantian moral law, which can be aligned with the Lacanian Symbolic Law,
is distinct from the superego because it is "beyond the master signifier," existing as an *unconscious* "enunciation without statement," and manifest only
as *affect* (anxiety, respect) (Zupančič, 2000: 140-169). According to Zupančič,
the matheme of the moral law is therefore also S(∅), indicating that this
"enunciation without statement" is an empty injunction to "do your duty,"
experienced by the subject as an unbearable anxiety ("respect," in proximity
to dread). Thus, according to her account, the pressures to conform to group
identifications, emanating from the superego agency—which for psychoanalytic theory are sometimes associated with criminal acts, for instance, with
"ethnic cleansing"—are always counter-balanced by the existence of moral
conscience. Consequently, the path towards resistance to regimes that vio-
late human rights runs through universality, and the subject can legitimately
be held responsible for their acts.

Political Impasse

Žižek is on the horns of a dilemma. The supremacy of the "non-universalisable singularity" of unconscious enjoyment—paradigmatically, that is, the
secret dependence of democratic politics on nationalist enjoyment—dictates
a politics torn between the alternatives of total capitulation or catastrophic rupture. On the one hand, democratic politics, discursive universality,
public legality, and so forth, are all lent their "ontological consistency" by
the hidden ballast of the "national Thing," which Žižek equates with a repressed "ethico-political Act" of social inauguration, and describes as "the
Political" (as opposed to mere everyday politics) (Žižek, 2000h: 187-191). Discursive formations are therefore relatively stable, because they are supported by the permanently vanished "political Act/national Thing/the Political," which persists as a kernel of enjoyment, structured by an unconscious
fantasy that somehow subsists beyond institutional relations. On the other
hand, the "Political/Act/Thing," the "kernel of the Real," has exclusively
sinister connotations, because Žižek aligns it with bureaucratic idiocy, illegal transgressions, racist *jouissance*, partiarchal sexism, and so forth. The
ballast of democratic politics therefore turns out to be the dead weight of
nationalist enjoyment, and so-called "ethnic cleansing" is revealed as the

"repressed truth" of liberal democracy (Žižek, 1993: 208). Worse, the nationalist fantasies that structure this hideous enjoyment are at once tenacious—they can apparently easily survive the destruction of the institutions that called them into being (Žižek, 1993: 209)—and so nebulous that we are enjoined not to fight them directly, but instead to promote alternative institutional arrangements altogether ... which would no doubt have their own secret fantasy support. Žižek's vision of modernity is relatively grim, then, and certainly lends little credibility to his claim (Žižek, 1989: 7), to defend the Enlightenment from the depredations of postmodern skepticism. To the contrary: Žižek reads like a late Romantic denunciation of modernity. Thus, on the surface of things, we have Enlightenment universality and modern liberty ... but beneath this veneer, the ghosts of the past and totalitarian *jouissance* reign supreme; by day, the modern subject is a perfect Dr Jekyll, but at night, a veritable Mr Hyde.

Grasping the democratic horn of the dilemma, it seemed that Žižek would opt for a politics of "enthusiastic resignation" to democratic invention (Žižek, 1990: 259)—including issuing Churchillian apologies for liberal parliamentarism (Žižek, 1991b: 28)—accompanied by the ethical strategy of "maintaining the gap" between politics and "the Political" (Žižek, 1991a). Turning aside from the foundation of the political field in the "national Thing" or the "revolutionary Act," leftwing theory would accept the consequences of human finitude, supplementing its politics with an ethically-based repudiation of the utopian fantasy of social harmony. Postmarxism, he claimed, defends the "inherently ethical" stance of eternal mourning for its historical defeats: the Left must return to and re-mark the trauma of the Lost Cause, and, by means of "empty" symbolic gestures, mark its impossibility (Žižek, 1991a: 273). Renouncing the lethal fascination with gestures of political institution, characteristic of, for instance, classical Marxism, postmarxism would remain on the field of hegemonic struggles marked out by the boundaries of liberal democracy. Eschewing the desire for a foundational political Act, the Left has to endlessly repeat the gesture of the missed encounter, acting as the perennial "vanishing mediator" in the victory of liberal democracy, within the field of the nation state (Žižek, 1991a: 271-273). Eternal bridesmaid, the Left is incapable of proposing a new social order and must "enthusiastically" resign itself to the role of loyal opposition. Beginning from such assumptions, however, it is equally elementary for Žižek to deduce that multicultural tolerance, political liberties, struggles for cultural recognition and even radical social reforms are all secretly supported by the unconscious enjoyment gained from compliance *in deed* (if not in words) with nationalistic rituals. Even radical reforms, in other words, are nothing but the "human face" of the obscene enjoyment generated by the capitalism-nationalism nexus. For instance, Žižek follows this logic to arrive at the classic ultra-left position that "the neo-Nazi skinhead's ethnic violence is not the 'return of the repressed' of the liberal multiculturalist tolerance, but *directly generated by it*, its own concealed true face" (Žižek, 2000h: 205). Instead of conceptualising the political field as struggles for hegemony, traversed by a shifting balance of forces (within which, reforms represent *concessions*, not tricks), Žižek describes politics in terms reminiscent of base-and-superstructure reductionism.

To appreciate the cruelty of Žižek's dilemma, it is worth considering the paradigmatic instance of the distinction between symbolic field and "obscene enjoyment," the division between democratic politics and nationalist enjoyment. The implication of Žižek's historicist position—the foundational role of the dominant ideology combined with the expressive conception of totality—is that democratic politics and nationalist enjoyment are inextricably bound. Thus, for instance, ultra-nationalism in Eastern Europe, Žižek wrote during the break-up of former Yugoslavia, "is returning to the West the 'repressed' truth of its democratic desire" (Žižek, 1993: 208). According to Žižek (and quite plausibly), "a nation only *exists* as long as its specific *enjoyment* continues to be materialised in a specific set of social practices and transmitted through national myths that structure these practices" (Žižek, 1993: 202). For Žižek (not so credibly), "the national Thing functions ... as a kind of *'particular Absolute' resisting universalisation*, bestowing its special 'tonality' upon every neutral, universal notion" (Žižek, 1993: 206-207). So, while Žižek provides an insightful analysis of the psychological mechanisms driving ethnic nationalism—"the late Yugoslavia offers a case study of ... a detailed network of 'decantations' and 'thefts' of enjoyment" (Žižek, 1993: 204)—the logic of his position determines that this concludes with the "speculative identity" of democratic politics and ethnic cleansing.[14]

Žižek's dilemma generates constant zigzags in his politics. Indeed, the stance of "enthusiastic resignation" is penetrated by ambivalence regarding liberal parliamentarism—indeed, it leads to an abstentionist position regarding the nationalist fantasy—and so a reversal into its opposite becomes, once catalysed by the horrors of the break-up of Yugoslavia, virtually inevitable. While many indices of this transformation exist—the Leninist party

---

14. Once again, Žižek is probably correct to assert that the imperialist intervention in Bosnia facilitated, rather than hindered, the process of ethnic cleansing, culminating in the reactionary solution of "ethnic cantonment". This is an empirical question, linked to the economic, political and military interests of the Western nations involved in the break-up of former Yugoslavia. Žižek elevates this into an *a priori* assertion, linked to the expressive conception of nationalist enjoyment as the inherent obverse of democratic politics. As with Lukács, this *philosophical* flattening of the *political* terrain can only lead to the collapse of democratic politics into liberal parliamentarism, leading to the search for "real democratic" alternatives (council communism, soviet power), as if the entire historical experience of the Bolshevik Revolution could be circumvented with a better grasp of psychoanalytically-enhanced Hegelianism.

(from fetish to analyst) (Žižek, 1995);[15] Stalinism (from perversion-instrumentalisation to tragic instrument of historical progress) (Žižek, 1989: 142-145; Žižek, 1991a: 170-173; Žižek, 2000h: 194, 379); Lenin (from Jacobin terrorist to decisionist "Master") (Žižek, 2000e)—the role of the Jacobin regicide is exemplary. This is because the "Jacobin paradox"—the problem of how to hold open the "empty place of power" in societies characterised by democratic invention, without inadvertently occupying (and thus, filling) this locus—is *the* conundrum of modern politics. As Žižek shifts back and forth between democratic politics and a direct assault on the "kernel of the Real," the Jacobin regicide travels the distance from being denounced as an "empty acting out" (Žižek, 1991a: 256), to its dramatic endorsement as a radical decision, expressing absolute freedom (Žižek, 2000h: 192). But even supposing that such a judgement were valid, how on earth would such a leap "into the Real" be accomplished?

For Žižek, only the "authentic Act" disturbs the reigning ideological fantasy and discloses the truth of the social totality (Žižek, 2000h: 369-392). Therefore, for Žižek, identification with the *sinthome*, the commission of an ethico-political Act and traversal of the fantasy are equivalent. As Žižek explains, the archetypal Act is a political revolution (Žižek, 2000h: 375). Yet, it follows from Žižek's construction of the opposition between Symbolic Order and the Real that this must happen "in the Real," through the unilateral declaration of a new social order. The consequences of conceptualising the distinction between hegemonic politics and the Act of institution of the "Political Thing" on these lines are relatively alarming—Žižek's exemplars, for instance, are increasingly drawn from fantasy and terrorism—and generate a constant vacillation between democratic politics and quasi-religious militarism.

Žižek defends his stance by means of the distinction between "acting out" and the "*passage à l'acte*," or Act. While "acting out is still a symbolic act ... addressed to the big Other ... a 'passage to the act' suspends the dimension of the big Other, as the act is transposed into the dimension of the Real" (Žižek, 1991a: 139). This distinction valorises what for many analysts indicates catastrophe, and neglects Lacan's distinction between "acting out" as impotent protest and the performative legitimacy of the symbolic act. For Žižek, quite explicitly, "the 'passage to the act' entails ... an exit from the symbolic network, a dissolution of the social bond" (Žižek, 1991a: 139). By becoming an incarnation of the object (*a*)—that is, an embodiment of an unconditional demand—subjects "separate" from the social field and liberate themselves from every master signifier (Žižek, 2001c: 69-105). Needless to say, however, there can be no question of performative felicity in the context of the complete dissolution of conventional authority (Austin, 1962). Hence

---

15. Compare this with (Žižek, 2001g).

Žižek's belief that the political Act involves an "impossible," unilateral performative, an inaugural declaration spoken in opposition to every existing convention (Žižek, 2001c: 96-99). Not surprisingly, as this aspect of Žižek's theory becomes central, the rhetoric of a "suicidal" and "psychotic" (Žižek, 1991a: 101) Act increases in stridency (Žižek, 1996b: 32-39; Žižek, 2000f: 151-156; Žižek, 2000h: 374-381).

Grasping the "political Act" horn of the dilemma, then, leads Žižek towards ambiguous references to the Khmer Rouge and Shining Path (Žižek, 1993: 224-225), coupled with the adoption of a Year-Zero-style rhetoric (Žižek, 2000e: 127), culminating in the advocacy of a militaristic, quasi-religious community, "beyond democracy". Is it necessary to add that this dichotomy—liberal parliamentarism or revolutionary totalitarianism—accepts, in advance, the legitimacy of the *Right's* construal of the political field? *Contra* Žižek, breaking the "*Denkverbot*" on revolutionary politics does not have to involve abandoning the notion of totalitarianism (Žižek, 2001b)—a gesture that can only fuel the worst sort of suspicions. Instead of an openness to the new social movements, Žižek's position is perilously close to an ultra-left refusal of the difference between capitalist democracy and military dictatorship, redolent of the politics of Third Period Stalinism.

Despite the elaborate conceptual apparatus that makes such deductions possible, Žižek's programmatic contributions display a certain "poverty of philosophy". Žižek's political impasse springs from the opposition between the democratic universal and nationalist singularity, leading to an oscillation between an "enthusiastic resignation" that smacks of cynical acceptance, and an ultra-left, voluntarist refusal of democratic politics. While Žižek's concept that nationalist enjoyment sustains parliamentary reformism indicates the importance of combining hegemonic politics with institutional reconstruction, he displays a supreme indifference to theories of alternative democratic forms, or indeed, to *any* theorisation of the institutional forms of popular sovereignty. If the Thing supports democracy, then to destroy the Thing, we have to destroy democracy, and replace it with a religious community (Žižek, 2000h: 177). Hence the exemplary status of the otherwise unintelligible references to the Hegelian Monarch and the Hegelian "ethical" (sometimes, "religious") community that pepper Žižek's work. The Hegelian Monarch is the "democratic" solution to the Jacobin problem, that is, a formal head of state who serves as a "rubber stamp" for parliamentary decisions. This must be interpreted as a form of plebiscitory presidential Bonapartism designed to protect democratic forms, while the "religious community" is the Hegelian organic totality beyond the nation-state (and therefore also beyond democracy). The oscillation between the advocacy of presidential Bonapartism and a religious commune determines the compass of Žižek's "politics".

Ethical Hesitations

Žižek's political vacillation is repeated on ethical terrain, as the hesitation between an ethics of desire, linked to the prohibition on disturbing the Thing, and the plunge into the "suicidal act," figured as an ethics of the Real. Žižek seeks to oppose a "spontaneous ideology of Lacanian psychoanalysis," according to which the endless metonymy of desire is the way to keep the lethal Thing at a minimal distance. This maintenance of the gap prevents the "danger of yielding to fascination with the Thing, and being drawn into its lethal vortex, which can only end in psychosis or suicidal *passage à l'acte*" (Žižek, 1996b: 96). According to the contemporary prolongation of the "New Philosophy" into an "ethical ideology"—a perspective apparently supported by conservative Lacanian interpretations of the ethics of desire—any act that aims to actually contribute to the good can only terminate in radical evil; hence, the role of ethics is to *prevent* any militant ethics and denounce any redistributive politics (Badiou, 2001).

By implication a Kantian ethics—involving the renunciation of the content of the Supreme Good for an ethics of universal duty—the "ethics of desire" promotes an ethical variant of the politics of "enthusiastic resignation" that we have just examined. Žižek denounces this as the logic of the "spurious infinity," the regulative ideal of the infinite perfectability of humanity which serves to mask an actual lack of empirical progress. This is, of course, arguably a complete misunderstanding of the concept of a regulative ideal, which does not at all imply an alibi for stagnation, but instead thinks the empirical approach to a conceptual ideal as asymptotic. Indeed, Žižek himself recognises that the Hegelian replacement for the regulative ideal, namely, the Notion, is definitionally unrealisable, because the Notion is characterised by turning into its opposite, once empirical reality achieves the ideal. His opposition to the postulate of a gap between phenomenal ethico-political striving and the strictly conceptual plane of regulative ideals is therefore, in actuality, grounded in other (highly metaphysical) considerations—as we will shortly see.

Žižek links the emergence of the modern subject to the advent of the nation state, through the event of the French Revolution, and especially, through Kantian philosophy, which he evidently regards (with Hegel) as its "highest expression". As is well known, Kantian ethics involves a rejection of every particular Supreme Good as a legitimate justification for ethical action, for a formal ethics of universality whereby the ethical basis for action is tested according to the principle of universalisability, and not against its ability to yield results in support of an ethico-political cause. Interpreting the problem of nationalism along these lines, Žižek argues that Kant both designates the space of the National Thing (the ideological Supreme Good) and prohibits the step into nationalism. Indeed, "filling out the empty place of the Thing by the Nation is perhaps the paradigmatic case of the inversion which defines radical Evil" (Žižek, 1993: 222). The utopian fantasy of the content of the Thing—the harmonious society beloved of totalitarian ideology—is to be opposed to the ethics of desire, which really means the maintenance of desire in *dis*-satisfaction. Reminiscent of Žižek's own postmarxian ethics from his radical democratic period of "enthusiastic resignation" (Žižek, 1991a: 270-273), this ethics characterises the political field in terms of the radically ambiguous relationship of the people to the national Thing, the kernel of the Real around which the life of the community revolves. But, asks Žižek, "how can we avoid recognising a reference to the contemporary political landscape, with its two extremes of unprincipled liberal pragmatism and fundamentalist fanaticism?" (Žižek, 1996b: 97).

Thus, for Žižek, the only alternatives opened by the "spontaneous ideology of Lacanian psychoanalysis" are political liberalism (supported by a psychoanalytically enhanced Kantian ethics) and its "inherent transgressions," ethnic nationalism, religious fundamentalism and so forth. In his recent statement of an ethics "beyond the Good," Žižek asks:

> Is not Lacan's entire theoretical edifice torn between ... two options: between the ethics of desire/Law, of maintaining the gap, and the lethal/ suicidal immersion in the Thing (Žižek, 1997b: 239)?

Whatever the case with Lacan, this certainly identifies the internal fissure in Žižek's work. When it comes to the decision, however, Žižek is for the "lethal/suicidal immersion in the Thing". In his recent insistence that diabolical evil and the supreme good are formally identical (Žižek, 1997b: 213-241)—because they represent the moment of ethico-political institution—Žižek aims, in his inimitably hyperbolic style, to oppose the deployment of Lacanian theory in support of an anti-radical ethics. By shifting the register, from Symbolic desire to the Real of the drives, Žižek hopes to open another path to a radical ethics. The starting point for this new ethics is nothing less than the Kierkegaardian trope of a "religious suspension of the ethical" (Žižek, 2001c: 82), which Žižek also figures as a "Leftist suspension of the Law" (Žižek, 2000h: 223). A blatant contradiction, this position makes sense only if we accept Žižek's assumptions: if discursive universality (and therefore everyday morality) is secretly supported by some venal enjoyment, then the only way to really defeat this racist/sexist/nationalist/etc. *jouissance* is to jump clear from the existing field of ethico-political universality altogether, in an ethico-politico-metaphysical "great leap forward". Not surprisingly, then, this road travels by way of the adoption of a curious rhetorical combination of messianic religious motifs and slogans reminiscent of Cultural-Revolution-period Maoism. Hence, we have the proletarian chiliasm of "Pauline materialism" and the injunction to "repeat Lenin" (Žižek, 2001g), the advocacy of the "gesture of the authentic master," the "irrational violence" that founds a new, spiritual community through a "supreme crime" (Žižek, 2000e), and so forth.

For Žižek, the consequences of his reconceptualization of the ethics of the Real are enormous: it "delivers us from guilt" and abolishes the objectivity of the distinction between Good and Evil (Žižek, 1996b: 98). If the origin of the ethical injunction—the moral law, and in the final analysis, the Other of the Symbolic Law—is itself incomplete, Žižek argues, perforated by the Real of enjoyment, then there exists no guarantee of the morality of the subject's actions. This is certainly true: there exists no *guarantee*, no certainty, that the actions of the subject are ethically legitimate—and it is for precisely this reason that Kant developed a series of testing procedures, not to deduce ethical maxims from pure concepts with apodictic certainty, as Hegel thought, but in order to rationally test the moral propositions that already exist in the field of the intersubjective debate over political affairs, moral problems, social questions, and so forth. Far from abolishing the distinction between ethical and unethical, right and wrong, a universal ethics leads us to accept that while most proposals for action are ethically legitimate (even though on other grounds we might disagree with them), there are some, branded somewhat archaically by Kant as "evil," that are simply illegitimate. These are the moral maxims that fail the tests of universality. Žižek is apparently only incidentally interested in this aspect of the question, however, for several other considerations are at work in this position, among them the Hegelian trope of ethical progress as necessitating a "crime" against ethical life (a transgression of social norms). Although Žižek's interpretation of Hegel is questionable,[16] it is probable that the principal consideration at work here is his supposition that it is possible to aim, not for the inherent transgressions of an ethico-political field, but for the "foreclosed" "kernel of the Real" that sustains the dialectics of social norm and moral transgression.

Žižek's exploration of this lethal plunge—the correlative to the political Act—happens through the trope of "diabolical evil" (Žižek, 1997b: 213-241). For Kant, evil exists as radical evil, which designates not a special class of

---

16. The Hegelian dialectics of crime as a demand for recognition and the expansion of the law are superbly (and completely unambiguously, unlike Žižek's unilateral "supreme crime") covered in the work of Williams and Honneth. (Honneth, 1995; Williams, 1997). In Hegel's own work, the role of Caesar in Rome, Socrates in Athens and Napoleon in Western Europe exemplify the "criminal" act that executes the "ruse reason" and leads to an expanded conception of ethical life. See (Hegel, 1956). These actions are justified in the light of a teleological conception of history: Hegel by no means condones unilateral violence or mere criminality, but instead suggests that certain *universal* conceptions were correct, despite their non-acceptance by the society of the time, and proposes that violence has historically been justified in their realisation. For a contemporary (neo-Hegelian) interpretation of the potential conflict between a universal ethical imperative and the concrete norms of social conduct in a given milieu, consult Agnes Heller's useful reconstruction of the concept of ethical life (Heller, 1988; Heller, 1990; Heller, 1996).

actions, but the root of the human condition in what we might call "patho-logical narcissism," that is, making the performance of ethical duty condi-tional upon some narcissistic satisfaction. Kant rules out the human com-mission of acts of "angelic good" or "diabolical evil" for the straightforward reason that in "diabolical evil," the noumenal moral law becomes phenom-enalised as an empirical action (Copjec, 1996: xvi-xx). What fascinates Žižek and cothinkers, however, is the interpretation of Kant's discussion of regi-cide, where "the state commits suicide," as the *locus classicus* of the suicidal-revolutionary act of "diabolical evil". In this act, it is the King's *sublime* body that is killed, through the formal act of execution. Zupančič, for instance, claims that Kant is "shaken" by this act of "diabolical evil" because "he is compelled by his argument to describe it in exactly the same words he used to describe and ethical act" (Zupančič, 2000: 85). Zupančič summarises: "diabolical evil, the highest evil, is indistinguishable from the highest good, and they are nothing other than the definitions of an accomplished ethical act" (Zupančič, 2000: 92). In terms of the structure of the ethical act, the difference between good and evil is irrelevant. Zupančič is simply echoing Žižek's claim that "the good is nothing but the name for the formal structure of action" (Žižek, 1997b: 213-241; Zupančič, 2000: 92).

Implied in Žižek's conception of the ethical act—apart from its explic-it moral relativism—are several consequences: the direct intrusion of the Symbolic Law into consciousness; the direct intervention of the noumenal realm into the phenomenal domain; and the obliteration of subjective divi-sion in the "act of an undivided subject".[17] These conditions equal an iden-tical subject-object. Žižek's reflections on Copjec's work, in a chapter sig-nificantly entitled "The Unconscious Law," might have launched a serious reconsideration of his "original insight," with its implicit equation of the Symbolic Law with the lower level of the Graph of Desire (Žižek, 1997b: 213-241). Instead, it formed a platform for the leap into the "abyss of freedom". Before following Žižek into the "abyss of freedom," though, where he will rehabilitate the doctrine of the identical subject-object, we have to observe the fall of the last barrier between Žižek and high metaphysics, namely, the collapse of the Lacanian relation of "aphanisis," or inverse proportionality, between subject and object.

Theoretical Uncertainty

Perhaps Žižek's best front cover is the dead octopus on *The Indivisible Remain-der* (1996). The indivisible remainder in question is, of course, the uncanny "subject before subjectivation"—and presumably the graphic alludes to "the materialist subject as the point at which nature 'runs amok' and goes off the

---

17. There are some signs that Žižek has begun to retreat from the pseudo-problem of "dia-bolical evil," without, however, retracting the identical subject-object that is its correlate.

rails" (Žižek, 1996b: 73). This subject is the abyss of freedom that differenti-
ates humanity from nature, a radical negativity in relation to all existence,
the void in the Symbolic field, the "vanishing mediator" in the historical
process. Indeed, this might be regarded as Žižek's fundamental theorem:
"the ultimate 'vanishing mediator' between nature and culture is the death
drive" (Žižek, 1991a: 207); and, as Žižek explains in a recent major work, "in
Lacanese, the subject prior to subjectivisation is the pure negativity of the
death drive prior to its reversal into the identification with some new master
signifier" (Žižek, 2000h: 160). If this unconscious "subject before subjectivation" were to meet the light of day (appearing, for instance, as a repulsive
dead octopus), it would open one baleful eye, fix the person with its dreadful gaze and pronounce the words of truth: "I am what is in you more than
yourself; I am the death drive".

Or would it? On a second pass, the death drive is not the divided subject,
but instead the object (a), the uncanny "extimate" thing within the "subject
beyond subjectivation". On this interpretation, the death drive is the traumatic kernel in the subject, and the divided subject, $, is, in the last analysis,
the subject divided as to the object (a), the Thing which both attracts and re-
pels the subject (Žižek, 1989: 180).

> The process of interpellation-subjectivation is precisely an attempt to
> elude, to avoid this traumatic kernel through identification: in assuming
> a symbolic mandate, in recognising himself in the interpellation, the
> subject evades the dimension of the Thing (Žižek, 1989: 181).

Now the subject before subjectivation is the void in the Symbolic field,
a subject that tries to avoid the encounter with the Thing that it is in the
Real, namely, the death drive in its rotary motion around the object (a). All
Symbolic identification happens not as a fundamental decision by the death
drive to adopt an existential project, but instead as a decision by the empty
"substanceless subjectivity" of the (unconscious) Cartesian subject to evade
the anxiety and disgust provoked by the encounter with the "rotary motion
of the drives".

In the recent account, then, $ = death drive. In the initial theory, how-
ever, (a) = death drive.

Between the two moments stands Žižek's speculative philosophy of the
Act. This metaphysics of the decision is explicitly posed as an exposition
of "dialectical materialism," that is, as isomorphic to the primordially repressed historical violence which founds that social field explored in "historical materialism" (Žižek, 1996b: 43). For Žižek, this means that the "ultimate speculative identity" happens when the "authentic Act" of the subject
suspends the existing Symbolic Order (coextensive with the social field, for
Žižek) only to inaugurate a new "big Other" (Žižek, 1996b: 144). This is
a metaphysical exploration of the problematic of the "great leap forward"

that we have already seen is the root of Žižek's political zigzags and ethical hesitations. Žižek constructs a chain of equivalences: first, the speculative identity of the object (*a*) with the Symbolic Order (Žižek, 1996b: 143-147); then, the speculative identity of the subject with the Symbolic Order. The clear implication is that in the Act, the subject and object are "speculatively" identical. Yet, this is "perhaps the hardest speculative nut to crack" for Žižek, and so he can only indicate that the Lacanian motif of creation *ex nihilo* means that:

> Although one has to be careful not to confound the Act *qua* Real with the performative gesture of the Master-Signifier, the two are nonetheless closely connected: the ultimate paradox of the process of signification, its "highest mystery," is the fact that the Act *qua* Real ... is simultaneously the "vanishing mediator" that *founds* the Symbolic Order. ... In short, the Act *qua* Real and the Master-Signifier are not "substantially" different (Žižek, 1996b: 146-147).

In other words, the historical subject, via the "highest mystery" of the transubstantiation of the death drive, creates the totality of the Symbolic Order (social field). The "ultimate paradox" of Žižek's theory is an identical subject-object of history.

IV.

According to the dustjacket of *The Ticklish Subject*, "Žižek argues for a radical politics ... unafraid to make sweeping claims in the name of a universal human subject". The concept of the unconscious subject as the "absent centre of political ontology" makes a lot of sense: central, as a universal, but constitutively absent because unconscious, the subject is the lynchpin of political resistance and the basis for an ethical conception of socialism. The problem lies in the execution, where "in a typical Žižekian inversion, the spectral Cartesian ego is reborn, but this time as its exact opposite, the id" (Eagleton, 2001: 50). To be precise, Žižek reconceptualises the id so as to attribute to it exactly the same properties (punctual unity, self-reflexivity, world-constituting agency) formerly assigned to the Cartesian "unified ego," the original "identical subject-object" in modern philosophy. This is the metaphysical root of the "antinomies of Žižek" that we have just encountered. Žižek thematises his metaphysics under the heading of the "abyss of freedom" and the "decision-event of Truth," and bases his claims to anti-historicism and anti-capitalism on the foundation of the world-constituting decision of the identical subject-object. Instead of a radical politics for the twenty-first century, I suggest, Žižek's metaphysical radicalism risks descent into irrationality and relativism.

The Abyss of Freedom

Žižek's lugubrious speculations on the undivided subject as incarnation of the death drive are supported by the high metaphysics of the "abyss of freedom," the encounter with the Romanticism of Schelling. According to Schelling's Romantic theological fantasy, the rational world of the *Logos* emerges from a divine decision to abandon the insane and formless vortex of cosmic creation, and enter temporality as the immortal substance. Nature, Schelling proposes, is the Odyssey of Spirit, finally reaching consciousness in humanity. Unhesitatingly projecting this creation myth onto humanity via the doctrine of "intellectual intuition," Schelling proposes that humanity is the "identical subject-object," because humanity is a formal incarnation of the divine substance (Schelling 1997). Žižek's delight at this speculative schema is evident. So is the fragility of his philosophical defense of this fantasy as rational solution to a serious cognitive problem. Straining credibility beyond the breaking-point, Žižek interprets Schellingian metaphysics as an anticipation of psychoanalysis, and recasts the divine decision as the contingent encounter with the Real of the drives, in the unconscious "choice of neurosis," equivalent to the Kantian original decision upon a moral disposition (Žižek, 1997a).

For Žižek, the drive is beyond the Symbolic Law (Žižek, 1997a: 78-79) and the rotary motion of the drives is a pre-symbolic antagonism (Žižek, 1997a: 19). At a stroke, this re-naturalises the drives, returning them, against Lacan, to biological instincts. "At the beginning proper stands a resolution, an act of decision that, by way of differentiating between past and present, resolves the unbearable tension of the rotary motion of the drives"—that is, makes the transition from drive to desire (Žižek, 1997a: 15). Schelling's pseudo-problem is that there is strictly no way to exit from the rotary motion of the drives unless the drives themselves are preceded by a mysterious "X" that "contracts" the drives. As we have seen, Schelling's "solution" is an identical subject-object who, through "intellectual intuition," posits both the totality and the distinction between subject and object. Let us once again examine why an advocate of Lacanian theory will encounter grave problems following Schelling.

Formally speaking, Žižek is able to prevent the emergence of an identical subject-object by proposing that the "subject before subjectivation" (symbolised by the Lacanian matheme, S) is in a relation of inverse proportionality with the "sublime object of ideology" (symbolised by the Lacanian matheme, object (a)), so that the approach of the object (a) means aphanisis (fading) of the subject, S. The only "identical subject-object" is the fantasy relation (symbolised as $S \Diamond a$), where the "losange," $\Diamond$, designates a relation of "internal exclusion" or "extimacy" between S and (a). So long as Žižek sticks to the Lacanian orthodoxy, then, he is quite immune to any allegation that he restores an identical subject-object.

Žižek, as we have just seen, exhibits a certain resistance to the consequences of crushing Lacanian theory in the speculative nutcracker. It is therefore left to Zupančič to make the full implications explicit. She claims the abolition of the division of the subject in the ethical Act—a subjectless act of a "full subject"—reveals the normal, pathological state of the divided subject by contrast with the Act. "The subject is 'realised,' 'objectified' in this act: the subject passes over to the side of the object. ... In an act there is no 'divided subject': there is the 'it' (the Lacanian *ça*) and the subjective figure that arises from it ... [which] follows the logic of what Lacan calls a 'headless subjectivation' or 'subjectivation without subject'" (Zupančič, 2000: 104). Less directly, Žižek states the same conclusion:

> [T]he authentic act that I accomplish is always by definition a foreign body, an intruder which simultaneously attracts/fascinates and repels me, so that if and when I come too close to it, this leads to my *aphanisis*, self-erasure. If there is a subject to the act, it is not the subject of subjectivisation, of integrating the act into the universe of symbolic integration and recognition, of assuming the act as "my own," but, rather, an uncanny, "acephalous" subject through which the act takes place which is "in him more than himself". *The act thus designates the level at which the fundamental divisions and displacements usually associated with the "Lacanian subject" ... are momentarily suspended* (Žižek, 2000h: 374-375 emphasis added).

This means that the Kantian objection to the intrusion of noumenal freedom into the phenomenal domain (the subject as moral author of the world is a god; correlatively, the intrusion of the noumenal realm implies that suspension of the subject's freedom, because this god manipulates all phenomenal events in line with a moral purpose) applies to the Act. For Kant, were God to intrude directly into the phenomenal world, humanity would become mere puppets of the Divine Will and not autonomous subjects. For Žižek, "the highest freedom coincides with ... a reduction to a lifeless automaton who blindly performs its gestures" (Žižek, 2000h: 375). Žižek therefore reinvents the doctrine of intellectual intuition by means of the claim that the punctual unity of the radical will is capable of unilaterally inaugurating a new social order.

Event of the Resolute Decision

As a consequence of the problematic of absolute freedom, Žižek's "philosophical manifesto of Cartesian subjectivity" (Žižek, 2000h: 2) necessarily leads to ethical decisionism and political voluntarism (Žižek, 2000h: 114-115), cognitive irrationalism (Žižek, 1997a: 76) and the transposition of individual psychology (madness) onto social formations (Žižek, 2000h: 34-41).

These are condensed, for Žižek, through the figure of a "voluntarist decisionism" combined with "Cartesian mechanism," into a "materialist theory of Grace" (Žižek, 2000h: 116-119). This position, as archaic as it is irrational, cannot possibly found a radical politics for the twenty-first century. To the contrary: it has strong neo-conservative affinities.

Decisionism—as exemplified by Carl Schmitt (Hirst, 1999: 7-17)— departs from a monological concept of subjectivity and postulates a prediscursive kernel that acts as the nucleus of decisions, without reference to ethical norms. On the basis of the theory of the "abyss of freedom," it is impossible for Žižek to avoid an ethical decisionism that intensifies the problems of Heidegger's theory of the "resolute decision" upon an existential project, elaborated in *Being and Time* (1927) (Heidegger, 1996: 233-277). Heidegger's conception of "anticipatory resoluteness" through the recognition of the "mineness of death" is overshadowed in contemporary debates by Heidegger's notorious Nazi entanglement. The major *philosophical* problem with *Being and Time* is not decisionism (Osborne, 1995: 168-175), however, but the transposition of the individual "resolute decision" onto the "historical destiny" of social collectives (Heidegger, 1996: 341-370 especially 352). As Žižek explains, the resulting neglect of the element of sociality means that the individual decision is ethically indifferent, while nations are treated as persons with a "destiny" (Žižek, 2000h: 11-22). Ethical decisionism might therefore not be Heidegger's problem—but it certainly is Žižek's, for Žižek supplements a theory of the "insane" decision, which results from the breaking of social bonds, with the postulate of a pre-symbolic kernel, in the form of a unitary will, that precedes the decision. This not only *neglects* the medium of sociality—an "inadequate deployment of the *Mitsein*"—it actively *negates* social existence and advocates the destruction of social norms and political legitimacy. On the basis of this theory, Žižek—the defender of Cartesian philosophical science against the onslaughts of the postmodern relativists—finds it difficult to discriminate between democracy and totalitarianism without resorting to a determination of social content that contradicts the asocial character of the Truth-Event (Žižek, 2000e: 138-139; Žižek, 2002: 39).

In the light of his thesis of the death drive as the undivided will of an identical subject-object, Žižek seeks to integrate Alain Badiou's concept of the Event of Truth into Žižek's post-Althusserian problematic of ideological interpellation (Žižek, 2000h: 128). Žižek salutes Badiou's resurrection of the metaphysical dimension of "the *politics of (universal) Truth*" (Žižek, 2000h: 132) and opposes this to the postmodern dogma that "events do not happen" (Žižek, 2000h: 135). For Žižek, this Truth can only be the repressed historical genesis of Being in a contingent political act of social inauguration, that is, a violent revolution. According to Žižek, "the truth-event consists in the elementary ideological gesture of interpellating individuals" (Žižek, 2000h:

141). Yet, the entailment of this position is that there exists no neutral gaze that might discern the Event and arbitrate any claim:

> Thus, there is no neutral gaze of knowledge that could discern the event in its effects: a decision is always-already there—that is, one can discern the signs of an Event in the situation only from a previous decision for Truth, just as in Jansenist theology, in which divine miracles are legible as such only to those who have already decided for Faith (Žižek, 2000h: 136).

Referring approvingly to Lukács (Žižek, 2000h: 137)—who claimed that real decisions precede knowledge of the situation and described his conversion to Communism as a "Pascalian wager"—Žižek proposes that the decision *precedes* any undecidability. This stance of irrational faith enables Žižek to impatiently dismiss the question of how to arbitrate whether a social movement is "truly the Event, not just another semblance of an Event" (Žižek, 2000h: 138). Accepting Badiou's anti-Enlightenment claim that religion is the formal model of political commitment, Žižek nonetheless feels compelled to ask how despite the fact that, today, religion is a pseudo-event, St Paul remains the *philosopher* of the formal conditions of the truth event. "Nonetheless, the problem remains of how it was possible for the first and still most pertinent description of the mode of operation of the fidelity to a Truth Event to occur apropos of a Truth Event that is a mere semblance, not an actual Truth" (Žižek, 2000h: 143). For Žižek, "from a Hegelian standpoint, there is a deep necessity in this, confirmed by the fact that in our century the philosopher who provided the definitive description of an authentic political *act* (Heidegger in *Being and Time*) was seduced by a political act that was undoubtedly a fake, not an actual Truth-Event (Nazism)" (Žižek, 2000h: 143). So—"what if what Badiou calls the Truth-Event *is*, at its most radical, a purely formal act of decision? [W]hat if the true fidelity to the Event is 'dogmatic' in the precise sense of unconditioned Faith?" (Žižek, 2000h: 144). In other words, Badiou does not sufficiently vigorously reject the Enlightenment position that politics is based on the demystification of religious illusions.

Nonetheless, sensing the relativist void opening before his feet, Žižek claims that the Hegelian position on the "singular universal," the element that embodies the void of the situation, is that it subverts the situation by "directly incarnating the universal" (Žižek, 2000h: 144). Hence, the problematic of proletarian chiliasm, the moment of the identical subject-object in a total revolution, is linked to the expressive totality and the direct incarnation of universality as the "solution" to the postmodern constellation. The truth-event is a Pascalian wager (Žižek, 2000h: 144), that involves a temporal loop (Žižek, 2000h: 144), which narrativises history as an evolutionary sequence, whereby the present is redeemed in the future thanks to the event

(Žižek, 2000h: 144). Which sounds like Žižek's description of the fantasy. Indeed, "is not the circular relationship between the Event and the subject … the very circle of ideology?" (Žižek, 2000h: 145).

The Decline of Symbolic Authority: Žižek's "Anti-Historicism"

It is therefore not surprising that Žižek's constant polemical denunciations of "historicism," for its lack of recognition of the "non-historical kernel of human existence," are laced with bold claims to have adopted a "dogmatic" stance, so that, for instance, we are informed that "Marxism and psychoanalysis are 'infallible' at the level of their enunciated content" (Žižek, 1994c: 183). To claim that Žižek remains within the gravitational field of historicism will perhaps generate consternation, for the dominant tendency in criticisms of Žižek is to take a position for or against his supposed *anti*-historicism. Crusader for Cartesian certainty, defender of the *cogito* and supporter of the Truth-Event of militant materialism (the October Revolution), Žižek has produced numerous critiques of "postmarxian historicism" and "postmodern sophism" (Žižek, 1993: 1-5; Žižek, 1996b: 214-218; Žižek, 2000c: 112-114; Žižek, 2001c: 80-81). In opposition to the historicist tendency of radical democratic postmarxism, Žižek has from the beginning proposed that "over-rapid historicisation makes us blind to the real kernel that returns as the same through diverse … symbolisations" (Žižek, 1989: 50). His position is that it is impossible to entirely contextualise a phenomenon: the dissolution of every event into its socio-historical context implies the positioning of the analyst in the "view from nowhere," the gods-eye position of pure, neutral metalanguage situated: "above" the historical texture. The apparently modest perspectival relativism of the historicist therefore masks an extraordinarily immodest claim to perfect neutrality, to possess the "master's gaze, which viewing history from a safe metalanguage distance, constructs the linear narrative of 'historical evolution'" (Žižek, 2001c: 80). Žižek connects the metanarrative of legitimation that supports historicism with the fundamental operation of ideology (Žižek, 1991a: 130) and regards deconstruction as the "highest expression" of contemporary historicism, because its endless recontextualisations engage precisely such a metalinguistic claim (Žižek, 1989: 153-155; Žižek, 1991a: 87-90). What historicism overlooks is the eternal return of the same of *difference itself* in every historico-symbolic text, conceptualised psychoanalytically as "lack" (the absence of a presence) (Žižek, 2000c: 114; Žižek, 2001c: 223). The problem is that this definition of the Symbolic as based in a pure, non-conceptual difference, besides having surprisingly Deleuzian overtones (Deleuze, 1994), coincides with Žižek's definition of the Real, collapsing "lack" into "loss," Symbolic into Real—and subject into object.

Žižek can salvage his position from relativism only on the basis of an explicit advocacy of expressive totality, that is, by undermining the non-metaphysical interpretation of Hegel. According to Žižek, there exists a structural homology between liberal capitalism and hysterical subjectivity (Žižek, 1993: 209-210). The basis for this assertion is the dubious theoretical identity between surplus value and "surplus-enjoyment," grounded in the "structural homology" between the self-transcending limit of capitalism and the relation between prohibition and transgression in psychoanalysis (Žižek, 1989: 49-53). The result is that, as Jason Glynos demonstrates, the "logic of desire *is* the motor of capitalism" (Glynos, 2001: 88). The substantive differences between the libidinal investments in the formation of social subjectivity, and the material basis in surplus labour-time for institutional relations, should warn us against any premature telescoping of the specificity of the ideological and economic. Žižek's position risks collapse into an insipid (and conservative) functionalism that denies the coefficient of resistance in social subjectivity, by suggesting that forms of individuation are *only* functional for capital accumulation (or *vice versa*, for Žižek's idealism). Žižek's precious formalism, which makes every form of structural imbalance somehow secretly "the same," licensing the collapse of structural regions into single generative mechanism, is exactly what Althusser criticised under the heading of "expressive totality" (Jameson, 1981: 34-37).

Žižek's indifference to Marxist theory leads to his endorsement of Hardt and Negri's baroque, Deleuze-inspired fantasia as a "new *Communist Manifesto*" (Hardt, 2000: dustjacket; Žižek, 2001d: 190-205), presumably on the basis that their exploration of the late capitalist desiring-machines of global empire supports his own conjecture that the flexible identities of the NSM correspond to "Spinozist late capitalism". Indeed, for Žižek, the proposition that "Spinozism"—by which Žižek means Deleuze and Guattari's *Anti-Oedipus* and *Thousand Plateaus*—is the "ideology of late capitalism" effectively displaces postmodern culture from that role (Žižek, 1993: 211-219). For Žižek, the postmodern celebration of dispersed, multiple subject-positions in the processes of deterritorialised global capitalism, "far from containing any kind of subversive potentials ... designates *the form of subjectivity that corresponds to late capitalism*" (Žižek, 1993: 216). The inconsistent modes of particularised enjoyment to which this "subject" surrenders are nothing but the operations of multinational capital. Hence, Žižek suggests, the alternatives of Althusserian Marxism and Deleuzian postmodernism are only the critical and celebratory aspects of a single process of late capitalism.

Unlike Lukács, for whom commodity reification was the mechanism of expressive unification of the capitalist totality, for Žižek (with Hegel), this mechanism is subjectivity. With the shift to late capitalism, perverse subjectivity supposedly emerges as the universal mode of subjection. According to Žižek, the break-up of the nuclear family correlative to globalisation leads to a decline in paternal authority and its replacement by the ferocious "maternal superego" (Žižek, 1991b: 97-104). This has potentially catastrophic results: because the father is connected to symbolic authority, society slides into a decline in symbolic efficiency where symbolic fictions are replaced by imaginary simulacra and the resort to the Real of violence (Žižek, 2000h: 315). The autonomous critical subject is increasingly replaced by the "path-ological narcissism" of a perverse subjectivity, which is paradoxically de-pendent upon the very authority it disavows, a resentful conformist whose failed rebellion drives in the direction of self-punishment or sadistic venge-ance upon others. In a revenge of the language on Lacanian hyperbole, then, we are presented with the spectacle of the "collapse" of a big Other who "does not exist" (Žižek, 2000h: 326). For Žižek, this signifies the col-lapse of the Symbolic Order, and its fragmentation into a multiplicity of do-mains of signification as *belief* in symbolic authority is destroyed by *knowledge* (Žižek, 2002).

Žižek therefore *accepts* the decline of Oedipus and the emergence of mul-tiple contingent identities, but *rejects* the narrative according to which this is a straightforward process of liberation: "the danger lies not in the remain-ders of the past, but in the obscene need for domination and subjection en-gendered by the new 'post-Oedipal' forms of subjectivity themselves" (Žižek, 2000h: 360). Žižek's position implies that political revolution is fundamen-tally a restoration of Oedipal subjectivity and a redemption of the "big Oth-er," redolent of a religious "cure" for postlapsarian wickedness. From this position it is impossible to evade the slide into self-instrumentalisation. Just as the Stalinist presents themselves as the instrument of the historical proc-ess destined to save modern culture from its descent into barbarism, Žižek opposes a redemptive universality "to come" to "globalisation-with-particu-larisation" and its perverted subjectivity.

Pauline Materialism: Žižek's "Anti-Capitalism"

According to Žižek, the new "end of history" of the post-Communist glob-al hegemony of American finance capital—the event-less reality of the New World Order—intensifies the depoliticisation characteristic of modernity. The result, Žižek suggests, is "postmodern post-politics," which:

> no longer merely represses the political, trying to contain it and pacify the "returns of the repressed," but much more effectively "forecloses" it, so that the postmodern forms of ethnic violence, with their "irrational" excessive character, are no longer simple "returns of the repressed" but, rather, represent a case of the foreclosed (from the Symbolic) which, as we know from Lacan, returns in the Real (Žižek, 2000h: 198).

The deadlock of the contemporary world, then, is that the declining ef-ficiency of symbolic authority and the post-political technocracy exemplified by the "global Third Way" of Anthony Giddens and Tony Blair, generate the combination of depoliticised apathy and anti-political fundamentalism that means that violence is increasingly the matrix for the resolution of social conflicts. This leads Žižek to the classic ultra-left position that "the neo-Nazi skinhead's ethnic violence is not the 'return of the repressed' of the liberal multiculturalist tolerance, but *directly generated by it*, its own concealed true face" (Žižek, 2000h: 205).

Žižek's effort to create an emancipatory politics capable of breaking through the supposed pseudo-dialectic of cynicism and violence leads him to declare himself a "Pauline materialist," or ethical Marxist. As he explains, "the New World Order, as in medieval times, is global, but not universal, since it strives for a new, global *order* with each part in its allocated place" (Žižek, 2000h: 176). Therefore:

> Today, more than ever, one has to insist that the only way open to the emergence of an Event is that of breaking the vicious cycle of globalisation-with-particularisation by (re)asserting the dimension of Universality *against* capitalist globalisation. ... [W]hat we need today is the gesture that would undermine capitalist globalisation from the standpoint of universal Truth, just as Pauline Christianity did to the Roman global Empire (Žižek, 2000h: 211).

Žižek's argument becomes increasingly incoherent from this point onwards. According to Žižek, and despite the assertion that capitalism replaces the universal with "globalisation-with-particularisation," there exist three universals today: the "Real universality" of international capitalism; the "Symbolic universality," the reigning symbolic fiction of multicultural tolerance; the "Imaginary universality" of the ideal of *égaliberté* (Žižek, 2000h: 213). This invokes a new "concrete universality" of "reflexive modernity," distinct from the concrete universal of the twentieth century, involving a "postmodern, post-nation state" form of globalised life supported by the reigning fiction of multicultural tolerance (Žižek, 2000h: 214). This allows Žižek—with proponents of "reflexive modernity"—to interpret neo-fascism and religious fundamentalism as desperate defenses against the new, rootless "void of universality" (Žižek, 2000h: 217).

The postulate of an expressive totality of late capitalism enables Žižek to interpret cultural and intellectual phenomena as mere aspects of a unitary process. On these lines, postmodern theory, postmarxian politics, multiculturalism, human rights, political liberties and parliamentary democracy are nothing but the "human face" of "capitalist globalism". Indeed, it licenses (for Žižek) practices of psychological labelling little different from the vulgar Marxist practice of premature class ascription. Žižek's discourse is generously larded with psychoanalytic "invective," so that highly respected interlocutors are described as "perverts" (Deleuze, Foucault, Butler) and "hysterics" (Derrida, Laclau). Multiculturalism involves a condescending distance towards the multiplicity of cultures that secretly relies upon a "neutral-universal" stance elevated beyond the militant particularisms—but this supposedly neutral stance is in actuality precisely based on capitalist globalisation and the universalisation of the Western form of life, before which every other culture appears as a particular (Žižek, 2000h: 216). Postmodern politics becomes entangled in the "unprecedented homogenisation of today's world" and a depoliticisation of social conflict, where "the price of this depoliticisation of the economy is the depoliticisation of politics … political struggle proper is transformed into the cultural struggle for the recognition of marginal identities and the tolerance of differences" (Žižek, 2000h: 218).

Žižek (quite correctly) criticises the situation where only the populist extreme Right now criticises capital, while the radical Left occupies itself with the struggle for cultural recognition on the basis of capitalism (Žižek, 2000h: 355). "Leftists support a strong State as the last guarantee of social and civil liberties against Capital; while Rightists demonise the State and its apparatuses as the ultimate terrorist machine" (Žižek, 2000h: 356). Yet, beyond the remedy of a "Leftist suspension of the Law," a suspension of the ethical in the name of a true universality to come (Žižek, 2000h: 223), Žižek is remarkably reticent regarding concrete alternatives. Žižek's opposition to the leftwing politics of enthusiastic resignation supposedly does not include hostility to the reform agenda of postmodern politics: "I am pleading for a 'return to the primacy of economy,' not to the detriment of the issues raised by postmodern forms of politicisation, but precisely in order to create the conditions for the more effective realization of feminist, ecological, and so on, demands" (Žižek, 2000h: 356). Yet, elsewhere, Žižek analyses the discursive form: "of course, …, but …," as the discourse of disavowal. He claims the real question is "how are we to reinvent the political space in today's conditions of globalisation?" (Žižek, 2000h: 222). I suggest that Žižek has no real answers—hence the rhetorical question.

Based on his conceptualisation of the "Lacanian Thing" as secretly identical to the Cartesian ego, Žižek can only lurch between the poles of an antinomy. For the postmarxian Žižek of the radical democratic period, the death drive (the Thing) represents the dimension of radical negativity that cannot be reduced to an expression of alienated social conditions. Therefore:

> it is not only that the aim is no longer to abolish this antagonism, but that the aspiration to abolish it is precisely the source of totalitarian temptation; the greatest mass murders and holocausts have always been perpetrated in the name of man as a harmonious being, of a New Man without antagonistic tension (Žižek, 1989: 5).

Indeed, this fantasy of the absolute crime that opens a New Beginning is *sadistic*. It is the fantasy that "it is possible to create new forms of life *ex nihi-*

lo, from the zero-point". From the vantage of Žižek's radical democratic period, it is "not difficult to see how all radical revolutionary projects, Khmer
Rouge included, rely on this same fantasy of ... the creation *ex nihilo* of a new
(sublime) Man, delivered from the corruptions of previous history" (Žižek,
1991a: 261). But, on the other hand, prohibition eroticises, and so there's an
irresistible fascination in the "lethal/suicidal immersion in the Thing" and
"creation *ex nihilo*"—at least for the hyper-Marxist Žižek of the period of
"Pauline Materialism". Hence, in the "unplugging" from the New World
Order by the "authentic psychoanalytic and revolutionary political collectives" that Žižek now urges (Žižek, 2000e: 160), "there is a terrifying *violence*
at work in this 'uncoupling,' that of the death drive, of the radical 'wiping
the slate clean' as the condition of the New Beginning" (Žižek, 2000e: 127).
This sort of "Year Zero" rhetoric may be meant as a provocation to the relativists, as a gesture of defiance towards the contemporary prohibition on
thinking about revolution (Žižek, 2001b). Nonetheless, I suggest that this
combination, of Leninist voluntarism and "irrational" Pauline materialism,
does not resist the postmodern couplet of cynical distance and irrational
fundamentalism, but repeats its terms.

Conclusion

Theories of Structuration, Theories of Ideology

Postmarxism lives its desire for radical social transformation as an exile. As before, with the Romantics and then the New Left, the failure of revolutionary hopes generated in the 1960s (and briefly renewed in 1989) has led to aesthetic compensations for political marginalisation. The failure of revolution now necessitates a detour—more or less permanent—through ideological manipulation, before it might once again be possible to return to mass politics: in a very familiar pattern, postmarxism seeks to transform political subjectivity where once it strove to change the world. Theorising political insurgency as a semi-divine force irrupting from a dimension "beyond" the "discursive formation," postmarxism is quick to add that this stands no chance of global success. As befits a generation for which messianic aspirations have cooled, the very best that can be hoped for is a localised shift in the balance of forces. Indeed, when postmodern anti-Enlightenment animus grips theorists of postmarxism, its positions resemble a "chemical wedding" of Structural Marxism with the "New Philosophy". Despite the hypostatisation of contingency and the insistence on the openness of the historical process, one thing is absolutely certain, flowing from the constitution of the political field with an iron necessity: because identities are formed through processes of exclusion and subordination, every victory is at once a fresh defeat; every liberation is automatically a new enslavement. At once radically libertarian and deeply cynical, postmarxism postulates a fundamental symmetry between the emancipatory politics of the oppressed and the repressive politics of domination. Hegemonic politics is theorised in radically "Machiavellian" terms, as a neutral technology of manipulation and domination that the Left would be well advised to learn to control. Because all social formations are fundamentally constructed upon exclusion and marginalisation, the real question becomes one of how to swap the leading personnel, rather than whether to transform the social order.

At the same time, however, postmarxism has really tried to preserve the radical impetus of socialist politics within a transformed historical conjuncture. Postmarxism secretes a deep desire for liberation, expressed as a radical disdain for everyday politics and the art of government, together with a privileging of "the political" as the moment of social antagonism and spontaneous plebeian rebellion. Many political positions oscillate between radicalised liberalism and an ultra-left refusal of everyday politics. A thoroughly progressive hostility towards every form of pseudo-natural domination animates the imprecations hurled at "essentialism," mistakenly considered by postmarxism to be a legacy of a now obsolete Enlightenment rationalism, rather than the enduring form of ideological mystification. While the turn to social subjectivity as a principle of structuration is reminiscent of Romantic theories, in postmarxian theory the analysis of hegemonic politics is linked to the problems of specifically *socialist* strategy. The defense of "the political" is aimed towards keeping alive exactly this strategic possibility in the context of postmodern culture and poststructuralist philosophy. The political has the status of the "postmarxian Thing," the forbidden and unnamed desire that animates the merely formal unity of a shared trajectory beginning in Althusserian social theory. "The political," as a moment of irruption and revolutionary openness, is counterposed to "the political field" of routine politics, characterised in modernity (for postmarxism) by democratic competition. From Laclau and Mouffe ("the political"), through Žižek ("the political Act"), to Butler ("resignification"), the post-Althusserian postmarxists are searching for a principle of transcendence that might reactivate the moment of social inauguration. Postmarxism at once yearns for a universal revolution ("the political" as the moment of social inauguration) and denies the validity of universality. It thereby organises the sabotage of its own programme and safeguards its unsatisfied desire. Accordingly, postmarxism is a protest politics designed to shift the new social movements to the left, but is not itself capable of generating new radical forms. Indeed, the recent rise of rightwing populism and religious fundamentalism exposes the reliance of postmarxism on a radicalised variant of liberal political theory, one which valorises social particularity, cultural difference and localised democratic initiatives, whilst becoming increasingly allergic to the equivalential logic of social confrontation. As with all radical forms of liberalism linked to protest politics, then, postmarxism expresses a hysterical demand to the political masters designed to force them to fix their system. For the perennial return and retreat of "the political" is the very locus of the postmarxian programme, dependent as it is upon the permanent deferment of the moment of "the political" for the effective sabotage of every "socialist strategy". This movement is perfectly expressed by Laclau's admission that radical democracy finally consists only of "the introduction of state regulation and democratic control of the economy, so that the worst effects of globalisation are avoided" (Laclau, 2000c: 206)—a "radical" programme not too distant from the policies of Third Way social democracy.

Postmarxism is a deeply contradictory phenomenon. On the one hand, postmarxism preserves a radical impulse that leads it to position itself on the leftwing of politics and to resist the drift "beyond Left and Right" that afflicts mainstream political parties and social theories. On the other hand, the historicist problematic that informs postmarxism leads it to reject political universality and engage forms of theoretical and moral relativism whose political implications are, at best, ambiguous, and at worst, reactionary. After the collapse of Communism, some ex-Marxists embraced the "criticism of actually existing democracy," announcing the perspective of "five hundred years of reforms" and the gradual maturation of political subjectivity before any substantial social transformations might once again become possible (Aronson, 1995). Post-Althusserian postmarxism—as the radical wing of postmodern politics—announced, by contrast, an urgent programme of "radical democracy" and "democratic citizenship" as the "corrective to the liberal vision," and declared that the very existence of "the political" was threatened by the imposition of the "New World Order" and its liberal-democratic consensus (Mouffe, 1992d: 1-8). Yet, postmarxism's hostility towards universality, resonating with some of the most reactionary themes of the "New Philosophy," leads its projected resistance to the New World Order astray every time. During the 1990s, postmarxism hailed the irruption of new ethnic nationalisms, religious fundamentalisms and political particularisms as a veritable "return of the political". Radically misreading this political conjuncture as a repudiation of universality (as it had strategically misread the late 1980s as a conjuncture of democratic advance instead of a political retreat before an ascendant neo-liberalism), postmarxism celebrated this "return of the repressed" as a break with the superficial consensus on "individualism, rationalism and universalism" (Mouffe, 1992d: 1-8). A decade later, and the leading theorists of postmarxism have discovered that without universality, there can be no resistance to domination—let alone a social alternative—for every modern demand for liberation expresses a claim on an empty (formal) universal. The titles of the contributions to *Contingency, Hegemony, Universality*—"Constructing Universality," "Competing Universalities," "The Role of Universality in the Construction of Political Logics," and so forth—should tell the story of a fundamental rethink, leading to a break with the historicist problematic. Until the underlying assumptions of historicism are theoretically confronted, however, every such effort to shift beyond political hermeneutics and ethical relativism only leads back into the charmed circle of ideology.

TOWARDS AN ALTERNATIVE AGENDA FOR THEORETICAL RESEARCH

I have demonstrated that the postmarxian field, as defined by the political strategy of radical democracy, is governed by the historicist problematic, which acts as a theoretical unconscious limiting the ability of Laclau and Mouffe, Butler and Žižek to think social complexity and radical strategy. I have sustained the thesis that the historicist problematic is characterised by five key positions: the relativisation of theory, the foundational character of ideology, the expressive conception of history, an identical subject-object and a theory of social practice modeled on individual praxis. In Chapter One, I showed that postmarxism's abandonment of the distinction between theory and ideology leads to a transposition of structures of ideological misrecognition onto theoretical formulations. In examining post-Fordism, the NSM and the history of Marxism, postmarxist theory betrays characteristically ideological structures of subject-centred descriptions, binary axiologies based on mirror relations and the occlusion of inconsistencies behind imaginary histories. Chapter Two showed that the major theoretical statements of Laclau and Mouffe rely upon a latent, expressive totality of history, centred on the master narrative of the unfolding of the "Democratic Revolution of Modernity". In Chapter Three, I proved that Butler's theory of "performativity" depends upon a conception of social practice modeled on individual praxis. Finally, Chapter Four, I demonstrated the existence of an impossible desire to resurrect the doctrine of the "identical subject-object of history" in Žižek's Lacanian dialectics, proposing that the theoretical advances in his work need to be systematically separated from his idealist speculations. This sequence was selected on the basis of choosing the theorist who best exemplified a particular aspect of the historicist problematic; while Laclau and Mouffe, Butler and Žižek all display symptoms of the influence of the entire matrix of the historicist problematic, this influence is unevenly developed, and cannot be said to somehow make them all "the same".

Indeed, there do exist real differences between Laclau and Mouffe, Žižek and Butler, and the best way to capture these is to reconsider the original problem of the historicisation of Althusser's "structural eternities". Postmarxian discourse theory is in search of a principle that might introduce historical transformation into the social formation, puncturing the structural necessity governing the totality with political contingency, and thereby rendering the social formation open, or incomplete. Political contingency therefore acts in postmarxian discourse theory as a principle of rupture, whose privileged location is, according to postmarxism, to be encountered in the realm of ideology (the formation of social subjectivity in the field of discourse). The divergences between the major theorists of post-structuralism—Derrida, Lacan and Foucault—are the basis for the different principles of rupture advanced by Laclau and Mouffe ("discursivity," equals *différance*), Žižek (the Real) and Butler (the dialogical structure of power and resistance), respectively.

The problem with all of the positions in the postmarxian field, however, is that they implicitly equate the transformation of social subjectivity with the historicity of social formations, thereby collapsing theories of structuration into theories of ideology. *HSS* is the most egregious instance of the transposition of an innovative theory of ideology onto the entire social field, by means of a novel concept of discursive practice that cannot withstand serious scrutiny. In actuality, postmarxian discourse theories are post-Althusserian theories of ideology, inflated beyond their capacity into theories of social structuration. By returning to the moment of Althusser's "ISAs essay" and recontextualising this within the constellation of theoretical problems it sought to solve, it becomes possible to grasp the limitations of making political subjectivity solely responsible for the transformation of social formations. Then it becomes possible to separate new insights into social structuration from the advances in the theory of ideology generated by postmarxism.

The significant advances in the Marxian theory of ideology generated in the movement from *Politics and Ideology in Marxist Theory*, through *HSS and Socialist Strategy*, to *The Sublime Object of Ideology*, need to be separated from the question of structuration and shorn of their historicist assumptions. Žižek's adaptation of Lacanian psychoanalysis not only stands at the end of this line of development (thereby benefiting from earlier breakthroughs), but seems the most promising from the perspective of the recognition of the role of the subject in social processes, and for an ethical basis for democratic socialism. Žižek's theory of ideology represents a major breakthrough, and one that, I have suggested, consists of two tendencies in a complex theoretical configuration. In Žižek's early, radical democratic incarnation, he presented a Lacanian theory of social subjectivity within a grasp of the ethico-political field that accepted the terms of debate of the opponent. Žižek's later, "Pauline Materialist" turn makes sometimes strident efforts to correct the political complacency of the early work, but in so doing inverts the theoretical constellation into a Hegelian teleology. It is therefore not just a question of opposing Žižek's early to the recent work, but rather of theoretically disentangling the many strands of his thinking.

At the same time, the insight that replacing labour as the model of social practice with a concept of discursive practice enables theorisation of the dialogical, or contested, existence of social relations, needs to be explored in depth. The concept of "discourse" as the selection and combination of differentially-related structural elements need not be limited by a literalisation of what is effectively the theoretical *metaphor* of speech. The restriction of discursive practice to metaphor and metonymy, equivalence and difference, arbitrarily constrains the thinking of social processes and can only model institutional formation at the cost of excessive abstraction. Once it is liberated from the constraints of a theoretical formalism that reflects Laclau and Mouffe's illegitimate transposition of ideological relations onto institutional structures, the concept of discursive practice can theorise the articulation of structural elements by social forces in the "field of social relations" (Poulantzas), within the horizon of action of a political conjuncture. Throughout my *investigation*, I have suggested an alternative agenda for theoretical research, seeking to radicalise and extend the historicised Structural Marxism known as Regulation Theory. Taking the historical *bricolage* of structural elements in a mode of social regulation as exemplary of a "hegemonic articulation," it becomes possible to think the structural constraints and institutional syntax that regulate "discursive practices," thereby moving beyond an exclusively linguistic conception of hegemonic articulation. Ideological discourses are one component of every hegemonic articulation, not the final horizon of all political strategy.

Bibliography

Abercrombie, Neal, Stephen Hill, *et al.* (1980). *The Dominant Ideology Thesis.* London: Allen & Unwin.

Aglietta, Michel (1979). *A Theory of Capitalist Regulation: The US Experience.* London: Verso.

Ahmad, Aijaz (1992). *In Theory: Classes, Nations, Literatures.* London and New York: Verso.

Althusser, Louis (1969). *For Marx.* London: New Left Books.

Althusser, Louis (1971). *Lenin and Philosophy and Other Essays.* London: New Left Books.

Althusser, Louis (1972). *Politics and History: Montesquieu, Rousseau, Hegel and Marx.* London: New Left Books.

Althusser, Louis (1976). *Essays in Self-Criticism.* London: New Left Books.

Althusser, Louis (1978). "What Must Change in the Party." *New Left Review*(109): 19-45.

Althusser, Louis (1990). *Philosophy and the Spontaneous Philosophy of the Scientists, and Other Essays.* London and New York: Verso.

Althusser, Louis (1994). *Sur la Philosophie: Entretiens avec Fernanda Navarro.* Paris: Gallimard.

Althusser, Louis (1995). *Machiavelli and Us.* London and New York: Verso.

Althusser, Louis and Étienne Balibar (1970). *Reading Capital.* London: New Left Books.

Amyot, Grant (1981). *The Italian Communist Party.* New York: St. Martin's Press.

Anderson, Perry (1974a). *Lineages of the Absolutist State.* London: New Left Books.

Anderson, Perry (1974b). *Passages from Antiquity to Feudalism.* London: New Left Books.

Anderson, Perry (1976). "The Antinomies of Antonio Gramsci." *New Left Review*(100): 5-78.

Anderson, Perry (1979). *Considerations on Western Marxism.* London: New Left Books.

Anderson, Perry (1980). *Arguments within English Marxism.* London: New Left

Books.

Anderson, Perry (1984). *In the Tracks of Historical Materialism*. Chicago and London: University of Chicago Press.

Anderson, Perry (1993). *A Zone of Engagement*. London and New York: Verso.

Antonian, Armen (1987). *Toward a Theory of Eurocommunism: The Relationship of Eurocommunism to Eurosocialism*. New York and London: Greenwood Press.

Antonio, Robert and Alessandro Bonanno (1996). "Post-Fordism in the United States: The Poverty of Market-Centered Democracy." *Current Perspectives in Social Theory*. **16**: 3-32.

Apollon, Willy and Richard Feldstein, Eds. (1995). *Lacan, Politics, Aesthetics*. New York: SUNY Press.

Arato, Andrew and Paul Breines (1979). *The Young Lukács and the Origins of Western Marxism*. London: Pluto Press.

Arato, Andrew and Jean Cohen (1992). *Civil Society and Political Theory*. London and Cambridge: MIT Press.

Aronowitz, Stanley (1988). "Postmodernism and Politics". *Universal Abandon? The Politics of Postmodernism*. Andrew Ross, ed. Minneapolis: University of Minnesota Press. 46-61.

Aronowitz, Stanley (1992). *The Politics of Identity*. New York: Routledge.

Aronowitz, Stanley (1994). "The Situation of the Left in the United States." *Socialist Review*. **93**(3): 5-79.

Aronson, Ronald (1995). *After Marxism*. New York: The Guilford Press.

Austin, J. L. (1962). *How To Do Things with Words*. Cambridge: Harvard University Press.

Badiou, Alain (2001). *Ethics: An Essay on the Understanding of Evil*. London and New York: Verso.

Bakhtin, Mikhail (1981). *The Dialogic Imagination: Four Essays*. Austin: University of Texas Press.

Balibar, Étienne (1973). "Self-Criticism." *Theoretical Practice*(7-8): 56-72.

Balibar, Étienne (1977a). "On the "Dictatorship of the Proletariat"". *On the Dictatorship of the Proletariat*. Étienne Balibar, ed. London: Unwin Brothers. 34-174.

Balibar, Étienne, Ed. (1977b). *On the Dictatorship of the Proletariat*. London: Unwin Brothers.

Balibar, Étienne (1978). "From Bachelard to Althusser: The Concept of 'Epistemological Break'." *Economy and Society*. **7**(3): 207-237.

Balibar, Étienne (1993). "The Non-Contemporaneity of Althusser". *The Althusserian Legacy*. Michael Sprinker and E. Ann Kaplan, eds. London and New York: Verso. 1-16.

Balibar, Étienne (1994a). "Althusser's Object." *Social Text*. **39**(2): 157-188.

Balibar, Étienne (1994b). *Masses, Classes, Ideas: Studies on Politics and Philosophy Before and After Marx*. London and New York: Routledge.

Balibar, Étienne (1994c). «Subjection and Subjectivation». *Supposing the Subject.* Joan Copjec, ed. London and New York: Verso. 1-15.

Balibar, Étienne (1995a). "Has the World Changed?" *Marxism in the Postmodern Age: Confronting the New World Order.* Antonio Callari, Steven Cullenberg and Carole Biewener, eds. London and New York: The Guilford Press. 405-414.

Balibar, Étienne (1995b). «The Infinite Contradiction.» *Yale French Studies.* **88**: 142-164.

Balibar, Étienne (1995c). *The Philosophy of Marx.* London and New York: Verso.

Balibar, Étienne (1996). "Structural Causality, Overdetermination and Antagonism". *Postmodern Materialism and the Future of Marxist Theory.* Antonio Callari and David Ruccio, eds. Hanover: Wesleyan University Press. 109-119.

Balibar, Étienne and Immanuel Wallerstein (1991). *Race, Nation, Class: Ambiguous Identities.* London: Verso.

Barnett, Stuart (1998). "Introduction: Hegel Before Derrida". *Hegel After Derrida.* Stuart Barnett, ed. London: Routledge. 1-32.

Barrett, Michèle (1980). *Women's Oppression Today: Problems in Marxist-Feminist Analysis.* London: Verso.

Barrett, Michèle (1991). *The Politics of Truth: From Marx to Foucault.* Cambridge: Polity Press.

Barrett, Michèle (1993). "Althusser's Marx, Althusser's Lacan". *The Althusserian Legacy.* E. Ann Kaplan and Michael Sprinker, eds. London and New York: Verso. 169-181.

Barthes, Roland (1972). *Mythologies.* New York: Hill & Wang.

Beck, Ulrich, Anthony Giddens, *et al.* (1994). *Reflexive Modernization.* Cambridge: Polity Press.

Bell, David, Jon Binnie, *et al.* (1994). "All Hyped Up and No Place to Go." *Gender, Place and Culture: A Journal of Feminist Geography.* **1**(1): 31-47.

Bellamy, Elizabeth (1993). "Discourses of Impossibility: Can Psychoanalysis be Political?" *Diacritics.* **23**(1): 24-38.

Benton, Ted (1984). *The Rise and Fall of Structuralist Marxism: Althusser and His Influence.* Basingstoke: Macmillan.

Bertens, Hans (1995). *The Idea of the Postmodern.* London and New York: Routledge.

Bertram, Benjamin (1995). "New Reflections on the 'Revolutionary' Politics of Ernesto Laclau and Chantal Mouffe." *boundary 2.* **22**(3): 81-110.

Best, Stephen and Douglas Kellner (1991). *Postmodern Theory: Critical Interrogations.* London: Macmillan.

Best, Stephen and Douglas Kellner (1997). *The Postmodern Turn.* New York and London: The Guilford Press.

Bhaskar, Roy (1978). *A Realist Theory of Science.* Hassocks: Harvester Press.

Bhaskar, Roy (1979). *The Possibility of Naturalism*. Brighton: Harvester Press.

Bhaskar, Roy (1989). *Reclaiming Reality: A Critical introduction to Contemporary Philosophy*. London: Verso.

Bhaskar, Roy (1991). *Dialectics: The Pulse of Freedom*. London and New York: Routledge.

Blackburn, Robin (1991). "Fin de Siècle: Socialism After the Crash". *After the Fall: The Failure of Communism and the Future of Socialism*. Robin Blackburn, ed. London and New York: Verso. 173-294.

Blackburn, Robin and Gareth Stedman Jones (1972). "Louis Althusser and the Struggle for Marxism". *The Unknown Dimension: European Marxism Since Lenin*. Dick Howard and Karl Klare, eds. London: Methuen. 365-387.

Bobbio, Norberto (1988). *Which Socialism?* Cambridge: Polity Press.

Bobbio, Norberto (1990). *Liberalism and Democracy*. London and New York: Verso.

Bobbio, Norberto (1996). *Left and Right: The Significance of a Political Distinction*. Cambridge: Polity Press.

Boggs, Carl (1976). *Gramsci's Marxism*. London: Pluto Press.

Boggs, Carl (1982). *The Impasse of European Communism*. Boulder: Westview Press.

Boggs, Carl (1986). *Social Movements and Political Power*. Philadelphia: Temple University Press.

Boggs, Carl (1993). *Intellectuals and the Crisis of Modernity*. Albany: SUNY Press.

Boggs, Carl (1995a). "Rethinking the Sixties Legacy: From New Left to New Social Movements". *Social Movements: Critiques, Concepts and Case Studies*. Stanford Lyman, ed. Boulder: Westview Press. 331-355.

Boggs, Carl (1995b). *The Socialist Tradition: From Crisis to Decline*. London and New York: Routledge.

Boggs, Carl (2000). *The End of Politics: Corporate Power and the Decline of the Public Sphere*. Boston: South End Press.

Boggs, Carl, and David Plotke, Eds. (1980). *The Politics of Eurocommunism*. Boston: South End Press.

Boothby, Richard (1991). *Death and Desire: Psychoanalytic Theory in Lacan's Return to Freud*. New York and London: Routledge.

Borch-Jacobsen, Mikkel (1991). *Lacan: The Absolute Master*. Stanford: Stanford University Press.

Bourdieu, Pierre (1977). *Outline of a Theory of Practice*. Cambridge: Cambridge University Press.

Bourdieu, Pierre (1984). *Distinction: A Social Critique of the Judgement of Taste*. London: Routledge and Kegan Paul.

Bourdieu, Pierre (1988). *Homo Academicus*. Cambridge: Polity Press.

Bourdieu, Pierre (1990). *The Logic of Practice*. Cambridge: Polity Press.

Bourdieu, Pierre (1991). *Language and Symbolic Power.* Cambridge: Polity Press.

Bourdieu, Pierre (1998). *Acts of Resistance.* Cambridge: Polity Press.

Bowles, Samuel and Herbert Gintis (1986). *Capitalism and Democracy: Property, Community and the Contradictions of Modern Social Thought.* New York: Basic Books.

Bowles, Samuel, David Gordon, *et al.* (1983). *Beyond the Wasteland.* New York: Doubleday/Anchor.

Boyer, Robert (1990). *The Regulation School: A Critical Introduction.* New York: Columbia University Press.

Boyer, Robert, Ed. (2000). *Japanese Capitalism in Crisis: A Regulationist Interpretation.* London and New York: Routledge.

Boynton, Robert (1998). "Enjoy Your Žižek!: An Excitable Slovenian Philosopher Examines The Obscene Practices Of Everyday Life - Including His Own." *Lingua Franca.* **8**(7).

Bracher, Mark (1994). "On the Psychological and Social Functions of Language: Lacan's Theory of the Four Discourses". *Lacanian Theory of Discourse: Subject, Structure and Society.* Mark Bracher, Marshall Alcorn, Ronald Corthell and Françoise Massardier-Kenney, eds. New York and London: New York University Press. 107-128.

Bracher, Mark, Marshall Alcorn, *et al.*, Eds. (1994). *Lacanian Theory of Discourse: Subject, Structure and Society.* New York and London: New York University Press.

Bramwell, Anna (1994). *The Fading of the Greens: The Decline of Environmental Politics in the West.* New Haven: Yale University Press.

Brandt, Karl-Werner (1990). „Cyclical Aspects of New Social Movements: Waves of Cultural Criticism and Mobilisation Cycles of New Middle-Class Radicalism". *Challenging the Political Order: New Social and Political Movements in Western Democracies.* Russell Dalton and Manfred Kuechler, eds. New York: Oxford University Press. 24-42.

Brannigan, John (1998). *New Historicism and Cultural Materialism.* New York: St Martin's Press.

Brenner, Robert (1998). "The Economics of Global Turbulence: A Special Report on the World Economy, 1950-1998." *New Left Review*(229): 1-265.

Brousse, Marie-Hélène (1995). «The Drive (I and II)». *Reading Seminar XI: Lacan's Four Fundamental Concepts of Psychoanalysis.* Richard Feldstein, Maire Jaanus and Bruce Fink, eds. New York: SUNY Press. 99-117.

Brown, Wendy (1995). *States of Injury: Power and Freedom in Late Modernity.* Princeton: Princeton University Press.

Brown, Wendy (2001). *Politics Out of History.* Princeton and Oxford: Princeton University Press.

Buci-Glucksmann, Christine (1980). *Gramsci and the State.* London: Lawrence and Wishart.

Burbach, Roger, Orlando Núñez, *et al.* (1997). *Globalisation and Its Discontents: The Rise of Postmodern Socialisms.* London and Chicago: Pluto Press.

Butler, Judith (1986). "Sex and Gender in Simone de Beauvoir's *Second Sex.*" *Yale French Studies.* **72**: 35-41.

Butler, Judith (1987a). *Subjects of Desire: Hegelian Reflections in Twentieth Century France.* New York: Columbia University Press.

Butler, Judith (1987b). "Variations on Sex and Gender: Beauvoir, Wittig and Foucault". *Feminism as Critique: Essyas on the Politics of Gender in Late-Capitalist Societies.* Seyla Benhabib and Drucilla Cornell, eds. Cambridge: Polity Press. 129-142.

Butler, Judith (1989a). "Foucault and the Paradox of Bodily Inscriptions." *Journal of Philosophy.* **86**(11): 601-607.

Butler, Judith (1989b). "Sexual Ideology and Phenomenological Description: A Feminist Critique of Merleau-Ponty's *Phenomenology of Perception*". *The Thinking Muse: Feminism and Modern French Philosophy.* Jeffner Allen and Iris Marion Young, eds. Bloomington: Indiana University Press. 85-100.

Butler, Judith (1991). "The Nothing That Is: Wallace Stevens' Hegelian Affinities". *Theorising American Literature: Hegel, the Sign, and History.* Bainard Cowan and Joseph Kronick, eds. Baton Rouge: Louisiana State University Press. 269-287.

Butler, Judith (1993a). *Bodies That Matter: On the Discursive Limits of "Sex".* London and New York: Routledge.

Butler, Judith (1993b). "Post-structuralism and Postmarxism." *diacritics.* **23**(4): 3-11.

Butler, Judith (1995). "Conscience Doth Make Subjects of Us All." *Yale French Studies.* **88**: 6-26.

Butler, Judith (1997a). *Excitable Speech: A Politics of the Performative.* London and New York: Routledge.

Butler, Judith (1997b). *The Psychic Life of Power: Theories in Subjection.* Stanford: Stanford University Press.

Butler, Judith (1998). "Merely Cultural." *New Left Review*(227): 33-44.

Butler, Judith (1999a). *Gender Trouble: Feminism and the Subversion of Identity.* New York and London: Routledge.

Butler, Judith (1999b). "Preface to the Second Edition". *Subjects of Desire: Hegelian Reflections in Twentieth-Century France.* Judith Butler, ed. New York: Columbia University Press. i-xxv.

Butler, Judith (2000a). "Competing Universalities". *Contingency, Hegemony, Universality: Contemporary Dialogues on the Left.* Judith Butler, Ernesto Laclau and Slavoj Žižek, eds. London and New York: Verso. 136-181.

Butler, Judith (2000b). "Dynamic Conclusions". *Contingency, Hegemony, Universality: Contemporary Dialogues on the Left.* Judith Butler, Ernesto Laclau and Slavoj Žižek, eds. London and New York: Verso. 263-280.

Butler, Judith (2000c). "Ethical Ambivalence". *The Turn to Ethics*. Marjorie Garber, Beatrice Hanssen and Rebecca Walkowitz, eds. London and New York: Routledge. 15-28.

Butler, Judith (2000d). "Restaging the Universal". *Contingency, Hegemony, Universality: Contemporary Dialogues on the Left*. Judith Butler, Ernesto Laclau and Slavoj Žižek, eds. London and New York: Verso. 11-43.

Butler, Judith, Ernesto Laclau, *et al.* (2000). «Introduction». *Contingency, Hegemony, Universality: Contemporary Debates on the Left*. Judith Butler, Ernesto Laclau and Slavoj Žižek, eds. London and New York: Verso. 1-4.

Butler, Judith (2001). *Antigone's Claim*. New York: Columbia University Press.

Calhoun, Craig (1993). "'New Social Movements' of the Nineteenth Century." *Social Science History*. **17**: 385-427.

Calhoun, Craig (1994). *Social Theory and the Politics of Identity*. Oxford and Cambridge: Blackwell.

Callari, Antonio, Carole Biewener, *et al.* (1995). "Marxism in the New World Order: Crises and Possibilities". *Marxism in the Postmodern Age: Confronting the New World Order*. Carole Biewener, Stephen Cullenberg and Antonio Callari, eds. New York: The Guildford Press. 1-10.

Callari, Antonio and David Ruccio, Eds. (1996). *Postmodern Materialism and the Future of Marxist Theory*. Hannover: Wesleyan University Press.

Callinicos, Alex (1976). *Althusser's Marxism*. London: Pluto Press.

Callinicos, Alex (1985). "Postmodernism, Post-Structuralism, Post-Marxism?" *Theory, Culture & Society*. **2**: 85-101.

Callinicos, Alex (1989). *Against Postmodernism: A Marxist Critique*. Cambridge: Polity Press.

Carrillo, Santiago (1978). *"Eurocommunism" and the State*. Westport: Lawrence Hill.

Carroll, William and Rudi Ratner (1994). "Between Leninism and Radical Pluralism: Gramscian Reflections on Counter-Hegemony and the New Social Movements." *Critical Sociology*. **20**: 3-26.

Castells, Manuel (2000). *The Rise of the Network Society*. Oxford: Blackwell.

Casteneda, Jorge (1993). *Utopia Unarmed: The Latin American Left After the Cold War*. New York: St. Martin's Press.

Chalmers, Alan (1990). *Science and Its Fabrication*. Buckingham: Open University Press.

Chodorow, Nancy (1978). *The Reproduction of Mothering: Psychoanalysis and the Sociology of Gender*. Berkeley: UCLA Press.

Claudin, Fernando (1975). *The Communist Movement: From Comintern to Cominform*. New York: Monthly Review Press.

Claudin, Fernando (1978). *Eurocommunism and Socialism*. London: New Left Books.

Clemens, Justin (2003). *The Romanticism of Contemporary Theory*. London: Ashgate.

Clement, Catherine (1983). *The Lives and Legends of Jacques Lacan*. New York: Columbia University Press.

Cloud, Dana (1994). "'Socialism of the Mind': The New Age of Post-Marxism". *After Postmodernism: Reconstructing Ideology Critique*. Michael Billig and Herbert Simmons, eds. London and New Delhi: Sage.

Cohen, Gerald (1978). *Karl Marx's Theory of History: A Defense*. New Jersey: Princeton University Press.

Cohen, Jean (1985). "Strategy or Identity: New Theoretical Paradigms and Contemporary Social Movements." *Social Research*. **52**: 663-716.

Collier, Andrew (1994). *Critical Realism: An Introduction to Roy Bhaskar's Philosophy*. London and New York: Verso.

Coole, Diana (2002). "The Dialectics of the Real". *Ideology After Poststructuralism*. Siniša Malešević and Ian MacKenzie, eds. London: Pluto Press. 111-133.

Copjec, Joan (1994a). "Introduction". *Supposing the Subject*. Joan Copjec, ed. London and New York: Verso. vii-xiii.

Copjec, Joan (1994b). *Read My Desire: Lacan Against the Historicists*. Cambridge: MIT Press.

Copjec, Joan (1996). "Evil in the Time of the Finite World". *Radical Evil*. Joan Copjec, ed. London and New York: Verso. i-xxvii.

Critchley, Simon (1993). *The Ethics of Deconstruction: Derrida and Levinas*. London: Blackwell.

Critchley, Simon (1999). *Ethics, Politics, Subjectivity: Essays on Derrida, Levinas and Contemporary French Thought*. London and New York: Verso.

Critchley, Simon (2002). "Ethics, Politics and Radical Democracy: The History of a Disagreement." *Culture Machine*(4): 1-6.

Cross, Gary (1993). *Time and Money: The Making of Consumer Culture*. London and New York: Routledge.

Croteau, David (1995). *Politics and the Class Divide: Working People and the Middle-Class Left*. Philadelphia: Temple University Press.

Cullenberg, Steven (1994). *The Falling Rate of Profit: Recasting the Marxian Debate*. London and Boulder: Pluto Press.

Dallmayr, Fred (1989). *Margins of Political Discourse*. New York: SUNY Press.

Dalton, Russell and Manfred Kuechler (1990). "The Challenge of the New Movements". *Challenging the Political Order: New Social and Political Movements in Western Democracies*. Russell Dalton and Manfred Kuechler, eds. New York: Oxford University Press. 3-20.

Daly, Glyn (1999). "Politics and the Impossible: Beyond Psychoanalysis and Deconstruction." *Theory, Culture & Society*. **16**(4): 75-98.

Davis, Mike (1999). *Prisoners of the American Dream. Politics and Economics in the History of the US Working Class*. London and New York: Verso.

Deleuze, Gilles (1994). *Difference and Repetition*. New York: Columbia University Press.

Derrida, Jacques (1971). *Positions*. Chicago: University of Chicago Press.

Derrida, Jacques (1978). *Writing and Difference*. Chicago: University of Chicago Press.

Derrida, Jacques (1981). *Dissemination*. Chicago: University of Chicago Press.

Derrida, Jacques (1982). *Margins of Philosophy*. Chicago: University of Chicago Press.

Derrida, Jacques (1987). *The Post Card: From Socrates to Freud and Beyond*. Chicago: University of Chicago Press.

Derrida, Jacques (1988). *Limited Inc*. Evanston: Northwestern University Press.

Derrida, Jacques (1994). *Spectres of Marx: The State of the Debt, the Work of Mourning and the New International*. London and New York: Routledge.

Descombes, Vincent (1980). *Modern French Philosophy*. Cambridge: Cambridge University Press.

Dews, Peter (1979). "The *Nouvelle Philosophie* and Foucault." *Economy and Society*. **8**(2).

Dews, Peter (1985). "The "New Philosophers" and the End of Leftism". *Radical Philosophy Reader*. Roy Edgley and Richard Osborne, eds. London: Verso. 361-384.

Dews, Peter (1987). *Logics of Disintegration: Post-Structuralist Thought and the Claims of Critical Theory*. London and New York: Verso.

Dews, Peter (1995a). *The Limits of Disenchantment: Essays on Contemporary European Philosophy*. London and New York: Verso.

Dews, Peter (1995b). "The Tremor of Reflection: Slavoj Žižek's Lacanian Dialectics". *The Limits of Disenchantment: Essays on Contemporary European Philosophy*. Peter Dews, ed. London and New York: Verso. 236-257.

Dicken, Peter (1998). *Global Shift: Transforming the World Economy*. Liverpool: Paul Chapman Publishing.

Dolar, Mladen (1993). "Beyond Interpellation." *Qui parle?* **6**(2): 75-96.

Dolar, Mladen (1996). "The Object Voice". *Gaze and Voice as Love Objects*. Slavoj Žižek and Renata Salecl, eds. Durham and London: Duke University Press. 7-31.

Dolar, Mladen (1998). "Cogito as the Subject of the Unconscious". *Cogito and the Unconscious*. Slavoj Žižek, ed. Durham and London: Duke University Press. 11-40.

Dollimore, Jonathan (1996). "Bisexuality, Heterosexuality, and Wishful Theory." *Textual Practice*. **10**(3): 523-539.

Donahue, Brian (2001). "Marxism, Postmodernism, Žižek." *Postmodern Culture*. **12**(2): 57 paragraphs.

Dor, Joël (1997). *Introduction to the Reading of Lacan: The Unconscious Structured*

Like a Language. New Jersey: Jason Aronson.

Dreyfus, Hubert and Paul Rabinow (1982). *Michel Foucault: Beyond Structuralism and Hermeneutics*. Chicago: University of Chicago Press.

Dryberg, Torben Bech (1997). *The Circular Structure of Power: Politics, Identity, Community*. London and New York: Verso.

Duyvendak, Jan (1995). *The Power of Politics: New Social Movements in France*. Boulder: Westview Press.

Eagleton, Terry (1976). *Marxism and Literary Criticism*. London: Methuen.

Eagleton, Terry (1990). *The Ideology of the Aesthetic*. Oxford and Cambridge: Blackwell.

Eagleton, Terry (1991). *Ideology: An Introduction*. London and New York: Verso.

Eagleton, Terry (1996). *The Illusions of Postmodernism*. Oxford: Blackwell.

Eagleton, Terry (2000). *The Idea of Culture*. Oxford: Blackwell.

Eagleton, Terry (2001). "Enjoy!" *Paragraph*(2): 40-52.

Easthope, Anthony (1983). "The Trajectory of *Screen*, 1971-1979". *The Politics of Theory. et. al.* Francis Barker, ed. Colchester: University of Essex. 121-133.

Easthope, Anthony (1988). "Film Theory". *British Post-Structuralism*. Anthony Easthope, ed. New York: Routledge. 34-70.

Ebert, Teresa (1996). *Ludic Feminism and After: Postmodernism, Desire and Labor in Late Capitalism*. Ann Arbor: University of Michigan Press.

Eder, Klaus (1993). *The New Politics of Class*. Newbury Park: Sage.

Eder, Klaus (1995). "Does Social Class Matter in the Study of Social Movements? A Study of Middle-Class Radicalism". *Social Movements and Social Class*. Louis Mahen, ed. London: Sage. 21-54.

Elliot, Patricia (1991). *From Mastery to Analysis: Theories of Gender in Psychoanalytic Feminism*. Ithaca and London: Cornell University Press.

Elliott, Anthony (1992). *Social Theory and Psychoanalysis in Transition: Self and Society from Freud to Kristeva*. Oxford: Oxford University Press.

Elliott, Gregory (1987). *Althusser: The Detour of Theory*. London and New York: Verso.

Elliott, Gregory (1995). "Intimations of Mortality: On Historical Communism and the 'End of History'". *Marxism in the Postmodern Age: Confronting the New World Order*. Antonio Callari, Steven Cullenberg and Carole Biewener, eds. London and New York: The Guilford Press. 415-425.

Elliott, Gregory (1998). "The Necessity of Contingency: Some Notes." *Rethinking MARXISM*. **10**(3): 74-79.

Elliott, Gregory (1999). "Introduction: In the Mirror of Machiavelli". *Machiavelli and Us*. Louis Althusser. London and New York: Verso. xi-xix.

Epstein, Barbara (1995). "Why Post-structuralism is a Dead End for Progressive Thought." *Socialist Review*. **25**(2).

Eschle, Catherine (2001). *Global Democracy, Social Movements and Feminism*.

Boulder: Westview.

Feenberg, Andrew (1981). *Lukács, Marx and the Sources of Critical Theory*. Oxford: Martin Robertson.

Feher, Férenc and Agnes Heller (1988). *The Postmodern Political Condition*. Oxford: Blackwell.

Feldstein, Richard, Bruce Fink, *et al.*, Eds. (1995). *Reading Seminar XI: Lacan's Four Fundamental Concepts of Psychoanalysis*. New York: SUNY Press.

Feldstein, Richard, Bruce Fink, *et al.*, Eds. (1996). *Reading Seminars I and II: Lacan's Return to Freud*. Albany: SUNY Press.

Felman, Shoshana (1983). *The Literary Speech Act: Don Juan with J. L. Austin, or, Seduction in Two Languages*. Ithaca and New York: Cornell University Press.

Fine, Ben and Frigga Haug (2002). *The World of Consumption: The Material and the Cultural Revisited*. London and New York: Routledge.

Fink, Bruce (1995a). *The Lacanian Subject: Between Language and Jouissance*. Princeton: Princeton University Press.

Fink, Bruce (1995b). "Reading *Hamlet* with Lacan". *Lacan, Politics, Aesthetics*. Richard Feldstein and Willy Apollon, eds. Albany: SUNY Press. 181-198.

Fink, Bruce (1995c). "The Real Cause of Repetition". *Reading Seminar XI: Lacan's Four Fundamental Concepts of Psychoanalysis*. Bruce Fink, Richard Feldstein and Maire Jaanus, eds. New York: SUNY Press. 223-229.

Fink, Bruce (1996). "The Subject and the Other's Desire". *Reading Seminars I and II: Lacan's Return to Freud*. Richard Feldstein, Bruce Fink and Maire Jaanus, eds. Albany: SUNY Press. 76-97.

Fink, Bruce (1997). *A Clinical Introduction to Lacanian Psychoanalysis: Theory and Technique*. London and Cambridge: Harvard University Press.

Flieger, Jerry (2001). "Has Oedipus Signed Off (or Struck Out)?: Žižek, Lacan and the Field of Cyberspace." *Paragraph*(2): 53-77.

Foreman, Ann (1977). *Femininity as Alienation: Women and the Family in Marxism and Psychoanalysis*. London: Pluto.

Forrester, John (1990). *The Seductions of Psychoanalysis: Freud, Lacan and Derrida*. Cambridge: Cambridge University Press.

Forster, Michael (1998). *Hegel's Idea of a Phenomenology of Spirit*. Chicago: University of Chicago Press.

Foucault, Michel (1972). *The Archaeology of Knowledge*. New York: Harper.

Foucault, Michel (1977). *Discipline and Punish: The Birth of the Prison*. Harmondsworth: Penguin.

Foucault, Michel (1991). "Politics and the Study of Discourse". *The Foucault Effect*. Michael Gordon and Miller Burchell, eds. London: Harvester. 53-72.

Fraad, Harriet, Stuart Resnick, *et al.* (1994). *Bringing It All Back Home: Class, Gender and Power in the Modern Household*. London and Boulder: Pluto.

Frank, Manfred (1989). *What Is Neo-Structuralism?* Minneapolis: University of Minnesota Press.

Fraser, Nancy (1995). "From Redistribution to Recognition: Dilemmas of Justice in a Post-Socialist Age." *New Left Review*(212): 68-93.

Fraser, Nancy (1996). *Justice Interruptus: Reflections on the "Postsocialist" Condition.* London and New York: Routledge.

Fraser, Nancy (1998). "Heterosexism, Misrecognition and Capitalism: A Response to Judith Butler." *New Left Review*(228): 140-149.

Fraser, Nancy (1999). "Ten Years After 1989 - Postcommunist Reflections." *Dissent.* **46**(4): 11-12.

Fraser, Nancy (2000). «Rethinking Recognition.» *New Left Review*(3): 107-120.

Freud, Sigmund (1984). *On Metapsychology: The Theory of Psychoanalysis.* London: Penguin.

Frow, John (1997). *Time and Commodity Culture: Essays in Cultural Theory and Postmodernity.* Oxford: Clarendon Press.

Gadamer, Hans-Georg (1998). *Truth and Method.* New York: Continuum.

Gallop, Jane (1985). *Reading Lacan.* Ithaca: Cornell University Press.

Garber, Marjorie (1996). *Vice Versa: Bisexuality and the Eroticism of Everyday Life.* New York: Schribner/Touchstone.

Garber, Marjorie, Beatrice Hanssen, *et al.*, Eds. (2000). *The Turn to Ethics.* London and New York: Routledge.

Gasché, Rodolphe (1986). *The Tain of the Mirror: Jacques Derrida and the Philosophy of Reflection.* London and Cambridge: Harvard University Press.

Gasché, Rodolphe (1994). *Inventions of Difference: On Jacques Derrida.* London and Cambridge: Harvard University Press.

Geras, Norman (1984). *Karl Marx and Human Nature: The Refutation of a Legend.* Cambridge: Cambridge University Press.

Geras, Norman (1987). "Post-Marxism?" *New Left Review*(163): 40-82.

Geras, Norman (1988). "Ex-Marxism without Substance: Being a Real Reply to Laclau and Mouffe." *New Left Review*(169): 34-62.

Geras, Norman (1990). *Discourses of Extremity: Radical Ethics and Post-Marxist Extravagances.* London and New York: Verso.

Giddens, Anthony (1984). *The Constitution of Society.* Cambridge: Polity Press.

Giddens, Anthony (1990). *The Consequences of Modernity.* Cambridge: Polity Press.

Giddens, Anthony (1991). *Modernity and Self-Identity.* Cambridge: Polity Press.

Giddens, Anthony (1992). *The Transformation of Intimacy.* Cambridge: Polity Press.

Giddens, Anthony (1994a). *Beyond Left and Right - the Future of Radical Politics.* Cambridge: Polity Press.

Giddens, Anthony (1994b). "Living in the Post-Traditional Society". *Reflex-*

ive Modernization. Ulrich Beck, Anthony Giddens and Scott Lash, eds. Cambridge: Polity Press.

Giddens, Anthony (1998). *The Third Way - A Renewal of Social Democracy.* Cambridge: Polity Press.

Giddens, Anthony (1999). *Runaway World.* London: Profile Books.

Giddens, Anthony (2000). *The Third Way and Its Critics.* Cambridge: Polity Press.

Giddens, Anthony, Ed. (2001). *The Global Third Way Debate.* Cambridge: Polity Press.

Gitlin, Todd (1994). "From Universality to Difference: Notes on the Fragmentation of the Idea of the Left". *Social Theory and the Politics of Identity.* Craig Calhoun, ed. Oxford and Cambridge: Blackwell.

Glowinski, Huguette, Zita Marks and Sara Murphy, Eds. (2001). *A Compendium of Lacanian Terms.* London and New York: Free Association Press.

Glucksmann, André (1972). "A Ventriloquist Structuralism." *New Left Review*(72): 61-92.

Glucksmann, André (1980). *The Master Thinkers.* New York: Harper and Row.

Glynos, Jason (2001). "'There is no Other of the Other': Symptoms of a Decline in Symbolic Faith, or, Žižek's Anti-Capitalism." *Paragraph*(2): 78-110.

Gowan, Peter (1999). *The Global Gamble: Washington's Faustian Bid for World Dominance.* London and New York: Verso.

Gramsci, Antonio (1971). *Selections from the Prison Notebooks.* London: Lawrence and Wishart.

Grigg, Russell (2001). "Absolute Freedom and Major Structural Change." *Paragraph*(2): 111-124.

Grosz, Elizabeth (1990). *Jacques Lacan: A Feminist Introduction.* London and New York: Routledge.

Habermas, Jürgen (1975). *Legitimation Crisis.* Boston: Beacon Press.

Habermas, Jürgen (1987). *The Philosophical Discourse of Modernity: Twelve Lectures.* Cambridge: Polity Press.

Habermas, Jürgen (1999). *Moral Consciousness and Communicative Action.* Cambridge: MIT Press.

Hall, Stuart (1980). "Nicos Poulantzas: *State, Power, Socialism.*" *New Left Review*(119): 60-69.

Hall, Stuart (1988). *The Hard Road to Renewal: Thatcherism and the Crisis of the Left.* London and New York: Verso.

Hall, Stuart (1992). "Cultural Studies and its Theoretical Legacies". *Cultural Studies.* Lawrence Grossberg, Cary Nelson and Paula Treichler, eds. New York and London: Routledge. 277-294.

Hall, Stuart, and Martin Jacques, Eds. (1983). *The Politics of Thatcherism.* London: Lawrence and Wishart in association with Marxism Today.

Hall, Stuart, and Martin Jacques, Eds. (1989). *New Times: The Changing Face of Politics in the 1990s.* London: Lawrence and Wishart.

Hamilton, Paul (1996). *Historicism.* London and New York: Routledge.

Hardt, Michael, and Antonio Negri (2000). *Empire.* London and Cambridge: Harvard University Press.

Harrington, Michael (1993). *Socialism: Past and Future.* London: Pluto Press.

Harris, David (1992). *From Class Struggle to the Politics of Pleasure: The Effects of Gramscianism on Cultural Studies.* London and New York: Routledge.

Harris, David (1996). *A Society of Signs?* London and New York: Routledge.

Hartmann, Klaus (1966). *Sartre's Ontology.* Evanston: Northwestern University Press.

Hartmann, Klaus (1972). „Hegel: A Non-Metaphysical View". *Hegel: A Collection of Critical Essays.* Alaisdair MacIntyre, ed. Garden City: Doubleday.

Hartmann, Klaus (1988). *Studies in Foundational Philosophy.* Amsterdam: Rodopi.

Hartsock, Nancy (1985). *Money, Sex and Power: Towards a Feminist Historical Materialism.* Boston: Northeastern University Press.

Harvey, David (1989). *The Condition of Postmodernity.* Oxford: Blackwell.

Haug, Wolfgang (1986). *Critique of Commodity Aesthetics: Appearance, Sexuality and Advertising in Capitalist Society.* Cambridge: Polity Press.

Heath, Stephen (1978). "Notes on Suture." *Screen.* **18**(4): 55-56.

Hebdige, Dick (1991). *Subculture: The Meaning of Style.* New York: Routledge.

Hegel, G. W. F. (1952). *The Philosophy of Right.* Oxford: Oxford University Press.

Hegel, G. W. F. (1956). *The Philosophy of History.* New York: Dover Publications.

Hegel, G. W. F. (1975). *Hegel's Logic.* Oxford: Clarendon Press.

Hegel, G. W. F. (1977). *Hegel's Phenomenology of Spirit.* London: Oxford University Press.

Hegel, G. W. F. (1995). *Lectures on the History of Philosophy, Vol.'s 1-3.* Lincoln and London: University of Nebraska Press.

Heidegger, Martin (1996). *Being and Time.* Albany: SUNY Press.

Heinämaa, Sara (1997). "What is a Woman? Butler and Beauvoir on the Foundations of the Sexual Difference." *Hypatia: Journal of Feminist Philosophy.* **12**(1): 20-39.

Heller, Agnes (1988). *General Ethics.* Oxford: Blackwell.

Heller, Agnes (1990). *A Philosophy of Morals.* Oxford: Blackwell.

Heller, Agnes (1996). *An Ethics of Personality.* Oxford: Blackwell.

Henrich, Dieter (1982). „Fichte's Original Insight". *Contemporary German Philosophy, Volume 1.* University Park: Pennsylvania State University Press. 15-53.

Herbold, Sarah (1995). "Well-Placed Reflections: (Post)modern Woman as

Symptom of (Post)modern Man." *Signs: Journal of Women in Culture and Society.* **21**(1): 83-115.

Hindess, Barry (1983). *Parliamentary Democracy and Socialist Politics.* London: Routledge and Kegan Paul.

Hindess, Barry, and Paul Hirst (1975). *Pre-Capitalist Modes of Production.* London: Routledge and Kegan Paul.

Hindess, Barry, and Paul Hirst (1977). *Mode of Production and Social Formation: An Auto-Critique of Pre-Capitalist Modes of Production.* London: Routledge and Kegan Paul.

Hirsch, Joachim (1988). "The Crisis of Fordism, Transformations of the 'Keynesian' Security State and New Social Movements." *Research in Social Movements, Conflicts and Change.* **10**: 43-55.

Hirst, Paul (1976). "Althusser's Theory of Ideology." *Economy and Society.* **5**(4): 385-411.

Hirst, Paul (1979). *On Law and Ideology.* London: Macmillan.

Hirst, Paul (1999). "Carl Schmitt's Decisionism". *The Challenge of Carl Schmitt.* Chantal Mouffe, ed. London and New York: Verso. 7-17.

Homer, Sean (1998a). *Fredric Jameson: Marxism, Hermeneutics, Postmodernism.* Cambridge: Polity Press.

Homer, Sean (1998b). "Psychoanalysis, Postmarxism and the Subject: From the Ethical to the Political." *PS: Journal of the Universities Association for Psychoanalytic Studies*(1): 18-28.

Honneth, Axel (1995). *The Struggle for Recognition: The Moral Grammar of Social Conflicts.* Cambridge: Polity Press.

Howarth, David (2000a). *Discourse.* London: Open University Press.

Howarth, David, Aletta Norval and Yannis Stavrakakis, Eds. (2000b). *Discourse Theory and Political Analysis: Identities, Hegemonies and Social Change.* Manchester and New York: Manchester University Press.

Howarth, David and Aletta Norval, Eds. (1998). *South Africa in Transition: New Theoretical Perspectives.* London: Macmillan.

Hughes, Alex and Anne Witz (1997). "Feminism and the Matter of Bodies: From de Beauvoir to Butler." *Body & Society.* **3**(1): 47-60.

Hull, Carrie (1997). "The Need in Thinking: Materiality in Theodor W. Adorno and Judith Butler." *Radical Philosophy*(84): 22-35.

Hutcheon, Linda (1988). *A Poetics of Postmodernism: History, Theory, Fiction.* New York: Routledge.

Hutcheon, Linda (1989). *The Politics of Postmodernism.* London and New York: Routledge.

Huyssen, Andreas (1986). *After the Great Divide: Modernism, Mass Culture, Postmodernism.* Bloomington: Indiana University Press.

Hyppolite, Jean (1974). *Genesis and Structure of Hegel's Phenomenology of Spirit.* Evanston: Northwestern University Press.

Inglehart, Ronald (1990a). *Culture Shift in Advanced Industrial Society.* Princeton:

Princeton University Press.

Inglehart, Ronald (1990b). "Values, Ideology and Cognitive Mobilisation in New Social Movements". *Challenging the Political Order: New Social and Political Movements in Western Democracies*. Russell Dalton and Manfred Kuechler, eds. New York: Oxford University Press. 43-66.

Inglehart, Ronald (1997). *Modernization and Postmodernization: Cultural, Economic and Political Change in 43 Societies*. Princeton: Princeton University Press.

Jaanus, Maire (1995). "The *Démontage* of the Drive". *Reading Seminar XI: Lacan's Four Fundamental Concepts of Psychoanalysis*. Bruce Fink, Richard Feldstein and Maire Jaanus, eds. New York: SUNY Press. 119-136.

Jameson, Fredric (1972). *The Prison House of Language: A Critical Account of Structuralism and Russian Formalism*. Princeton: Princeton University Press.

Jameson, Fredric (1981). *The Political Unconscious: Narrative as a Socially Symbolic Act*. Ithaca: Cornell University Press.

Jameson, Fredric (1990). *Late Marxism: Adorno, Or, The Persistence of the Dialectic*. London and New York: Verso.

Jameson, Fredric (1991). *Postmodernism, Or, The Cultural Logic of Late Capitalism*. Durham: Duke University Press.

Jameson, Fredric (1992). *The Geopolitical Aesthetic: Cinema and Space in the World System*. London: BFI Publishing.

Jameson, Fredric (1994). *The Seeds of Time*. New York: Columbia University Press.

Jay, Martin (1984). *Marxism and Totality: The Adventures of a Concept from Lukács to Habermas*. Berkeley and Los Angeles: UCLA Press.

Jay, Martin (1992). *Force Fields*. Berkeley and Los Angeles: UCLA Press.

Jenkins, Craig and Bert Klandermans, Eds. (1995). *The Politics of Social Protest: Comparative Perspectives on States and Social Movements*. Minneapolis: University of Minnesota Press.

Jessop, Bob (1985). *Nicos Poulantzas: Marxist Theory and Political Strategy*. London: Macmillan.

Jessop, Bob (1990). *State Theory: Putting the Capitalist State in Its Place*. Cambridge: Polity Press.

Jessop, Bob, Ed. (1991a). *The Politics of Flexibility: Restructuring State and Industry in Britain, Germany and Scandinavia*. Brookfield: Edward Elgar.

Jessop, Bob (1991b). "Thatcherism and Flexibility: The White Heat of a Post-Fordist Revolution". *The Politics of Flexibility: Restructuring State and Industry in Britain, Germany and Scandinavia*. Bob Jessop, ed. Brookfield: Edward Elgar. 135-161.

Jessop, Bob, Kevin Bonnett, *et al.*, Eds. (1988). *Thatcherism: A Tale of Two Nations*. Cambridge: Polity Press.

Jones, Gareth Stedman (1971). "The Marxism of the Early Lukács: An Evaluation." *New Left Review*(70): 27-64.

Julien, Philippe (1994). *Jacques Lacan's Return to Freud: The Real, the Symbolic and the Imaginary*. New York: New York University Press.

Kant, Immanuel (1993). *Critique of Pure Reason*. London: Everyman.

Keane, John (1988). *Democracy and Civil Society*. London: Verso.

Kellner, Douglas (1995). "The End of Orthodox Marxism". *Marxism in the Postmodern Age: Confronting the New World Order*. Antonio Callari, Steven Cullenberg and Carole Biewener, eds. London and New York: The Guilford Press. 33-41.

Kojève, Alexandre (1980). *Introduction to the Reading of Hegel*. Ithaca: Cornell University Press.

Koopmans, Ruud (1995). *Democracy From Below: New Social Movements and the Political System in West Germany*. Boulder: Westview Press.

Kriesi, Hanspeter (1995). *New Social Movements in Western Europe: A Comparative Analysis*. Minneapolis: University of Minnesota Press.

Kuhn, Annette and AnnMarie Wolpe, Eds. (1978). *Feminism and Materialism: Women and Modes of Production*. London: Routledge and Kegan Paul.

Kuhn, Thomas (1970). *The Structure of Scientific Revolutions*. Chicago: Chicago University Press.

Kuhn, Thomas (1977). *The Essential Tension*. Chicago: Chicago University Press.

Lacan, Jacques (1972). "The Seminar on the "Purloined Letter"." *Yale French Studies*. **48**: 38-72.

Lacan, Jacques (1974). *The Seminar of Jacques Lacan, Book XX: Encore*. London and New York: Norton.

Lacan, Jacques (1977). *Écrits: A Selection*. London and New York: Norton.

Lacan, Jacques (1986). *The Seminar of Jacques Lacan, Book VII: The Ethics of Psychoanalysis*. New York and London: Norton.

Lacan, Jacques (1987). *Television: A Challenge to the Psychoanalytic Establishment*. New York: Norton.

Lacan, Jacques (1988a). *The Seminar of Jacques Lacan, Book I: Freud's Papers on Technique*. New York: Norton.

Lacan, Jacques (1988b). *The Seminar of Jacques Lacan, Book II: The Ego in Freud's Theory and the Technique of Psychoanalysis*. New York: Norton.

Lacan, Jacques (1989a). *The Seminar of Jacques Lacan, Book V: The Formations of the Unconscious*. Translation by Cormac Gallagher, PhD. Dublin.

Lacan, Jacques (1989b). *The Seminar of Jacques Lacan, Book VI: Desire and Its Interpretation*. Translation by Cormac Gallagher, PhD. Dublin.

Lacan, Jacques (1993). *The Seminar of Jacques Lacan, Book III: The Psychoses*. London and New York: Norton.

Lacan, Jacques (1996). "Position of the Unconscious". *Reading Seminar XI: Lacan's Four Fundamental Concepts of Psychoanalysis*. Bruce Fink, Richard Feldstein and Maire Jaanus, eds. Albany: SUNY Press.

Lacan, Jacques (1998). *The Seminar of Jacques Lacan, Book XI: The Four Funda-*

mental Concepts of Psychoanalysis. London and New York: Norton.

Laclau, Ernesto (1977). *Politics and Ideology in Marxist Theory*. London: New Left Books.

Laclau, Ernesto (1985). "New Social Movements and the Plurality of the Social". *New Social Movements and the State in Latin America*. Ken Slater, ed. Amsterdam: CEDLA. 27-42.

Laclau, Ernesto (1988). "Politics and the Limits of Modernity". *Universal Abandon? The Politics of Postmodernism*. Andrew Ross, ed. Minneapolis: University of Minnesota Press. 63-82.

Laclau, Ernesto (1989). "Preface". *The Sublime Object of Ideology*. Slavoj Žižek. London and New York: Verso. ix-xiv.

Laclau, Ernesto (1990). *New Reflections on the Revolution of Our Time*. London and New York: Verso.

Laclau, Ernesto (1993). "Discourse". *The Blackwell Companion to Contemporary Political Philosophy*. Oxford: Blackwell.

Laclau, Ernesto (1995a). *Emancipation(s)*. London and New York: Verso.

Laclau, Ernesto (1995b). "Subject of Politics, Politics of the Subject". *Emancipation(s)*. Ernesto Laclau, ed. London and New York: Verso. 47-65.

Laclau, Ernesto (1995c). "The Time is Out of Joint." *diacritics*. **25**(2): 89-96.

Laclau, Ernesto (1996a). "The Death and Resurrection of the Theory of Ideology." *Journal of Political Ideologies*. **1**(3): 201-220.

Laclau, Ernesto (1996b). "Deconstruction, Pragmatism, Hegemony". *Deconstruction and Pragmatism*. Chantal Mouffe, ed. London and New York: Routlledge. 47-68.

Laclau, Ernesto (2000a). "Constructing Universality". *Contingency, Hegemony, Universality: Contemporary Dialogues on the Left*. Judith Butler, Ernesto Laclau and Slavoj Žižek, eds. London and New York: Verso. 281-307.

Laclau, Ernesto (2000b). "Identity and Hegemony: The Role of Universality in the Constitution of Political Logics". *Contingency, Hegemony, Universality: Contemporary Dialogues on the Left*. Judith Butler, Ernesto Laclau and Slavoj Žižek, eds. London and New York: Verso. 44-89.

Laclau, Ernesto (2000c). "Structure, History and the Political". *Contingency, Hegemony, Universality: Contemporary Dialogues on the Left*. Judith Butler, Ernesto Laclau and Slavoj Žižek, eds. London and New York: Verso. 182-212.

Laclau, Ernesto (2002). "Ethics, Politics and Radical Democracy: A Reply to Simon Critchley." *Culture Machine*(4): 1-5.

Laclau, Ernesto and Chantal Mouffe (1985). *Hegemony and Socialist Strategy: Toward a Radical Democratic Politics*. London: Verso.

Laclau, Ernesto and Chantal Mouffe (1987a). "History of Marxism." *New Left Review*(166): 79-106.

Laclau, Ernesto and Chantal Mouffe (1987b). "Post-Marxism without Apologies." *New Left Review*(163): 40-82.

Laclau, Ernesto and Chantal Mouffe (1990). "Phronesis Manifesto". *New Reflections on the Revolution of Our Time*. Ernesto Laclau. London and New York: Verso.

Laclau, Ernesto and Chantal Mouffe (2000). "Phronesis Manifesto". *(Dis) figurations: Discourse/Critique/Ethics*. Ian Angus. London and New York: Verso.

Laclau, Ernesto and Lilian Zac (1995). «Minding the Gap: The Subject of Politics». *Emancipation(s)*. Ernesto Laclau, ed. London and New York: Verso. 11-39.

Lacoue-Labarthe, Philippe and Jean-Luc Nancy (1992). *The Title of the Letter: A Reading of Lacan*. New York: SUNY Press.

Lakatos, Imré (1978). "History of Science and Its Rational Reconstruction". *Imré Lakatos: Philosophical Papers, Volume I: The Methodology of Scientific Research Programmes*. John Currie and George Worrall, eds. Cambridge: Cambridge University Press.

Landry, Donna and Gerald MacLean (1991). "Rereading Laclau and Mouffe." *Rethinking MARXISM*. 4(4): 41-60.

Laplanche, Jean and Jean Pontalis (1973). *The Language of Psychoanalysis*. New York: Norton.

Larrain, Jorge (1979). *The Concept of Ideology*. London: Hutchinson.

Larrain, Jorge (1983). *Marxism and Ideology*. London: Macmillan.

Larrain, Jorge (1994). *Ideology and Cultural Identity: Modernity and the Third World Presence*. Cambridge: Polity Press.

Lash, Scott and John Urry (1987). *The End of Organised Capitalism*. Cambridge: Polity Press.

Lash, Scott and John Urry (1994). *Economies of Signs and Space*. London: Sage.

Laurent, Éric (1995). «Alienation and Separation (I and II)». *Reading Seminar XI: Lacan's Four Fundamental Concepts of Psychoanalysis*. Bruce Fink, Richard Feldstein and Maire Jaanus, eds. New York: SUNY Press. 19-38.

Leader, Darian (1996). *Why Do Women Write More Letters than They Post?* New York: Basic Books.

Leader, Darian (1998). *Things Lovers Say Once it Gets Late*. New York: Basic Books.

Leader, Darian (2001). *Stealing the Mona Lisa: What Art Prevents Us From Seeing*. New York: Basic Books.

Lear, Jonathan (2000). *Happiness, Death and the Remainder of Life*. Cambridge and London: Harvard University Press.

Lecourt, Dominique (1975). *Marxism and Epistemology: Bachelard, Canguilhem and Foucault*. London: New Left Books.

Lecourt, Dominique (2001). *The Mediocracy: French Philosophy Since the Mid-1970s*. London and New York: Verso.

Lee, Martyn (1993). *Consumer Culture Reborn: The Cultural Politics of Consumption.* New York: Routledge.

Lefort, Claude (1986). *The Political Forms of Modern Society.* Cambridge: Polity Press.

Lefort, Claude (1988). *Democracy and Political Theory.* Cambridge: Polity Press.

Leledakis, Kanakis (1995). *Society and Psyche: Social Theory and the Unconscious Dimension of the Social.* Oxford and Washington: Berg Publishers.

Lemaire, Annika (1977). *Jacques Lacan.* London: Routledge.

Levine, Andrew, Eric Olin-Wright, *et al.* (1992). *Reconstructing Marxism.* London: Polity Press.

Lévy, Bernard-Henri (1982). *Barbarism with a Human Face.* New York: Harper and Row.

Lipietz, Alain (1985). *The Enchanted World.* London: Verso.

Lipietz, Alain (1987). *Mirages and Miracles: The Crisis of Global Fordism.* London: Verso.

Lipietz, Alain (1992). *Towards a New Economic Order: Post-Fordism, Democracy and Ecology.* Oxford: Polity Press.

Lipietz, Alain (1995). *Green Hopes: The Future of Political Ecology.* Cambridge: Polity Press.

Lloyd, Moya (1999). "Performativity, Parody, Politics." *Theory, Culture & Society.* **16**(2): 195-213.

Luhmann, Niklas (1995). *Social Systems.* Stanford: Stanford University Press.

Lukács, Georg (1970). *Lenin: A Study on the Unity of his Thought.* London: New Left Books.

Lukács, Georg (1971). *History and Class Consciousness.* London: Merlin.

Lukács, Georg (1975). *The Young Hegel: Studies in the Relations Between Dialectics and Economics.* Cambridge: MIT Press.

Lukács, Georg (1978). *The Ontology of Social Being: Marx's Basic Ontological Principles.* London: Merlin.

Lukács, Georg (1980). *The Ontology of Social Being: Labour.* London: Merlin.

Lupton, Julia and Kenneth Reinhard (1993). *After Oedipus: Shakespeare in Psychoanalysis.* Ithaca and London: Cornell University Press.

Lyotard, Jean-François (1997). *The Postmodern Condition: A Report on Knowledge.* Minneapolis: University of Minnesota Press.

Macchiochi, Maria Antonietta (1973). *Letters from Inside the Italian Communist Party to Louis Althusser.* London: New Left Books.

Macherey, Pierre (1978). *A Theory of Literary Production.* London: Routledge and Kegan Paul.

MacPherson, C. B. (1962). *The Political Theory of Possessive Individualism: From Hobbes to Locke.* London: Oxford University Press.

MacPherson, C. B. (1972). *The Real World of Democracy.* New York: Oxford University Press.

MacPherson, C. B. (1973). "Post-Liberal Democracy". *Democratic Theory: Essays in Retrieval.* C. B. MacPherson, ed. Oxford: Clarendon Press.

MacPherson, C. B. (1977). *The Life and Times of Liberal Democracy.* New York: Oxford University Press.

Malone, Kareen and Stephen Friedlander, Eds. (1988). *The Subject of Lacan: A Lacanian Reader for Psychologists.* New York: State University of New York Press.

Mandel, Ernest (1978a). *From Stalinism to Eurocommunism: The Bitter Fruits of 'Socialism in One Country'.* London: New Left Books.

Mandel, Ernest (1978b). *Late Capitalism.* London: Verso.

Marchais, Georges (1977a). "In Order to Take Democracy Forward to Socialism". *On the Dictatorship of the Proletariat.* Étienne Balibar, ed. London: Unwin Brothers. 182-192.

Marchais, Georges (1977b). "Liberty and Socialism". *On the Dictatorship of the Proletariat.* Étienne Balibar, ed. London: Unwin Brothers. 161-164.

Marini, Marcelle (1992). *Jacques Lacan: The French Context.* New Brunswick: Rutgers University Press.

Marx, Karl (1962a). *Capital, Vol. 2.* Moscow: Progress Publishers.

Marx, Karl (1962b). *Capital, Vol. 3.* Moscow: Progress Publishers.

Marx, Karl (1963). *Capital, Vol. 1.* Moscow: Progress Publishers.

Marx, Karl (1973). *Grundrisse.* Harmondsworth: Penguin.

Marx, Karl (1986a). „Preface to *A Contribution to the Critique of Political Economy*". *Marx-Engels Selected Works in One Volume.* Karl Marx and Frederick Engels. Moscow: Progress Publishers. 311-331.

Marx, Karl and Frederick Engels (1986b). *Marx Engels Selected Works.* Moscow: Progress Publishers.

Marzani, Carl (1980). *The Promise of Eurocommunism.* Westport: Lawrence Hill.

Mastnak, Tomaz (1994). "From Social Movements to National Sovereignty". *Independent Slovenia: Origins, Movements, Prospects.* Jill Benderly and Evan Kraft, eds. New York: St. Martin's Press.

Mathews, John (1988). *A Culture of Power: Rethinking Labour Movement Goals for the 1990s.* Leichhardt: Pluto Press.

Mathews, John (1989a). *The Age of Democracy: The Politics of Post-Fordism.* Melbourne: Oxford University Press.

Mathews, John (1989b). *Tools of Change: New Technology and the Democratisation of Work.* Sydney: Pluto Press.

McAdam, John, John McCarthy and Mayer Zald, Eds. (1996). *Comparative Perspectives on Social Movements: Political Opportunities, Mobilising Structures.* New York: Cambridge University Press.

McGee, Daniel (1997). "Postmarxism: The Opiate of the Intellectuals." *Modern Language Quarterly.* **58**(2): 200-226.

McHale, Brian (1987). *Postmodernist Fiction.* London: Methuen.

McInnes, Neil (1976). *Eurocommunism.* Los Angeles: Sage Publications.

McLennan, Gregor (1996). "Post-Marxism and the 'Four Sins' of Modernist Theorising." *New Left Review*(218).

McNay, Lois (1994). *Foucault: A Critical Introduction.* Cambridge: Polity Press.

McNay, Lois (1999). "Subject, Psyche and Agency: The Work of Judith Butler." *Theory, Culture & Society.* **16**(2): 175-193.

Melucci, Alberto (1989). *Nomads of the Present: Social Movements and Individual Needs in Contemporary Society.* Philadelphia: Temple University Press.

Melucci, Alberto (1994). "A Strange Kind of Newness: What's "New" in New Social Movements?" *New Social Movements: From Ideology to Identity.* Enrique Laraña, Hank Johnston and Joseph Gusfield, eds. Philadelphia: Temple University Press.

Melucci, Alberto (1996). *Challenging Codes: Collective Action in the Information Age.* Cambridge: Cambridge University Press.

Metz, Christian (1982). *The Imaginary Signifier.* Bloomington: Indiana University Press.

Miklitsch, Robert (1995). "The Rhetoric of Post-Marxism: Discourse and Institutionality in Laclau and Mouffe, Resnick and Wolff." *Social Text.* **14:4**(45): 167-196.

Miklitsch, Robert (1996). "The Commodity-Body-Sign: Toward a General Economy of 'Commodity Fetishism'." *Cultural Critique*(33): 5-40.

Miklitsch, Robert (1998a). *From Hegel to Madonna: Towards a General Economy of «Commodity Fetishism».* Albany: SUNY Press.

Miklitsch, Robert (1998b). „'Going Through the Fantasy': Screening Slavoj Žižek." *South Atlantic Quarterly.* **97**(2): 475-507.

Miliband, Ralph (1970). "The Capitalist State - Reply to Nicos Poulantzas." *New Left Review*(59): 53-60.

Miliband, Ralph (1973). "Poulantzas and the Capitalist State." *New Left Review*(82): 83-92.

Miliband, Ralph (1985). "The New Revisionism in Britain." *New Left Review*(150): 5-26.

Miller, Jacques-Alain (1978). «Suture (Elements of the Logic of the Signifier).» *Screen.* **18**(4): 24-34.

Miller, Jacques-Alain (1994). «Extimité». *Lacanian Theory of Discourse.* Mark Bracher, Marshall Alcorn, Ronald Corthell and Françoise Massardier-Kenney, eds. New York and London: New York University Press. 74-87.

Mitchell, Juliette (1974). *Psychoanalysis and Feminism.* Harmondsworth: Penguin.

Močnik, Rastko (1993). "Ideology and Fantasy". *The Althusserian Legacy.* E. Annie Kaplan and Michael Sprinker, eds. London and New York: Verso. 139-156.

Molyneux, Maxine (1979). "Beyond the Domestic Labour Debate." *New Left*

Review(116): 83-125.

Montag, Warren (1995). "'The Soul is the Prison of the Body': Althusser and Foucault, 1970-1975." *Yale French Studies*(88): 53-77.

Montag, Warren (1998). "Althusser's Nominalism: Structure and Singularity." *Rethinking MARXISM.* **10**(3): 64-73.

Moody, Kim (1988). *An Injury to All: The Decline of American Unionism.* London and New York: Verso.

Moody, Kim (1997). *Workers in a Lean World: Unions in the International Economy.* London and New York: Verso.

Morgan, Michael and Susan Leggett, Eds. (1996). *Mainstream(s) and Margins: Cultural Politics in the 1990s.* Westport: Greenwood Press.

Moriarty, Michael (2001). "Žižek, Religion and Ideology." *Paragraph*(2): 125-139.

Mouffe, Chantal (1979a). «Hegemony and Ideology in Gramsci». *Gramsci and Marxist Theory.* Chantal Mouffe, ed. London: Routledge and Kegan Paul. 168-205.

Mouffe, Chantal (1979b). «Introduction: Gramsci Today». *Gramsci and Marxist Theory.* Chantal Mouffe, ed. London: Routledge and Kegan Paul. 1-18.

Mouffe, Chantal (1987). "Rawls: Political Philosophy without Politics." *Philosophy and Social Criticism.* **13**(2): 105-123.

Mouffe, Chantal (1988). "Radical Democracy: Modern or Postmodern?" *Universal Abandon? The Politics of Postmodernism.* Andrew Ross, ed. Minneapolis: University of Minnesota Press. 31-46.

Mouffe, Chantal (1990). "Radical Democracy or Liberal Democracy?" *Socialist Review*: 57-66.

Mouffe, Chantal (1991). "Democratic Citizenship and the Political Community". *Community at Loose Ends.* Miami Theory Collective, ed. Minneapolis: University of Minnesota Press. 70-82.

Mouffe, Chantal (1992a). "Citizenship and Political Identity." *October*(61): 28-32.

Mouffe, Chantal (1992b). "Democratic Citizenship and the Political Community". *Dimensions of Radical Democracy: Pluralism, Citizenship, Community.* Chantal Mouffe, ed. London and New York: Verso. 225-239.

Mouffe, Chantal (1992c). «Introduction: For an Agonistic Pluralism». *The Return of the Political.* Chantal Mouffe, ed. London and New York: Verso. 1-8.

Mouffe, Chantal (1992d). «Preface: Democratic Politics Today». *Dimensions of Radical Democracy: Pluralism, Citizenship, Community.* Chantal Mouffe, ed. London and New York: Verso. 1-14.

Mouffe, Chantal (1992e). *The Return of the Political.* London and New York: Verso.

Mouffe, Chantal (1996a). "Deconstruction, Pragmatism and the Politics of

Democracy". *Deconstruction and Pragmatism*. Chantal Mouffe, ed. London and New York: Routledge. 1-12.

Mouffe, Chantal (1996b). «Democracy, Power and the 'Political'». *Democracy and Difference*. Seyla Benhabib, ed. Princeton: Princeton University Press. 245-256.

Mouffe, Chantal (1996c). «Radical Democracy or Liberal Democracy?» *Radical Democracy: Identity, Citizenship and the State*. David Trend, ed. London and New York: Routledge. 1-25.

Mouffe, Chantal (1999). "Carl Schmitt and the Paradox of Liberal Democracy". *The Challenge of Carl Schmitt*. Chantal Mouffe, ed. London and New York: Verso. 39-55.

Mouffe, Chantal (2000). "Which Ethics for Democracy?" *The Turn to Ethics*. Marjorie Garber, Beatrice Hanssen and Rebecca Walkowitz, eds. London and New York: Routledge. 85-94.

Mouzelis, Fred (1978). "Ideology and Class Politics: A Critique of Ernesto Laclau." *New Left Review*(112): 45-61.

Mouzelis, Fred (1988). "Marxism or Postmarxism?" *New Left Review*(167): 107-123.

Mujal-Léon, Eusebio (1983). *Communism and Political Change in Spain*. Bloomington: Indiana University Press.

Mulgar, Geoff (2000). *Politics in an Anti-Political Age*. Oxford: Clarendon Press.

Mulhall, Stephen and Adam Swift (1996). *Liberalism and Communitarianism*. London: Blackwell.

Muller, John and William Richardson (1982). *Lacan and Language: A Reader's Guide to "Écrits"*. New York: International Universities Press.

Napolitano, Georgio (1977). *The Italian Road to Socialism*. Westport: Lawrence Hill.

Nash, Kate (2000). *Contemporary Political Sociology: Globalisation, Politics and Power*. Oxford: Blackwell.

Nealon, Jeffrey (1998). *Alterity Politics: Ethics and Performative Subjectivity*. Durham and London: Duke University Press.

Newman, Saul (2000). "Universalism/Particularism: Towards a Poststructuralist Politics of Universality." *New Formations*(41): 94-108.

Newton-Smith, W. H. (1981). *The Rationality of Science*. Boston and London: Routledge.

Nicol, Brian (2001). "As If: Traversing the Fantasy in Žižek." *Paragraph*(2): 140-155.

Norris, Christopher (1987). *Derrida*. London and Cambridge: Harvard University Press.

Norris, Christopher (1990). *What's Wrong with Postmodernism: Critical Theory and the Ends of Philosophy*. Baltimore: Johns Hopkins University Press.

Norris, Christopher (1991). *Spinoza and the Origins of Modern Social* Theory.

Oxford and Cambridge: Blackwell.

Norris, Christopher (1992). *Uncritical Theory: Postmodernism, Intellectuals and the Gulf War*. Amherst: University of Massachusetts Press.

Norris, Christopher (1993). *The Truth About Postmodernism*. Oxford: Blackwell.

Norris, Christopher (1996). *Reclaiming Truth: Contribution to a Critique of Cultural Relativism*. London: Lawrence and Wishart.

Norris, Christopher (1997). *New Idols of the Cave: On the Limits of Anti-Realism*. Manchester and New York: Manchester University Press.

Norris, Christopher (2001). *Against Relativism: Philosophy of Science, Deconstruction and Critical Theory*. Oxford: Blackwell.

Norris, Christopher (2002). *Truth Matters: Realism, Anti-Realism and Response-Dependence*. Edinburgh: Edinburgh University Press.

Norval, Aletta (1996). *Deconstructing Apatheid Discourse*. London and New York: Verso.

Nussbaum, Martha (1999). *The Professor of Parody*. The New Republic. http://www.tnr.com/archive/0299/022299/nussbaum022299.html.

Offe, Claus (1985). "New Social Movements: Challenging the Boundaries of Institutional Politics." *Social Research*. **52**: 817-868.

O'Neill, John (1995). *The Poverty of Postmodernism*. London: Routledge.

Osborne, Peter (1991). "Radicalism without Limit?" *Socialism and the Limits of Liberalism*. Peter Osborne, ed. London and New York: Verso. 201-225.

Osborne, Peter (1995). *The Politics of Time: Modernity and Avant-Garde*. London and New York: Verso.

Osborne, Peter, Ed. (1996). *In a Critical Sense: Interviews with Intellectuals*. New York: Norton.

Palmer, Bryan (1990). *Descent into Discourse: The Reification of Language and the Writing of Social History*. Philadelphia: Temple University Press.

Patton, Paul (1998). "Foucault's Subject of Power". *The Later Foucault*. Jeremy Moss, ed. London: Sage. 64-77.

Petrey, Sandy (1990). *Speech Acts and Literary Theory*. New York and London: Routledge.

Pettigrew, David and François Raffoul, Eds. (1996). *Disseminating Lacan*. New York: SUNY Press.

Pfaller, Robert (1998). "Negation and Its Reliabilities: An Empty Subject for Ideology?" *Cogito and the Unconscious*. Slavoj Žižek, ed. London and Durham: Duke University Press. 225-246.

Pinkard, Terry (1989). *Hegel's Dialectic: The Explanation of Possibility*. Philadelphia: Temple University Press.

Pinkard, Terry (1994). *Hegel's Phenomenology: The Sociality of Reason*. Cambridge: Cambridge University Press.

Piore, Michael and Charles Sabel (1984). *The Second Industrial Divide: Possibilities for Prosperity*. New York: Basic Books.

Pippin, Robert (1989). *Hegel's Idealism: The Satisfactions of Self-Consciousness.* Cambridge: Cambridge University Press.

Pippin, Robert (1999). *Modernism as a Philosophical Problem: On the Dissatisfactions of European High Culture.* Oxford: Blackwell.

Plotke, David (1990). "What's So New About New Social Movements?" *Socialist Review.* **20**: 81-102.

Plotke, David (1995). "What's So New About New Social Movements?" *Social Movements: Critiques, Concepts and Case Studies.* Stanford Lyman, ed. New York: New York University Press. 125-166.

Porter, Robert (2002). "A World Beyond Ideology? Strains in Slavoj Žižek's Ideology Critique". *Ideology After Poststructuralism.* Ian MacKenzie and Siniša Maleševic, eds. London: Pluto Press. 43-63.

Poulantzas, Nicos (1973). *Political Power and Social Classes.* London: New Left Books.

Poulantzas, Nicos (1974). *Fascism and Dictatorship.* London: New Left Books.

Poulantzas, Nicos (1975). *Classes in Contemporary Capitalism.* London: New Left Books.

Poulantzas, Nicos (1976). *The Crisis of the Dictatorships: Portugal, Greece, Spain.* London: New Left Books.

Poulantzas, Nicos (1978). *State, Power, Socialism.* London: New Left Books.

Priest, Graham (1987). *In Contradiction: A Study of the Transconsistent.* Dordrecht: Nijhoff.

Priest, Graham (1995). *Beyond The Limits of Thought.* Cambridge and Melbourne: Cambridge University Press.

Probyn, Elspeth (1995). "Lesbians in Space: Gender, Sex and the Structure of Missing." *Gender, Place and Culture: A Journal of Feminist Geography.* **2**(1): 77-84.

Prosser, Jay (1998). *Second Skins: The Body Narratives of Transsexuality.* New York: Columbia University Press.

Przeworski, Adam (1985). "Social Democracy as a Historical Phenomenon". *Capitalism and Social Democracy.* Adam Przeworski, ed. Cambridge: Cambridge University Press. 7-46.

Ragland-Sullivan, Ellie (1986). *Jacques Lacan and the Philosophy of Psychoanalysis.* Urbana and Chicago: University of Illinois Press.

Rawls, John (1971). *A Theory of Justice.* Cambridge: The Belknap Press of Harvard University.

Rawls, John (1993). *Political Liberalism.* New York: Columbia University Press.

Ray, Larry (1993). *Rethinking Critical Theory: Emancipation in the Age of Global Social Movements.* London: Sage.

Reinhard, Kenneth (2001). „Coming to America: Psychoanalytic Criticism in the Age of Žižek." *Paragraph*(2): 156 164.

Resch, Robert (1992). *Althusser and the Renewal of Marxist Social Theory.* Berkeley and Oxford: University of California Press.

Resch, Robert (1999). "Running on Empty: Žižek's Concept of the Subject." *JPCS: Journal for the Psychoanalysis of Culture & Society.* **4**(1): 92-99.

Resch, Robert (2001). "The Sound of Sci(l)ence: Žižek's Concept of Ideology-Critique." *JPCS: Journal for the Psychoanalysis of Culture & Society.* **6**(1): 6-19.

Resnick, Stuart, and Robert Wolff (1987). *Economics: Marxian versus Neoclassical.* Baltimore: Johns Hopkins University Press.

Resnick, Stuart and Robert Wolff (1987). *Knowledge and Class: A Marxian Critique of Political Economy.* Chicago: University of Chicago Press.

Ricoeur, Paul (1970). *Freud and Philosophy: An Essay on Interpretation.* New Haven and London: Yale University Press.

Ricoeur, Paul (1988). *Time and Narrative, Volume Three.* Chicago and London: University of Chicago Press.

Rigby, S. H. (1998). *Marxism and History: A Critical Introduction.* Manchester and New York: Manchester University Press.

Rosenau (1992). *Postmodernism and the Social Sciences: Insights, Inroads and Intrusions.* Princeton: Princeton University Press.

Ross, Andrew (1988). "Introduction". *Universal Abandon? The Politics of Postmodernism.* Andrew Ross. Minneapolis: University of Minnesota Press. *vii-xxviii.*

Ross, George (1980). "The PCF and the End of the Bolshevik Dream". *The Politics of Eurocommunism.* Carl Boggs and David Plotke, eds. Boston: South End Press. 112-135.

Roustang, François (1990). *The Lacanian Delusion.* New York: Oxford University Press.

Ruigrok, Winfried and Rob van Tulder (1995). *The Logic of International Restructuring.* London and New York: Routledge.

Rustin, Michael (1988). "Absolute Voluntarism: Critique of a Post-Marxist Concept of Hegemony." *New German Critique*(43): 147-173.

Rustin, Michael (1989). "The Politics of Post-Fordism: or, the Trouble with 'New Times'." *New Left Review*(175).

Ryan, Michael (1988). "Postmodern Politics." *Theory, Culture and Society.* **5**.

Salecl, Renata (1994). *The Spoils of Freedom: Psychoanalysis and Feminism After the Fall of Socialism.* London and New York: Routledge.

Salecl, Renata (1998). *(Per)Versions of Love and Hate.* New York: Verso.

Salecl, Renata, Ed. (2000). *Sexuation.* Durham: Duke University Press.

Salih, Sara (2002). *Judith Butler.* London and New York: Routledge.

Salvadori, Massimo (1979). *Karl Kautsky and the Socialist Revolution: 1880-1938.* London: New Left Books.

Sandler, Blair and Jonathan Diskin (1995). "Postmarxism and Class". *Marxism in the Postmodern Age: Confronting the New World Order.* Antonio Callari, Steven Cullenberg and Carole Biewener, eds. London and New York:

The Guilford Press. 178-187.

Sartre, Jean-Paul (1969). *Being and Nothingness*. London: Routledge.

Sassoon, Donald (1981). *The Strategy of the Italian Communist Party*. London: Frances Pinter.

Saussure, Ferdinand de (1966). *Course in General Linguistics*. New York: Mc-Graw-Hill.

Saville, John (1990). "*Marxism Today*: An Anatomy." *Socialist Register*: 35-59.

Schelling, F. W. J. von (1997). „The Ages of the World". *The Abyss of Freedom*. Slavoj Žižek, ed. Ann Arbor: University of Michigan Press.

Schmidt, Alfred (1981). *History and Structure: An Essay on Hegelian-Marxist and Structuralist Theories of History*. Cambridge: MIT Press.

Schneiderman, Stuart (1983). *Jacques Lacan: The Death of an Intellectual Hero*. Cambridge: Harvard University Press.

Schrift, Alan (1997). "Foucault's Reconfiguration of the Subject: From Nietzsche to Butler, Laclau/Mouffe and Beyond." *Philosophy Today*. **41**(1): 153-159.

Schrift, Alan (2001). "Judith Butler: Une Nouvelle Existentialiste?" *Philosophy Today*. **45**(1): 12-23.

Scott, Alan (1990). *Ideology and the New Social Movements*. London and Boston: Unwin Hyman.

Searle, John (1969). *Speech Acts: An Essay in the Philosophy of Language*. Cambridge: Cambridge University Press.

Searle, John (1979). *Expression and Meaning: Studies in the Theory of Speech Acts*. Cambridge: Cambridge University Press.

Searle, John (1983). *Intentionality: An Essay in the Philosophy of Mind*. Cambridge: Cambridge University Press.

Shannon, Thomas (1989). *An Introduction to the World System Perspective*. Boulder: Westview Press.

Sharpe, Matthew (2001a). "*Che Vuoi*? What Do You Want? The Question of the Subject, the Question of Žižek." *Arena Journal*(16): 101-120.

Sharpe, Matthew (2001b). *A Little Piece of the Real*. Ashworth Centre for Social Theory. Melbourne: University of Melbourne.

Sim, Stuart (1998). "Spectres and Nostalgia: *Post*-Marxism/Post-*Marxism*". *Post-Marxism: A Reader*. Stuart Sim. Edinburgh: Edinburgh University Press. 1-15.

Singer, Daniel (1970). *Prelude to Revolution*. New York: Hill and Wang.

Smith, Anna Marie (1994). *New Right Discourse on Race and Sexuality: Britain 1968-1990*. Cambridge: Cambridge University Press.

Smith, Anna Marie (1998). *Laclau and Mouffe: the Radical Democratic Imaginary*. New York and London: Routledge.

Smith, Tony (1989). *The Logic of Marx's Capital: Replies to Hegelian Objections*. New York. SUNY Press.

Sohn-Rethel, Alfred (1978). *Intellectual and Manual Labour: A Critique of Episte-*

mology. London: Macmillan.

Soja, Edward (1989). *Postmodern Geographies: The Reassertion of Space in Critical Theory*. London: Verso.

Sokal, Alan and Jean Bricmont (1998). *Fashionable Nonsense: Postmodern Intellectuals and the Abuse of Science*. New York: Picador.

Soto-Crespo (2000). "'Scars of Separation': Psychoanalysis, Marxism and Loss." *Textual Practice*. **14**(3): 439-456.

Sprinker, Michael (1987). *Imaginary Relations: Aesthetics and Ideology in the Theory of Historical Materialism*. London and New York: Verso.

Staten, Henry (1985). *Wittgenstein and Derrida*. Oxford: Blackwell.

Stavrakakis, Yannis (1999). *Lacan and the Political*. New York and London: Routledge.

Steinmetz, George (1994). "Regulation Theory, Post-Marxism and the New Social Movements." *Comparative Studies in Society and History*(36): 176-212.

Suchting, Wallis (1986). *Marx and Philosophy: Three Studies*. Basingstoke: Macmillan.

Tarrow, Sydney (1994). *Power in Movement: Social Movements, Collective Action and Politics*. Cambridge: Cambridge University Press.

Taylor, Charles (1975). *Hegel*. Cambridge: Cambridge University Press.

Therborn, Göran (1978). *What Does the Ruling Class Do When It Rules?* London: New Left Books.

Therborn, Göran (1980). *The Power of Ideology and the Ideology of Power*. London: New Left Books.

Thompson, Edward (1963). *The Making of the English Working Class*. New York: Vintage.

Thompson, Edward (1978). *The Poverty of Theory and Other Essays*. New York: Monthly Review Press.

Torfing, Jacob (1999). *New Theories of Discourse: Laclau, Mouffe and Žižek*. Oxford: Blackwell.

Touraine, Alain (1977). *The Self-Production of Society*. Chicago: University of Chicago Press.

Touraine, Alain (1985). "An Introduction to the Study of Social Movements." *Social Research*. **52**: 749-787.

Trend, David, Ed. (1996). *Radical Democracy: Identity, Citizenship and the State*. New York and London: Routledge.

Trotsky, Leon (1991). *The Revolution Betrayed: What Is the Soviet Union and Where Is It Going?* Detroit: Labor Publications.

Tucker, Kenneth (1991). "How New Are the New Social Movements?" *Theory, Culture and Society*. **8**(2): 75-98.

van Pelt, Tamise (2000). *The Other Side of Desire: Lacan's Theory of the Registers*. New York: SUNY Press.

Vattimo, Gianni (1988). *The End of Modernity: Nihilism and Hermeneutics in Post-*

modern Culture. Baltimore: Johns Hopkins University Press.

Vattimo, Gianni (1992). *The Transparent Society*. Baltimore: Johns Hopkins University Press.

Veltmeyer, Henry and James Petras (1999). *The Dynamics of Social Change in Latin America*. New York: St. Martin's Press.

Vološinov, V. N. (1973). *Marxism and the Philosophy of Language*. London: Harvard University Press.

Wallerstein, Immanuel (1990). "Antisystemic Movements: History and Dilemmas". *Transforming the Revolution*. Giovanni Arrighi, Samir Amin, André Gunder Frank and Immanuel Wallerstein, eds. New York: Monthly Review Press. 13-53.

Walzer, Michael (1983). *Spheres of Justice: A Defense of Pluralism and Equality*. New York: Basic Books.

Weber, Henri (1978). "Eurocommunism, Socialism and Democracy." *New Left Review*(110).

White, Alan (1983). *Absolute Knowledge: Hegel and the Problem of Metaphysics*. Columbus: Ohio University Press.

Wilden, Anthony (1968). "Lacan and the Discourse of the Other". *The Language of the Self: The Function of Language in Psychoanalysis*. Anthony Wilden, ed. Baltimore and London: The Johns Hopkins Press.

Williams, John and Wendy Harrison (1998). "Trouble with Gender." *The Sociological Review*. **46**(1): 73-94.

Williams, Robert (1992). *Recognition: Fichte and Hegel on the Other*. Albany: SUNY Press.

Williams, Robert (1997). *Hegel's Ethics of Recognition*. Berkeley and Los Angeles: UCLA Press.

Wilson, Elizabeth (1977). *Women and the Welfare State*. London: Tavistock.

Winfield, Richard (1988). *The Just Economy*. New York: Routledge, Chapman & Hall.

Wolff, Richard (1996). "Althusser and Hegel: Making Marxist Explanations Anti-Essentialist and Dialectical". *Postmodern Materialism and the Future of Marxist Theory: Essays in the Althusserian Tradition*. Antonio Callari and David Ruccio, eds. Hanover and London: Wesleyan University Press. 150-163.

Wolpe, Harold, Ed. (1980). *The Articulation of Modes of Production*. London: Routledge and Kegan Paul.

Wood, Ellen (1995). *Democracy Against Capitalism: Renewing Historical Materialism*. Cambridge: Cambridge University Press.

Wood, Ellen (1997a). "What is the "Postmodern" Agenda?" *In Defense of History: Marxism and the Postmodern Agenda*. Ellen Wood and John Foster, eds. New York: Monthly Review Press.

Wood, Ellen (1998). *The Retreat From Class: A New "True" Socialism*. London and New York: Verso.

Wood, Ellen, and John Foster, Eds. (1997b). *In Defense of History: Marxism and the Postmodern Agenda.* New York: Monthly Review Press.

Wright, Edmond (2001). "Introduction: Faith and the Real." *Paragraph*(2): 5-23.

Wright, Eric Olin (1978). *Class, Crisis and the State.* London: New Left Books.

Wright, Eric Olin (1985). *Classes.* London and New York: Verso.

Young, Robert (1990). *White Mythologies: Writing History and the West.* London and New York: Routledge.

Zaretsky, Eli (1976). *Capitalism, the Family and Personal Life.* London: Pluto Press.

Zerilli, Linda (1998). "This Universalism Which Is Not One." *diacritics.* **28**(2): 3-20.

Žižek, Slavoj (1989). *The Sublime Object of Ideology.* London and New York: Verso.

Žižek, Slavoj (1990). "Beyond Discourse Analysis." *New Reflections on the Revolution of Our Time.* Ernesto Laclau, ed. London and New York: Verso. 249-260.

Žižek, Slavoj (1991a). *For They Know Not What They Do: Enjoyment as a Political Factor.* London and New York: Verso.

Žižek, Slavoj (1991b). *Looking Awry: An Introduction to Jacques Lacan Through Popular Culture.* Cambridge and London: MIT Press.

Žižek, Slavoj (1992a). "Eastern Europe's Republics of Gilead." *Dimensions of Radical Democracy: Pluralism, Citizenship, Community.* Chantal Mouffe, ed. London and New York: Verso. 193-207.

Žižek, Slavoj, Ed. (1992b). *Everything You Always Wanted to Know About Lacan (But Were Afraid to Ask Hitchcock).* London and New York: Verso.

Žižek, Slavoj (1993). *Tarrying with the Negative: Kant, Hegel and the Critique of Ideology.* London and New York: Verso.

Žižek, Slavoj (1994a). "A Hair of the Dog That Bit You." *Lacanian Theory of Discourse: Subject, Structure and Society.* Mark Bracher, Marshall Alcorn, Ronald Corthell and Françoise Massardier-Kenney eds. New York and London: New York University Press. 46-73.

Žižek, Slavoj (1994b). "Is There A Cause of the Subject?" *Supposing the Subject.* Joan Copjec, ed. London and New York: Verso. 15-36.

Žižek, Slavoj (1994c). *The Metastases of Enjoyment: Six Essays on Woman and Causality.* London and New York: Verso.

Žižek, Slavoj (1994d). "The Spectre of Ideology." *Mapping Ideology.* Slavoj Žižek, ed. London: Verso. 1-33.

Žižek, Slavoj (1995). "The Fetish of the Party." *Lacan, Politics, Aesthetics.* Richard Feldstein and Willy Apollon, eds. Albany: SUNY Press. 3-29.

Žižek, Slavoj (1996a). "'I Hear You with My Eyes'; or, The Invisible Master." *Gaze and Voice as Love Objects.* Slavoj Žižek and Renata Salecl, eds. Durham and London: Duke University Press. 90-127.

Žižek, Slavoj (1996b). *The Indivisible Remainder: An Essay on Schelling and Related Matters.* London and New York: Verso.

Žižek, Slavoj (1997a). *The Abyss of Freedom.* Ann Arbor: University of Michigan Press.

Žižek, Slavoj (1997b). *The Plague of Fantasies.* London and New York: Verso.

Žižek, Slavoj (1998a). "The Cartesian Subject versus the Cartesian Theatre." *Cogito and the Unconscious.* Slavoj Žižek, ed. Durham and London: Duke University Press. 247-274.

Žižek, Slavoj, Ed. (1998b). *Cogito and the Unconscious.* London and New York: Verso.

Žižek, Slavoj (1998c). "Four Discourses, Four Subjects." *Cogito and the Unconscious.* Slavoj Žižek, ed. Durham: Duke University Press. 74-113.

Žižek, Slavoj (1998d). "Psychoanalysis in Post-Marxism: The Case of Alain Badiou." *South Atlantic Quarterly* **97**(2).125-184.

Žižek, Slavoj (1999). "Carl Schmitt in the Age of Post-Politics." *The Challenge of Carl Schmitt.* Chantal Mouffe, ed. London and New York: Verso. 18-37.

Žižek, Slavoj (2000a). *The Art of the Ridiculous Sublime: On David Lynch's Lost Highway.* Seattle: Walter Chapin Simpson Centre for the Humanities.

Žižek, Slavoj (2000b). "The Cartesian Subject without the Cartesian Theatre." *The Subject of Lacan: A Lacanian Reader for Psychologists.* Kareen Malone and Stephen Friedlander, eds. Albany: SUNY Press. 23-40.

Žižek, Slavoj (2000c). "Class Struggle or Postmodernism? Yes, Please!" *Contingency, Hegemony, Universality: Contemporary Dialogues on the Left.* Judith Butler, Ernesto Laclau and Slavoj Žižek, eds. London and New York: Verso. 90-135.

Žižek, Slavoj (2000d). "*Da Capo senza Fine.*" *Contingency, Hegemony, Universality: Contemporary Dialogues on the Left.* Judith Butler, Ernesto Laclau and Slavoj Žižek, eds. London and New York: Verso. 213-262.

Žižek, Slavoj (2000e). *The Fragile Absolute - Or, Why Is the Christian Legacy Worth Fighting For?* London and New York: Verso.

Žižek, Slavoj (2000f). "Georg Lukács as the Philosopher of Leninism." *A Defense of History and Class Consciousness.* Georg Lukács. London and New York: Verso. 151-156.

Žižek, Slavoj (2000g). "Holding the Place." *Contingency, Hegemony, Universality: Contemporary Dialogues on the Left.* Judith Butler, Ernesto Laclau and Slavoj Žižek, eds. London and New York: Verso. 308-329.

Žižek, Slavoj (2000h). *The Ticklish Subject: The Absent Centre of Political Ontology.* London and New York: Verso.

Žižek, Slavoj (2001a). "Chance and Repetition in Kieslowski's Films." *Paragraph*(2). 23-39.

Žižek, Slavoj (2001b). *Did Somebody Say Totalitarianism? On the Abuses of a Term.* London and New York: Verso.

Žižek, Slavoj (2001c). *Enjoy Your Symptom! Jacques Lacan in Hollywood and Out.* London and New York: Routledge.

Žižek, Slavoj (2001d). "Have Michael Hardt and Antonio Negri Rewritten the Communist Manifesto for the Twenty-First Century?" Rethinking MARXISM **13**(3/4). 190-205.

Žižek, Slavoj (2001e). "The Only Good Neighbour is a Dead Neighbour." Melbourne: University of Melbourne.

Žižek, Slavoj (2001f). "Psychoanalysis and Politics: Did Lenin Love His Neighbours?" Melbourne: Lacan Circle of Melbourne.

Žižek, Slavoj (2001g). "Repeating Lenin". Truth in the Postmodern, Berlin. http://lacan.com/replenin.html.

Žižek, Slavoj (2002). *On Belief.* London and New York: Verso.

Žižek, Slavoj and Renata Salecl, Eds. (1996). *Gaze and Voice as Love Objects.* London and New York: Verso.

Zupančič, Alenka (2000). *Ethics of the Real: Kant, Lacan.* London and New York: Verso.

Index of Proper Names

Lightning Source UK Ltd.
Milton Keynes UK
UKHW010859030223
416423UK00001B/34